The Complete Book of
Babycare

The Complete Book of
Babycare

Edited by
Barbara Nash
Associate Editor of Mother magazine

Photography by
Sandra Lousada

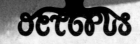
octopus

The Authors

Michael Brudenell
MB BS FRCS FRCOG
Consultant Obstetrician and
Gynaecologist at
King's College Hospital
London

Malcolm Chiswick
MD MRCP DCH
Consultant in Charge at the
Special Care Baby Unit at
St Mary's Hospital Manchester

Barbara Nash
Associate Editor of Mother magazine

Patricia Gilbert
MB BS DRCOG
Senior Clinical Medical Officer
Warwickshire

Janet Smy
Staff writer at Mother magazine

This edition first published exclusively in paperback
for Marks and Spencer Limited in 1980 by
Octopus Books Limited
59 Grosvenor Street
London W1
Third impression, 1980
© 1978 Octopus Books Limited

ISBN 0 906320 38 0

Printed in Hong Kong

The complete Book of Babycare was
published previously by Octopus Books Limited
in 1978 in hardback edition.

Foreword

However many times it may have happened to somebody in the past and however many times it may happen to someone in the future, conception —the development of an infinitesimal seed into a perfectly formed human being—remains a miracle. An everyday miracle it may be, but a miracle nevertheless. Conception and birth are uniquely awe-inspiring for the two people most closely concerned. As one father expressed it at the birth of his first child, 'It is like watching an act of God. She's so perfect she could not be anything else.' He was, as he admitted later, very surprised by his response—he had always prided himself on being free of such sentiments.

Like all the great events and momentous moments in life, the addition of the titles father and mother to that of husband and wife, raises many questions. Some of these questions are concerned with the physical development—the mother-to-be's and the child's; some with the mental development of parents and child; some with the emotional aspects of parenthood and childhood; and some are profoundly spiritual in origin.

Between the time that pregnancy is confirmed and the baby is born and placed in his parents' arms, thousands of questions pass through the minds of expectant mothers and fathers. Some are quickly resolved; some linger, cause fear and anxiety and will not rest until a satisfactory answer is found; some may never be answered except within the annals of a lifetime's quest.

The authors and publishers of good babycare books foresee as many of the questions as they can. They understand the doubts, the fears and the confusion that can cast shadows over the joy of conception, pregnancy, birth and development. They appreciate that any babycare book worth reading, needs to concern itself not only with the physical, mental, emotional and spiritual development of a baby, but with the development and birth of parents.

If, in addition, the writers and compilers always bear in mind that every human being is different; that no two parents and no two children are the same, the stage is set for a really worthwhile book that can be packed with information, guidance and hints certain to help any parent—be he or she about to have a first, second, third or fourth child.

With the best will in the world, a babycare book cannot answer all the questions or predict precisely what will arise and when. It can, however, give excellent guidance, deepen understanding and point the way.

What remains, in fact, paramountly clear when compiling and working on a babycare book, such as this—a book which takes parents from conception through the three most important years of their own and their child's development—is that everybody can learn from experience—their own and others. A little knowledge does, indeed, go a long way and will always hold us in good stead.

Knowing what to expect during pregnancy and the first three years of a child's life is invaluable. What may be learned within these pages will, in our view, help to prepare every parent for what is, after all, the most important and most fulfilling role offered to any human being—that of being mother or father and therefore responsible for the physical, mental, emotional and spiritual development of a brand new human being.

Barbara Nash

Contents

In the Beginning

Man and Woman
From Puberty to Adulthood

In the very early embryo there is little visible evidence of what he or she will eventually look like. At this stage of life all individuals look the same. Nevertheless, the genetic material in the chromosomes, which have come from the mother's egg and father's sperm cells, is beginning to work and whether or not an individual will become a superb athlete or a slightly built dancer is already decided. Environmental factors, both during the time in the womb and after birth, may cause changes in the eventual appearance of a mature adult but, in the main, the pattern is fixed and is already taking shape.

Although the sex of the baby is decided at conception, the foetus is not recognizably male or female until the seventh week. By this stage the germ cells, which make up the sex glands, have come together to form the testes in the male child and the ovaries in the female. During the remaining months of life in the uterus, the testes make

their way slowly down the body of the male foetus into the groin and eventually into the scrotum. The final descent into the scrotum is sometimes delayed until well after birth. This condition is known as undescended testes. The female ovaries likewise descend in the developing body cavity, but they stop in the pelvic region where they remain for the rest of the individual's life.

The importance of the sex glands is that they produce hormones—chemical substances—which bring about the formation of the external sexual characteristics of male and female. The male hormones, mainly testosterone, are produced by the adrenal gland and by the testes. The female hormones, oestrogens, are also produced by the adrenals and by the ovaries.

Male and female hormones are not present in any significant quantity at the beginning of life. They make their appearance at puberty when the ovaries and the testes become active. Whether a

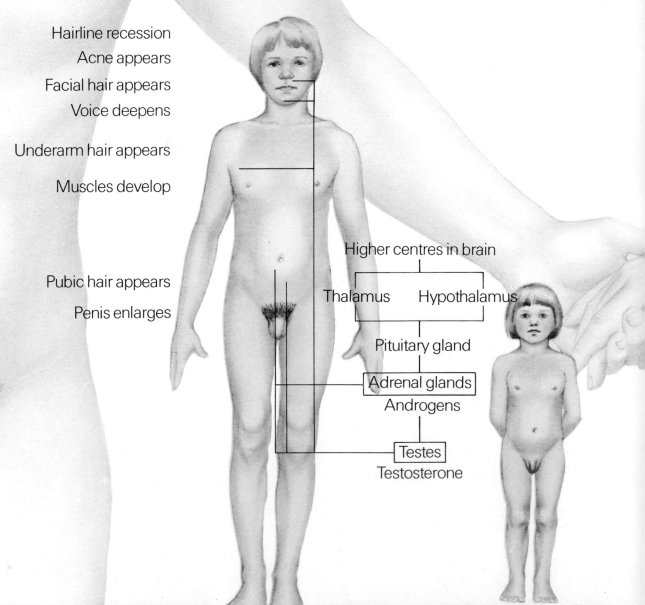

Hairline recession
Acne appears
Facial hair appears
Voice deepens

Underarm hair appears

Muscles develop

Pubic hair appears
Penis enlarges

Higher centres in brain

Thalamus   Hypothalamus

Pituitary gland

Adrenal glands
Androgens

Testes
Testosterone

baby is to be a male or female child is decided by the fact that, in the case of a boy, male hormones bring about the development of the scrotum, testes and penis. The female child, lacking male hormones, is born with unfused labia instead of a scrotum and a small clitoris instead of a penis. These differences apart, the physical form of a male and female child is identical. For this reason, although doting parents may feel that their infant looks just like the boy (or girl) he (or she) is, the unbiased observer may be forgiven for mistaking the baby's sex!

The similarity in external physical appearance continues in early childhood. With the onset of puberty, however, physical changes begin to take place. The actual age ot puberty varies widely but, in any given population, tends to be earlier in girls than in boys. The mechanisms by which these changes are brought about are shown below.

The speed with which puberty changes take place also varies a great deal. The earlier physical development of girls in their early teens is often reflected in their mental attitudes, which tend to be more mature than boys of equal age. Interest in the opposite sex usually starts earlier in girls, but, here again, individuals vary considerably. A group of normal fourteen-year-old girls, for example, may vary from a physically and emotionally immature girl-child to full-blown voluptuousness.

Environment plays an important part in both physical and mental development. Good nutrition encourages the growth of good physique, whilst education and parental influence play an important part in psychological attitudes. Puberty is a time of change and is often a time of trial for the individual concerned. A knowledge of the changes that are taking place and an understanding approach by older members of a family help to smooth the sometimes difficult path from childhood, through the turbulence of adolescence, to adulthood.

BODY STRUCTURE

The finished product of puberty, the adult body, clearly exhibits the physical differences between male and female which no amount of sex equality legislation can blur! Changing social conditions and, in particular, a woman's aspirations towards a life other than that of wife and mother may modify the aims of the male/female pair in relation to reproduction and the size and timing of a family, but it does not alter the physical situation of either partner or their inborn sex drive.

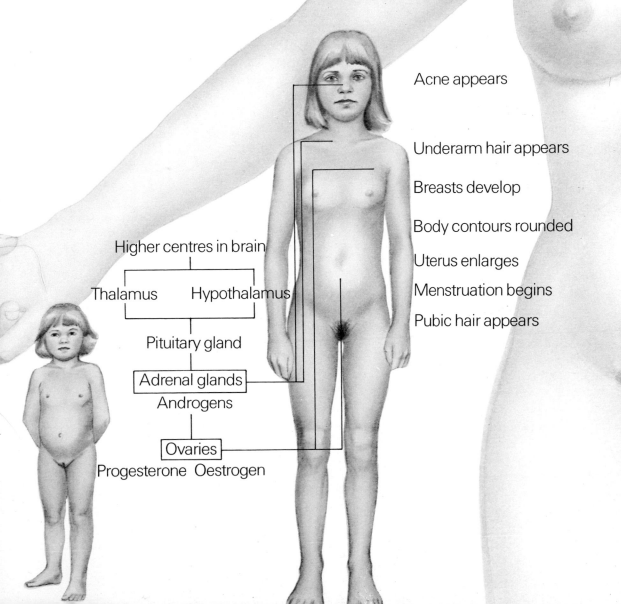

Acne appears

Underarm hair appears

Breasts develop

Body contours rounded

Uterus enlarges

Menstruation begins

Pubic hair appears

Higher centres in brain

Thalamus   Hypothalamus

Pituitary gland

Adrenal glands

Androgens

Ovaries

Progesterone Oestrogen

Male Sexual Anatomy

The external genitalia of the adult male comprise a penis, scrotum, testes, epididymis and part of the vas deferens. The internal genitalia comprise the remainder of the vas deferens, the ejaculatory ducts, the seminal vesicles and prostate gland.

EXTERNAL GENITALIA

☐ **Penis** This executive organ of sexuality is made up of glans, shaft and root. It is traversed by the penile urethra, which serves as a passageway for both urine and semen. The urethra is surrounded by three parallel tubes of erectile tissue which is made up like a sponge with innumerable spaces. When the erectile tissue becomes engorged with blood the penis becomes distended, rigid and erect.

☐ **Glans** The glans is the tip of the penis and is covered by the protective fold of skin, known as the foreskin or prepuce. The rite of circumcision —surgical removal of the foreskin—has been practised by Jews and Moslems and by many other peoples throughout the world. The origin of the operation is related to old ideas that the normal secretions which accumulate under the foreskin if it is not retracted and washed regularly were unhygienic. In some races the operation is carried out at puberty to signify the boy's emergence into manhood. Circumcision is rarely indicated on medical grounds although it is still widely practised in many countries such as Australia. It is not true that the circumcised penis is less sensitive and that the circumcised male is more likely to suffer premature ejaculation; during intercourse the foreskin is retracted and stays this way as long as the penis is in the vagina.

☐ **Shaft** The shaft of the penis varies in length and diameter, and connects the glans to the root. Some men are very preoccupied with penile size, but there is a good deal of normal variation. Average penises range in length between seven and eleven cm (three to four-and-a-half ins), in the flaccid state and fourteen to eighteen cm (five to seven-and-a-half ins), in the erect state. This variation in size is not usually related to the size of the man, i.e., small men do not necessarily have small penises and large men do not necessarily have large penises.

The fact that a small flaccid penis gets relatively bigger than a large flaccid penis means that the size when erect cannot be gauged by the size when the penis is in a flaccid condition.

☐ **Root** The root of the penis is situated where the glans joins the body. It is composed of erectile tissue, continuous with that of the shaft, and is covered by muscles which contract strongly at the time of orgasm and cause the ejaculation of semen from the external opening of the urethra at the tip of the penis.

☐ **Scrotum** This is the pouch of skin which hangs down from the root of the penis. It is divided into two compartments, each of which contains a testis. The scrotum has an important part to play in keeping the temperature of the testes constant, slightly below normal body temperature. In cold weather, muscle fibres just below the surface of the scrotal skin contract and make it very wrinkled. This draws the testes up nearer the body thereby reducing the amount of heat lost. In warmer conditions, the muscles are relaxed, the skin is smoother and the testes hang lower down. It is thought that the temperature of the testes is important in relation to sperm production. If the temperature of the testes becomes too high, for example, if the testes have not descended into the scrotum, or if the man wears too close-fitting underpants, the production of fertile sperm is inhibited.

☐ **Testes** The testes, which lie on each side of the scrotum, perform two important functions. They produce sperm and the male hormone testosterone. Testosterone passes directly into the blood stream to exert its action throughout the body. The sperm, which are formed from cells lining a series of tubes, known as the seminiferous tubules, then pass down these tubes into collecting tubes, known as the efferent ducts. The ducts then convey them into the epididymis.

☐ **Epididymis** This is a dilated tube which is loosely attached to the testes from which it receives the efferent ducts. The lowest part of the epididymis is continuous with the vas deferens, a firm cord-like tube, which runs up from the scrotum into the groin and then internally into the pelvic cavity.

INTERNAL GENITALIA

☐ **Vas deferens** Having started in the scrotum as part of the external genitalia, the vas becomes part of the internal genitalia when it enters the pelvis and joins the prostate gland. As it enters the prostate, it receives the secretions from the separate duct, known as the seminal vesicle. The final ejaculation of semen comprises the sperm from the testes, together with the secretions from the seminal vesicle, prostate and bulbo-urethral glands.

☐ **Bulbo-urethral and Prostate glands** The prostate gland, which is the size of a walnut, surrounds the urethra and is situated just below the bladder.

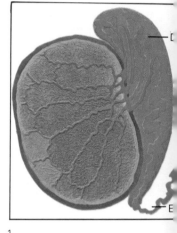

1

Key:
A Penis
B Erectile tissue
C Penile urethra
D Epididymus
E Vas deferens
F Bladder
G Prostate gland
H Seminal vesicle

It contains muscle fibres which contract during sexual activity and squeeze the clear prostatic secretion into the urethra through a number of small ducts. Below the prostate, two pea-sized glands, known as the bulbo-urethral glands, add their secretions to the urethra.

☐ **Seminal vesicles** The two seminal vesicles are situated on either side of the back of the bladder and their ducts pass through the prostate and into the urethra.

It is thought that the secretions of the prostate, seminal vesicles and bulbo-urethral glands play an important part in enhancing sperm motility (their ability to move) and the ability of the sperm to fertilize. In the absence of sexual stimulation, the urethra remains empty except when urine is passed. When sexual stimulation occurs, the penis becomes erect and at the time of male orgasm the prostate muscles contract and squeeze the sperm and glandular secretions into the urethra. The muscles at the root of the penis then contract and the mixture is propelled through the penis and ejaculated through its tip into the vagina.

1 A cross-section of the testis, showing the seminiferous tubules, a mass of convoluted tubes in which the sperm cells are produced. The sperm pass through the efferent ducts to the epididymus.

urethral glands. These secretions are thought to play a part in enhancing sperm motility.

3 Diagram to show the relative positions of the male external and internal genitalia.

2 The sperm travel from the testes to the penis along the vas deferens. The final ejaculation of semen contains sperm cells and secretions from the seminal vesicle, prostate and bulbo-

2 3

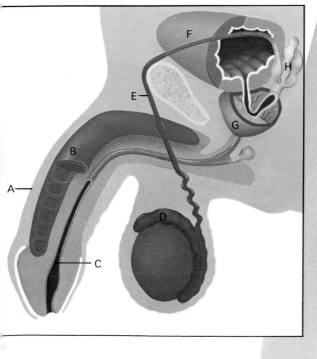

Female Sexual Anatomy

The external genitalia of a female comprise the vulva, which includes mons pubis, major and minor lips, clitoris, vestibule and vaginal orifice. The internal female genitalia comprise a vagina, uterus, the two uterine (Fallopian) tubes and the two ovaries.

EXTERNAL GENITALIA (VULVA)

☐ **Mons pubis** This is a fibro-fatty pad which lies, covered in pubic hair, in front of the pubic bone.

☐ **Labia** The labia (lips) are folds of skin—one outer large (majora) pair and an inner smaller (minora) pair. The labia majora are composed of fat covered by hair-bearing skin. The labia minora are composed of erectile tissue similar to that of the penis and are covered with hairless skin.

☐ **Clitoris** The labia minora meet at the top of the entrance to the vagina and form the clitoris which is the female equivalent of the penis. Like the penis, the clitoris is made of skin covered with erectile tissue and has a glans with a covering fold of skin, the prepuce. The clitoris is the most sexually sensitive part of the vulva. When stimulated, it brings about a secretion of vaginal fluid which lubricates both the vagina and the vestibule. The size of the clitoris varies considerably in different women and is unrelated to sexual responsiveness.

☐ **The Vestibule** is the space enclosed by the labia minora, at the entrance to the vagina. At its upper end is the opening of the female urethra; at its lower end, it has the entrance to the vagina proper. Opening into the vestibule, from the inner surface of each labia minor, is the duct of vestibular (Bartholin's) glands. These pea-sized glands are placed, each side, in the substance of the labia minora. The secretions of the vestibular glands play a minor part in lubrication during the later stages of intercourse.

1

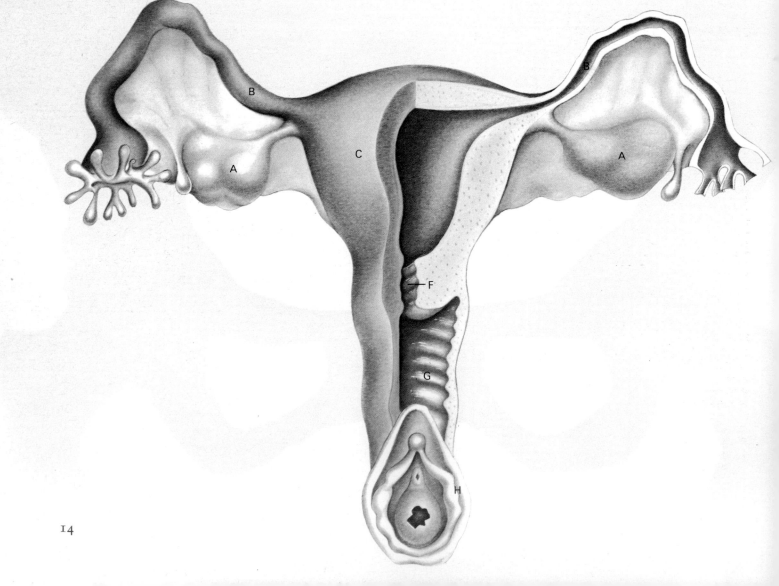

INTERNAL GENITALIA

☐ **Vagina** The vagina is a hollow tube, of about eight cm (three ins) long, which extends upwards and backwards from the vestibule at its lower end to the cervix at its upper end. At the lower end there is a membraneous fold, known as the hymen. The hymen varies considerably in thickness, elasticity and in the size of its central opening. In a virgin the opening will usually only admit the tip of a little finger but, after stretching to allow the insertion of a tampon, or after the first intercourse, when it is usually torn, two fingers can be inserted without difficulty.

1 Diagram to show the essential parts of the female reproductive organs, viewed from the front, showing the ovaries, the Fallopian tubes, the uterus and the uterine wall, the vagina and the vaginal wall, the labia and the vestibule.

2 Diagram to show the position of the female internal and external reproductive organs, viewed from the side.

3 Diagram to show the relative positions of the female internal reproductive organs within the pelvis.

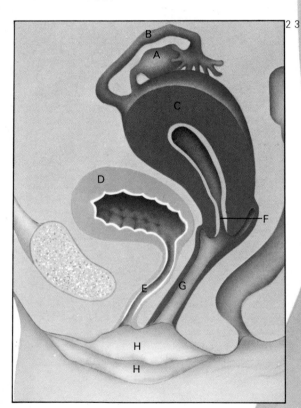

Key:
A Ovary
B Fallopian tube
C Uterus
D Bladder
E Urethra
F Cervix
G Vagina
H Labia

The vagina is lined by normal skin which is thrown into numerous folds. The elasticity of the vaginal walls allow it to be distended and elongated very considerably during intercourse.

☐ **Uterus (womb)** The uterus is a hollow muscular organ, the size and shape of an inverted pear. It is placed in the pelvis at the top of the vagina and is normally angled forward from it (anteversion). About twenty per cent of women have a uterus which is tilted backwards. This condition is called retroversion, but it is not usually of any importance.

The lowest part of the uterus, the cervix (neck of the womb) protrudes into the vagina. The central opening (the external os) leads up a short canal through an inner opening (the internal os) into the cavity of the uterus. The cavity of the uterus is lined by a special membrane, known as the endometrium, which responds to the ovarian hormones. This is shed once a month if fertilization does not occur. The shed endometrium, together with a variable amount of blood which escapes at the time of shedding, make up the menstrual flow which passes down the cervical canal and into the vagina.

☐ **Uterine tubes (Fallopian tubes)** The uterine (Fallopian) tubes are two hollow structures the diameter of thick string. They extend outwards from the uterus on either side to the ovaries. Each tube is about eleven cm (four-and-a-half ins) long. The muscles in the walls of the tubes are arranged so that their contents are squeezed towards the uterus. The tube is narrowest where it enters the uterus and widest at its outer end close to the ovary.

The outer end of the tube has a number of finger-like projections which stretch out towards the ovary and help to pick up the egg cell after it is released and conduct it into the tube. Fertilization occurs in the tube and the fertilized egg is then passed down it into the uterus where development of the baby takes place.

☐ **Ovary** The ovaries are the female equivalent of the testes and lie, one on each side of the pelvis, near to the outer end of the uterine tubes. Like the testes, the ovaries serve two functions. They produce egg cells (ova) and the female hormones, oestrogen and progesterone. Each ovary contains about two hundred thousand ova in early life, but the numbers decrease with age and all remaining ova disappear after the menopause. Only about four hundred ova actually develop fully and are eventually released at monthly intervals into the adjacent uterine tube.

It is thought that ova are released from alternate ovaries each month. At the start of each menstrual cycle a controlling (gonadotrophic) hormone from the pituitary gland causes one egg cell in one or other ovary to enlarge and mature. As it does so, the space in which it sits becomes distended with fluid and moves close to the surface of the ovary. This fluid-filled space and the egg cell it contains is called the Graafian follicle.

The follicle secretes the female hormone, oestrogen, and ruptures under the influence of another controlling hormone to release the egg cell from the ovarian surface into the outer end of the uterine tube. The Graafian follicle persists for some time after the egg cell has been shed and is then called the corpus luteum. This name comes from the yellow pigment which accumulates in it at this time. The corpus luteum secretes the female hormones oestrogen and progesterone which act on the lining of the uterus and build it up.

If fertilization does not occur the corpus luteum degenerates and stops producing its hormones. When this happens the lining breaks down and is shed, giving rise to menstruation (period), after which the cycle begins all over again.

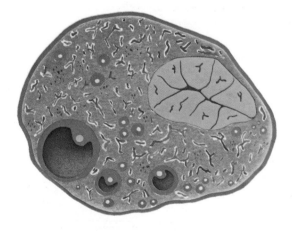

Cross-section through an ovary. As an ovum (egg cell) enlarges and matures, the area around it becomes distended and filled with fluid. This fluid-filled area and the ovum it contains is known as the Graafian follicle. The Graafian follicle moves closer to the surface of the ovary and finally ruptures, releasing the mature ovum into the outer end of the Fallopian tube. The follicle persists for a time after this and is then known as the corpus luteum.

Infertility

Most normal women who have sexual intercourse two or three times a week, become pregnant within a year of normal married life. There is, however, no need to worry if pregnancy does not occur *immediately* after starting to try for a baby. If nothing has happened by the end of a year, a doctor should be consulted. Infertility means being unable to conceive and may result from a number of causes which will need investigation.

THE BEST TIME TO CONCEIVE

Conception is most likely to occur when intercourse takes place about the time of ovulation (see page 18). When a woman has a normal twenty-eight day menstrual cycle, ovulation usually occurs on the fourteenth day, counting the first day of the menstrual period as day number one. Intercourse about this time is most likely to be successful, especially if the man is 'rested', i.e., has not had intercourse for a few days before this time.

The temperature chart refers to women who have a twenty-eight day menstrual cycle, i.e., four weeks from the start of one period to the start of the next. Many normal women have a longer cycle, five or six weeks from the start of one period to the start of another. In these women, ovulation is delayed and occurs, on average, fourteen days before the *start* of the next period.

Although conception is most likely to occur following intercourse on the expected day of ovulation, it is important to realize that pregnancy can result from intercourse at any time during the menstrual cycle because ovulation does not always take place at the expected time.

IMPROVING CHANCES

The younger and healthier a couple is, the greater their chances of starting a family when they want to. Couples who are overweight, overtired, worried, who eat, drink or smoke too much, will find it both more difficult to achieve a pregnancy and to have a really healthy baby.

Some women who do not become pregnant as quickly as they wish become over-anxious. This, in turn, makes pregnancy even less likely. Reassurance from a doctor, proper investigations and treatment, if necessary, are, of course, important. Equally important, however, is the necessity to remain calm and to get on, as philosophically as possible, with the business of living and loving.

Couples who plan to have sexual intercourse too strictly in accordance with a fertility chart may become too tense to cope.

CAUSES OF INFERTILITY

It is a fact that many couples who fail to achieve a pregnancy are normal by all present-day tests. This indicates that there is still a great deal to be learned about human infertility.

Of the known causes, the following are the most important:—

☐ **HIM   Too few sperm** This may be a congenital defect or may be the result of an earlier infection, especially gonorrhoea or mumps which involves inflammation of the testicles. A low sperm count may also result from poor general health.

☐ **Impotence** The inability to have sexual intercourse is usually due to a temporary psychological upset.

☐ **HER   Failure to ovulate** The failure of the ovary to produce an egg results from a hormonal disturbance involving the pituitary gland. In this instance the gland fails to stimulate the ovary to ovulate.

☐ **Blocked tubes** This results from an infection in the tubes (salpingitis). It may occur as a complication of gonorrhoea or after a termination of pregnancy or spontaneous abortion.

☐ **Cervical mucus** In some women the mucus secreted by the glands of the cervix is abnormal, and prevents the sperm from passing through into the uterus.

INVESTIGATING INFERTILITY

As infertility can be caused by either partner, it is vital for both to be investigated. Likewise, it is important that the problems and proposed investigations or treatment should be discussed with both partners.

☐ **HIM** The husband should be seen and examined by a male fertility specialist. The most important test is an examination of the seminal fluid. For this a sample of semen, obtained by masturbation, is analysed to ascertain the number of sperm present. The activity of the individual sperms and presence of abnormal sperms are also noted.

☐ **HER** The wife should be seen and examined by a gynaecologist who has a special interest in infertility problems. There are tests which are designed to show if and when ovulation is occurring. The tubes are also tested to see if they are open. Quite often, nowadays, the tests are combined in a single procedure called laparoscopy. In this instance, the woman is admitted to hospital for forty-eight hours, a few days before a period is due. Under an anaesthetic a pencil-sized telescope (laparoscope) is passed into the abdomen through a tiny cut that is made just below the

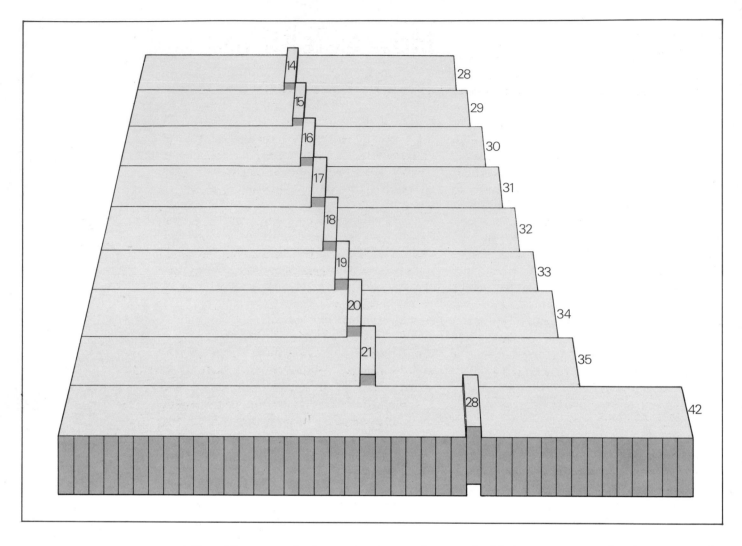

umbilicus. The gynaecologist can then inspect the tubes and ovaries to see if they are normal and, at the same time, take a blood sample and a sample from the lining of the womb—endometrium—to check that ovulation is occurring.

A post-coital test can also be carried out on the woman a few hours after intercourse has taken place at the time of ovulation. A sample of the secretion in the neck of the womb—cervix—is taken and examined under the microscope to see if living sperm are present. In a normally fertile woman plenty of active sperm can be seen, but in some women the secretion is too sticky or contains some substances harmful to the sperm (sperm antibodies) so that only a few dead sperm are present.

TREATMENT

When no abnormality is found, no treatment is necessary. In fact, pregnancy often follows soon after the investigations have been completed and reassurance given.

☐ **HIM** Drugs can be given to the husband to improve his sperm count and quality of semen. Occasionally a minor surgical operation may be needed. Psychological difficulties, which have resulted in impotence, can often be overcome by discussion between the couple and a sympathetic psycho-sexual counsellor.

☐ **HER** Failure of ovulation can be treated by fertility drugs. With some drugs twins are the worst hazard! With other much stronger stimulants greater care is needed to avoid multiple ovulation resulting in multiple births. Such drugs should only be given in specialized clinics that have the facilities to get the dose exactly right.

When the cervical mucus is hostile to the husband's sperm, a small dose of the female hormone, oestrogen, given in the middle of the menstrual cycle can improve the receptivity of the mucus.

Blocked tubes can sometimes be unblocked surgically and, with modern techniques using an operating microscope, results are improving all the time. The success rate of tubal surgery is, however, still low. The best way to avoid blocked tubes is to avoid the inflammation—salpingitis—which causes them. For this and other reasons do not risk gonorrhoea or have a pregnancy terminated unnecessarily. If a termination is essential or if a spontaneous abortion does occur, make sure that it is properly dealt with by an expert.

ADOPTION

When all reasonable investigations and treatment have failed to enable a couple to have a baby of their own, adoption can, of course, be considered as an alternative. It is important, however, not to leave the consideration of adoption too late. It is often extremely difficult to adopt a child these days and the sooner a couple begin the procedure and get on to the waiting list of an adoption society, the better. Adoption societies, currently faced with too great a demand for too few babies, tend to favour young couples whose only medical problem is infertility. Handicapped babies or babies of mixed racial origin are easier to adopt than other babies.

It is *not* true that adopting a baby is often followed by the couple producing one of their own, although this does sometimes happen. It *is* true that it does not matter if the eventual family consists of adopted and natural children, provided the children are told the truth and provided that love is seen to be fairly distributed.

ARTIFICIAL INSEMINATION

Artificial insemination can be performed using either the husband's semen or semen from a donor. Artificial insemination, using the husband's semen, AIH, is rarely of value except when the man is unable to have intercourse properly with his partner because of an anatomical abnormality or a psycho-sexual problem which cannot be resolved. AIH may also be used when the woman's cervical mucus is hostile to the husband's sperm and cannot be improved with hormone treatment. Putting the husband's semen directly into the uterus, so that contact with the cervical mucus is avoided, does sometimes result in pregnancy. The results of this approach, however, have so far been disappointing.

Because of the difficulties involved in adoption nowadays, artificial insemination, using donor semen, AID, is being increasingly used in cases where the husband has no sperm or only a very small number of sperm. For AID, semen from anonymous donors of proven fertility is injected into the wife's vagina at the time of ovulation. Selection of infertile couples for this method of treatment has to be done very carefully and can only be carried out if both husband and wife are in full agreement about its desirability. An attempt is usually made to match the donor's physical characteristics such as race, height, colouring, with that of the husband. The success rate in properly selected women is high and, so far, no obvious disadvantages have emerged. The legal and ethical problems, however, remain to be fully resolved.

How to Tell If You are Pregnant

Pregnancy is one of the most commonly mis-diagnosed conditions in medical practice. Some women who think they are pregnant are not, while others go through half a pregnancy (or more!) before they realize what is happening. Doctors diagnose pregnancy when it is not present, or fail to diagnose it when the patient's symptoms suggest other conditions! The possibilities for error are enormous. Yet, for the vast majority of women, the diagnosis is perfectly straightforward.

SIGNS AND SYMPTOMS OF PREGNANCY

☐ **Cessation of normal monthly periods** For a woman who usually has a normal regular menstrual cycle, a missed period is the most important and reliable symptom of pregnancy. If the periods are usually irregular, however, it may be a while before the absence of periods is noticed. By this time, other symptoms will be drawing attention to the situation.

The answer to whether or not a woman can have normal periods when pregnant is no. Any woman who is having normal regular periods is not pregnant. Slight bleeding may occur at intervals during the first three months of pregnancy, but this is not the same as having a period, and is best regarded and treated as a threatened miscarriage. Heavier bleeding should certainly be so treated. Women who claim that they have 'normal periods' when pregnant have usually had a repeated threatened miscarriage which has cleared up and allowed the pregnancy to continue normally.

☐ **Enlarged, tender breasts** The breasts often become a little enlarged and tender before a period is due; these breast changes are even more noticeable as soon as pregnancy occurs and the first period is missed. Once the pregnancy is fully established it is usually possible to express a yellow fluid called colostrum from the nipples.

☐ **Sickness** Most but not all pregnant women suffer from some degree of nausea in early pregnancy which may make them vomit. Early morning sickness is a traditional pregnancy symptom, but in reality the nausea and vomiting may occur at any time of the day.

☐ **Tiredness** Early pregnancy is often associated with a feeling of fatigue and a desire to sleep for longer periods than usual. The answer is to give the body what it needs—rest.

1 With the aid of a simple examination, the doctor can confirm a pregnancy within eight weeks of the last menstrual period.

2 It is a very thrilling moment when a woman can tell her husband that pregnancy has been confirmed.

☐ **Micturition** In early pregnancy the enlarging uterus presses on the bladder and the result is more frequent trips to the lavatory! The pregnant woman also drinks more to quench an increased thirst, and this, too, makes for a greater production of urine.

☐ **Vaginal discharge** A slight white vaginal discharge, which does not cause any local soreness or irritation, is not due to any infection in the vagina. It results from an increase in the normal vaginal secretions.

☐ **Pigmentation** During first pregnancy, the skin on the nipples turns brown because of an increase in the amount of brown pigment. Although the brown colour fades after the pregnancy is over, it never goes completely. As well as changing colour, the small lubricating glands around the nipple increase in size and can be seen as small projections from the surface of the skin. These are known as Montgomery's tubercles, named after the doctor who first described them.

Pigmentation also occurs in a thin line stretching from the pubic bone to the lower end of the breast bone (sternum). This dark line (linea nigra) is more obvious between pubis and navel.

Pigmentation of the face around the eyes, on the cheeks and forehead, is usually present to some degree in most women, but it is not usually very noticeable. Occasionally it is very prominent and the mother-to-be may look as though she is wearing a mask—the so-called mask of pregnancy. Both abdominal and facial pigmentation fade once the pregnancy is over.

DIAGNOSING PREGNANCY

If a woman thinks she may be pregnant she should, of course, consult her doctor. He will usually want to confirm whether or not she is pregnant by doing an examination to see if the uterus (womb) is enlarged. In the early stages of pregnancy this can only be done by a vaginal examination.

1

2

□ **Vaginal Examination** Many women dread the thought of a vaginal or internal examination. The idea that the doctor is going to insert his fingers into the vagina is, for some women, very upsetting and embarrassing. It is, however, a simple examination which is usually painless and, at worst, only slightly uncomfortable. For the doctor it is as normal a part of his routine as, for example, looking into the ear of a patient with earache.

It is very important to be relaxed because if the pelvic and abdominal muscles are tense the examination is much more difficult for the doctor and much more likely to be painful for the patient. If you find you are becoming tense, breathe slowly and steadily with your mouth open. This will help to keep the relevant muscles relaxed.

The examination may be carried out with the woman lying on her back with her knees drawn up, or lying curled up on her left side. The doctor

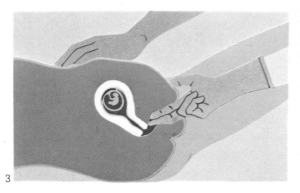

3

will put on a plastic glove and insert one or two fingers gently into the vagina to feel the womb. At the same time, he will press his other hand gently on the lower part of the woman's abdomen. To the experienced doctor, the enlarged soft uterus of pregnancy is easily detectable by about six to eight weeks after the last menstrual period. By estimating the size of the uterus, the doctor can also give an expected date of delivery.

The examination is more easily conducted in thin women than in overweight women. In the latter, the uterus may not be easy to feel in early pregnancy. Provided the patient relaxes completely, however, a confident diagnosis can usually be made by eight weeks even in the plumpest ladies.

□ **The Pregnancy Test** The change that takes place in a woman's hormones when she becomes pregnant provides an easy reliable method of pregnancy testing. The particular hormone that is used for this purpose at the present time is called gonadotrophin. Six weeks from the first day of the last menstrual period, or approximately four weeks after conception has occurred, this appears in the urine in sufficient quantity to be detected. The test can be performed on any clean specimen of urine, but a specimen taken from the first urine passed in the morning gives the most reliable

results. Although the actual performance of the tests is simple, reading the result, especially in the very early stages of pregnancy, can be more difficult. For this reason the test is best done by someone with experience. The local hospital laboratory is usually the most reliable place to have a pregnancy test performed, but many reputable chemists offer a reasonable pregnancy testing service, as do the larger pregnancy advisory services. Do-it-yourself kits are best avoided if other testing facilities are available.

Unfortunately it is in the very early days of pregnancy that test results are least reliable and this can lead to much unnecessary confusion and distress. A test which shows a woman to be pregnant when she is not sometimes arises in women approaching the menopause. This is because the hormonal changes of menopause are similar in some ways to those of early pregnancy. A test which shows the woman not to be pregnant when she is, is most likely to occur in very early pregnancy, between six to eight weeks after the first day of the last menstrual period.

□ **Listening to the Baby's Heart** Once twelve weeks have passed from the first day of the last period, the top of the uterus can be felt in the lower part of the abdomen just above the pubic bone. Feeling the enlarged uterus is, in itself, a good way to diagnose pregnancy, but by using an ultrasonic foetal heart detector the baby's heartbeat can be demonstrated. This provides the most dramatic evidence of all that not only is the woman pregnant, but that the baby is alive and 'ticking'!

□ **Ultrasound** A more complicated ultrasonic machine can be used to diagnose pregnancy from a very early stage, but this sort of ultrasound examination will normally only be carried out at this stage of pregnancy if the other diagnostic measures are inconclusive. See page 36.

□ **X-rays** X-rays are rarely used nowadays to diagnose pregnancy. The baby only shows up on the X-ray after sixteen weeks and by this time the diagnosis is usually obvious by other symptoms and signs. Occasionally a pregnant woman is X-rayed as part of an investigation into other diseases and the baby shows up on the X-ray picture as a surprise intruder! In well-run X-ray departments this will never happen because the radiologist will make quite sure that every woman who is X-rayed is not pregnant. The reason for this is that there is a very slight risk to the baby if an X-ray of the mother's abdomen is taken in early pregnancy. The best general rule is that *a woman who needs an X-ray of the lower abdomen or pelvis should only have it taken in the first ten days of the menstrual cycle.* In this way there will be little risk of X-raying an unsuspected early pregnancy.

3 A vaginal or internal examination is quite painless. The doctor will wear a plastic glove and gently insert one or two fingers into the vagina. By pressing your tummy gently with his other hand he will be able to feel the enlarged uterus of early pregnancy.

Chromosomes and Genes

Almost as soon as pregnancy has been confirmed, every parent becomes fascinated by whether their baby will be a boy or girl, whether he (or she) will have blond, brown, red or dark hair, or blue, green, grey or brown eyes, and whether he will eventually look like his mother or father.

The answers to all these questions are determined in the very moment that the mother's egg cell unites with the father's sperm cell to form a baby. The reason is that both the mother's egg cell and the father's sperm cell contain twenty-three minute, thread-like structures which are known as chromosomes. These chromosomes are responsible for all hereditary characteristics.

The fertilized egg, known as a zygote, has forty-six chromosomes and is, therefore, an equal mixture of both mother and father. Although the fertilized egg cell, containing the forty-six chromosomes, will eventually multiply into innumerable cells which make up a baby, every cell is, of course, a descendant of the original fertilized egg cell and continues to contain forty-six chromosomes arranged in twenty-three pairs.

Of the forty-six chromosomes, forty-four (twenty-two maternal and twenty-two paternal) determine all the hereditary physical structure and function, and one pair, known as the sex chromosomes, determines whether the fertilized egg is to be a girl or boy baby.

SEX CHROMOSOMES

The egg cells of a woman are present when she is born. As they ripen, they divide into cells each of which contains a single sex chromosome called the X chromosome. In contrast, a man's sperm cells do not develop until puberty, when two types of cells are formed in equal proportions. Some of the male sperm cells contain the X chromosome and others contain a Y chromosome.

The actual sex of a baby depends entirely on which type of sperm cell unites with the egg cell. If it is an X-containing sperm, then an XX zygote or female baby will result. If, however, a Y-containing sperm happens to reach the woman's egg cell first, then an XY zygote or male baby will result. It is remarkable that a baby's sex and, therefore, his whole lifestyle is determined by a chance happening at the moment he is conceived!

WHAT ARE GENES?

Each chromosome consists of hundreds of molecules of nucleo-proteins which are known as genes. These 'units of information' are arranged in pairs along the length of each chromosome.

Each pair is situated so that a maternal gene, on a maternal chromosome, is opposite a paternal gene on a paternal chromosome. Each pair of genes accounts for a particular characteristic of an individual, such as a physical feature like hair colouring or an aspect of internal function—metabolism. A gene, depending on its strength, is known as dominant or recessive. For example, the gene which determines the growth of dark hair is known as a dominant gene, while the gene which determines red hair is known as recessive. If, therefore, a baby inherits both these genes from his parents he will have dark hair. He will, however, be a carrier of the gene for red hair and might well pass this gene on to his children. Because the gene for red hair is recessive and, therefore, able to be overpowered by a dominant gene, a red-haired baby will only occur if the gene is inherited from both parents.

WHEN CHROMOSOMES GO WRONG

Unfortunately, at conception, things do occasionally go wrong with chromosomes and genes. Nature, however, has her own way of dealing with many of these abnormalities and imperfections, and approximately one-half of all conceptions are spontaneously aborted.

Careful examination, for example, has revealed that as many as six out of ten aborted foetuses have abnormal chromosomes in each cell, i.e., forty-seven instead of forty-six. Although chromosomes can now be individually labelled, the type of extra chromosome present in these instances varies from case to case.

Another type of abnormality is the absence of a particular chromosome. Here it is usually one of the sex chromosomes that is missing in a baby girl, so that there is only one X chromosome instead of two. Although the external genitalia are perfectly formed, affected individuals are subsequently infertile.

Occasionally, babies with chromosome abnormalities are not spontaneously aborted and are born in the normal way. In rare cases the chromosome abnormality causes malformation of many different organs and these babies usually die soon after birth. Other types of chromosome abnormality are, however, compatible with life, although the affected babies might have abnormal characteristics which remain. The most common example is mongolism, also known as Down's syndrome. There are also very slight chromosome abnormalities which would only be detected if the chromosomes were analysed for some reason.

1 A child's facial features, colour of skin, eyes and hair are determined at the moment of conception by the type of genes carried on the maternal and paternal chromosomes. The development of many other personal characteristics depend on the environment. For example, a child's intelligence is strongly influenced by the amount of opportunity there is to explore and learn.

2 Every human cell has 46 chromosomes —23 from each parent. Forty-four of these determine all hereditary characteristics such as hair colour. The remaining pair determine sex. If two X chromosomes combine the baby will be a girl; if one X and one Y chromosome combine, as in this case, the baby will be a boy.

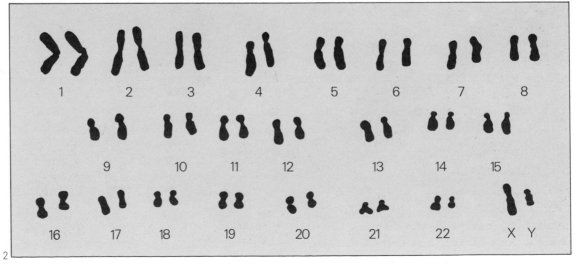

2

A baby may have normal chromosomes and yet have an abnormality of a single gene or pair of genes. Abnormal genes, just like normal genes, may be dominant or recessive. In conditions caused by an abnormal dominant gene, such as congenital dwarfism, affected individuals may inherit the gene from either a mother or father who suffers from the same disorder, although both parents may be normal. In these cases the gene abnormality in the offspring is called a mutation and the gene is known as a mutant gene.

On rare occasions, a baby may be born with a metabolic disturbance—an abnormality of internal bodily function. Many chemical reactions in the body rely on enzymes to trigger them off and a pair of genes controls the development of individual enzymes. These are recessive genes, so that if both genes of the pair are faulty, one from the mother and one from the father, the appropriate enzyme does not develop. This leads to a metabolic disturbance. Neither the mother nor the father shows signs of any disturbance because they have only one abnormal gene which is matched by a normal gene. The parents are called carriers. The diseases in question are fortunately rare because there is only a small chance that a carrier of a particular disease would happen to choose a partner who is also a carrier.

Unfortunately, in most of these diseases, there is no way of telling who is a carrier until a baby is born with the disease. Phenylketonuria is an example of a metabolic disease caused by a pair of abnormal recessive genes. Here the baby cannot metabolize a chemical called phenylalanine which is present in milk and other food. Fortunately this condition can be controlled with the help of a special diet.

Another example of disease caused by a pair of abnormal recessive genes is cystic fibrosis. Affected babies fail to grow properly because of malabsorption of food and repeated chest infection. Although this is probably the most common of the inherited metabolic disorders, affecting one in two thousand babies, the precise biochemical cause of the disturbance is unknown.

Finally, if a single abnormal recessive gene happens to be situated on an X chromosome, it will cause problems. In a male (XY) it will behave like a dominant gene and cause disease. In contrast, if a female (XX) has a single abnormal recessive gene on one of her X chromosomes, the disease will not manifest but she will be a carrier. Examples of diseases that occur in males and are carried by apparently normal females, are haemophilia, one type of muscular dystrophy and colour blindness.

1

1,2 Quite commonly a baby's facial features and even the colour of his hair or eyes alter with growth; a resemblance between him and other members of the family may only develop later. A mother might wonder how tall her baby will be. Height is one genetically determined characteristic that is modified by the environment in childhood. Over-eating will not make a baby taller. However, if a child is seriously under-nourished, he may not achieve his genetically intended height. A child's personality is also influenced by the environment in the early years. The laughter that lights up a child's face generally reflects a happy home environment.

Genetic Counselling

Even before conception many people worry about the risk of a baby being born with a certain abnormality. A couple may, for example, already have an abnormal baby, or a relative may have an abnormality. In these circumstances a genetic counsellor can often estimate the risk of a particular disorder occurring in a baby. The accuracy of a prediction can, however, only be made with a reasonable certainty if the precise nature of the disorder in question is known. The parents are usually seen in an out-patient clinic where a detailed family history is taken. This enables a family tree to be drawn up indicating any members of the family who may have suffered from the disorder.

Most abnormalities are not inherited in a simple dominant or recessive way. Indeed many of the fortunately rare congenital abnormalities result from a complex interplay of genetic and environmental factors. Examples include hare lip, cleft palate and congenital dislocation of the hip joint, all of which can be successfully treated in the first twelve months of life. In such cases, the counsellor can only give a very approximate risk of the abnormality occurring. However, even when there is a family history, the risk of it recurring is usually small.

Genetic counselling and the diagnosis of abnormality in the unborn baby early in pregnancy are complementary services. Sometimes parents, having received genetic counselling, decide to have a baby knowing that it will be possible to detect the abnormality and terminate the pregnancy should this prove necessary. Unfortunately, only a few abnormalities can be diagnosed early in pregnancy. When this approach is feasible it does, at least, give the parents a chance of having a baby free from the defect in question.

The most common reason for genetic testing is when a mother is at risk of giving birth to a baby with spina bifida or mongolism. There are various types of spina bifida, but basically the abnormality means that some of the bones of the vertebral arches have failed to form their usual protective role of encasing the spinal cord. In this rare instance, a segment of spinal cord, usually in the lower part of the back, becomes exposed on the surface of the skin.

When this happens, a chemical, known as alpha fetoprotein, is present in large quantities in the waters (amniotic fluid) that surround the unborn baby. A sample of the fluid can be removed at about the sixteenth week of pregnancy and analysed. Although a very high level of alpha fetoprotein suggests that spina bifida is present, the level does not always rise in some of the milder forms of the condition.

Cells from the skin of an unborn baby are continually shed into the fluid. If a specimen of this fluid is removed by amniocentesis (see p. 38) the cells can be separated and grown in a special broth. After two weeks, if the cells are looked at with a powerful microscope, the chromosomes in each cell can be seen and counted. It is possible to diagnose mongolism in this way. This test is generally performed for women who have a somewhat greater risk of giving birth to a mongol, namely those over thirty-five years, and those who have already given birth to a mongol.

The results of chemical tests done on cells that an unborn baby has shed into the amniotic fluid can reveal certain rare metabolic disorders. These tests are only applicable to women who have already given birth to a baby with a rare metabolic disorder, because both parents carry an abnormal recessive gene.

If a mother is a carrier of the rare disease of haemophilia there is a one in two chance that male babies born to her would be affected. Chromosome analysis of the unborn baby's skin cells enables the sex of the baby to be determined early in pregnancy. A mother may feel that if she is carrying a boy in these circumstances she is justified in having the pregnancy terminated.

Pregnancy

Fertilization and Pregnancy
Conception

From the moment when a sperm penetrates into the egg cell (ovum) and their nuclei join together, pregnancy begins. Before fertilization can take place, however, the sperm have to reach the outer part of the tube in which the egg cell is deposited from the ovary about the middle of each menstrual cycle. Semen, containing many millions of sperm, is deposited at the top of the vagina at the time of male orgasm. Once deposited the sperm face a difficult journey to reach the egg. Most of the semen, in fact, containing the majority of the sperm, leaks out of the vagina soon after it has been deposited and most of the sperm are killed off by the acid vaginal secretion. Women often worry that the loss of semen and the acidity of the vaginal secretion may be the cause of their failure to become pregnant. This is not the case, however, for the successful sperm escape the effect of vaginal acidity by reaching the cervical canal very shortly after having been deposited in the vagina.

The cervical canal is blocked by cervical mucus through which the sperm must penetrate in order to make their way up into the uterus. Although the sperm swim actively, their journey into the uterus and the Fallopian tube is most likely to be the result of movement of the uterus and tubes which tends to suck them up and out towards the egg cell. Of the millions of sperm present in the original ejaculation, only a few hundred reach the outer end of the tube after a few minutes. Once in the outer part of the tube the sperm undergo a process called capacitation. As a result of this process, chemical substances—enzymes—are produced which enable the successful sperm to dissolve the outer membrane surrounding the egg cell and penetrate into its centre. As the solitary survivor of an army of many millions, the successful sperm is very highly selected. Once the egg cell has been penetrated by the sperm, it changes its outer coat so that no further penetration by the other sperm in the outer part of the tube can occur. In this way multiple fertilization by a number of sperm is avoided. The timing of fertilization is very precise because the egg cell only lives for twenty-four hours after being shed and entering the tube, and the sperm do not survive for much longer than this after ejaculation. It follows that for fertilization to occur intercourse must take place within twenty-four hours of ovulation.

THE FERTILIZED EGG

The fertilized egg starts the process of development immediately. During the first five days, whilst the early stages of growth are taking place, the developing egg moves down the tube and into the uterus. At the same time, it starts to produce hormones which, together with the mother's own ovarian hormones, help to prepare the lining of the uterus to receive it. The process by which the normal lining—endometrium—of a non-pregnant woman is changed to the much thicker lining of

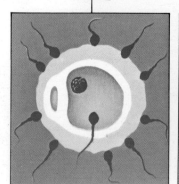

Fertilization

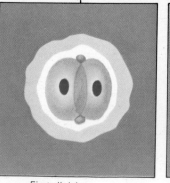

First division
30 hours

pregnancy—decidua—is very important, for once the egg has reached the uterus it must implant itself into this lining.

In order for implantation to occur, more enzymes are called into play. These enable the developing egg to penetrate fully into the lining and then start the process by which a placenta is formed. The placenta is the vitally important organ which nourishes the baby during the whole of its life in the uterus. Implantation of the fertilized egg is completed by about eight days after fertilization has occurred. Over the succeeding twelve weeks the egg grows to fill the cavity of the uterus. As the egg grows, the uterus enlarges under the influences of the hormones produced by the developing egg and by the mother's ovaries. In twelve weeks the uterus is completely filled by the developing pregnancy, which has become a foetus with umbilical cord and placenta.

TEST-TUBE BABIES

Recently much work has been done to try to help women in whom the Fallopian tubes have previously been blocked or destroyed by disease. In order to enable these women to have a baby, an egg has been taken from the ovary and fertilized by the husband's semen in a test-tube. The fertilized egg is then reimplanted into the uterus by artificial means. The process by which the lining of the uterus is prepared for the egg is very elaborate and so far only a few successful implantations leading to the birth of live babies have been reported. The low success rate of this and the surgical procedures to open blocked tubes emphasise the importance of avoiding tubal infection which causes the damage in the first place.

Fertilization takes place in the outer end of the uterine tube. The fertilized egg then passes along the tube to the uterus where it implants.

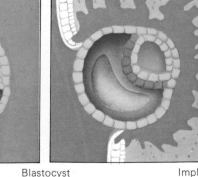

Blastocyst
5–6 days

Implantation
7 days

Foetal Development

The development of the human baby from a single cell, which is formed when the ovum is fertilized by a sperm, remains the greatest miracle of nature. The whole process takes an average of only two hundred and sixty-nine days, from the day of fertilization. This is the same as saying two hundred and eighty-two days, forty weeks or ten lunar months from the first day of the last menstrual period. During this short time, the single cell becomes a complex structure of many millions of cells, each of which is highly developed to perform a specialized function within the baby's body. By the time the baby is born, it is six billion times heavier than the egg from which it came.

What happens inside the uterus throughout pregnancy is now clearly understood, but little is known about how and why the baby develops as it does. What is known is that development is controlled by the genes and the chromosomes which make up the nucleus of the fertilized egg. These genes, derived half and half from mother and father (see page 23), determine the steps in development and the eventual physical and mental form and character of the baby. As human individuals, we are then, what our parents' genes have made us; but the environment in which we live in the uterus before birth, and in the world afterwards, can modify the effects of heredity very considerably. This is especially true during the forty weeks of life in the uterus when we are entirely dependent upon our mother's ability to supply us with the oxygen and all nutrition which is essential to healthy growth and development.

THE FIRST TWELVE WEEKS

During the first twelve weeks of life, whilst the transformation from fertilized egg to fully formed embryo is proceeding, the embryo is particularly sensitive to outside influences. Everyone has heard of thalidomide babies or babies rendered blind or deaf because the mother caught German measles —rubella—in early pregnancy. These are two classic examples of the adverse effects which external influences may have on the developing baby. It is probable, however, that many other agents can produce lesser effects. Virus infections, like 'flu, may cause an effect upon the baby, although the effects are far less serious than those caused by German measles. Similarly, other drugs may have an adverse effect, although the serious effects of thalidomide are fortunately restricted to that particular drug. The importance of maintaining the best possible standard of health and of avoiding any unnecessary drugs during the early part of pregnancy cannot be over-emphasized.

To calculate the expected date of delivery: look at the date when the last menstrual period began on the top lines of figures in light type. The expected date of delivery appears immediately underneath in dark type. This date is only approximate.

OBSTETRIC TABLE
To calculate the expected date of delivery

	1	2	3	4	5	6	7	8	9	10	11	12	13	14	15	16	17	18	19	20	21	22	23	24	25	26	27	28	29	30	31	
January / **OCTOBER**	8	9	10	11	12	13	14	15	16	17	18	19	20	21	22	23	24	25	26	27	28	29	30	31	1	2	3	4	5	6	7	January / **NOVEMBER**
February / **NOVEMBER**	8	9	10	11	12	13	14	15	16	17	18	19	20	21	22	23	24	25	26	27	28	29	30	1	2	3	4	5				February / **DECEMBER**
March / **DECEMBER**	6	7	8	9	10	11	12	13	14	15	16	17	18	19	20	21	22	23	24	25	26	27	28	29	30	31	1	2	3	4	5	March / **JANUARY**
April / **JANUARY**	6	7	8	9	10	11	12	13	14	15	16	17	18	19	20	21	22	23	24	25	26	27	28	29	30	31	1	2	3	4		April / **FEBRUARY**
May / **FEBRUARY**	5	6	7	8	9	10	11	12	13	14	15	16	17	18	19	20	21	22	23	24	25	26	27	28	1	2	3	4	5	6	7	May / **MARCH**
June / **MARCH**	8	9	10	11	12	13	14	15	16	17	18	19	20	21	22	23	24	25	26	27	28	29	30	31	1	2	3	4	5	6		June / **APRIL**
July / **APRIL**	7	8	9	10	11	12	13	14	15	16	17	18	19	20	21	22	23	24	25	26	27	28	29	30	1	2	3	4	5	6	7	July / **MAY**
August / **MAY**	8	9	10	11	12	13	14	15	16	17	18	19	20	21	22	23	24	25	26	27	28	29	30	31	1	2	3	4	5	6	7	August / **JUNE**
September / **JUNE**	8	9	10	11	12	13	14	15	16	17	18	19	20	21	22	23	24	25	26	27	28	29	30	1	2	3	4	5	6	7		September / **JULY**
October / **JULY**	8	9	10	11	12	13	14	15	16	17	18	19	20	21	22	23	24	25	26	27	28	29	30	31	1	2	3	4	5	6	7	October / **AUGUST**
November / **AUGUST**	8	9	10	11	12	13	14	15	16	17	18	19	20	21	22	23	24	25	26	27	28	29	30	31	1	2	3	4	5	6		November / **SEPTEMBER**
December / **SEPTEMBER**	7	8	9	10	11	12	13	14	15	16	17	18	19	20	21	22	23	24	25	26	27	28	29	30	1	2	3	4	5	6	7	December / **OCTOBER**

Antenatal Care

Until the beginning of the twentieth century, unless complications developed, a pregnant woman did not consult her midwife or doctor until she went into labour. The idea of antenatal care arose from the realization that many complications could be prevented if mothers-to-be were seen and examined throughout pregnancy. Modern antenatal care starts early and aims not only at preventing complications, but also at keeping the mother-to-be fit and happy. Today she can approach labour with the quiet confidence that comes from proper antenatal care and a knowledge of what will happen to her in labour and who will be looking after her. With this understanding of what is happening during pregnancy, women are better equipped to take care of their health and that of their unborn child. Since knowledge relieves many of the common anxieties, it is very important that during the antenatal period the mother-to-be comes to understand the processes of pregnancy and labour.

ATTENDANCE AT THE ANTENATAL CLINIC

Regular antenatal examinations are the cornerstone of modern obstetric care, so regular visits to the antenatal clinic, however boring or tedious they may seem, are vital to the expectant mother's and baby's well-being. If the mother-to-be is unable to keep a particular appointment, she should tell the doctor or midwife so that an alternative appointment can be arranged. Failure to do this is not only unfair to the doctor or midwife, but to the baby and the mother-to-be herself.

As soon as a woman thinks she may be pregnant she should consult her doctor and have the pregnancy confirmed (see page 20). This will normally be two to three weeks after the first period is missed, i.e. six to seven weeks after the last menstrual period. Once pregnancy has been diagnosed, an appointment should be made for the first proper antenatal visit. In most cases this will involve a trip to the hospital booking antenatal clinic. This usually takes place ten to twelve weeks after the last menstrual period. Women who feel well in early pregnancy often postpone the first visit to the doctor, but this is misguided. A simple examination in early pregnancy is very helpful in detecting complications and establishing that the foetus is developing normally.

The first visit to the antenatal clinic is an exciting event for every pregnant woman—exciting because having succeeded in becoming pregnant she will be anxious to be reassured that all is well

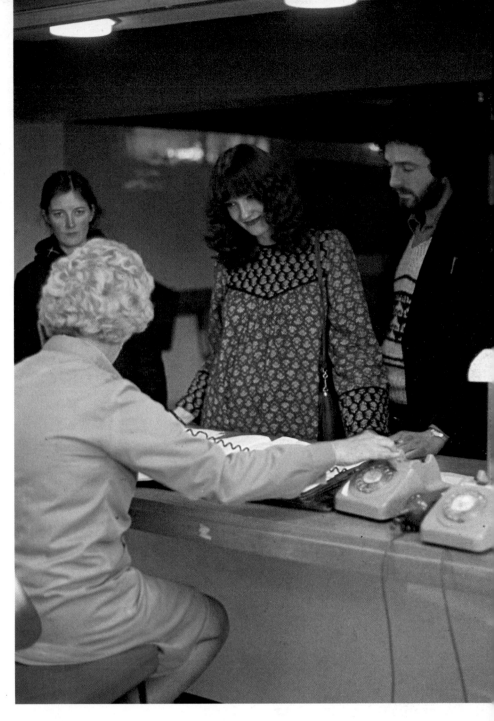

and that she has nothing to fear in the six months or so that follow. Antenatal clinics are usually very busy and, unfortunately, harassed doctors and midwives sometimes overlook the fact that the woman making her first visit may be apprehensive and worried. Fortunately, however, most clinics are happy places and the large number of patients, overcrowded accommodation and insufficient staff and equipment are cheerfully accepted by the team running them. A welcoming attitude by the staff helps to make the long wait more acceptable and certainly allays apprehension. Fear of what may happen to her may make the antenatal patient *im*patient and aggressive so that friction develops. An understanding of the problems by both sides leads to better relationships and, incidentally, more efficient antenatal care which, after all, is to the final benefit of expectant mother, baby and clinic staff.

Antenatal clinics are busy places but all the staff are concerned to provide the best care possible for the mother-to-be and her baby.

The First Visit

Inevitably, a form will need to be filled in. The form, in this case, is an antenatal record sheet. On it the midwife or doctor interviewing the patient will enter the essential details of past medical or obstetric problems and of the history of the present pregnancy so far. It helps if the patient can remember the details of her medical history and especially the date of her last menstrual period which is important in calculating the expected date of delivery. The simple sum, assuming a regular twenty-eight day cycle, is first day of last menstrual period, plus seven days, minus three calendar months, equals expected date of delivery e.g. LMP 13.4.78 = EDD 20.1.79.

Once the form is filled, the clinical examination and various tests will be carried out. What the doctor wants to know about a pregnant woman is (1) is she healthy? (2) is the pregnancy proceeding normally?

In order to answer the first question the doctor will carry out a general examination of the woman, paying particular attention to the heart and lungs and breasts. Weight and height are also important and will be measured.

The second question is answered by the doctor examining the abdomen to feel if the uterus is growing up from the pelvis as it should do from twelve weeks onwards. The size of the uterus has to be confirmed by a vaginal examination. For this, the doctor inserts his first (or first and second) fingers into the vagina and feels the uterus between his fingers and his other hand which is placed on the lower part of the abdomen (see page 21). The vaginal examination also gives the doctor a chance to feel the ovaries and tubes alongside the uterus and detect any abnormality, such as an ovarian cyst. Finally, the doctor will feel the bony part of the woman's pelvis to try to assess whether or not it is likely to be big enough to allow the passage of a normal sized baby in labour. As well as the clinical examination a series of special tests will be carried out on every mother-to-be to check that everything is going well with her and the foetus.

1 Keeping the important record of weight gain throughout pregnancy is begun at the first visit. The expectant mother will be weighed at each visit.

2

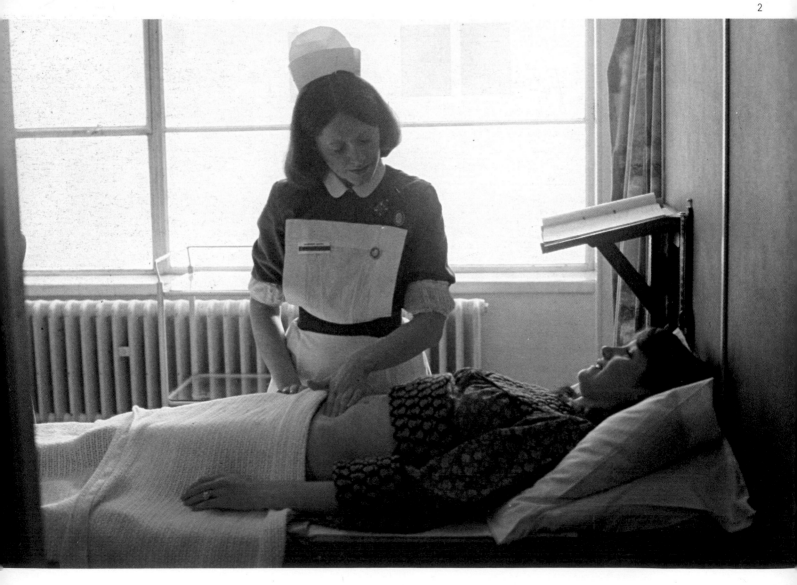

URINE TESTING

At every antenatal visit a specimen of urine is tested for protein (albumin) and glucose (sugar). This is a simple way of knowing if the patient is developing toxaemia or diabetes. Sugar in the urine is common in pregnancy, but *sometimes* it is due to the fact that the mother-to-be is developing diabetes. Because infection of the urine is more common in pregnancy than at other times, many hospitals also test urine for germs at the first visit.

BLOOD TESTING

A sample of blood is taken by inserting a needle into the vein in the front of the arm and drawing a small quantity of blood into a syringe. A number of tests are then carried out on the blood.

☐ **Blood Group** It is very important to know the blood group of the mother-to-be in case a transfusion should be needed. The blood group is in two parts: the A, B, O group, in which the patient is either group A or O (the commonest) or B or AB (the least common). The second part of the blood group is the rhesùs group and the patient is either rhesus positive or rhesus negative. Being

3

rhesus negative used to be quite a serious matter because rhesus antibodies could sometimes form in second and subsequent pregnancies in rhesus negative women and harm a rhesus positive baby causing anaemia and jaundice. This can now be prevented by a suitable injection after delivery (see page 68).

☐ **Haemoglobin** The amount of haemoglobin in each blood cell determines its ability to carry oxygen around the body. When the haemoglobin level is low the patient is anaemic. Anaemia results from a lack of iron and folic acid in most cases. In such cases the haemoglobin level falls below the normal one hundred per cent. In pregnant women a haemoglobin of eighty per cent or more is normal because retention of water during pregnancy dilutes the blood.

☐ **Test for Syphilis** Although syphilis is very uncommon nowadays, in pregnant women, it is, nevertheless, such a serious condition that all pregnant women's blood is tested to make sure that they are free of syphilitic infection. The test that is usually carried out is called the Kahn test. This ensures no undiagnosed infection.

2 There is not much of a 'bump' for the midwife or nurse to feel at the first antenatal clinic, but once 12 weeks have passed, a 'bump' certainly is there, if only a small one at first.

3 Measuring the blood pressure at the first antenatal visit is important because a high level at later visist may indicate toxaemia.

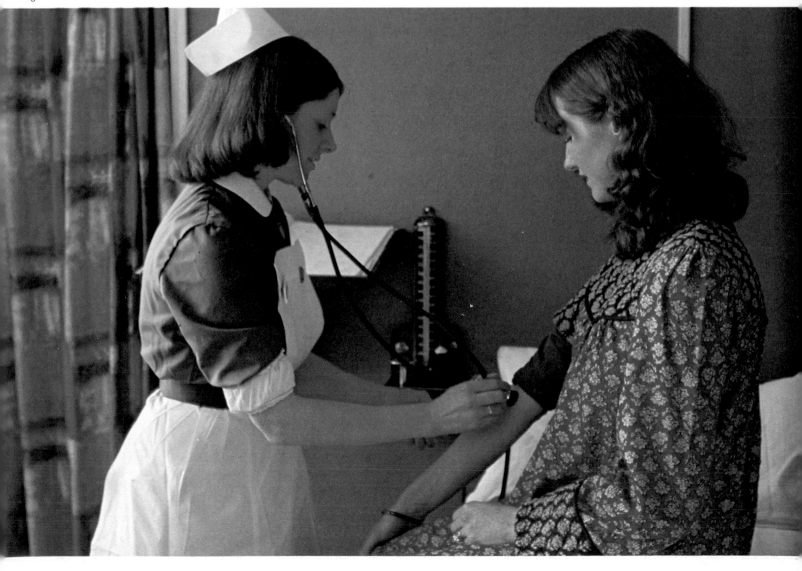

8 weeks

The fertilized egg takes about seven-to-eight days to pass down the Fallopian tube and implant itself into the decidua—the thickened lining of the uterus. Thereafter, rapid growth and development occurs so that, by eight weeks, a recognizable embryonic baby is present, in a bag of fluid called the amniotic sac.

This sac is formed by two membranes which develop from cells on the outside of the fertilized egg. The outer of the two membranes is called the chorion and it encloses the inner membrane, the amnion, which contains the amniotic fluid.

By eight weeks the body has formed with limbs, and fingers and toes are starting to be visible. The ear, nose and mouth openings are present. The eyes have formed, but are covered by the eyelids. They do not open until about twenty-four weeks. The heart forms very early in development and, by six weeks, beats actively and visibly. By eight weeks the blood vessels, which carry blood between the embryo and the developing placenta, are coming together at the site of the future navel to form the main umbilical vessels. The developing heart pumps blood through the umbilical arteries to the placenta where oxygen and nutrients are picked up from the maternal circulation. Thereafter, the blood returns and nourishes the embryo through the umbilical vein. At this stage the baby's size is approximately 2.5 cm (1 in) long; its weight is about 2 gm (0.070 oz).

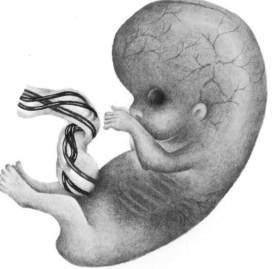

The eight week embryo is already recognizable as a 'baby'. The cord has formed and the placental circulation is developing. The small drawing shows the embryo at actual size.

☐ **Rubella (German Measles) Test** This is carried out to see whether or not the mother-to-be has previously had rubella. If so she is likely to be immune from any further infection, so there is no worry that an attack of rubella in early pregnancy will harm the unborn baby. If the patient has not had rubella previously this will be shown by the test. If she subsequently develops rubella during pregnancy this, too, can be confirmed by a second rubella test which will show a higher level of rubella antibodies than in the test taken before she developed the infection. Women who have not previously had rubella may be vaccinated at the end of the pregnancy.

☐ **Test for Spina Bifida** When the foetus has a deformed spine an abnormal substance called alpha foetoprotein appears in the blood stream. Many women will have their blood tested for this substance in the hope that it will prove a useful method of detecting possible spina bifida foetuses. When this blood test is positive an ultra-sound examination and amniocentesis should be performed.

☐ **Test for Sickle Cell Disease** Sickle cell disease may affect women of African or Asian origin and a similar condition, called thalassaemia, may affect women of Mediterranean origin. The blood of these women is, therefore, tested to see if they have any evidence of these diseases. If they have there is no need for any immediate treatment, but the pregnancy needs to be managed particularly carefully to avoid any complications.

CERVICAL SMEAR TEST

Cancer of the cervix is very uncommon in pregnant women, but the earliest changes of this condition may already be present and can be detected by the cervical smear test. The test, is, therefore, commonly carried out during the first antenatal visit (or sometimes at the postnatal visit). To carry out the test the doctor passes a small metal instrument called a vaginal speculum into the vagina so that he can actually see the cervix. He then gently scrapes the surface of the cervix with a thin wooden strip called a cervical spatula. The spatula picks up cells from the surface of the cervix which can then be examined under a microscope. Although the great majority of smear tests in pregnancy are negative, a positive or doubtful smear may call for further investigation to establish the exact nature of the abnormality. This may entail a visit to hospital and a short general anaesthetic to enable a small part of the cervix to be taken away for further microscopic examination. The smear test is widely used as a screen for cervical cancer in pregnancy, but it is important to realize that cancer of the cervix is extremely rare at this time in a woman's life.

12 weeks

The embryo is now called the foetus, a Latin word which means a young one. In appearance it is much more like a full-term baby, although the head is still disproportionately large. Movements of the limbs are more co-ordinated (although the mother-to-be cannot feel them) and swallowing of the amniotic fluid takes place. As if to compensate for the taking of this fluid, the foetus passes a small amount of urine back into the amniotic sac. The foetal heart is beating strongly and, although it cannot be picked up by a conventional foetal stethoscope yet, it can be heard by means of an ultrasound detector. The external genitals appear, making the sex of the baby obvious. Fingers and toes are fully formed.

The length of the foetus is difficult to measure from the head to the feet because it tends to be curled up for most of the time. The length from the top of the head to the foetal bottom, called the crown-rump length, is more easily measured and is about 11 cm (4½ in); the foetal weight is about 14 gm (0.493 oz).

Ultrasound Examinations

One of the most exciting developments in modern obstetrics is the use of high-frequency sound-waves to produce 'pictures' of the foetus within the uterus. This method was pioneered by the British obstetrician, Professor Ian Donald, and is based on the principle that when high-frequency sound waves strike a solid object, the waves can be picked up by a suitable receiver and converted into pictorial form. (The history of ultrasound is interesting because it was first applied to the detection of submarines, by surface warships, during World War I. The modern diagnostic ultrasound machine is a development of these earlier uses, so, not for the first time, a wartime invention has been put to peaceful use.)

THE USE OF ULTRASOUND IN VERY EARLY PREGNANCY

An ultrasound picture of the developing embryo can be obtained by about five to six weeks after the last menstrual period. By eight weeks, a clearly defined foetal echo can be shown on the ultrasound screen. Ultrasound is most often used in cases of threatened abortion in early pregnancy to determine if the embryo is continuing to grow and develop. It can also be used at this stage in pregnancy if there is reason to think that the baby may be abnormal.

ULTRASOUND EXAMINATION AFTER THE FIRST TWELVE WEEKS

Ultrasound examination is becoming more and more widely used and it seems likely that, in future, all pregnant women will have at least one ultrasound examination during the course of a pregnancy. At present, ultrasound examination is used in the following conditions.

☐ **Twins** The ultrasound picture of twins is characteristic and a diagnosis can be made very early. In most cases twins will not be suspected before sixteen to twenty weeks, even later in some cases, and an ultrasound scan, at this time, will quickly establish the diagnosis. Triplets, quads and even quins can also be diagnosed.

☐ **Uncertain Dates** When a woman is unsure of the date of her last menstrual period, or has irregular periods, it is difficult to estimate when the baby is due. In this event, an ultrasound scan will measure the diameter of the foetal head and will give a good indication of the maturity of the foetus and hence the expected date of delivery. This examination is most accurate when done at about twenty-eight to thirty weeks. The measurement of the length of the foetus, crown-rump length, may also be used, as may the circumference of the foetal chest, to give an indication of the likely birthday.

☐ **Foetal Growth** Successive ultrasound scans, at weekly intervals during the last ten weeks of pregnancy, to measure the foetal head diameter give a useful indication of how well the foetus is growing. Slow growth suggests that the foetus is not receiving all the oxygen and nourishment that it should from the placenta. This situation sometimes calls for early delivery of the foetus to avoid the risk of a more severe lack of oxygen as the pregnancy progresses. A baby that is smaller than it should be is said to be 'small for dates'. Ultrasound scans are frequently used to detect the 'small for dates' situation and to measure subsequent foetal growth as the pregnancy progresses.

☐ **Breech Presentation** An ultrasound scan shows clearly which way round the foetus is and enables a breech presentation to be diagnosed.

☐ **The Position of the Placenta** The placenta is usually placed in the upper part of the uterus where it will not interfere with the foetus as it passes down through the cervix in labour. If the placenta is placed low down in the uterus, it may obstruct the passage of the foetus and, becoming separated, cause vaginal bleeding. This is the condition known as placenta praevia (see page 67). It can be detected by an ultrasound scan which will demonstrate clearly where the placenta is placed in the uterus.

☐ **Foetal Abnormality** Major foetal abnormalities, especially those involving the head—too large a head—hydrocephalus, or failure of development of the upper part of the head—anencephalous—and spine—spina bifida—can be detected by ultrasound scans. If the diagnosis is made sufficiently early in pregnancy, the pregnant woman can be offered a termination. Other abnormalities can be diagnosed by amniocentesis or foetoscopy.

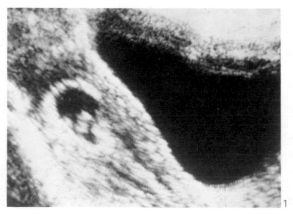

1 Pregnancy of 7 weeks gestation, showing the foetus (left centre).

2 Ultrasound scan showing the placenta (top) and the foetus (centre).

3 Pregnancy of 18 weeks gestation showing the placenta, the foetal body, head, heart and legs.

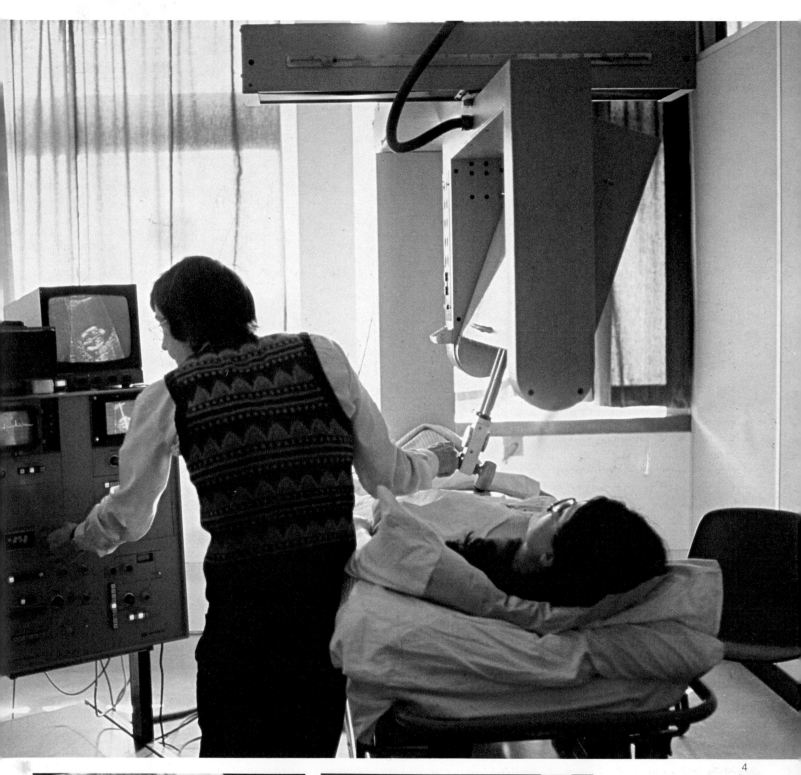

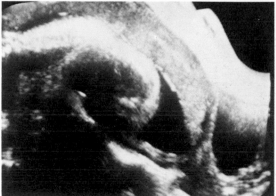

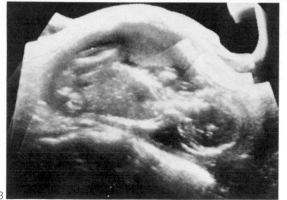

4 An ultrasound scan in progress. The procedure is painless and the picture is a beautiful way of showing the mother that she really does have a baby!

The Placenta

The placenta —afterbirth —develops during the first twelve weeks and is the means by which the foetus breathes, eats and disposes of its waste products. The foetus and placenta between them also produce a number of very important hormones which are essential for normal growth and healthy pregnancy. The placenta grows on part of the chorion, the outer of the membranes surrounding the developing embryo, and is made up of a large number of finger-like projections, called villi, which burrow into the lining of the uterus, the decidua, and come to lie in a space called the intervillus space. In this space the mother's blood flows past the projecting villi, oxygen and nutrients, then cross into the foetal blood stream. Carbon dioxide and waste products are collected. The free passage of these substances from the maternal blood stream to the foetal blood stream is the vital link between mother and foetus on which the life of the foetus depends. If the blood supply from the mother to the intervillus space is reduced, as it may be, for example, in women with high blood pressure, the foetus starves and will be smaller than it should be. If there is a serious reduction in the maternal blood flow past the villi, the foetus suffers from lack of oxygen and may die as a result.

Apart from the normal nutrients in the maternal blood stream, like glucose, amino acids and fatty acids, any drugs that are in the mother's blood supply may also pass into the foetus. Substances made up of large molecules, such as protein, will not be able to get across the wall of the villi. It is important to note that there is no mixing of the maternal and foetal blood streams. Each blood stream is separate and the substances passing from mother to foetus, and

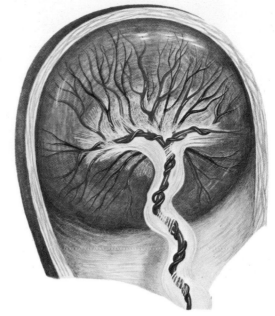

vice versa, have to come out of one blood stream, cross the villi, and enter the other blood stream. The placenta is fully formed by about twelve weeks and thereafter grows steadily with the baby.

At forty weeks the placenta is as big as a small dinner plate and weighs about one-sixth of the weight of the baby so that a 3-kg (6 lb 9 oz-) baby will have a placenta weighing approximately 0.5 kg (1 lb). The health and well-being of the foetus is very much dependent upon how well the placenta is made and functions. As individuals we are only as good as our placentas made us and each placenta is only as good as the blood supply from the mother into the intervillus space where the essential transfers take place.

Specialized Tests

AMNIOCENTESIS

This is the name given to the procedure in which a needle is inserted through the abdominal wall into the amniotic sac in the uterus. A sample of the amniotic fluid can then be withdrawn and examined in the laboratory. Before the needle is inserted, an ultrasound scan is done to show the position of the placenta and the baby so that neither is damaged by the needle.

AMNIOCENTESIS IN EARLY PREGNANCY

The procedure is used in the first half of pregnancy, usually at about fourteen to sixteen weeks to detect mongol and spina bifida babies.

☐ **Mongolism (Down's Syndrome)** is diagnosed by taking some of the baby's skin cells, contained in the amniotic fluid, and growing them on a suitable culture medium. The body cells of mongols have a different chromosome count from normal individuals and this can be demonstrated in the nuclei of the growing cells. It takes between two and four weeks to complete the test. As the culture does not always take the first time round, the test might have to be repeated. The risk of having a mongol baby is about one in a thousand in women up to the age of thirty-five. For women over this age, and for women who have a family history of the condition or who have previously had one mongol child, the risk is greater. By the time a woman is forty the risk of having a mongol child is one in eighty. For this reason, it is now recommended that all women over the age of

The Umbilical Cord

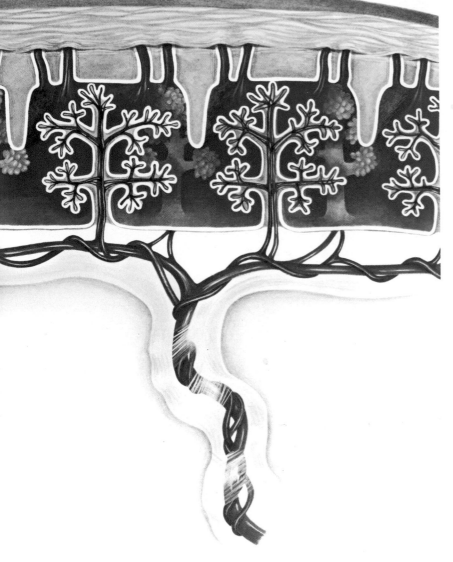

The blood vessels in the placenta join together and emerge from the centre of its foetal surface as two arteries carrying blood from the foetus to the placenta and one vein carrying blood the other way. These three blood vessels are surrounded by a special jelly-like substance and enclosed by an outer membrane to form the umbilical cord, which stretches out from the placenta to enter the foetus at the site of its future navel. There, the blood vessels from the placenta join up with those of the foetus. The foeto-placental circulation is thus completed. The foetal heart can now pump blood through the umbilical arteries to the placenta and receive blood back from it in the umbilical vein.

At the end of pregnancy the umbilical cord is about 50 cm (20 in) long and is the vital link between the baby and its placenta. Astronauts walking in space refer to the pipe which connects them to the space craft as their umbilical cord. The comparison is very apt, since, in both cases, the individual is dependent upon the oxygen brought to it through the connecting link.

---

thirty-five should have an amniocentesis to exclude mongolism.

Although the amniocentesis procedure itself carries a slight risk of causing a miscarriage, the advantage of knowing that the baby is not going to be a mongol outweighs this risk in most women with an increased chance of having one.

□ **Spina Bifida** This condition can be detected by an ultrasound examination alone but, in most cases, it will be necessary to confirm the diagnosis by examining the amniotic fluid for alpha foeto-protein. The test can be carried out quickly, unlike the test for mongolism, and the result is available within a few days. Alpha foeto-protein can also be detected in the blood and it is hoped that by doing this blood test on all pregnant women those with a possible spina bifida foetus will be picked up.

An amniocentesis to detect spina bifida is only done at present where the blood test is positive, there is a family history or where the woman has already given birth to a spina bifida baby.

Before having an amniocentesis to detect mongolism or spina bifida, it is important that the woman concerned decides that if the test is positive, she will be prepared to have a termination.

AMNIOCENTESIS IN LATE PREGNANCY

Amniocentesis is used in late pregnancy principally to detect bile pigment or lecithin and sphingomyelin in the fluid.

□ **Bilirubin** is the bile pigment present in the fluid when the foetus has become severely jaundiced as a result of rhesus incompatibility (see page 68). When the level is high steps must be taken to lower the level or deliver the baby.

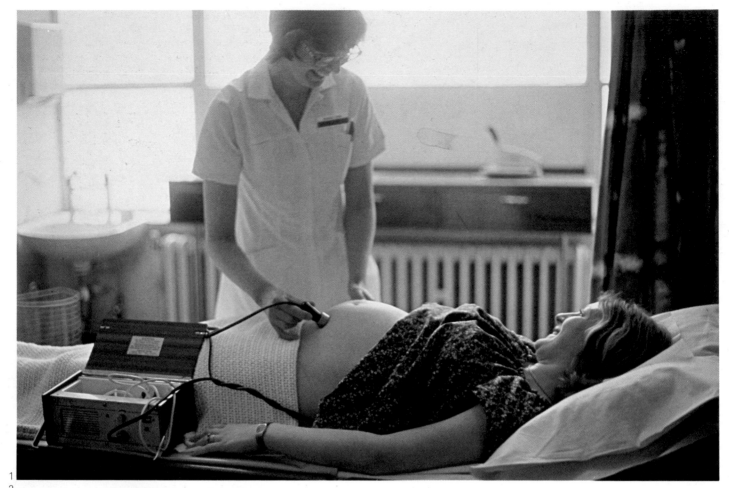

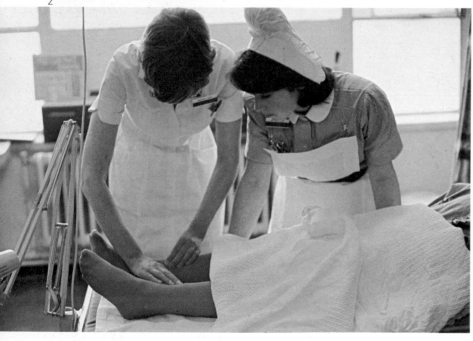

1 Listening to the foetal heart with a simple ultra-sound detector. The happy smiles indicate that both mother and midwife can hear it.

2 Some slight swelling of the ankles, feet and fingers occurs in most normal pregnancies. More severe swelling can be a sign of toxaemia so it is always checked at the antenatal visits.

3 Checking the blood pressure forms a regular part of the programme of antenatal care. Thus any signs of complications can be quickly detected.

□ **Lecithin and Sphingomyelin** These substances are present in the baby's lungs and enable the lungs to open up after delivery when the baby takes its first breath. A lack of lecithin and sphingomyelin leads to great difficulty in breathing and the baby sometimes dies of the condition known as the respiratory distress syndrome or hyaline membrane disease. Premature babies may lack the necessary lecithin and sphingomyelin to enable their lungs to function properly. For this reason, when a woman threatens to go into labour prematurely, or when it is thought advisable to deliver the baby early, a sample of amniotic fluid will often be taken and examined for these substances. If they are not present in adequate amounts, steps will be taken to increase the levels by medical means, or to delay delivery.

FOETOSCOPY

The foetoscope is a large needle that acts as a telescope and allows the operator to examine the baby inside the amniotic sac. The procedure is in the early stages of development at present, but holds great promise for the future. In addition to enabling abnormalities such as hare lip and cleft palate to be diagnosed, it may also be possible to obtain a sample of the foetal blood and test it for congenital blood diseases.

ANTENATAL FOETAL HEART MONITORING— FOETAL BREATHING

This is a new antenatal test to see if the baby is getting adequate oxygen from the placenta. Using a special ultrasound detector, placed on the mother's abdomen over the region of the foetal back, the foetal heart sound can be picked up and recorded on a moving paper strip. A normal foetal heart rate and rhythm indicates that all is well with the baby.

Sometimes another recording device is placed on the mother's abdomen at the same time and this records when the uterus contracts. The effect of the contractions on the foetal heart rate and rhythm can then be seen on the graph paper. Although not generally used as yet, this sort of test is likely to become more common in the future especially as ultrasound machines become more sophisticated. Thus, it is already possible to use ultrasound to observe and measure the breathing movements which every foetus makes inside the womb during pregnancy. Although in the unborn baby breathing does not take place in the same way as it does after birth, the breathing movements on the foetal chest wall are thought to be an important aspect of normal foetal activity. An absence or lessening of these movements may indicate that the foetus is suffering from a lack of oxygen.

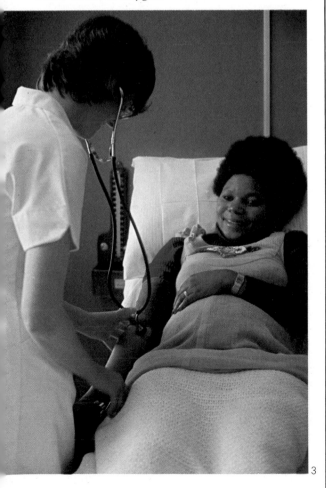

3

20 weeks

The foetus has grown considerably and the details of the human form appear at this stage. It is covered by a fine downy hair called lanugo and some coarser hair now appears on the head and eye-brows. The eyes remain covered by the eyelids and are, therefore, still firmly closed. The foetus moves about freely in the amniotic sac and, by this stage, the mother is usually aware of the movements. The crown-rump length has extended to some 16 cm (6½ in) and the weight is about 300 gm (10.58 oz).

Communicate

When being examined and while the tests are being carried out, the mother-to-be should always ask what is being done and why. She should also take the opportunity to voice any fears she has about the pregnancy and to ask questions. The doctors and midwives in the clinic welcome such questions as it gives them an opportunity to allay anxiety and to build up the woman's confidence in herself and in them.

At the end of the first visit the patient will usually be given a supply of tablets containing iron and folic acid. These will help her to meet the extra demand for these substances made by the growing baby. Without them anaemia may develop. Finally, an appointment will be made for the next antenatal visit, usually in four weeks' time. Although the antenatal clinic appointments are made at fixed intervals, it should be clearly understood that the woman can go to the antenatal clinic or to her own doctor if she develops any unusual symptoms. A telephone call to the clinic Sister is a useful way of getting advice on whether or not an extra visit to the clinic or to the doctor is necessary.

SHARED ANTENATAL CARE

The majority of women nowadays are delivered in hospital, in a maternity unit supervised by a consultant obstetrician (see page 58). Some hospital deliveries are carried out in general practitioner maternity units. These are run by general practitioner obstetricians with help and advice from consultant obstetricians as required. Mothers-to-be who are booked for delivery in general practitioner units, and some women booked for delivery in consultant units, will receive their antenatal care from their own general practitioner or from one of his partners. Only women who are likely to go through pregnancy without complications are suitable for delivery in general practitioner maternity units. This also applies to women whose antenatal care is shared between the hospital consultant and the general practitioner.

The advantage of shared antenatal care is that it is usually more convenient for the woman to visit her own doctor in his surgery than to go to the hospital antenatal clinic. One or two of the routine antenatal visits should, however, be made to the hospital, especially towards the end of the pregnancy. This allows the mother-to-be to get to know the doctors and midwives there and to benefit from their specialized experience and knowledge. Arrangements for antenatal care

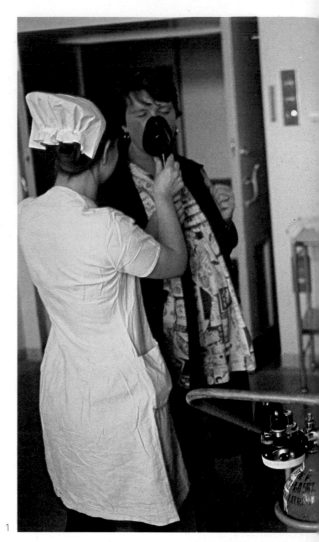

differ from area to area and a pregnant woman should enquire about the local conditions from her family doctor. The ideal set-up is one which allows her to be looked after by the same team throughout pregnancy and labour. The family doctor is often the best person to do this, but he can only be expected to manage a normal pregnancy and labour. When booking for confinement in a general practitioner unit, it is important for the mother-to-be to ensure that there is adequate provision for specialist back-up should complications develop. This is already ensured for mothers-to-be who are booked for confinement in a hospital consultant unit, who if they wish can ask for their antenatal care to be shared by their own family doctor. Whenever more than one doctor or midwife is involved in the care of a pregnant woman, it is important that each knows the results of the other's examination. For this reason, a woman who is having shared antenatal care should be given a co-operation card to carry with her. This should be filled in by the doctor or midwife at every antenatal visit. The co-operation card should be carried by the woman and taken with her when she is admitted to hospital when she is in active labour.

28 weeks

By this time the foetus has developed to a stage where it is considered capable of surviving if it is born. This is a legal definition only. The foetus born before twenty-eight weeks is classed as an abortion, or miscarriage. After twenty-eight weeks it is classed as a baby. Survival after a premature birth at this time is by no means guaranteed although many babies do survive nowadays. Occasionally, babies born before twenty-eight weeks also survive, but this is unusual. In appearance the foetus is still very wrinkled and red, but the skin is now covered by a white soapy substance, known as the vernix to prevent the skin from becoming waterlogged. As there is still plenty of room for the foetus to move about, it does so vigorously. The foetal head and limbs can easily be felt through the mother's abdominal wall at this time and the foetal heart can now be heard with an ordinary foetal stethoscope. The length of the crown-rump is now 24 cm (9½ in); the weight 1.050 gm (2 lb 5 oz).

1 Mothers being shown around the maternity unit can try out the gas and oxygen machine.

2 Regular checks detect too small a weight gain as well as too large a gain.

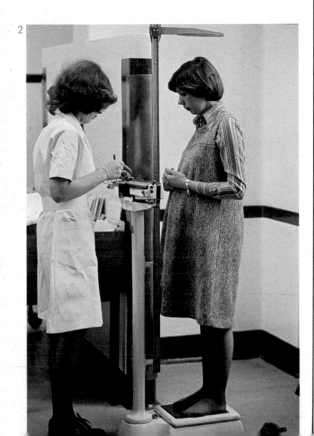

Regular Antenatal Visits

Visits to the clinic or the doctor's surgery usually take place at four-week intervals up to twenty-eight weeks of the pregnancy and, after that, at two-week intervals up to thirty-six weeks and then weekly. If complications develop, more frequent visits will be needed.

At each visit, weight, blood pressure and urine tests will be repeated and a simple examination made of the enlarging uterus. This is done by the doctor (or midwife) feeling the uterus to determine how much it has enlarged in size since the previous visit. He will also be able to feel the baby inside the uterus to check that it is growing normally. The presentation of the baby, that is which part is coming first, is only important after about thirty-four weeks. By this time the head should have settled down into the lower part of the uterus. The crown of the head is called the vertex, hence this is known as vertex presentation. If the buttocks of the baby presents, this is called a breech presentation. It is diagnosed by feeling the hard round baby's head in the upper part of the uterus. Breech presentation is common up to thirty-four weeks, but after that time is uncommon. Attempts are usually made to turn the baby round to the correct head-down vertex position.

The abdominal examination will be completed by the doctor or midwife placing a foetal stethoscope over the lower part of the uterus in order to listen to the baby's heart beat. Using the simple traditional trumpet-like foetal stethoscope, the heart cannot be heard before twenty-four weeks. With the aid of an ultrasound stethoscope, the heart can be heard as soon as the uterus is large enough to be felt in the lower part of the abdomen, usually about twelve weeks. Although listening to the baby's heart is a traditional part of the antenatal visit, it only confirms what the woman herself already knows from feeling the baby's movements—that her baby is alive and well!

For a woman who has already had a baby and knows what to expect movements of the baby are usually first felt between sixteen and eighteen weeks. For a woman who is pregnant for the first time, twenty weeks is more common. There is a considerable normal variation, however, and movements may be felt earlier or later in some individuals.

Movements are a good indication of a baby's well-being and, tiresome though they may be at night, hearty kicks and thumps indicate a vigorous baby. The pattern of foetal movements may change during pregnancy and it may be more active at some times than at others. In general, provided the baby has a spell of good activity two or three times a day, all is well. If a baby, which has been very active, becomes much less so over a period of one or two days, this fact should be reported to the doctor or midwife so that a check can be made to see that all continues well. Please note, *one or two days, not one or two hours*, of inactivity. The baby will often sleep inside the uterus for several hours at a time.

REPEAT ANTENATAL TESTS

Unless the expectant mother is anaemic, no further blood tests will be needed after the first antenatal visit, until about thirty weeks. A haemoglobin estimation will be needed at this time to check on possible anaemia. In the case of rhesus negative women, the blood sample will also be examined to see if any rhesus antibodies are developing.

☐ **Hormone Tests** As the baby's well-being depends on the placenta, and as the placenta produces hormones which can be measured in the woman's blood or urine, hormone tests are often carried out to confirm that the placenta is functioning normally and keeping the baby properly supplied with oxygen and nourishment. If there is any doubt, following a simple abdominal examination at the clinic, that the foetus is not growing as it should, these tests are done as a precautionary measure. A number of tests are needed at weekly intervals for any conclusions to be reached. The fact that the doctor decides to

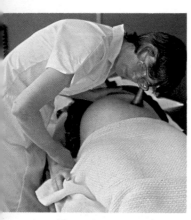

1 Listening to the foetal heart using the conventional foetal stethoscope.

2 The nurse or midwife feels for the foetal head.

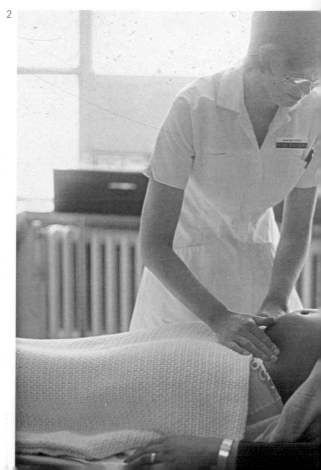

have them done should not be a cause for anxiety. They are part of the antenatal system of checks to confirm that all is going well and to detect any possible complications long before the baby suffers any harm. Different hospitals do different tests, but the common hormones to be measured are *oestriol*, which comes from both baby and placenta and is measured most often in a complete twenty-four hour specimen of urine from the mother, and *human placental lactogen* (H.P.L.) which comes from the placenta alone and is measured in a sample of the mother's blood.

☐ **X-rays** are rarely needed in mid-pregnancy except, occasionally, to diagnose twins or to confirm a breech presentation. Ultrasound is increasingly preferred to X-rays for this purpose.

DON'T BE AFRAID TO ASK

At each antenatal attendance, take the opportunity to tell the doctor or midwife about any unusual symptoms or discomforts, and ask about any aspect of pregnancy that is worrying you. It is a good idea to jot questions down on a piece of paper as they arise and take the paper with you to the clinic. This avoids the 'I know there was something else I wanted to ask you, doctor, but I can't remember what it is' situation. Be persistent! The doctor or midwife should be able to answer your questions and allay your worries. Politely, but firmly, refuse to be fobbed off with any answers that you do not understand or that do not relieve your anxiety. Antenatal visits are a time to get to know the doctors and midwives and to build up a confident bridge of understanding which will stand you in good stead in labour.

36
weeks

The birthday is fast approaching! The foetus has become plumper and the earlier wrinkled appearance has disappeared. The vernix is still present, but is less prominent and the soft lanugo —body hair—is starting to disappear. Space is much more confined, so the foetus has less room to move about. The head now occupies its correct position in the lower part of the uterus, so that, in labour, the crown of the baby's head —the vertex—will appear in the vagina first. In obstetric parlance, this is a vertex presentation. The crown-rump length is now 31 cm (12$\frac{1}{2}$ in); the weight 2.4 kg (5 lb 4 oz).

The Last Antenatal Visit

By the time thirty-six weeks have elapsed from the last menstrual period, the mother-to-be will have come to understand the meaning of the phrase 'Heavy with child'! The last four weeks of pregnancy are often an uncomfortable time and apprehension about labour will often increase as the expected date of delivery draws near. Late pregnancy is a time to strive for a tranquil existence. Cut routine jobs down to a minimum and rest. During the last few antenatal visits, greater attention will be paid to excessive weight gain, swelling of the legs and hands, protein in the urine or a raised blood pressure, since these signs are a warning of toxaemia. At the same time, the presentation of the baby is carefully checked to ensure that the head is properly down in the lower part of the uterus—vertex presentation.

As well as checking the presentation, the doctor will want to check as far as possible that the head of the baby will pass through the mother's pelvis. The pelvis has an inlet, a cavity and an outlet. The inlet is the narrowest part of the pelvis so that if the baby's head will go through the pelvis inlet it will usually go through the cavity and emerge at the outlet.

At about thirty-six weeks, in the case of a woman having her first baby, the head passes through the inlet and into the pelvis to become engaged. The mother-to-be will notice less pressure in the upper part of the abdomen. There is no need for anxiety if your baby's head has not engaged by thirty-seven weeks. In the first place, engagement of the head at this time usually only occurs with the first baby and, even then, not invariably. With second and subsequent babies, engagement occurs later and may not take place until labour has actually begun.

When the head is not engaged, the doctor may carry out a simple test in which he presses gently down on the baby's head to see if it will go into the pelvis. The head that is not engaged when the mother-to-be lies down often becomes so when she sits or stands up. This is because gravity pulls the baby's head down in the direction to which the uterine contractions will make it go when labour starts.

If there is any doubt about the presentation or about the ability of the foetus to pass through the pelvis, the doctor will carry out a vaginal examination. This will enable him to feel the baby's head and to confirm that it will come down into the pelvis when the mother-to-be sits up or when gentle abdominal pressure is exerted on it. Occasionally, in cases of real doubt, an X-ray may be ordered so that the exact size of the pelvis can be measured. As a result of these examinations, it will usually be clear that there is not likely to be any problem about the foetus passing through the pelvis and delivering normally.

SPECIAL TESTS IN LATE PREGNANCY

At thirty-six weeks, a repeat blood test will be performed to ensure that you have not become anaemic during the preceding six weeks since the last blood test. In the case of rhesus negative women a further test for rhesus antibodies will be performed at the same time.

☐ **Hormone tests** In order to confirm that the placenta is continuing to function well, it may be necessary to check the level of oestriol in the urine or of H.P.L. in the blood. If the foetus does not seem to be growing as it should, and if the tests indicate that the placenta is failing, labour will often be induced in order to deliver the baby from what is becoming an increasingly unfavourable environment.

☐ **X-Rays** Apart from the occasional use of an X-ray to measure the size of the pelvis mentioned above X-rays are rarely needed at this stage of the pregnancy. They may sometimes be done to confirm presentation, for example, when the expectant mother is very overweight and the foetus therefore difficult to feel.

BE PREPARED

The mother-to-be should, of course, know how to tell when labour starts (see page 87) and what to do when it does. In particular, you should know how to contact your husband if you go into labour when he is out at work. If he cannot take you to hospital, you should know, in advance, how to call for an ambulance or a neighbour to transport you. Hospitals are often confusing places with several entrances, so it is wise for the mother-to-be to know which entrance to use and which ward you are to be admitted to. Most antenatal clinics run a series of classes in relaxation exercises and mothercraft which include a visit to the labour and postnatal wards. It is very reassuring to familiarize yourself in advance with the surroundings in which such an important event as your baby's birth will take place. A bag containing all essential items that you will need in hospital should be packed and ready by the thirty-eighth week. The clinic will supply you with a check-list of items. The antenatal period may end at any time after that and give way to the climax of pregnancy—having the baby!

40 weeks

All is now ready for labour to start. The head has moved down further into the lower part of the uterus. In many cases it has passed through the entry into the bony pelvis and is said to be engaged. Because it has descended, the mother-to-be notices less pressure in the upper part of her abdomen. This phenomenon is known as 'lightening'. Unfortunately, the pressure is now transferred to the bladder so frequent trips may have to be made to the lavatory to pass urine.

The appearance of the foetus is now that of a normal baby. It has well-formed features, open eyes and a heart beat which can be easily heard with a simple foetal stethoscope. Foetal movements are vigorous and the mother-to-be may find her offspring as disturbing at night in the uterus as he or she will be after the birth, when muscular activity is replaced by vocal activity! Foetal movements do not normally diminish at this time. Usually they continue up to the start of labour, after which they are naturally less noticeable.

Malpresentation

Inside the uterus the foetus is characteristically curled up with its arms and legs flexed up alongside its body. The lie of the foetus describes how its long axis is placed in relation to the long axis of the uterus. Most often, the lie is longitudinal but it may be transverse or oblique, especially when the uterus is of abnormal shape or is very 'floppy' as it may be in women who have had several previous pregnancies.

The presentation of the foetus refers to that part of it which presents at the lower part of the uterus. With a normal flexed foetus, that is a foetus that is lying longitudinally, the top of the head will present. This is known as a vertex presentation, sometimes also called a cephalic presentation. If the foetus has its head in the upper part of the uterus, the bottom presents. This is known as a breech presentation. When the foetus lies transversely or obliquely, the lower shoulder presents. This is known as a shoulder presentation. Very rarely the foetus may have its head thrown back, thus producing a face or brow presentation.

Breech Presentation

This is the commonest malpresentation seen during the antenatal period. The foetus often presents as a breech up to about thirty-four weeks. At this time, most kick themselves around to the vertex presentation. If they have not done so by this time, it is usually because the legs, instead of being flexed have become extended and act as a splint.

If a breech presentation is discovered at thirty-four weeks, the doctor will endeavour to turn the foetus gently round —an operation called external version. This can be done without risk to the foetus and, if successful, avoids the necessity for a breech delivery. If attempts at version are unsuccessful by thirty-six weeks, no further attempts will be made. Further attempts are not made because, by then, the foetus will, in most cases, be too big and a decision will have to be made on how best to deliver it. If the mother-to-be has a small pelvis or if there are other complications, such as toxaemia or a difficult past obstetric history, a Caesarean section will be preferred.

Shoulder, brow and face presentations only arise in labour and complicate delivery considerably. Shoulder and brow presentations usually require a Caesarean operation, but most face presentations can be delivered in the normal way.

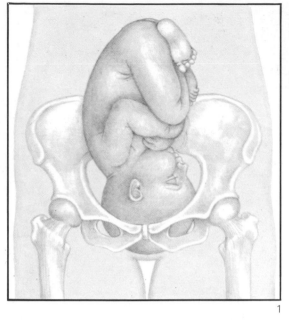

1 The normal situation — longitudinal lie and vertex (head) presentation.

2 'Upside down' —the lie is longitudinal, but the presentation is breech.

3 Transverse lie —the foetus lies across the uterus.

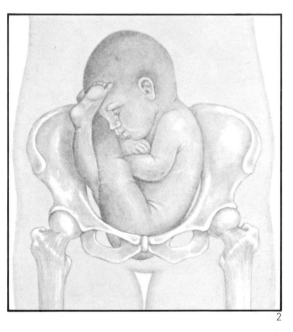

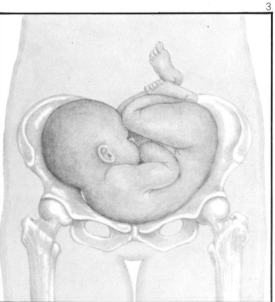

Health in Pregnancy

For most women the desire to become pregnant is one of the strongest driving forces in life. Not surprisingly, therefore, pregnancy is a time of great fulfilment and happiness. It is, however, also a time of physical and mental change and it is important to understand these changes if unnecessary worry is not to mar the happiness. Fortunately, most women remain happy and healthy during pregnancy, but there are a few 'do's' and 'don'ts' to heed if fitness and contentment are to remain at their peak. Perhaps the best advice to any woman who is contemplating having a baby should be to ensure that she is fit and well *before* commencing pregnancy. Every gardener understands that it pays to prepare and nourish the soil carefully before planting the seed, and the same is true of pregnancy. The ideal that every woman should aim for before she becomes pregnant is to be in good health, to be the right weight, to eat the right diet, to take plenty of physical exercise and to stop smoking. It also helps, but is not essential, if she is between the ages of eighteen and twenty-five for the first baby.

Body Changes during Pregnancy

Pregnancy involves the building of a baby in the uterus from the time that the fertilized egg enters, until the time that the fully formed baby leaves at the end of the labour. In order that all this may be achieved successfully, changes occur in the body to enable it to supply all a baby needs for healthy growth and development.

CHANGES IN THE BLOOD

Pregnant women have about 2 litres (4 pts) more blood than non-pregnant women, which is needed to supply the baby with the oxygen and nourishment that he requires. In order to make more blood the pregnant woman has to manufacture more haemoglobin—the essential component of red blood cells. Haemoglobin contains iron and in order to make the extra haemoglobin required for pregnancy, the mother-to-be draws upon iron which is usually stored in the body. If there is not enough iron in store, the woman cannot make enough haemoglobin, the blood becomes more diluted than it should be, and the woman is said to be anaemic. Anaemia in pregnancy, is, therefore, mainly due to a lack of enough iron to make

the haemoglobin available for the essential extra blood cells.

Folic acid—a constituent of the Vitamin B complex which influences red blood cell formation—is also needed to build haemoglobin. Although less important than iron, lack of folic acid can also cause anaemia in pregnancy.

Anaemia can be detected by checking the amount of haemoglobin in the blood and this is always done on several occasions during pregnancy. If anaemia is to be avoided it is obviously important for the pregnant woman to have adequate amounts of iron and folic acid in her diet. Most women, however, need to take a small dose of iron and folic acid every day from twelve weeks of pregnancy onwards.

CHANGES IN THE HEART AND LUNGS

Because of the increased amount of blood present in the body, the heart has to work a good deal harder in pregnancy, especially in the later stages. At the same time the lungs get pushed up by the uterus as it increases in size. As a result of these changes the pregnant woman gets out of breath more easily and is also more liable to feel faint from time to time. These are normal happenings in pregnancy and should not be a cause for alarm. Also normal is a rapid heart beat which may be noticed from time to time during pregnancy. Such bursts of heart activity are due to the sudden need for the heart to work harder to keep up the increased output. Heart failure is very rare in pregnant women and no woman with a normal heart need worry about its ability to meet the need of increased activity during pregnancy or labour. Pregnant women with heart disease do, of course, need special medical care to ensure that the heart is not put under too much strain.

CHANGES IN THE KIDNEYS AND URINARY SYSTEM

Pregnant women drink more fluid (water, tea, coffee, fruit juice, etc.). As a result, the kidneys produce more urine and the mother-to-be has to go to the lavatory to pass urine more often. This is particularly noticeable in early pregnancy when the enlarging uterus presses on the bladder; and in late pregnancy when the baby's head does the same thing. Unfortunately, pregnancy is also a time when infection of the urine is more likely to occur and it is sometimes difficult for a woman to distinguish between frequency of micturition (passing water) due to the pregnancy and frequency due to an infection involving the bladder

A full understanding of the physical changes taking place during pregnancy will help the mother-to-be to adjust and adapt to the new demands on her body. This understanding, combined with common sense and proper antenatal care, will do much to ensure a trouble-free, healthy and enjoyable pregnancy.

(cystitis) or kidney (pyelonephritis) or both. When infection is present the urine seems to burn, or scald, or sting, as it passes and this helps to draw attention to the infection.

CHANGES IN STOMACH AND BOWELS

Feeling sick and being sick is common during early pregnancy, and this is due to the effect of increased hormone levels. As the pregnancy proceeds, the sickness wears off and most women are not troubled by it after about twelve to fourteen weeks. It does persist for longer than this in some women, but it is rarely very troublesome in middle or late pregnancy. Some women find that they can relieve the feeling of sickness by eating snacks between meals.

Apart from feeling sick, many women develop an increased appetite in pregnancy. The reason for this is not clear.

Some foods are less attractive than others during pregnancy. Fried fatty foods are often avoided because they are more prone to cause indigestion or heartburn. Heartburn is a burning sensation behind the lower part of the breast bone and is caused by acid secretions from the stomach getting up to the lower part of the oesophagus (gullet). This happens because the little mechanism that normally operates where the oesophagus and stomach join is less efficient in pregnancy. For this reason acid may splash up from the stomach, especially when the pregnant woman lies flat or bends over.

A craving for certain foods often occurs during pregnancy. Fruit usually features high on the list of cravings and highly flavoured or spicy foods, pickles, cheese or kippers are also popular. Cravings can also include unlikely items, such as coal, soap and toothpaste!

The bowels are inclined to be sluggish during pregnancy and constipation is, therefore, very common. Unless the constipation causes discomfort it can be ignored. (See page 60.)

CHANGES IN THE MOUTH

The gums may become a little swollen and spongy in pregnancy and they may bleed more easily than normal. Contrary to popular belief, the teeth do not lose calcium during pregnancy, not even when the pregnant woman's diet is deficient in calcium. Pregnancy does not, therefore, damage the teeth directly. It does, however, seem to increase the risk of starting caries and of increasing the extent of existing caries. Dental check-ups are, therefore, especially important at this time.

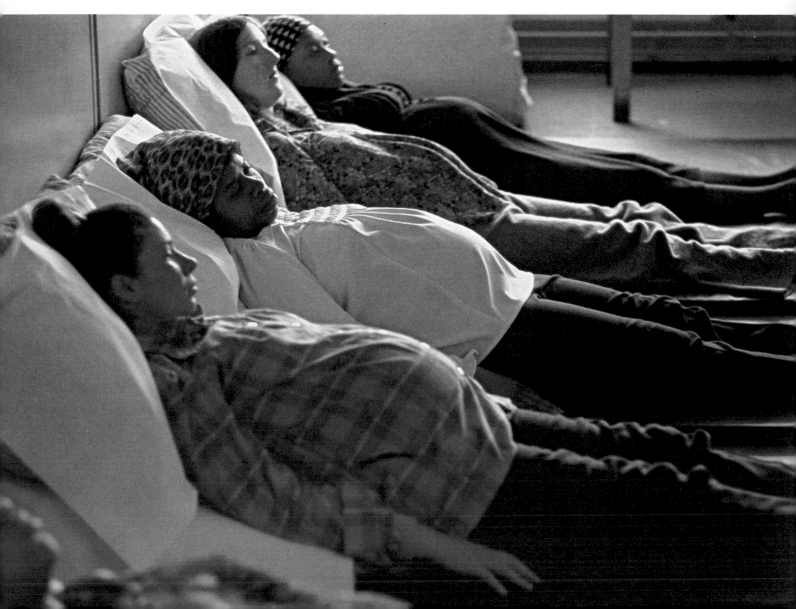

1 It is very reassuring for an expectant mother to visit the maternity unit where her baby will be delivered and many hospitals nowadays welcome such visits. Mothers-to-be can visit the rooms, meet the staff and even try out some of the equipment. Familiarity with her surroundings will help the mother relax when she goes into hospital.

2,3 Regular relaxation classes during the antenatal period also help to prepare the mother-to-be both physically and mentally for the birth.

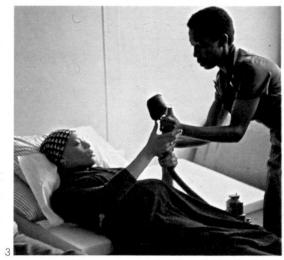

Another widely held belief is that women make more saliva than usual when pregnant. However, measurement of the amount of saliva secreted does not support this idea. A possible explanation is that because some mothers-to-be feel sick they do not swallow the saliva and, therefore, have an excess of it in the mouth.

CHANGES IN BONES AND JOINTS

Pregnancy hormones cause a softening of ligaments around the joints, especially in the back and pelvis. This looseness of back and pelvic joints, and the strain of walking about with an increasing weight of baby, often causes backache and pain in the sacro-iliac joints where the back joins the pelvis. Pain, low down in the back or pelvis, is often blamed on the baby 'pressing on a nerve', but it is more probable that the effect of the pregnancy on the bones and joints is responsible.

SKIN CHANGES

During pregnancy the blood vessels in the skin are more open than usual and this leads to the skin feeling warmer. This warmth is comforting in cold weather and may lead to disagreements between husband and wife about how wide the bedroom window should be kept open! In warm weather the feeling of heat is less welcome. The skin all over the body shares in the change, including the skin lining of the nose. The increased blood flow here may lead to occasional nose bleeds or, if the skin lining is thickened by the change, to a tendency to snore. For this reason the poor husband may not only be cold at night, but kept awake!

Some women complain that they become more prone to skin blemishes and spots during pregnancy, but for the most part the skin remains in good condition. Some pigmentation of parts of the skin, particularly on the face around the eyes and on the abdomen, has already been noted as a sign of pregnancy on page 20. Stretch marks are dealt with on page 61.

HAIR AND NAILS

The hair and nails grow more quickly in pregnancy, but this is not usually a problem. It does mean, however, that when the pregnancy is over the excess hair will fall out. Not surprisingly this can cause alarm, but it is a normal happening which never leads to baldness.

CHANGES IN BREASTS

A sensation of fullness and tenderness in the breasts is an early symptom of pregnancy and is followed by enlargement of the breasts as the pregnancy progresses. Enlargement is caused by an increase in the size and amount of the milk-secreting glands and also by an increase in the amount of fat surrounding the breasts. Because of this increase in size it is advisable, throughout pregnancy, to wear a comfortable brassiere that gives good support to the breasts. The secretion of normal breast milk after the birth of the baby is dealt with in the breastfeeding section on page 105.

PSYCHOLOGICAL CHANGES IN PREGNANCY

Whole books have been written on the subject of psychological changes during pregnancy. But, in simple terms, there is no golden rule to apply to these. Many factors have to be taken into consideration, but the two most important are whether or not the baby is wanted and, later, on how much the mother-to-be is worried about the outcome of the pregnancy—i.e., will my baby be normal?; will I survive/endure/enjoy labour?; will I be able to cope with looking after the baby?; will my husband still love me? etc.

As a general rule, it can be stated that attitudes to life tend to be exaggerated in pregnancy—the happy woman becomes happier, the anxious woman worries more and the depressed woman becomes even more depressed. The majority of women, the happy ones, will find, therefore, that pregnancy is a time of increased happiness, but even they may occasionally become anxious and depressed for no very obvious reason. Provided the mother-to-be understands that the sudden changes of mood are normal, no harm results and a little sympathetic reassurance from an understanding husband is often the only treatment that she will require.

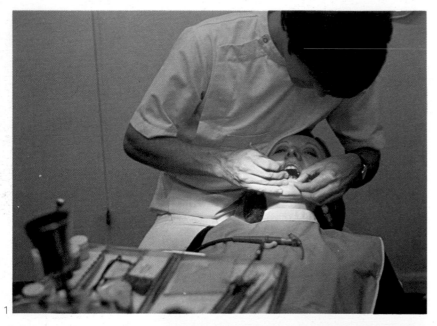

1 While it is absolutely untrue that a woman loses one healthy tooth for every baby, pregnancy does seem to increase the risk of caries to any teeth that have been neglected in the past. Therefore, regular dental check-ups are essential during pregnancy.

2 There is no reason why a woman's hair should not look as beautiful and healthy during pregnancy as at any other time. Hair, like nails, does grow more quickly during pregnancy, but this does not give rise to any problems and is a good excuse for more frequent visits to the hairdresser.

Staying Healthy Throughout Pregnancy

A woman who is healthy at the start of her pregnancy is likely to remain so throughout, provided she understands what is going on and applies her natural common sense to the three important aspects of pregnancy.
1: *Rest, Work and Exercise*
2: *Food, Drink and Smoking*
3: *Proper Medical Care.*

REST, WORK AND EXERCISE

In a nutshell, the soundest advice is to rest when you feel tired and take regular simple exercise when you do not! This sounds simple and reasonable but, in practice, many women find it hard and expect to be able to do all the things they normally do in addition to being pregnant. This is often possible in the first thirty weeks or so of pregnancy, but it is important to recognize that pregnancy is an extra strain and that the carrying out of a normal routine may make the mother-to-be very tired. If you feel tired, do not grit your teeth and struggle on; stop and take a rest.

It is not possible to lay down hard-and-fast rules about the amount of rest to be taken in pregnancy because different women will need different amounts. If the simple 'rest when you are tired' maxim is applied, you will feel much better than if you try to soldier on. The basis of rest must be a good eight hours' sleep every night. Thereafter, the amount of rest can be regulated according to how each individual feels. A rest in the afternoon is often beneficial, especially in late pregnancy, but it is not necessary for the woman who does not feel tired without it.

A woman's work is never done, we say, and this applies to pregnant women especially. It is, however, important to remember that the pregnant woman may not be able to do all the work she would normally do or, indeed, would like to do. Strenuous physical work is unlikely to cause harm, but should not be carried out to excess. Again this simply means that you should stop when you start to feel tired. It is impossible to dictate the best time for a mother-to-be who has a job to give it up; to some extent this is governed by the nature of the work, but more importantly by the feelings of the individual. Some women work happily up to the day of delivery, while others are ready to take it easy from the seventh month.

The woman with small children as well as

3 Getting the right measure of work, rest and play is essential at any time in life, but even more so during pregnancy. A wise mother-to-be accepts that pregnancy can place an extra strain on her physical capabilities and that, at various times, ordinary routines will leave her feeling rather depleted and tired. Only the individual mother-to-be knows how she is feeling at any one time and, therefore, when it is necessary for her own and her baby's sake, to drop everything and lie down for a really lovely rest.

husband and home to look after, may find it very difficult to reduce her workload during pregnancy, but she and the rest of the family will benefit considerably if she is able to avoid becoming unduly tired. A work-weary woman cannot feel her best, cannot look after the rest of the family as she would like to do and her pregnancy is likely to be a burden in every sense. Pregnancy is a family event and every member of the family should be aware of the need to give that extra bit of help with ordinary day-to-day chores.

If too much work is undesirable, the same can be said of too little exercise. Being fit before pregnancy is not enough. Keeping fit during pregnancy is equally important. Here, again, however, common sense must be used and exercise limited to what is enjoyable. Certainly it should not be pursued to the point of exhaustion. Within reason, practically any normal sporting activity can be followed during pregnancy but, for the average woman, a daily walk, a regular game of tennis, badminton or golf, or a session of swimming two or three times a week, will provide the necessary exercise. In late pregnancy, walking may be the only exercise that can be carried out comfortably and it should be continued as long as it is enjoyable. Some complications of pregnancy call for restriction of physical activity, but normal pregnancy does so only within the limits of common sense.

☐ **Sex in Pregnancy** Many women experience a loss of sexual desire during pregnancy, while others enjoy lovemaking as much as ever. Some men find their pregnant wives very attractive, others do not. Whatever your reactions, pregnancy can be a time for strengthening your relationship by loving communication of both your needs and feelings. From a medical point of view, sexual intercourse can usually take place throughout much of a *normal* pregnancy without fear of harming either mother or foetus but intercourse should be avoided in early pregnancy if the woman has previously had an abortion or has bled at any time during the pregnancy. Normal sexual relations can be resumed after twelve weeks, but if you are in doubt, ask your doctor's opinion.

As the uterus grows in size it will become increasingly uncomfortable for the woman if her partner lies on top of her. Towards the end of pregnancy it is, therefore, more comfortable if the woman lies on her side with her husband lying behind her. Even in this position, deep penetration may be uncomfortable in late pregnancy. Sexual intercourse in the few days before the baby is due may sometimes cause labour to start, because semen contains substances which can cause the uterus to contract. No harm results when labour is started off in this way.

54

Because every mother-to-be is an individual, there are no hard-and-fast rules about rest, exercise and when to stop work. The important thing is for the individual woman to know her own capabilities, acknowledge her own natural limitations, and to respond to the information that her own body will, day by day, feed back. Certainly, it is never wise to grit your teeth and, come what may, carry on. It is far better to accept that pregnancy does bring physical, mental and emotional changes, and that to keep fit you you must ensure that you have exactly the right measure of rest, work, food and exercise.

1 There is no doubt that with proper care and consideration, most mothers-to-be have a very healthy and trouble-free pregnancy. Indeed it can be a very enjoyable time —a time when one can make the most of the days at home and seek out restful pursuits such as sewing and dressmaking, to help make the necessary preparations for the new baby.

FOOD, DRINK AND SMOKING

Over the years pregnant women have been bombarded with advice as to what they should or should not eat or drink. Once again, common sense rules. Provided the diet is healthy and balanced before pregnancy, the mother-to-be need not alter it significantly during pregnancy. A normal balanced diet is one that contains *carbohydrate* (bread, potatoes, cereals, rice), *fat* (butter, margarine, milk, cream, cheese, cooking fat), *protein* (meat, fish, nuts, cheese, lentils, egg), *roughage* (green vegetables, bran) and fresh *fruit*.

Many women eat more than usual during pregnancy and, not surprisingly, this causes them to become heavy with excess fat as well as with the weight of the child. One problem about over-eating in pregnancy is that its effect may not become fully apparent until after the baby is born. Then the mother suddenly realizes that, in spite of having had the baby, she is very overweight. Losing weight by dieting can be uphill work. A much wiser plan is to avoid over-eating during pregnancy, so that the total weight gain does not exceed 10–11 Kg (22–24 lbs). This makes it easy for the mother to get back to her pre-pregnancy weight within two or three months after the baby's birth.

Every pregnant woman knows that she should drink milk during pregnancy, but there is much conflicting advice on how much. The strange thing is that people who advocate strict attention to not putting on too much weight are often the same people who prescribe two pints of milk per day! The truth is that two pints of milk, drunk in addition to a normal balanced diet, is guaranteed to increase anybody's weight, pregnant or otherwise. The point about milk is that it contains calcium and calcium is needed in pregnancy for the formation of the baby's bones and teeth. If the mother-to-be drinks an extra 250 ml ($\frac{1}{2}$ pt) per day over and above whatever milk is taken in tea, coffee and cooked foods, this will be a perfectly adequate intake. Apart from this small extra amount of milk, the pregnant woman can drink whatever she pleases, provided she remembers that sweet drinks are fattening. Alcohol, in moderation, is not harmful in pregnancy.

☐ **Alcoholism and Drug Addiction** Women who are addicted to alcohol or drugs, such as cannabis or heroin, should on no account become pregnant. If they do, they should seek medical advice at once because both alcohol and drugs in excess are harmful to the developing foetus and can cause congenital abnormality. Even when the baby is normal in other respects it will have become addicted whilst in its mother's womb and may suffer serious withdrawal symptoms shortly after birth. To see a tiny baby suffering like an adult addict, cut off from the supply of drugs, is very distressing. No woman should risk inflicting such a terrible experience on her child. Overcoming the addiction before becoming pregnant is the only safe and humane course of action.

☐ **Smoking** Evidence that smoking in pregnancy is harmful to the baby is now overwhelming. Babies born to smokers are, on average, smaller than those whose mothers are non-smokers. There may be other harmful effects, but these are more difficult to measure for certain. Women who smoke should try and stop before they become pregnant. If that is impossible, they should stop as soon as they become pregnant. The sooner they stop smoking or, at least, reduce the number of cigarettes, the less effect there will be on the baby. Pregnancy is, therefore, a good time to give up smoking. If it can be given up permanently the mother will live longer to enjoy not only her child but also her child's child.

PROPER MEDICAL CARE

Pregnancy is a normal occurrence which could, theoretically, proceed without outside assistance. Unfortunately some complications and problems do arise and so medical care is essential.

The first object of medical care is to ensure that the mother-to-be keeps as healthy as possible throughout the pregnancy and goes on to have an uncomplicated normal labour and a healthy baby.

The second object is to detect complications at as early a stage as possible and act quickly to prevent minor problems from becoming more serious. Doctors are sometimes accused of interfering unnecessarily, but they only do so when they believe that the mother and baby will benefit as a result. The fact that having a baby is such a safe and easy process nowadays is partly due to modern medical care.

Father's Role

Like most of life's great events, the knowledge that one is to be a father brings its own special joys, rewards, anticipations and anxieties.

The first thing for a father-to-be to remember, is that all the chemical and glandular changes that are a natural accompaniment of early pregnancy, can play havoc with his wife's body and feelings. She may, for example, suffer from nausea, sickness, tiredness, rise to great heights of happiness and plunge just as quickly into insecurity and despair. All this can, of course, be very bewildering and wearing for a husband, but it is essential for him to remain rational, understanding, supportive and loving. Nothing is more damaging to a marriage than the turmoil of an action/reaction situation. As the onus of bodily and emotional changes is on the mother-to-be, it is clearly important that the father-to-be should accept the onus for remaining calm and rational.

Some wives remain sexually responsive throughout pregnancy; others experience a lessening of sexual desire. Whatever the situation, a wife's wishes should be respected and given first consideration. Fears that the loss of interest is permanent or that the sexual relationship will never be the same again are quite unfounded. Pregnancy is a unique time during which a couple's love and devotion can be expressed in ways other than sex. Far from undermining a relationship, this can, in fact, deepen the love that a husband and wife have for each other.

A mother-to-be also needs time to adjust to the changes in circumstances. If, for example, she has been used to a career, she will, for a while, miss the working routine and all the friendships which this involves. She may feel very lonely at times, insecure about the new routine or the need to make new friends. Daily opportunities for quiet understanding conversation will do much to speed the necessary psychological and emotional adjustment.

The more a father-to-be knows about pregnancy, childbirth and parenting, the better it will be for him and his wife. Family life is essentially a sharing of love and interests and pregnancy is a very good time to start.

The decision of whether or not a father-to-be is to attend the birth should never be based on, or biased by, what others do, but childbirth preparation classes and films are invaluable in helping a husband and wife decide. The important thing is that neither should feel pressurized.

At least three weeks before the baby is expected, a father-to-be should make sure that he has

the telephone numbers of the doctor, midwife, hospital and ambulance service. If he is to drive his wife to the hospital, he should keep cushions and blankets in the car, check the petrol gauge and tyres each evening, and work out, in advance, the shortest route to the hospital and the precise location of the admissions' desk.

Remember that father-love, like mother-love, may not be instantaneous. Some parents need time to get to know their baby. Newborns rarely look as beautiful as babies in television commercials and photographs. A father-to-be who takes time to study photographs of how a baby looks immediately after the birth will not be alarmed if, initially, his own baby looks like a red or purple wizened old man or woman.

Remember, too, that after all the excitement of labour and birth, the next few days may seem something of an anti-climax. Once again, as the onus of physical adjustment is on the wife, the onus of remaining rational and supportive should be with the husband.

There is no doubt that pregnancy, childbirth and becoming a parent entails major adjustments for men and women, but both can be immeasurably enriched by the experience.

The maxim, 'It is a wise man who knows his own child' is as true today as ever it was. Equally, a wise man makes a point of knowing his own wife—and draws on this knowledge when deciding whether to be lenient or firm, vociferous or silent. Above all, he never forgets to bring reason to bear on a situation, whether during pregnancy or at any other time in his marital and family life.

2 There is nothing like shared moments and shared interests for bringing a husband and wife closer together. Pregnancy is essentially a time when the love and consideration which a man and woman have for each other can expand and grow to include and welcome a new life. Daily opportunities for quiet understanding conversation do much to smooth the passage for all the psychological and emotional adjustments that are a natural and essential part of any transition period, including, of course, the period when husband and wife are slowly but surely transforming themselves into their new roles of father and mother.

Who's Who

The medical world—in common with many other professions—has a language of its own. This even applies to the names given to various people (both doctors and nurses) with whom you will come into contact during pregnancy, delivery and babyhood days. Here is a quick run-down to help you sort out who is who.

OBSTETRICIAN

An obstetrician is a doctor who, after taking a qualifying medical degree, has specialized and taken further qualifications in caring for pregnant women and their babies. He is the man you will see at intervals during your pregnancy when you attend for your routine antenatal checks. The obstetrician will always see you on your first visit, and will give you a complete examination to ensure that there is no reason why your baby should not be delivered normally. Unless anything unforeseen happens often he will not see you again until the thirty-sixth week of pregnancy. He—or one of his registrars or housemen (doctors carrying out their specialized obstetric training under the close supervision of the consultant)—will be available to carry out any unusual procedures, such as forceps delivery, a breech delivery or a Caesarean section, for example, which may be necessary when the time comes for your baby to be born.

GYNAECOLOGIST

A gynaecologist is a doctor who has specialized, and taken further degrees in, diseases which are particular to women, especially diseases which occur during the woman's reproductive years.

This work is combined with the work of the obstetrician so that the consultant you would see if, for example, you had any condition specific to your reproductive system, would be the same person under whose care you were placed when your baby was born.

The road to becoming a consultant obstetrician/gynaecologist is a long one—ten to fifteen years after the initial six years of basic medical qualification.

PAEDIATRICIAN

Paediatricians are doctors who have specialized in the treatment of the diseases of children, after obtaining their basic medical qualification. The training to become a consultant paediatrician takes ten to fifteen years after qualification, and further post-graduate examinations must also be taken. Most paediatricians work in hospitals but,

increasingly, as acute illness in children lessens, they are to be found working in the community, in child health clinics, medical centres, schools and assessment centres.

NEO-NATOLOGIST

A neo-natologist is a paediatrician who specializes in the care of the newborn baby. As medicine becomes more complex, the areas of specialization increase and a doctor's working life can easily—and usefully—be devoted to one small aspect of care.

Perhaps the most vulnerable time in our lives is the first week of life. In a relatively short space

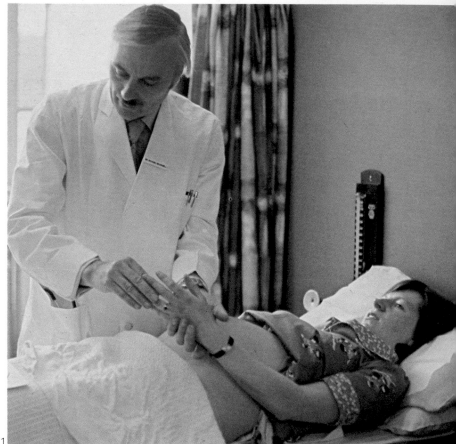

of time, our body is subjected to a completely new environment. Much change has to occur for lung and digestive systems, to mention just two facets, to work in an entirely different way. Problems can arise at this time, particularly if there are any congenital defects present. It is then that the highly specialized skills of the neo-natologist are needed, both for diagnosis and treatment.

☐ **Perinatology** is concerned with the well-being of the baby during the actual birth process—that vital six to forty-eight hours upon which so much depends. All obstetricians and most paediatricians are concerned with the perinatal period. Any minor degree of oxygen lack or injury at any stage of birth can affect a child's whole life.

During the course of labour the baby's heart

1 The obstetrician is a specialist in the care of pregnant women and their babies. He will see you at intervals during the antenatal period to ensure that your pregnancy is proceeding smoothly towards a trouble-free delivery.

beat and other physiological functions are carefully monitored—frequently by a complex range of instrumentation. If any variations from the normal are observed, action will be taken to ensure the delivery of a healthy baby.

GENERAL PRACTITIONERS

A general practitioner is a doctor who has decided to spend his working life in the community caring for the whole range of age groups in the family. After qualification, and a certain time spent in hospital medicine, he will become a trainee in an established partnership of doctors. After this time —usually one to two years—he will become a junior partner in a group practice and will take the examination to become a member of the newly created College of General Practitioners. An increasing number of doctors these days operate from a health centre. Here, under one roof, one can find the doctor's consulting rooms, the health visitors and district nurses and, often, in larger practices, a small operating theatre and many other personnel such as speech therapists, physiotherapists, and so on.

This forms the basis of the primary care team, and it is here that all patients must first attend, when ill or in need of advice about their health.

In practice, each doctor often has a particular area of interest. For example, one of the partners may have an especial interest in children; another may have an especially sympathetic way of dealing with the elderly.

2 The health visitor plays an important part in the community health services in Britain. She is able to give advice on many different aspects of caring for your new baby at home.

3 The paediatrician is a specialist in the care of children. He will perform the first medical check-up on your new baby and is also responsible for babies who need special care.

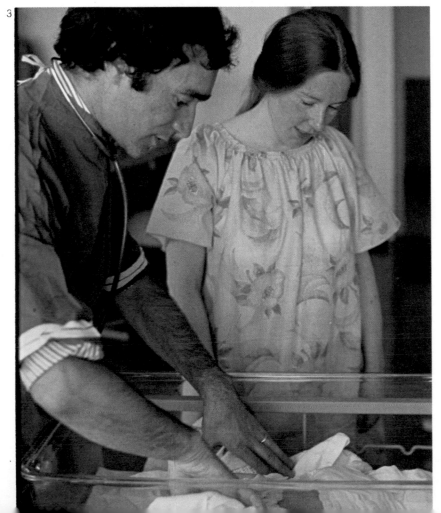

MIDWIVES

Midwives are nurses who have undergone further training in midwifery, that is, the delivery of babies and their immediate post-natal care. To be a midwife, the nurse must have obtained her SRN (State Registered Nurse) qualification, and passed a further examination at the end of her midwifery course to become an SCM (State Certified Midwife).

The normal delivery of a baby in hospital is undertaken by a midwife or a pupil midwife under the immediate supervision of a trained midwife. If complications of any kind occur, such as the need to deliver a baby with the use of forceps, the midwife will call one of the obstetric team.

The role of the midwife does not end with the birth. She is responsible for the care of the baby and the mother until they leave hospital. So, as well as being fully conversant with the delivery of women, the midwife must also have a sound working knowledge of newborn babies.

District midwives still exist, although in fewer numbers than when many mothers had their babies at home. With today's policy of early discharge from hospital (forty-eight hours) district midwives are busy with the home care of the new mother and the young baby.

When the baby is ten days old, however, the care of both mother and baby is handed over to the health visitor.

HEALTH VISITOR

A health visitor is an SRN who has had midwifery experience and who has undertaken a further year's training in all aspects of nursing and social care in the community.

Her work ranges from the very young to the very old, and she is a mine of information on the social aspects of community care.

She will be in charge of the child health clinics and will run developmental assessment clinics in conjunction with either a general practitioner or a local authority community doctor. She will visit the homes of mothers with young babies and will be on call to them if any problems arise. Feeding, sleeping and behaviour problems are all within her scope. Mothers rely on their health visitor's expertise to help them over the potentially worrying days at home with their new baby.

Most health visitors, these days, are attached to a group of local doctors and work closely with them. So when a mother chooses her doctor she will also be choosing her health visitor.

As the babies grow into school children, the health visitor will have much to offer by way of advice to both parents and school doctor and teachers. Her knowledge of the family can ease many stresses in the school situation.

Pregnancy Discomforts

Although pregnancy is a happy time, there is no disguising the fact that it may also be an uncomfortable one. Some of the discomforts have already been mentioned in discussing health in pregnancy, but here are a few more common discomforts.

VARICOSE VEINS

The pregnant woman has more blood in circulation than a non-pregnant woman; because of this, the blood vessels may become dilated. This change is especially noticeable in the veins of the legs which become increasingly prominent as pregnancy advances. In many women, one or two veins may become so dilated and prominent as to warrant the label 'varicose'.

A varicose vein is simply a vein which has become stretched and dilated to carry more blood. Most varicose veins that occur in pregnancy will disappear in two or three months after delivery, but one or two may persist and require treatment. This is especially true of women who have had a number of pregnancies with only a short space between each. Whilst it is true that there is a familial tendency to varicose veins, so that if a woman's mother has varicose veins she is more likely to get them herself, no-one, nowadays, need have the sort of varicose veins which were common twenty years ago.

The important preventive measures for varicose veins in pregnancy are:—

1: Avoid being on your feet for too long periods —two separate half days' shopping are better than one long day trudging around with little rest. When sitting down, especially in the second half of pregnancy, put your feet up so that the veins are relieved to some extent of the pressure on them.
2: Avoid constricting garters or elastic-topped stockings or socks.
3: If varicose veins seem to be developing, consult the doctor or midwife about the advisability of wearing support stockings. Properly fitted elastic stockings provide the best support, but they are rather hot and unsightly. Reinforced nylon stockings or tights are often a reasonable compromise.
4: If varicose veins are still present three months after delivery, consult the doctor, or, better still, a varicose vein specialist. The treatment of mild varicose veins is, of course, easier than the treatment of the more advanced kind. For this reason, it is important not to let mild varicose veins become severe. Seek advice on treatment before embarking on the next pregnancy.

☐ **Varicose veins of the vulva** Occasionally, vulval varicose veins appear in late pregnancy, either on their own or in association with varicose veins of the leg. They cause a good deal of aching discomfort. They appear as an irregular swelling on one of the labia majora and are most noticeable when the expectant mother is on her feet for any length of time. The swelling and discomfort quickly subside when she lies down. Rest is the only satisfactory treatment for it is not possible to give support to the vulva and supporting tights do not usually give much relief. Fortunately, these uncomfortable and irritating veins do not cause any difficulty during delivery and disappear completely, without treatment, shortly after delivery.

☐ **Small Varicose Veins** Very small veins in the legs, known as venules, may become dilated and cause small patches of blue tracery which can look rather unsightly. (Support stockings do not, unfortunately, make any difference.' They do, however, disappear almost completely as soon as the pregnancy is over.

☐ **Ruptured Varicose Veins** Very occasionally a varicose vein ruptures during pregnancy, and the bleeding can be very alarming. The way to stop the bleeding is *not* to bend over and apply pressure to the bleeding point, but to lie down and elevate the leg in the air. This empties the vein and the bleeding stops at once. Having taken this measure, a doctor should, of course, be consulted.

☐ **Piles (haemorrhoids)** Piles are varicose veins situated at the entrance to the anus (back passage). They often develop in late pregnancy and can be very uncomfortable, especially in the first few days after delivery when they are usually at their most prominent. In most cases, like varicose veins in the legs, they disappear completely within three months after delivery. They are worse after long periods of standing and are improved by lying down. Constipation also aggravates them and may cause bleeding when hard faeces are passed. The constipation can be eased by including bran cereals, wholemeal bread, fresh green vegetables, etc. in the diet.

By avoiding prolonged standing and constipation, the discomforts of piles can be reduced, but if they are troublesome the doctor or midwife should be consulted. Soothing ointments and suppositories will help. If piles persist for longer than three months after delivery, a doctor or preferably a specialist in piles should be consulted. A good time to mention this problem to your doctor is at the post-natal check-up.

ANAL FISSURES

An anal fissure is a crack in the skin of the anus. Because it causes local discomfort and bleeding it is sometimes mistaken for a pile. It most commonly occurs after delivery and characteristic symptoms are pain and bleeding on passing a motion. It can easily be treated by suitable local applications or a simple surgical procedure. If it does not quickly clear up on its own, seek the doctor's advice.

LEG CRAMP

Leg cramp, which is common in mid-pregnancy, is a violent contraction of the calf muscles and sometimes also the muscles of the sole of the foot. It occurs less frequently in late pregnancy, but may persist and even occur during labour. Cramp most often occurs during the night or on first waking. It is triggered by sudden stretching of the leg. The spasm that follows is very painful and may last for one or two minutes. The cause of this is unknown. Putting the foot to the ground and rubbing the knotted muscles are the best first-aid treatments. A loud yell to wake up husband and to get him to do the rubbing is recommended! A good preventive measure is to avoid stretching the leg muscles suddenly in bed. Leg cramps in pregnancy are not a sign of lack of calcium or salt, as is sometimes suggested.

STRETCH MARKS

The skin over the abdomen, breasts, buttocks and thighs stretches during pregnancy. As a result, stretch marks—striae gravidarum is the medical term—often appear. They are caused by a tearing of the deeper levels of skin and look rather red and angry when they first appear. They persist after pregnancy is over, but become paler and much less noticeable. There is a popular idea that the skin can be made more supple and stretch marks avoided by rubbing olive oil or more elaborate and expensive preparations into the skin every day. Alas, there is no evidence that such measures do any good. The simple fact is that some women seem to have a more elastic skin than others. The lucky elastic ones remain free of stretch marks, whilst their less elastic friends do not. Of course, the bigger the baby, and the greater the weight gain, the more the skin will be stretched and the more stretch marks will appear. Women who have twins or large babies, and who gain a great deal of weight, will therefore be most at risk.

NUMBNESS AND TINGLING

During pregnancy numbness and tingling often occur in the hands, especially in the region of the thumb, index and middle fingers. This area is supplied by the median nerve which swells slightly because of fluid retention towards the end of pregnancy. As a result, the nerve becomes compressed across the front of the wrist and hand. This pressure produces pins and needles, loss of sensation in the affected parts of the hand and a weakness of the hand muscles. The symptoms are most noticeable on waking up in the morning, but generally improve during the day. Although inconvenient, the condition does not usually require treatment, although, in severe instances, splinting the wrist overnight to prevent movement may be helpful, as may a simple pain-relieving tablet.

The nerve which supplies the outer part of the thigh may also become compressed as it passes through a ligament in the groin on its way to the leg. As a result, numbness and tingling may affect the outer part of the thigh. No treatment is required.

HEARTBURN AND INDIGESTION

Heartburn is especially common in middle and late pregnancy. The causes are described on page 50. Avoid bending over from the waist, by bending from the knees instead, and avoid lying flat (use one or two extra pillows). When it does occur, heartburn can be relieved by swallowing a small dose, 10–15 ml., of a suitable alkaline mixture, or by chewing an alkaline indigestion tablet.

Indigestion is also common in pregnancy. The best solution is to avoid those foods—usually fatty foods—which cause discomfort. Eating small rather than large amounts of food at any one mealtime is less likely to cause indigestion, especially towards the end of pregnancy.

VAGINAL DISCHARGE

Vaginal secretions increase during pregnancy, so a slight extra moistness is normal. However, if the discharge entails wearing extra protection and especially if it causes irritation of the vulval skin, the mother-to-be should consult her doctor.

☐ **Thrush** This is the commonest cause of irritation and excessive vaginal discharge in pregnancy. It is caused by a yeast-like germ, called *Candida albicans*. The organism is a frequent inhabitant of the skin of normal healthy women and men, but it only causes symptoms and discomfort in conditions of warmth, moisture and sugar, all of which are present in a pregnant woman's vaginal and vulval skin. Sometimes the germ is passed on from the skin of the husband's penis and he may also complain of a skin irritation. The discharge is white or yellow and looks rather like milk curds. The irritation is often severe and is especially uncomfortable in bed at night. Fortunately, there are a number of effective treatments, the best

During early pregnancy and during the last few weeks before delivery increased rest and decreased activity are the simple answers to avoiding fatigue and unnecessary strain on the back, abdominal and leg muscles. Common discomforts of pregnancy, such as varicose veins and piles (haemorrhoids) can be eased by avoiding prolonged periods of standing and being on your feet and remembering to balance working periods in the kitchen, house or known of which is nystatin. Putting a pessary of this substance into the vagina every night, and rubbing nystatin cream into the itching skin night and morning for a week, will usually clear up the symptoms rapidly. Recurrence is, however, common, and pessaries and cream should be kept readily available, so that a further course of treatment can be started as soon as the symptoms reappear. Patients sometimes become discouraged in the first few days of treatment because the discharge does not show immediate improvement. It is important to remember that some discharge can be expected until the treatment is completed. Irritation should clear up within a day or two of starting treatment.

garden, by putting your feet up and enjoying a real rest!
No discomfort should be considered too small to mention to the doctor. It is, for example, far easier to treat mild varicose veins than severe ones. Discomforts which are mentioned and, therefore checked in the early stages —as soon as you you are aware of their presence —are far easier to treat and put right than something which is ignored and allowed to develop.

□ **Trichomonal Infection** A vaginal infection caused by a trichomonas vaginalis germ is quite common in pregnancy. This causes an unpleasant vaginal discharge and irritation of the vulval skin. The infection comes from an infected man who often does not have any symptoms himself.

The treatment is a course of antibiotic tablets. The tablets are taken by mouth and the male partner needs to be treated at the same time if re-infection is to be avoided.

□ **Gonococcal Infection** Gonorrhea is a common venereal disease which can occur in pregnant as well as non-pregnant women. It causes an excessive vaginal discharge, but no irritation. The germ involved is the gonococcus and the only way that it can enter the vagina is by the woman having intercourse with an infected man.

Any pregnant woman who experiences a heavy, yellow, vaginal discharge which does not irritate,

or who thinks she may have had intercourse with an infected partner, should seek immediate medical advice. The infection can easily be cleared up with an injection or a course of injections of penicillin. Unless the infection is cleared up before delivery, the baby's eyes may be infected and permanently damaged.

□ **Herpes Infection** Very occasionally the herpes virus, which causes cold-sores on the lips, can infect the vulval skin and vagina. The small blisters that form are very painful and may cause a watery vaginal discharge. This condition usually clears up within ten to fourteen days without treatment, but the doctor should always be consulted in order to ensure that the infection is completely cleared up before the baby is delivered. In this way, infection of the baby can be avoided.

□ **Blood-Stained Discharge** A blood-stained discharge may indicate a threatened abortion in early pregnancy or the onset of labour in late pregnancy. In mid-pregnancy a blood-stained discharge may follow intercourse if the patient has a cervical erosion. Cervical erosions occur on the cervix and are the result of thinning of the normal cervical skin covering. The thinner skin looks red and bleeds readily when rubbed. Apart from causing a blood-stained discharge, the erosion does no harm and will often clear up spontaneously after the pregnancy is over.

□ **Watery Discharge** A watery discharge in late pregnancy may be the result of ruptured membranes. In the normal course of events, there is a definite small gush of clear fluid when the membranes rupture, but sometimes the rupture is very small and the usual gush is replaced by a watery drip. Labour is likely to start soon after, so the doctor should be consulted. If there is any doubt the woman should go into hospital.

TIREDNESS AND INSOMNIA

Strangely enough these two symptoms often go together. The pregnant woman feels very tired and yet when she goes to bed, finds herself unable to sleep. Pregnant women get tired more easily, especially in early pregnancy and in the last few weeks before delivery. Increased rest and decreased work are the simple answers, but this may not be so easy in practice. A good night's rest— not less than eight hours—is essential to avoid over-tiredness, but sometimes sleep will not come. Unless the insomnia is so persistent that the woman is losing a great deal of sleep, drug treatment should be avoided because sedatives given to the mother also sedate the foetus. A warm drink and a good book are all that are needed in most cases. Serious insomnia may be due to worry. In this case, seek the doctor's help so that he can, as far as possible, allay any anxieties.

Maternity and Child Benefits

Most of the developed countries of the world have a system of maternity benefits, usually linked to the national insurance contributions of the mother and her husband. In Britain maternity benefits come under two headings—the maternity grant and the maternity allowance. All leaflets and forms mentioned are available from your local social security office.

MATERNITY GRANT

This is a lump sum paid to the mother by giro-cheque. Although the amount payable is not very large, it is designed to help cover the general expenses of having a baby. This grant is payable on a woman's own National Insurance contributions if she works, or on her husband's contributions if she is a full-time housewife.

☐ **To qualify** for the grant either you or your husband must have paid Class 1, 2 or 3 National Insurance contributions on earnings at least twenty-five times the lower weekly earnings limit. Also, there must have been paid, or credited, the same amount of contributions in the previous tax year. (Detailed instructions regarding the lower weekly earning limit are listed in leaflet N1 17A.)

☐ **To claim** you must fill in a form (BM4). The time to claim is any time from the beginning of the fourteenth week *before* your baby is expected, and up to three months *after* the birth. If you do not claim the grant by the time your baby is three months old, you will lose it.

MATERNITY ALLOWANCE

This is paid by a book of orders which can be cashed at the post office every week. The amount is usually increased with each Budget.

☐ **To qualify** for the maternity allowance you must have paid your own National Insurance contribution. Maternity allowance is not payable on a husband's National Insurance. The exact details of how many insurance contributions need have been paid are variable according to individual circumstance. (See leaflet N1 17A.) Check with your wages' department at work for information regarding your own particular contribution status.

☐ **Claiming your allowance** The allowance is payable for eighteen weeks. This starts at the eleventh week before the week in which your baby is expected, continues through the week of the birth and finishes when your baby is six weeks old if you claim before your confinement. (It is wise to claim as soon as possible after the fourteenth week before your baby is due, so that you will be able to receive the allowance for the full length of time.) If you do not claim until after your baby is born, you will only be entitled to the allowance for the week of your confinement and the following six weeks.

The allowance is only payable for the days in which you do no paid work. Even if you receive maternity pay from your employer, you will also in addition receive the maternity allowance, as long as no paid work is done.

EARNINGS RELATED BENEFIT

These are extra monies, paid weekly, that you can claim if you have fulfilled the conditions for the maternity allowance—i.e. have paid your own standard rate class 1 contributions amounting to more than fifty times the lower earnings limit. (See leaflet N1 155A.) This supplementary benefit usually starts in the third week of your maternity allowance and continues for one hundred and fifty-six days. You will not be entitled to this benefit if you are self-employed, or are married and have opted out of paying full National Insurance contributions.

MATERNITY PAY

This is a comparatively new concept in Britain, which came into force April 1975 as part of the 1975 Employment Protection Act. This money from your employer will be calculated in the following way: 90 per cent of your basic salary *plus* earnings related benefit, if you are eligible for this, but, *minus* the state maternity allowance. (This latter deduction applies whether or not you are eligible to claim it in respect of your own National Insurance contributions.)

Your employer actually pays you the cash, but he will claim the full amount back from the Maternity Pay Fund into which he (and he alone) has been paying increased social security contributions.

This payment is continued for six weeks; but before you are entitled to receive it you:

1: Must have been working for the same employer for two years by the time that the eleventh week before your baby is due has been reached.

2: Must actually work up to the eleventh week before your baby is due.

3: Must be able to supply your employer with a certificate showing the expected date of your baby's birthday if he requires it.

4: Must have notified your employer at least three weeks before you leave that you are doing so because you are pregnant.

SPECIAL CASES

A number of special circumstances may alter the position with regard to maternity benefits.

☐ **Twins** If you have more than one baby you can claim maternity grant for each child who lives longer than twelve hours.

☐ **Single women** can claim the maternity grant only on their own National Insurance contribution.

☐ **Widows** expecting their late husband's child can claim either on his contributions or their own.

☐ **Divorced women** can only claim on their own contributions, unless married to the man on whose contribution she is claiming for any part of the period starting eleven weeks before, and ending with, the expected date of the baby's birth.

☐ **Girls under sixteen** are not eligible for maternity grant or maternity allowance.

☐ **Babies who are born abroad** There are reciprocal arrangements regarding social security benefits between Britain and a number of other countries. Make enquiries from the Department of Health and Social Security, in Newcastle-on-Tyne, if this applies to you. If your baby is born unexpectedly abroad, you can claim your maternity grant after he is born.

☐ **Stillborn babies** The maternity grant is still payable if the pregnancy has lasted at least twenty-eight weeks.

☐ **Other dependants** Increased allowance may be payable for certain adults or other children who are dependent on you.

All this sounds very complicated and confusing, but it will resolve itself when you apply the rules to your own specific set of circumstances. The staff of your local Social Security office are always willing to help unravel the mysteries.

OTHER FAMILY BENEFITS

In Britain, there are various other benefits to which you may be entitled.

☐ **1: Child benefit** is paid for all children under sixteen, or under nineteen if still a full-time student at school or college. The initial claim should be made on a special form from your local Social Security office. You will then receive an order book, which contains tokens that can be cashed at the post office.

☐ **2: Free dental and prescription charges** for expectant mothers and women who have a child less than one year old. Children and families on a low income also benefit in this way.

☐ **3: Free milk and vitamins** for expectant mothers and children under eleven years, some larger families and people on a low income.

☐ **4: Free Family Planning** through family planning clinics or your general practitioner.

☐ **5: Low income families** can benefit from free spectacles and free school meals.

Again, your local Social Security office will be able to give you full details regarding exact entitlements and ways of claiming.

RIGHTS AND DUTIES

☐ **Home or hospital confinement?** Although a mother-to-be has the right to choose a home rather than an hospital confinement, the medical profession strongly recommends a hospital birth. In a hospital there are ancillary services and staff for coping with any unexpected complication or emergency situation. Whilst it is possible for a woman in labour, or a newly-delivered mother to be transferred from home to hospital, a delay of as little as half an hour can, in some situations, prove the difference between life and death.

☐ **Induction** Induction is a term that is used when labour is started artificially. Medical reasons for induction include, among others, pre-eclampsia, placental insufficiency, diabetes, hypertension and Rhesus incompatability. Hospital authorities frequently stress that induction is *not* used for the convenience of medical staff.

☐ **Fathers At The Birth** Most hospitals today welcome a father, especially if he has attended the father's evenings given by the wife's antenatal classes and, therefore, knows what to expect and how he can best help to support and encourage her during the various stages of labour. Provided all is progressing well, some maternity units allow fathers to remain for the actual delivery.

☐ **Registering The Birth** For hospital purposes, you may be asked for your baby's first names soon after the birth, but the *Registration* of the birth is your responsibility. This should be done within six weeks (or within three weeks in Scotland) at the office of the Registrar of Births. Details of how to register your baby's birth will be given during your stay in the hospital post-natal ward.

☐ **Single Parent Families** A useful organization, which offers help and guidance on every sort of problem that the single parent is likely to meet, is: The National Council for One-Parent Families, 255 Kentish Town Road, London, NW5 2LX. (The Council is also trying to get services and conditions improved for the single parent.)

Gingerbread is another self-help organization for one-parent families. It has local groups throughout the country. For further information, write to: 35 Wellington Street, London, WC2.

Pregnancy Complications

Although most pregnancies are absolutely normal, a few mothers-to-be develop complications which require special care and treatment. Such complications are usually diagnosed in the antenatal clinic and can be successfully treated without any harm having resulted to mother or foetus. Regular attendance at the antenatal clinic is vital as late diagnosis of complications is a serious matter.

TOXAEMIA

This is perhaps the best known complication. It occurs in late pregnancy, usually after thirty-six weeks, and is sometimes called pre-eclampsia or pre-eclamptic toxaemia. Pre-eclampsia consists of hypertension (raised blood pressure), proteinuria (protein—mostly albumin—in the urine) and oedema (swelling of the legs, hands and face). The normal blood pressure of a healthy pregnant woman is usually about 110/80. Hypertension is usually said to be present when the pregnant woman's blood pressure has risen to 140/90.

Proteinuria is not normally present in pregnancy or in early cases of toxaemia, but if the hypertension is allowed to continue, the kidneys will be damaged and will be unable to continue their normal functions, including keeping the protein in the blood from spilling over into the urine. The presence of proteinuria, which is tested for at every antenatal visit, is an indication that toxaemia is becoming more severe.

Oedema (swelling) of the ankles and feet can be expected by all pregnant women at some time in pregnancy because of a retention of fluid in the body. Fingers and hands also sometimes swell.

☐ **The Management of Toxaemia** As the cause of toxaemia is unknown, the management is aimed at control of the symptoms until the foetus is mature enough to be delivered. After delivery the signs of toxaemia quickly disappear and there is no permanent damage. The main initial treatment is rest and this is often all that is needed in mild cases to keep the blood pressure down and to stop proteinuria and oedema developing. Rest in bed at home is allowed in mild cases, but more severe cases require rest in hospital. The importance of admission to hospital in all but the mildest cases of toxaemia lies in the fact that mild toxaemia may sometimes progress quickly to severe toxaemia and the change can only be detected if frequent observations are made on the patient's blood pressure. Patients with toxaemia are often reluctant to go into hospital because they feel well, but to ignore medical advice in this situation is to risk letting the condition progress unchecked from mild to severe toxaemia or even to eclampsia. Severe pre-eclamptic toxaemia is a serious complication which requires sedative and anti-hypertension drugs. As soon as the blood pressure is under control in severe pre-eclampsia, steps will be taken to deliver the baby. This is done either by inducing labour, or in very severe cases, by performing a Caesarean section operation.

When a woman has had toxaemia during a first pregnancy she will naturally be concerned about suffering the same complication during a second pregnancy. About fifty per cent do, unfortunately, develop toxaemia with the second pregnancy, but it is usually much less severe than during the first pregnancy.

☐ **Eclampsia** This form of toxaemia is the end product of untreated or inadequately treated severe pre-eclampsia. In addition to hypertension, oedema and proteinuria, the patient develops severe headaches and fits. Because eclamptic fits endanger both mother and foetus, every effort is made to prevent mild pre-eclampsia from becoming severe and severe pre-eclampsia from progressing to eclampsia.

VAGINAL BLEEDING IN LATE PREGNANCY

Vaginal bleeding after twenty-eight weeks is called antepartum haemorrhage. This is a serious complication because the bleeding usually comes from the site where the placenta is attached to the uterus. The blood lost is almost invariably from the mother's circulation, but because the placenta

Most women have slight swelling of the hands and fingers in late pregnancy. More severe swelling is a sign of toxaemia.

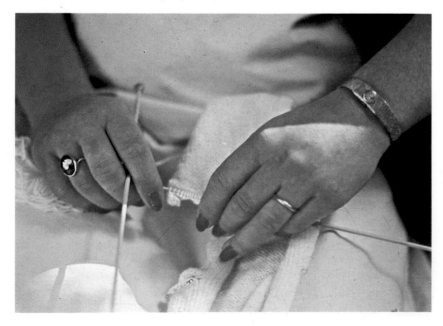

gets separated from its attachment to the uterus, the foetus is endangered by lack of oxygen. There are two main types of antepartum haemorrhage, depending on where the placenta is attached to the uterus. (See below).

☐ **Placenta Praevia** This is the term given to the placenta when it is attached to the lower part of the uterus (see diagram). In this situation the placenta is in the path of the foetus when the foetus tries to make its way down through the cervix. If the uterine contractions separate the placenta from its attachments, severe bleeding will occur. There are varying degrees of placenta praevia. If the placental attachment is only partly in the way of the foetus, the bleeding will be less serious and a normal birth may be possible. Usually, placenta praevia causes an antepartum haemorrhage some time before labour starts. When this happens there is a sudden, small, bright red blood loss from the vagina between thirty and thirty-six weeks of pregnancy. There is no associated pain and the bleeding clears up quickly. If the warning is ignored a much larger haemorrhage may occur and will require urgent treatment. For this reason, any vaginal bleeding in late pregnancy must be taken seriously and reported to the doctor at once so that the woman can be admitted to hospital for investigations. Investigation will aim at showing the site of the placenta. This is most commonly done nowadays by means of an ultrasound scan. Once the diagnosis has been established and the severity of the placenta praevia decided, plans can be made for delivery. In all but the mildest cases a Caesarean birth will be necessary and the woman will be kept in hospital until the foetus is sufficiently mature to be delivered, usually any time after thirty-six weeks.

☐ **Abruptio placentae** This is the term given to antepartum haemorrhage which occurs when a normally situated placenta partly separates from its attachment. The cause of separation is not usually clear, although, on rare occasions, it may result from a direct blow to the mother's abdomen.

As with placenta praevia, urgent admission to hospital is needed for abruptio placentae, so that the woman can have the loss of blood replaced by blood transfusion and the baby's condition can be assessed.

Abruptio placenta is a serious complication that requires expert care in hospital. Fortunately it is rare for a woman who has suffered it in one pregnancy to get it in another. This is also true of placenta praevia. Because of the potential dangers, a pregnant woman who notices any vaginal bleeding in late pregnancy should report the occurrence to her doctor as soon as possible.

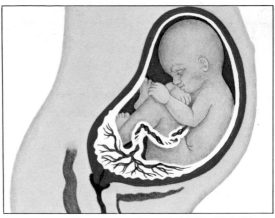

COMPLICATIONS AFFECTING THE BLOOD

☐ **Anaemia** This is the commonest blood problem in pregnancy and it arises when the mother's iron and folic supplies cannot keep up with the extra demand (see page 49, Health in Pregnancy). It should not arise in a woman who takes a balanced diet and the iron and folic acid tablets provided by the antenatal clinic.

Anaemia will be detected by the routine antenatal blood tests and can be treated effectively with additional iron and folic acid. The importance of anaemia in pregnancy is not only that the anaemic woman suffers from extra tiredness and is unable to carry on her normal physical activity without getting very out of breath, but also in the event of a haemorrhage the anaemic woman, already short of blood, will be unable to meet the extra demand. In a very severely anaemic woman even a small haemorrhage can be very dangerous. The moral is, please eat sensibly and take the iron tablets!

☐ **Thrombosis** Thrombosis is the formation of a blood clot within a blood vessel. It is fortunately uncommon in pregnancy. When it does occur, the veins deep in the calves are most likely to be affected and will cause local pain and swelling of the leg and foot beyond the site of the blockage. The most likely time for a deep vein thrombosis to occur is in the first two weeks after the baby has been born. It is more common after complicated deliveries, especially Caesarean operations. Anticoagulants—substances which stop the blood clotting—are used to stop the blood clot spreading and to help its absorption. They need to be continued for some weeks and the dose has to be carefully controlled by regular blood tests.

☐ **Thrombophlebitis** This is a much less serious condition than deep vein thrombosis. It results from an inflammation of the walls of a varicose vein. It may occur after the vein has been damaged by a knock or sometimes without provocation. Although the inflammation causes the blood to clot in the vein and the vein becomes painful and tender, it will usually settle down quickly with rest and a supporting crepe bandage.

Placenta Praevia is a serious, but fortunately uncommon, condition. The placenta lies in the path of the foetus. It can then become partially or wholly separated from the uterine wall. This can result in a severe loss of blood and endanger the lives of both the mother and the foetus. It is usually diagnosed with an ultrasound scan and action for immediate delivery, usually a Caesarean birth, is taken.

1 The majority of normal women carry the Rhesus factor in their red blood cells and are said to be Rhesus positive. Those whose blood does not contain this factor are said to be Rhesus negative. If a Rhesus negative woman becomes pregnant with a Rhesus positive foetus there is a danger that, during delivery, some of the foetal red blood cells will escape into her circulation. This may stimulate her to produce antibodies which, in later pregnancies, may attack the red blood cells of the foetus, causing anaemia and jaundice.

This combination of a Rhesus negative mother and a Rhesus positive foetus can only occur when the mother is Rhesus negative and the father is Rhesus positive.

The Rhesus blood group of all pregnant women is tested in early pregnancy as a matter of routine. Also the Rhesus blood group of the baby is tested immediately after the birth if the mother is Rhesus negative. If the baby is Rhesus positive the mother is given an injection of anti-D gamma globulin to prevent the formation of antibodies and avoid any complications in later pregnancies.

1

☐ **The Rhesus Factor in Pregnancy** About eighty-five per cent of normal women carry a special factor in their red blood cells called the Rhesus factor and they are said to be Rhesus positive. The remaining fifteen per cent of women have no Rhesus factor in their red blood cells and are said to be Rhesus negative.

The Rhesus negative woman who marries a Rhesus negative husband is fortunate, because since both father and mother are negative, the children will also be Rhesus negative and no problems will arise. If, however, the Rhesus negative woman does become pregnant with a Rhesus positive foetus, there is a danger, especially at the time of delivery, that some of the foetal red blood cells will escape into the mother's circulation and stimulate her to produce anti-Rhesus positive antibodies. These antibodies will then attack and destroy any Rhesus positive red blood cells which they come into contact with. As Rhesus positive antibodies are only likely to be formed in the mother after the baby is born, a first baby is unaffected. However, the antibodies remain in the mother's blood and if she becomes pregnant again with a Rhesus positive foetus, the anti-Rhesus positive antibodies will cross the placenta and attack and destroy the foetal red cells and cause the baby to become anaemic and jaundiced. After birth, the destruction of the blood cells will continue because the antibodies persist for some time in the baby's circulation. In this event, the newborn baby becomes even more anaemic and jaundiced. In severe cases, it will need an exchange transfusion. This entails changing the baby's blood and supplying it with fresh blood which does not contain any antibodies.

The Rhesus blood group of every pregnant woman is tested as part of the routine blood test in early pregnancy. Where a woman is Rhesus negative, further tests will be taken to see if she is developing Rhesus antibodies. If she does, and this is only likely with a second or subsequent Rhesus positive foetus, the concentration of antibodies will be measured. If repeated tests show that the level of antibodies is rising, it may be necessary to take a sample of the amniotic fluid to see if the baby is becoming jaundiced. If it is, then it may have to be delivered prematurely so that an exchange transfusion can be carried out.

Sometimes the foetus is affected very early in pregnancy when premature delivery is not advisable. In this instance, the baby can be given a simple transfusion of Rhesus negative blood. This procedure, called an intra-uterine transfusion, is done under X-ray control by very experienced doctors. It is rarely necessary nowadays and is only performed for a very badly affected foetus.

☐ **Prevention of Rhesus Disease** As the result of a discovery that antibody formation in Rhesus negative women after delivery can be prevented, Rhesus problems in pregnancy are fortunately very much on the decrease nowadays. Today, immediately after a Rhesus negative woman has delivered her child, a sample of blood is taken from the baby to see if it is Rhesus positive. If it is Rhesus positive, then a sample of blood is taken from the mother to see how many of the baby's Rhesus positive blood cells have entered her circulation during delivery. Depending upon the number, she is given an injection of a substance called anti-D gamma globulin which attacks and destroys the Rhesus positive cells before they can initiate the formation of anti-bodies by the mother. In this way, the Rhesus negative woman can enter her next pregnancy without anti-Rhesus positive antibodies. Provided that she is given a further injection of anti-D gamma globulin after her next delivery, (if the baby is also Rhesus positive) she will never have a chance to form them. As an additional safeguard, anti-D gamma globulin is also now given to Rhesus negative women who have a miscarriage, an ectopic pregnancy or a termination.

FIBROIDS

A fibroid is a benign growth that arises from the muscle wall of the uterus. It grows slowly and forms a firm, white, rounded tumour which may vary in size from a pea to a football. Fibroids are very common, but do not usually give rise to symptoms until a woman is over the age of thirty. They may cause lower abdominal discomfort and heavy menstruation. Occasionally, they may be responsible for a failure to become pregnant or for repeated miscarriages. When a woman with fibroids does become pregnant, the fibroids increase in size but usually return to their previous size when the pregnancy is over. They do not usually give rise to symptoms.

Surgical removal of a fibroid has to be avoided in pregnancy because the operation is very likely to cause miscarriage or premature labour.

OVARIAN CYSTS

The ovaries are sometimes the site of cysts. These are fluid-containing swellings, which, like fibroids, can become very large indeed. An ovarian cyst can occur at any age and, in older women, may be malignant. In pregnant women, ovarian cysts are very unlikely to be malignant but, unfortunately, they do show a tendency to become twisted round in pregnancy so that their blood supply is interfered with. If untreated, peritonitis then develops and the woman becomes very ill. For this reason, unlike fibroids, an ovarian cyst should be surgically removed, even during pregnancy.

The diagnosis of an ovarian cyst is usually made when the doctor examines the patient in early pregnancy and finds the cyst alongside the uterus. The operation to remove the cyst is best carried out at about fourteen to sixteen weeks. By this time, the pregnancy is well established, but the uterus has not become too large to make the operation difficult. Done at this time, the removal of the cyst does not disturb the pregnancy or harm the foetus.

MULTIPLE PREGNANCY

This is the term given to twins, triplets and all the other multiples up to the record octuplets (eight babies). Twins occur in about one pregnancy in eighty in most white races, but are more common in some black races. Family history of twins, on either a mother's or father's side, makes twins more likely, although the father's influence only applies to identical (uniovular) twins.

A woman who has already given birth to twins has about a one in ten chance of having a second set. Triplets occur once in six thousand births and quads about once in five hundred thousand births. As a result of women receiving treatment with fertility drugs the incidence of multiple births has increased in modern times. This is because it is sometimes difficult to avoid over-stimulating the ovaries with fertility drugs.

☐ **Identical and non-identical Twins** Identical or uniovular twins develop from one ovum (egg cell) which divides into two separate cells shortly after being fertilized by a single sperm. When the separation of the cells has not been complete, conjoined or Siamese twins result. This is, however, extremely rare.

Identical twins are always the same sex and are usually very alike in physical and mental characteristics. They share the same placenta inside the uterus and are enclosed by a common outer membrane (chorion) although they have their own separate inner membranes (amnion).

Non-identical or binovular twins develop from two ova, which are released instead of the normal one. Each ova is fertilized by a separate sperm and the two fertilized ova then develop normally. This form of twinning is more common than the uniovular type and the resulting babies can be of different sexes and resemble one another only in the same way that brothers and sisters do. Inside the uterus each twin has its own separate placenta and membrane.

☐ **Diagnosing Twins** In the normal course of events, twins should be diagnosed by sixteen weeks because, by this time, the mother's abdomen is much more distended than it should be. This results from the double burden that the uterus is carrying. As the pregnancy proceeds, the head of each twin can be felt and two heartbeats heard. Sometimes the diagnosis is not made until later in pregnancy and, occasionally, especially in women who have firm abdominal muscles or who are fat, not until the first twin has been delivered!

2 Non-identical or binovular twins (left) develop from two fertilized ova. Each foetus has its own placenta and they have separate outer membranes (chorion) as well as separate inner membranes (amnion). The resemblance between binovular twins is only as great as that between any brothers and sisters. They may be different sexes.

Identical or uniovular twins (right) develop from one ovum which divides shortly after fertilization. They share the same placenta and outer membrane (chorion). They have separate inner membranes (amnion). The resemblance between uniovular twins is very great and they are always the same sex.

3 This ultrasound scan clearly shows three distinct foetal heads in the uterus. Ultrasound is the most certain and the safest way of diagnosing multiple pregnancies—in this case, triplets.

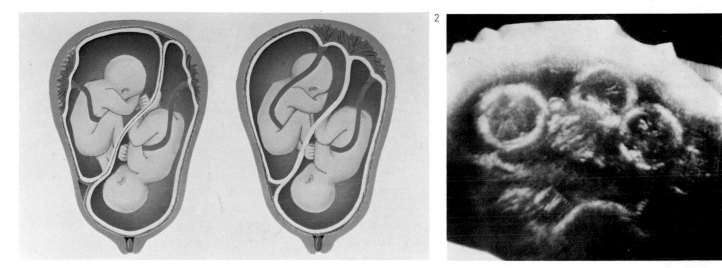

2

3

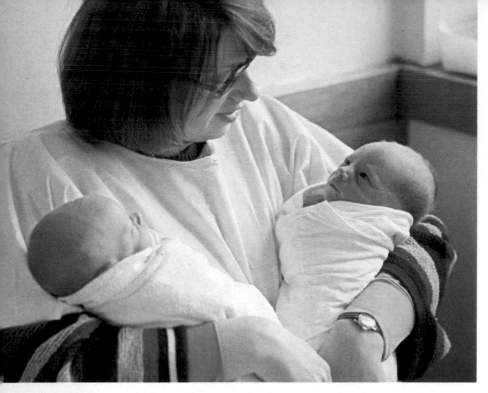

A twin pregnancy can usually be diagnosed by the sixteenth week. Proper obstetric care is essential in this case because both pregnancy and labour are more likely to be complicated than a normal single pregnancy. Breech presentation is quite common and twin labour often occurs prematurely. With proper care, however, there should be no problems and having two additions to the family at once can be very exciting and rewarding for parents and brothers and sisters.

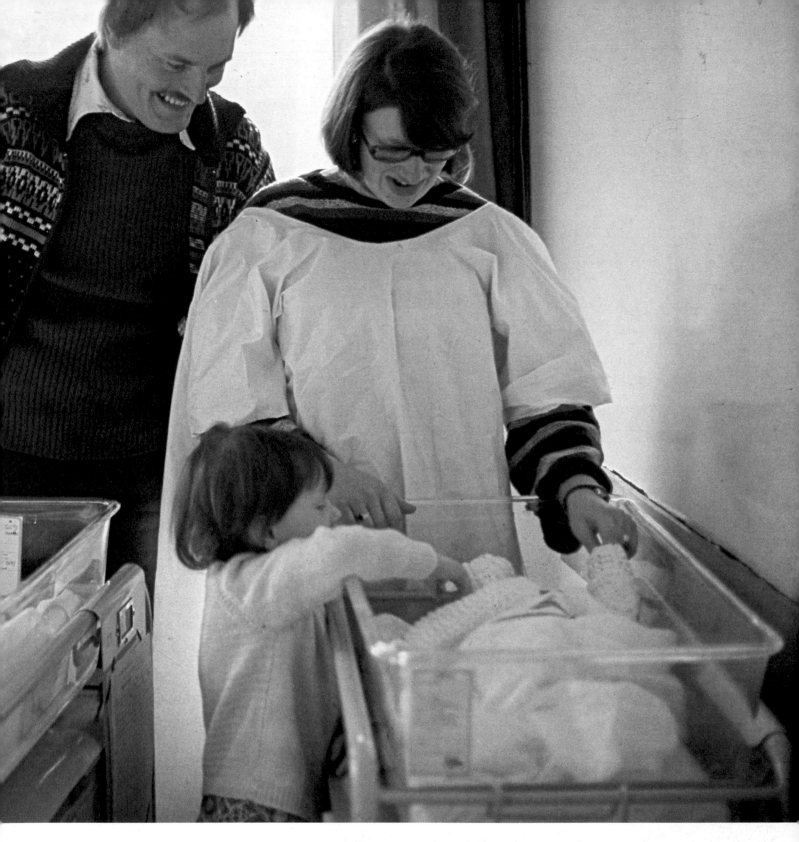

If twins are suspected early in pregnancy, an ultrasound scan or an X-ray will confirm the diagnosis.

☐ **Twin pregnancy** Although most women are delighted to be having twins, twin pregnancy is more likely to be complicated. Apart from the discomfort of the distended abdomen, anaemia, toxaemia and premature labour are all more likely to occur in a twin pregnancy. Accordingly, women who have a twin pregnancy need extra rest, and extra iron and folic acid if they are to avoid anaemia. Admission to hospital may well be needed to ensure that the patient does rest. This will certainly be necessary if toxaemia develops.

☐ **Twin labour** Twin labour is likely to be anything up to eight weeks premature, although with luck and good antenatal care it will not occur before thirty-eight weeks. Skilled obstetric care is needed and confinement in a hospital which has a special-care baby unit for premature babies, is a must. Twin labour does not usually last longer than with a single baby, but breech presentation, that is, when the buttocks rather than the vertex present, is more common.

ABORTION

In the eyes of the law at the present time a baby is not considered to be capable of a separate existence before the completion of the twenty-eighth week of pregnancy. If pregnancy ends for some reason before this time, it is said to have aborted or miscarried. The terms miscarriage and abortion both mean the same thing, the ending of a pregnancy before the twenty-eighth week, but the word abortion is more commonly used to refer to pregnancies which have been deliberately terminated.

Termination of pregnancy or induced abortion is, nowadays, performed legally for a variety of reasons—for example, when the health or welfare of the woman or her family is threatened or when there is risk that the baby may be deformed.

□ **What causes miscarriage?** Miscarriage occurs in about one in every five conceptions. There are many causes but, perhaps, the most important is a failure of the pregnancy to develop normally. When the baby is likely to be very severely deformed, nature often intervenes, development ceases and the woman miscarries.

Severe illness of many sorts in the mother can cause miscarriage. For example, a severe attack of gastro-enteritis, a sudden emotional shock like the death of a near relative, extremes of physical activity, may all cause miscarriage. At the same time, it is remarkable how some pregnancies will survive the most hair-raising adventures in both a medical and non-medical sense!

Deficiency of the hormone, progesterone, has been blamed for some miscarriages, especially as a shortage of progesterone is most likely to occur at about twelve weeks when a miscarriage quite often takes place.

Miscarriage after twelve to fourteen weeks is most often due to an abnormality in the shape of the uterus or to a weakness in the cervix.

Sexual intercourse in the early months of pregnancy may, occasionally, cause slight bleeding, but it rarely causes miscarriage. However, if intercourse does cause bleeding in early pregnancy, it should be avoided until after twelve weeks. Quite often no cause can be found for a particular miscarriage and, in such a case, the woman's next pregnancy is often perfectly normal.

□ **Miscarriage—signs and symptoms** Most miscarriages occur in the first twelve weeks of pregnancy, but a small proportion occur later. Usually the first sign that something is wrong is painless bright red vaginal bleeding. To start with, the loss is slight and may stop after a few hours. This is medically termed a threatened miscarriage. If the bleeding continues, however, the miscarriage becomes inevitable and the blood

loss can be severe. In this case the bleeding is accompanied by griping pains, like severe period pains, in the lower part of the abdomen and back. If the foetus, with its sac of membranes and developing placenta, passes intact, the bleeding will stop after some hours and the pain will cease. This is known as a complete miscarriage.

If parts of the foetus and membranes are left behind in the uterus, the bleeding and pain continue and a small operation is necessary to clean out the uterus. This operation—evacuation of the uterus—is carried out under a short general anesthetic and entails a one- to two-day stay in hospital. If much blood has been lost, a blood transfusion will be given.

A careful examination should always be made by a doctor after a miscarriage has occurred to confirm that there are no remnants left inside the uterus. If these are not removed, infection may occur in the uterus and the woman will, as a result, become seriously ill. This is known as septic miscarriage or septic abortion.

In the type of miscarriage known as a missed abortion, the foetus dies at about ten or twelve weeks or later, but is not expelled immediately. In such a case the woman stops feeling pregnant and, after a few days, develops a brown discharge from the vagina. Eventually, usually after two or three weeks, but sometimes longer, bleeding occurs and any remaining parts of the pregnancy are expelled to the accompaniment of some vaginal bleeding and abdominal pain. If missed abortion is suspected and the diagnosis is confirmed by a negative pregnancy test and an ultrasound examination (see page 36) the patient is admitted into hospital and the contents of the uterus evacuated, as in the case of an incomplete miscarriage.

□ **Repeated miscarriage** Any woman who has had a miscarriage will be worried about the prospects of subsequent pregnancy. If a careful examination, following a single miscarriage, has not revealed any abnormality and if the miscarriage is not the result of a permanent problem for that particular woman, it is reasonable for her to try to become pregnant again as soon as she desires to do so. The risk of another miscarriage, in this instance, is small. It is, however, sensible for such a woman to wait until she feels fully recovered from the effect of the miscarriage and has had one or two normal periods again. No special treatment is needed when she does become pregnant again, but heavy physical work should be completely avoided and she must have adequate rest—for example, one hour's rest on a bed or couch in the middle of the day and ten hours' sleep at night. To avoid even the slightest risk of disturbing the pregnancy, sexual intercourse is best avoided during the first twelve weeks of pregnancy.

☐ **Reactions to miscarriage** Once miscarriage is complete, all pain should cease and the vaginal bleeding should clear up in a few days. Two or three days after a late miscarriage the breasts may fill up with milk and feel swollen and tender for a day or two. They quickly return to normal without treatment in most cases. Rhesus negative women should receive an injection of anti-D gamma globulin (see page 68) to avoid the slight risk of rhesus sensitization.

Ovulation occurs between two and three weeks after a miscarriage and, provided the woman does not immediately become pregnant again, the first period will start a few weeks after ovulation, i.e. four to five weeks after the date of the miscarriage. Thereafter the normal menstrual cycle is resumed.

The disappointment of losing the baby often leaves a woman feeling depressed. This is a normal reaction to an unhappy event and needs sympathetic handling by the husband and close friends. The husband himself will often be as disappointed as his wife, but shared sorrow is more easily borne. Reassurance that miscarriage is very common and that it is unlikely to recur in a subsequent pregnancy is helpful. Persistent depression needs expert medical advice and a doctor should always be consulted if the natural sadness that follows a miscarriage lasts longer than two or three weeks.

☐ **Recurrent miscarriage** In a few rare instances, miscarriage occurs more than once. When this happens the woman should be referred to a gynaecologist for investigation. Improvement in general health, operations to correct an abnormally shaped uterus, stitching the cervix in early pregnancy and sometimes hormone treatment, are steps that may be taken. These are usually successful nowadays in overcoming the problems of recurrent miscarriage. The important point is that women who have had two successive miscarriages should be properly investigated before they try to become pregnant again.

☐ **Ultrasound in early pregnancy** Nowadays, high frequency sound-waves are often used during late pregnancy to obtain a "picture" of the baby inside the uterus. This enables doctors to measure the baby's size and maturity (see page 36). Recently ultrasound has also been applied to the study of early pregnancy. The developing foetus can be identified as early as four weeks after conception and when there is a threat of miscarriage, an ultrasound examination will determine whether or not a miscarriage is actually inevitable. When a miscarriage has occurred, an ultrasound examination will reveal whether or not it is complete.

ECTOPIC PREGNANCY

Once in every hundred or so pregnancies the fertilized egg unfortunately implants itself in the Fallopian tube instead of in the uterus. This is termed an ectopic pregnancy.

Once implanted it tries to develop, but because of the space cannot grow normally. The tube becomes very stretched at the site of the pregnancy and then either splits, medically termed ruptured ectopic, or squeezes the pregnancy back along the tube the way it came which is known as tubal abortion. In both cases the foetus dies and the mother suffers some internal bleeding.

☐ **How to recognize an ectopic pregnancy** The most important symptom of ectopic pregnancy is pain on the site of the affected Fallopian tube. This usually starts one or two weeks after the first period is missed and becomes increasingly severe. Normal symptoms of pregnancy are present and a pregnancy test is usually positive. As the pregnancy grows in the tube there will often be some vaginal bleeding. If much internal bleeding occurs, as it may in the case of a ruptured tube, the woman becomes very pale and may collapse with a very low blood pressure. Some lower abdominal pain is not uncommon in early normal pregnancy, but it is mild compared with the pain of an ectopic pregnancy and does not last. The pain of an ectopic pregnancy is both severe and persistent. Any woman who gets a pain to one side or the other of the lower abdomen in early pregnancy should consult her doctor at once. Diagnosis of ectopic pregnancy can often be made by a simple vaginal examination. If there is doubt, the patient is admitted immediately to hospital and is examined under a general anaesthetic. The anaesthetic enables the gynaecologist to do a much more thorough vaginal examination without causing the patient pain. If there is still doubt about the diagnosis, a narrow telescope, known as a laparoscope, can be passed through a tiny incision made just below the umbilicus. This enables the Fallopian tubes and ovaries to be inspected.

☐ **Treatment of ectopic pregnancy** When an embryo is present in a tube, the woman needs an operation to remove both the embryo and the affected tube. Unfortunately, as the tube itself is often too badly damaged to be left in place, it is not possible to remove only the embryo. If there has been much internal bleeding the woman will need a blood transfusion. Removal of one tube does not, of course, mean the end of the woman's child-bearing career.

Ectopic pregnancy is a very serious condition. The important thing is to seek medical advice at once if severe abdominal pain develops during early pregnancy.

Using the Time before Birth

First Things First

Pregnancy is a time for planning, for looking ahead and for making any preparations and changes that will help the days run more smoothly when the baby arrives. A well ordered home is a boon to a busy mother and gives a baby, however young, a sense of security, of feeling well cared for and at home in his surroundings. As rest is such an essential part of caring for the unborn baby, pregnancy brings many opportunities to sit down and plan ahead. Rest periods are also ideal times for embarking on practical preparations, like knitting baby clothes.

The months of pregnancy are an ideal opportunity for a mother-to-be to look at her home environment and ask: 'How can I run this home to the advantage of the family and myself?'.

The art of running a household successfully lies in having an organized, but flexible routine. A measured routine can make an incredible difference to a mother's, father's and child's day. The simplicity, for example, of being able to say: 'We always do this now' is a very effective way of dealing with family dissension. Such a routine is also the beginning of discipline for a child and it is always worth remembering that a child's sense of security stems from a well-ordered routine, from knowing what he can expect from his surroundings and what, in turn, is expected of him.

ORGANIZING THE HOME

A home needs to be comfortable, free of clutter, clean and hygienic. If it is free of clutter, then it will be comfortable and easy to clean; if it is easy to clean it will be hygienic because germs collect and thrive where there is dust and dirt.

In running a home, it is the feet, legs and back that take most of the strain, and any equipment that lessens this strain is worth having. The most expensive equipment is not necessarily the best; choose items carefully, first making sure that they will save you time and energy.

For instance, an ironing board should be firm, steady and adjustable, so that you can sit down to iron. A principle for motherhood is never to stand when you can sit. Plan working surfaces so that they are comfortable to stand or sit at; shop around for electrical equipment that is not irritatingly noisy when in use. All these points save time, energy, tension and strain and, therefore, add up to a happy mother and family.

PLANNING THE SHOPPING

Take a good look at your home, stock up the larder and earmark a cupboard that can be used for reserve stocks. Fill a store cupboard with essential 'dry' supplies, such as lavatory paper, soap, soap powder, disinfectant, and so on, so that you will not need to include these in your weekly shop during the early weeks of motherhood. If you have a freezer, stock up on prepared dishes that you can draw upon in the first few weeks after the birth.

Try to find, in advance of the birth, a mother or grandmother who would be happy to look after your baby while you go shopping.

Be prepared to accept that the first few weeks after your baby's birth will be an expensive time. It is better to spend less money on equipping your baby with splendid new things, and more on someone to help with the ironing, cooking or cleaning. This will enable you to reserve your vital energy for feeding, caring for and generally getting off to a good start with your baby. In this way you will more quickly build up your own energy and will be more relaxed and happy!

See whether there are any stores that will deliver to your home, or whether a neighbour or school-girl can help with essential day-to-day shopping. Make use of mail order catalogues.

GETTING THINGS RIGHT

Once your baby is born, you will spend even more time than normal in the kitchen. Ask yourself 'how labour-saving is this kitchen?'. This question is answered not so much in terms of how many gadgets are contained in it, but how much time and effort is spent in crossing from one side of the room to the other. Ideally, you should not need to take a single step further than is necessary and the most essential pieces of equipment—food stores, draining board, sink, working surfaces and cooker should all be next to each other. If possible, a washing machine or spin-dryer should fit under the working surface next to the sink so that hand-washing can be easily put into it for rinsing.

The average height of working surfaces is 91 cm (36 in) above the floor. You will also need a slightly lower surface of about 81 to 84 cm (32 to 33 in) which is the height at which pastry- or bread-making or chopping vegetables is most easily carried out. Wall cupboards need to be about 38 cm (15 in) above a working surface, preferably with narrow shelves, so that everything is easily accessible and cannot get hidden. Drawers need to be shallow, so that you can see everything at a glance, and dry shelves and cupboards above arm's reach should be kept for rarely used equipment or items which are dangerous to children at the toddling stage.

Attention to detail, when you are pregnant, will save you much precious time and energy (and temper) in the years to come. It is particularly helpful to plan ahead because once children arrive, spare money usually goes towards their clothing, education and holidays rather than the home.

The Baby's Room

Once the kitchen is streamlined, then consider the room which your baby will occupy. Often this is the box room. It is, however, well worth remembering that a baby grows quickly into a toddler who needs lots of space to move and play and into a child who wants an enormous railway set!

In the early years, a toddler is not happy for long playing out of view or earshot of his mother, so it is important to consider the room as a place where you will need to spend time reading, writing, sewing or knitting while your child plays. It is wiser to plan for this, rather than to allow the child to get into the habit of bringing his toys into the kitchen.

The kitchen, unless part of it is partitioned off, is rarely a safe place for play and a child cannot be expected to respect a sitting-room until he is older.

HEATING

If the home is centrally heated, see that it is also equipped with humidifiers. Those that are electrically operated can be very helpful in relieving a dry atmosphere. They will also ease chest ailments, eczema and other skin conditions. From birth, a baby needs a room which is continually heated to about 21°C (70°F). If you do not have central heating, the best and safest alternative is a thermostatically controlled electric radiator or a convector heater with a child-proof grid.

FLOORING

Floor coverings for a child's room need to be easy to clean, safe to walk or crawl on, good for the efficient running of clockwork toys—and not too precious, because accidents will happen!

DECORATION

Walls are best covered with emulsion paints which can be wiped clean and easily repainted, or with a washable paper. Painted walls can be livened up with nursery friezes, paintings or collages.

When choosing curtains, look for subtle colours and simple designs which give the room a restful appearance. The true function of curtains is to keep out cold and draughts—they are, therefore, best lined and interlined.

CHANGING TOP

A top priority is a working surface on which to change and dress the baby. This could be a waist-high chest of drawers, or a steady table, padded with a folded towel, a terry-towelling mattress or a ready-made changing mat. Alternatively, you could buy a specially-designed baby dresser and storage unit. A bed is not suitable. It is normally too low for comfortable use and causes unnecessary strain on a mother's back.

If you are going to feed the baby in his room, then you will also need a low, comfortable armless chair.

THE FIRST BED

Until your baby is about six months old, or unable to sit up, he can sleep in a Moses basket, carrycot, pram body, cradle or even a drawer! Anything, in fact, that he feels secure and comfortable in and which protects him from draughts. Whatever your choice, make sure that your baby sleeps on a firm mattress and non-wobbly surface.

If a wooden drawer is to be used, it should be carefully investigated for splinters and then well-padded. Wicker cradles and Moses baskets should be lined to protect the baby from draughts. A carrycot, with non-porous lining, should have its sides lined or padded with a blanket to prevent the possibility of the baby rolling to the side of the cot and being suffocated.

FULL-SIZE COT

By about six months of age, or when he can sit up, your baby will need a full-size cot. This should have a safety catch to prevent the sides being let down; and the vertical bars should be spaced close enough together to prevent any chance of the baby getting his head stuck. The cot should be sturdy enough to stand up to vigorous shaking; there should be no harmful inner projections and no horizontal bars which could be used as a step-ladder for climbing out! *Any paint used should be lead-free.*

☐ **Mattresses** The mattress should be firm and a perfect fit for the cot so that there is no danger of the baby becoming wedged in a gap between the mattress and the cot. It is best covered from top to toe with a waterproof cover. One side of it could have a porous lining. Making a mattress from foam rubber is not recommended.

☐ **Waterproof Sheets** An unprotected mattress must be protected by a waterproof sheet. This needs to cover the whole mattress, as a baby's urine spreads across quite a wide area. For the baby's comfort, an underblanket or flannelette sheet should be placed between the waterproofing and bottom sheet. Choose waterproof sheets that can be boiled.

☐ **Bedding** A pillow should not be used for the first twelve months of a baby's life. The baby does not need it, and the possible risk of suffocation is enough to ban its use. Fitted stretch terry sheets are comfortable and make bed-making easy;

It is, of course, only natural, when preparing for a longed-for baby, to want the best of everything and to crave the kind of money that the best costs. But remember that babies quickly outgrow one set of clothes and circumstances. They soon become toddlers and toddlers quickly become children, schoolchildren and teenagers!

If money is in short supply, a few imaginative touches will more than compensate. For example, a coat of non-toxic, lead free paint and a second-hand piece of furniture will transform any room and provide a royal welcome fit for any baby.

flanelette sheets are warmer than cotton but take longer to dry and will not last as long. Cotton sheets can easily be made from the unworn outside sections of full-sized sheets.

☐ **Blankets** Cotton cellular blankets are light but warm, they are also machine-washable and can be boiled. Some woollen blankets can be machine-washed. Old blankets cut to size can be used. Blankets should be bound with satin to protect a baby's face and neck from irritation. Fringes are best avoided on blankets because the baby will suck them. Shawls can be used, but avoid those with an open-work lacy pattern in which a baby can catch his fingers and toes. Cot-size blankets can be folded and used doubled in the crib or

pram. The number of blankets needed will depend on how warm the room is; they should not be piled on. You will need to allow sufficient for frequent washing and changing.

☐ **Continental Quilts** Only from the time a baby can sit up should these be used for prams and cots. Choose washable Terylene quilts made to British Standard specifications, of the correct size.

☐ **Sleeping Bags** These are especially useful for travelling. They need to be large enough for a baby to stretch his legs, and should not be tight round the neck or wrists. They should be easily washable. If you use a sleeping bag regularly you will need more than one.

Basic Equipment

CHOOSING A PRAM

If you live in a hilly area, choose a pram that is light to push and soft-bodied; if you have lots of roads to cross, look for one with large wheels; if you have to negotiate many steps or stairs, choose a pram with small wheels. The higher a pram, the easier it is to attend to a baby; it also keeps him out of reach of friendly dogs! If you are under 1.5 m (5 ft), however, take this into account or you will spend all your time peering over the sides. Put the pram hood up before buying the pram to find out whether you can see over the top! If you travel a great deal, then choose a pram that is light and easy to dismantle. Remember, however, that a light-weight pram is not always the most comfortable for long walks.

Whatever your choice, there are essential points to check before making your purchase: Can you reach the brake easily, when, for example, holding the handle with one hand? A brake is more effective when it works on two wheels rather than on one. The hood should collapse easily, but the body should not. Harness attachments must be safely anchored and the pram must be strong enough not to tip over when rocked by a baby. If you expect to carry heavy shopping, then look for a model which will safely support a pram tray. The harness should be designed to go over the baby's shoulders and fastened so that he cannot stand up. Are the pram and harness large enough to use until your baby is ready for a pushchair?

The list of things that a baby appears to require may seem never-ending when you first consider layettes, prams and feeding equipment. But, in reality, a baby's needs are very simple and there are many ways in which you can economize while still ensuring his good looks and comfort. It helps to remember that man-made fibres are not comfortable for babies and that it is far wiser to buy natural fabrics, such as cotton and wool. Prams should be carefully chosen, keeping your own locality in mind.

BUYING SECONDHAND

All the items mentioned above and on the previous page can be bought secondhand through advertisements in local newspapers, clinics, shops or through friends. Always remember to examine the goods carefully, looking for safety factors such as splintered wood, flaking paint and the possibility of needing replacement parts.

TOILETRIES

Choose the purest kind of toilet soap, free from perfume, and always rinse it off with plenty of water. Alternatively, use a specially prepared baby liquid in the bath. You will also need:
baby shampoo
cotton-wool for cleaning the face and buttocks
soft towels
cotton swabs for umbilicus
cream for buttocks.
Talcum powder is not essential and can be dangerous if a toddler inhales it.

CLOTHES

A new baby needs to be dressed in several layers of light clothing rather than a few bulky garments.
A basic layette consists of:
2 dozen nappies
3 pairs of plastic pants
3 stretch suits or long gowns
3 cotton or cotton and wool vests
2 cardigans
2 hats
2 pairs of mittens (for cold weather)
1 shawl
2 angel tops
2 blankets
3 cot sheets
3 pram sheets and 2 pram blankets
6 terry-towelling bibs

When choosing a layette, avoid garments that are made entirely of man-made fibres. These cut off the supply of air, do not allow a baby's skin to breathe, cause perspiration and are not as warm as natural fibres. Stretch suits are fine but make sure that they are roomy enough for the baby to move freely. Choose simple, shift-style nightgowns with raglan sleeves. Choose cardigans made from a closely worked pattern which button all the way up. Avoid jumpers until your baby is happy to have things pulled over his head.

FEEDING AND STERILIZING EQUIPMENT

The section on bottle-feeding describes the bottles, teats and sterilizing equipment needed. Even if you are breastfeeding, you will need at least two bottles for the occasional feed and for water. If bottle-feeding, you will need between four and six bottles. See page 130.

Labour and Birth

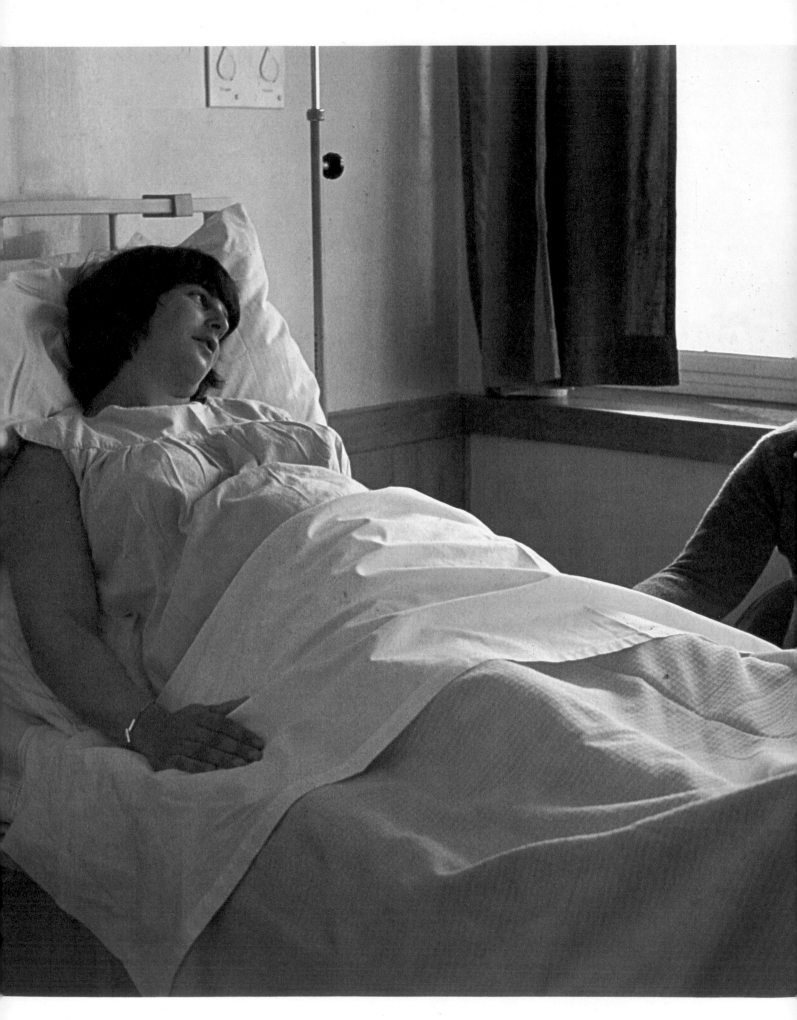

Labour and Birth

Pain Relief in Labour

However delighted a mother is, childbirth is always tiring and to some extent uncomfortable. Many women require some form of pain relief and it is important to accept this and to be prepared to use whatever methods are appropriate.

DRUGS

Many pain-relieving drugs have been used in labour, but the most commonly used nowadays are pethidine (known as demerol in some countries) and morphia in various preparations of which Omnopon is, perhaps, the most common. Both these drugs, when given in adequate dosage, are effective in relieving pain. They do, however, pass across the placenta and, having entered the foetus's circulation, tend to depress the foetus's breathing. This can delay the onset of normal breathing when the baby is born. For this reason, pethidine and morphia are not usually given in late labour, say two hours before the birth. Given earlier in labour, they are perfectly safe for both mother and baby. Pethidine is often combined with a mild sedative in order to encourage sleep and this also increases the pain-relieving effect. Both pethidine ' and morphia are given by injection and start to work after fifteen to twenty minutes. The mother-to-be will then be less aware of the contractions and will usually feel rather drowsy. The effects wear off after three or four hours when a repeat injection can be given if necessary and if the birth is not imminent.

GAS AND OXYGEN

A mixture of fifty per cent nitrous oxide (laughing gas) and fifty per cent oxygen has replaced the earlier gas and air mixture. It is administered through a special face mask which the mother-to-be holds herself. The breathing of this gas mixture slightly anaesthetizes the mother-to-be so that pain is relieved without her becoming completely unconscious. (It is very important for proper instructions to be given in how to use the machine —otherwise it will be ineffective.) As soon as the contraction starts the mother-to-be should place the face mask *firmly* against her face, covering both mouth and nose, and should then breathe deeply, drawing as much gas into the lungs as quickly as possible. The gas should be breathed throughout the contraction, but not between contractions or else she will become too drowsy.

Gas and oxygen is most often used for the end of the first stage and during the second stage of labour. When the woman is in the second stage she should take only two or three quick deep breaths of gas before holding her breath and starting to push. Gas and oxygen causes the woman to feel slightly 'drunk' at the time she is using it, but it is completely safe and does not cause any harmful effects to the foetus. It is most unlikely to stop the baby breathing normally at birth.

LOCAL ANAESTHESIA

A local anaesthetic can be injected into the perineal tissues to make them numb and so relieve the perineal pain of the second stage of labour. Such an injection should always be given before carrying out an episiotomy or when stitches are inserted to repair a perineal tear.

☐ **Pudendal Block** The pudendal block is an injection of local anaesthetic on each side of the lower vagina wall. This will anaesthetize the pudendal nerve which supplies the perineum and the lower vagina. It is most often used when a simple forceps delivery or vacuum extraction is required. (See pages 100 and 101.)

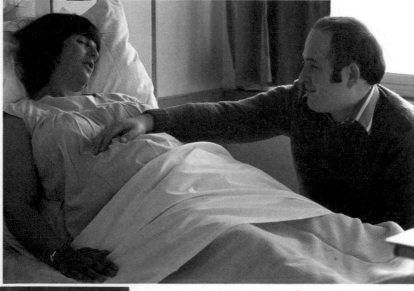

1 A couple look forward to the happy event together. His presence means so much, especially during the waiting time of the first stage of labour.

2 The hardness of the uterus during a contraction can be very easily felt—even by a first-time expectant father.

'Le Boyer' births are becoming more wide-spread in many European hospital hospitals.

1 During the birth, both husband and midwife encourage the mother to push with each contraction.

2 Once the head and shoulders have been delivered, the baby's body slips out easily.

3 The first external contact between the mother and her baby is when he is gently placed on her tummy immediately after the birth, with the cord still attached.

☐ **Epidural Block** Epidural block is a relatively new method of relieving pain during the first and second stages of labour. It consists of an injection of a long-acting local anaesthetic and is given through a needle introduced into the lower part of the back. The tip of the needle is usually inserted into the spinal canal close to the nerves that carry painful sensations from the uterus to the spinal cord above. Because the injection is given low down there is no risk of damaging the spinal cord itself. In addition to anaesthetizing the uterine and vaginal nerves, the perineum and leg nerves are also affected. This means that as well as relieving pain from uterine contractions, the epidural makes the legs and perineum numb and may temporarily stop the woman being able to move her legs properly.

In the modern form of epidural, once the needle has been placed in position a fine soft plastic catheter (tube) is passed down through it and the needle is then withdrawn leaving the catheter in place. This remains in place throughout labour, so that, when the effect of the first injection wears off, subsequent injections can be given without difficulty. This enables the pain relief to be continued throughout labour.

There is no doubt in my mind that at the present time the epidural block is the most effective method of pain relief in labour. The pain is abolished completely without any loss of consciousness on the part of the mother or drug effect on the baby. Failure of the method is rare in the experienced hands of an anaesthetist and nerve damage is almost unknown. A fall in blood pressure, which causes the mother to feel faint and sick, may occur after the injection has been given. This, however, is quickly corrected by turning the mother on her side and giving intravenous fluid. This means that an intravenous drip must always be set up when the epidural catheter is being put into place.

One disadvantage of the method is its very effectiveness. Because all the painful sensations are abolished the mother may not be aware of contractions during the second stage of labour and will need to be told when to push. This lack of sensation may lead to an increased chance of needing a simple low forceps' delivery, but with

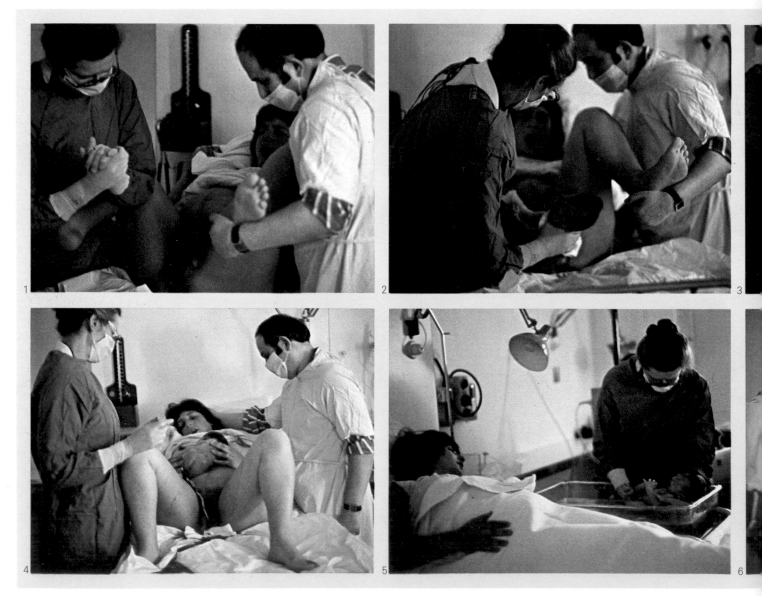

the epidural block this is easily done without risk to either mother or baby. Some mothers feel cheated if they do not experience the pain and sensations of childbirth and for them the epidural is an anathema. For women who desire pain relief without being drugged, however, I regard the epidural block as a very satisfactory solution to the problem of labour pains.

☐ **The Caudal Block** The caudal block is very similar to the epidural except that the injection is made lower down. It is less popular than the epidural, but equally good results can be obtained.

☐ **Spinal Anaesthesia** Epidural and spinal anaesthesia are often confused. A spinal anaesthetic is given through a needle inserted in the same place as for an epidural, but the tip of the needle is advanced further so that the injection of local anaesthetic is given into the cerebro-spinal fluid. Pain relief is complete, as with epidural, but lasts for only two or three hours and cannot then be repeated. Muscle paralysis is much more profound and the anaesthetic sometimes causes a headache. It is a very safe and useful anaesthetic but it has no advantage over epidural.

NATURAL CHILDBIRTH

Since childbirth is a natural process many people, including doctors and midwives, have suggested that it should be kept as natural as possible and that medical intervention should be reduced to a minimum. This is sound in theory and every midwife or doctor who looks after a mother-to-be who does not need pain relief, and who delivers her baby naturally with the minimum of assistance, is delighted. However, in practice, such mothers are comparatively uncommon. For most women, nature is given some assistance, both in the easing of pain and the ensuring of the mother's and baby's safety. Without such assistance I believe that most modern women would find labour a painful and unpleasant experience.

The late Dr Grantly Dick Read pioneered the concept of natural childbirth, based on the observation that fear produced tension and that tension caused labour to be much more painful than it need be. He advocated a series of relaxation exercises, based on controlled breathing, which helped the patient to relax and thereby relieve pain. Dr Lamaze, in Paris, and in Russia,

4 It only takes a short time for breathing to become established. The cord is clamped and cut when it stops bleeding.

5 In order to minimise the differences between life inside and outside the uterus, 'Le Boyer' babies are bathed in warm water.

6 Most babies have an instinctive desire to suck when brought into contact with the mother's breast.

7 'Fixing' the baby's mouth on to the nipple sometimes needs a little help at first.

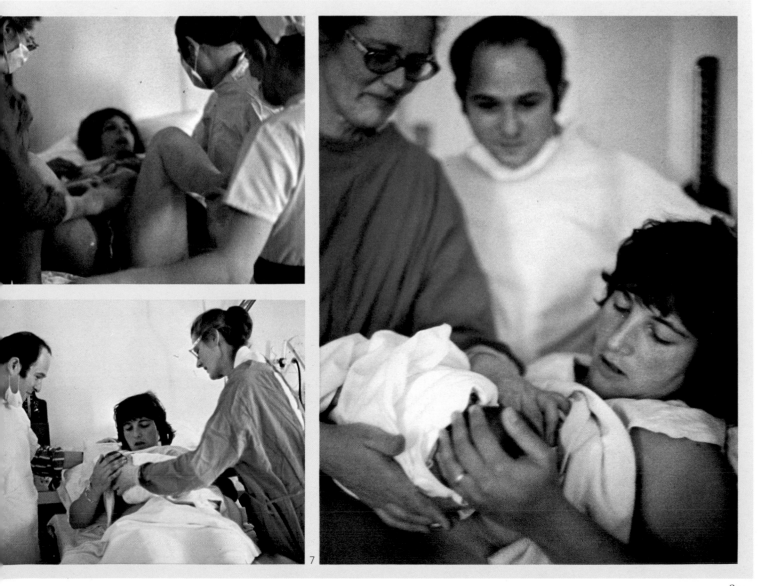

7

Dr Nicolaiev developed a similar system, called psychoprophylaxis, which also consists of relaxation exercises. Psychoprophylaxis is widely used, especially in Europe and in Russia.

All these methods involve educating the mother-to-be in the process of labour, and also in the idea that uterine contractions are not painful if the correct relaxation exercises are followed. In Britain, at the present time, the National Childbirth Trust teaches relaxation as well as giving instruction on all other aspects of pregnancy and labour.

There are a number of techniques for controlling and overcoming discomfort and pain in labour taught and used very successfully. All of these are dependent on a full understanding of the physical process and the use of controlled breathing. The intention of the various techniques of natural childbirth is to enable the mother to cope with the increasing intensity of her uterine contractions by identifying her own particular needs and progressing through several stages or levels of controlled breathing. Most hospitals run such clinics, but these tend to lay greater stress on mothercraft—i.e., caring for the baby after the birth. Most women find instructional classes helpful and are, as a result, able to some extent to relieve the pain in labour by relaxation. For some, this method is all that is needed to cope with labour and delivery, and for them the sense of achievement is considerable. It is, however, important that those who are unable to use the method without additional assistance should not feel that they have failed in some way. Labour and the birth of a healthy baby is always a success, no matter how or with what help it is achieved.

In recent years Dr Leboyer, in France, has written and spoken extensively on the need for peace and calm at the time of birth and the effect that such conditions, or a lack of them, will have on the birth and subsequent development of the child. That a tranquil birth produces a tranquil person is a most attractive theory, but, in my view, the necessary proof is lacking at present and much more research is needed before further conclusions can be drawn.

Home Confinement

The idea of having a baby at home, in the family setting, attended by the local midwife and general practitioner, is very attractive to many mothers-to-be who do not feel at ease in hospital surroundings. Although safe home delivery is perfectly possible for some women, the problem is how to know which women will be safe and which will not. Some of the complications of labour cannot be predicted and when things go wrong specialist help and equipment is urgently needed. For example, foetal distress during labour requires all the medical facilities that are necessary to rescue the baby quickly. This may involve a forceps' delivery or a Caesarean section. Post-partum haemorrhage is another complication which may require a life-saving blood transfusion and all the necessary facilities and equipment to give it. Not so long ago, when there were insufficient maternity beds in hospitals and some women had to be delivered at home, arrangements were made to send help out from the hospital to those women who developed complications. The help came in the form of an obstetric flying squad which consisted of an obstetrician and anaesthetist and one or two midwives, plus the necessary medical equipment. Unfortunately, even the most practised flying squad could not reach the patient's home without some delay and, during this time, the mother or baby could die.

Although the risks of home confinement are slight, most doctors and midwives think that they are sufficiently great to recommend a hospital delivery. In hospital, the necessary medical and obstetric help is available on the spot and so are the facilities for operative delivery and resuscitation of the baby. Early discharge from hospital after delivery, and the free access which most maternity units now give to fathers to be present and the family to visit, may not be quite so satisfying as home confinement, but a hospital confinement is safer for both mother and baby.

If you decide on a home confinement, you will be given a list of equipment required and information about the most suitable conditions. The room and equipment will, of course, need to be prepared well in advance.

Labour

The Onset of Labour

During pregnancy the uterine muscle contracts intermittently and the uterus as a whole becomes hard, usually without causing any discomfort. Indeed, the mother-to-be may not be aware that this is occurring. In late pregnancy these contractions become more frequent and powerful and the mother-to-be may feel them and be deceived into believing that labour has started. This phenomenon, called 'false labour', is more common in women who are having a second or subsequent baby and may cause an unnecessary trip to the hospital.

True labour begins when the uterine contractions become regular and cause a progressive dilatation (opening up) of the cervix and descent of the foetus through the pelvis. As a result of dilatation commencing the membranes around the internal os (opening) of the cervix separate from their attachment and slight bleeding occurs. Sometimes this slight bleeding or 'show', as it is called, is the first thing that a woman notices. The contractions then become obvious later. Occasionally, rupture of the membranes, in which a small amount of fluid is released, is the first obvious sign that labour has started.

The most usual sequence of events is the onset of regular contractions followed by a slight blood loss. Rupture of the membranes does not normally occur until a later stage.

☐ **What Causes Labour to Begin?** The onset of labour represents the culmination of a series of complicated hormonal changes that are probably instituted by the foetus itself. The exact mechanism in the human being is not known, but the hormone, oxytocin, and the substances known as prostaglandins, play an important part in making the uterus contract.

WHEN TO GO INTO HOSPITAL

In most cases the onset of labour will be clearly recognized. Sometimes, however, the mother-to-be is uncertain and delays going into hospital. In practice, as soon as regular contractions, say one in every ten minutes, have occurred for more than one hour, labour should be assumed to have started even if no bleeding has occurred and the membranes have not ruptured. Slight bleeding alone is not strong enough evidence and, in this instance, the mother-to-be should wait for the contractions to begin before going in to hospital. Rupture of the membranes, however, is always a clear indication that the baby is on the way and the mother-to-be should go to the hospital.

If there is any doubt about whether or not labour has started, a telephone call, asking for advice, should be made to the doctor, or midwife, or labour ward sister at the hospital. The important principle is: if in doubt, go in. Going in on a false alarm is far wiser than being delivered in an ambulance!

THE STAGES OF LABOUR

Traditionally, labour is divided into three stages.

The first stage extends from the onset of labour until the time when the cervix is fully dilated, that is when the cervix is sufficiently open to allow the foetal head to pass through. When the cervix is fully dilated, the first stage has come to an end.

The second stage of labour lasts from full dilatation of the cervix until the completion of delivery of the baby.

The third stage of labour extends from the time of the completion of the delivery of the baby until the completion of the delivery of the placenta.

The duration of the first stage of labour varies considerably, but a first stage which lasts from four to twelve hours would be considered normal for a primipara (a mother giving birth to her first baby) or two to six hours for a multi-para (a mother who has had more than one baby). There is a good deal of individual variation, however, and shorter or longer labours occur.

The duration of the second stage of labour should never be longer than two hours and it is often much shorter, especially for second or subsequent babies. The duration of the third stage of labour is shortened in modern obstetric practice by an injection which causes a very powerful contraction of the uterus. This helps to expel the placenta and, as a result, the third stage of labour rarely lasts more than five minutes.

DILATATION OF THE CERVIX

The uterine muscle is stronger in the upper segment of the uterus than in the lower segment. As a result, when the uterus contracts, the stronger upper segment draws the lower segment and cervix up over the foetal head and, at the same time, drives the head downwards into the pelvis. Continuing contractions then stretch and dilate the os (opening) until the opening is large enough to allow the baby's head to pass through.

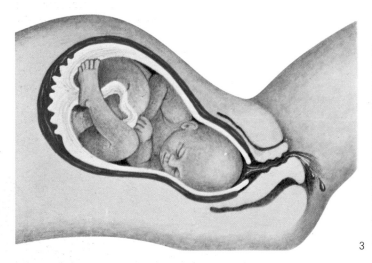

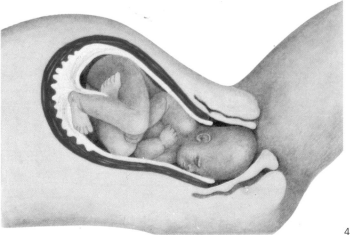

1

2

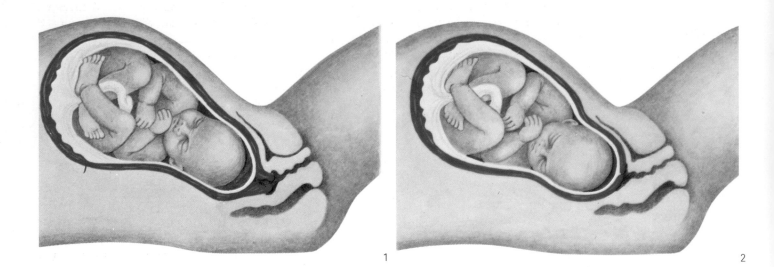

3

4

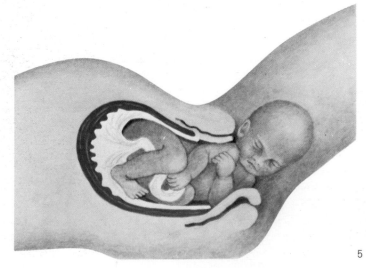

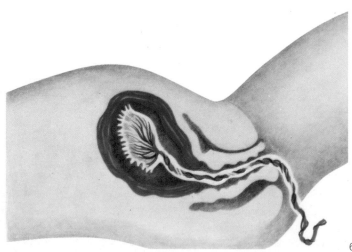

5

6

1 Towards the end of pregnancy, the baby is usually positioned head downwards in the uterus —vertex presentation.

2 At the very start of the first stage of labour, the baby's head begins to descend. The cervix is flattening out, sometimes called 'taking up'.

3 During the first stage of labour, the strong contractions of the uterine muscles gradually dilate the cervix. The membranes have ruptured.

4 By the end of the first stage of labour, the cervix is fully dilated— ten centimetres or five fingers breadths. This marks the beginning of the second stage of labour, the birth of the baby. The baby's head can be seen by the obstetrician or the midwife and the mother feels a strong desire to push downward with each contraction.

5 The uterine contractions, combined with the mother's efforts, push the baby down the vagina. Most of the work in the second stage of labour is involved with the birth of the head. Once the head is born, face downwards, it turns and the shoulders and body slip out fairly easily.

6 In the third stage of labour, the placenta separates from the wall of the uterus and is delivered with just one more contraction.

7 The baby's head usually looks slightly elongated at birth with a small swelling (caput) at the back. It soon assumes a normal round shape.

The vagina is not directly affected by the uterine contractions, but it is very easily distended in labour and allows the foetus to pass through without difficulty. This occurs during the second stage of labour when the mother is playing an active role in helping to push the foetus down in time with the uterine contractions. This continues until the delivery is completed. Although the vagina easily distends to allow the passage of the baby, the vulva and lower pelvic muscles may require an episiotomy (incision). This is easily repaired with stitches (see below).

After the birth of the baby the uterus contracts and retracts, that is it shrinks down in size, sheering the placenta (after-birth) from its attachment and pushing it down into the lower uterine segment and upper vagina. From this site, the placenta is delivered either by the obstetrician drawing on the umbilical cord, or by the mother pushing down as she did when having the baby. Once the placenta is delivered, labour is completed.

In general, labour takes some twelve hours or so for a first baby and six hours or so for second and subsequent babies.

MECHANISM OF LABOUR

In order to pass through the cervix and out through the vagina, the foetal head has to negotiate and squeeze through the bony tunnel of the mother's pelvis. Squeeze is the right word, for, even in normal labour, the head is a tight fit in the pelvis.

The passage of the head is brought about by a series of movements which, collectively, form the mechanism of labour. Firstly, the foetal head engages in the maternal pelvis; by this is meant the passage of the widest diameter of the foetal head through the entrance to the pelvis. For a mother-to-be having a first baby, this normally occurs before the onset of labour. For second and subsequent babies, it may not occur until labour has actually started. Once labour has started and the head has engaged it descends slowly through the pelvis, turning as it does so. As a result, the baby is facing backwards when born.

After the birth of the head, the baby's shoulders also turn inside the pelvis. This causes the head to turn to one side or the other. Once the shoulders are born, the rest of the baby's body passes easily out.

Almost all of the first and second stages of labour are spent in bringing about the birth of the head in the manner described. The birth of the rest of the baby's body is accomplished in less than a minute.

☐ **Moulding and Caput** Because the baby's head is such a tight fit in the mother's pelvis, it is

squeezed or moulded into the best possible shape to enable it to pass through. The baby's head can change shape in this way because, at the time of birth, the skull bones have not fused together. The moulding of the head gives it an elongated appearance which is made somewhat stranger-looking by a sort of bruise, called the caput, which develops on the top of the head during labour. Do not worry—both the moulding and the caput subside quickly, so that, within twenty-four to forty-eight hours after birth, the baby's head assumes its normal rounded shape.

TEARS, EPISIOTOMY AND STITCHES

A small tear of the perineum is very common, especially during the birth of first babies. Obstetricians have long believed that if there is a chance of anything more than a small tear developing, it is better to make an incision—episiotomy—since this causes much less damage to the skin tissues than a jagged tear and is easier to stitch accurately. The vagina is always a little less tight after having a baby, but provided excessive tearing is avoided by the proper use of episiotomy and provided that careful stitching is carried out, the difference will only be slight.

Stitches are put in under a local anaesthetic and are so placed as to draw the tissues and skin together so that they do not have to be taken out. The knots on the outside fall off within a few days and may be noticed on the pad or in the bath. The number of stitches varies greatly. Anything from two to ten stitches is quite normal.

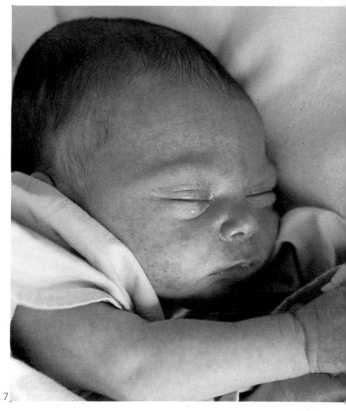

Going into Hospital

Going into hospital in labour can be a frightening experience, especially when one remembers what some of our more ancient hospitals look like in the middle of the night! The important thing to remember is that everyone in the hospital wants the mother-to-be to have an easy labour and a successful delivery of a healthy baby. Everything is, therefore, done with this in mind.

Sometimes you will not understand why certain steps are being taken. If so, however busy the midwife or doctor may be, they should always spare the time to explain what is happening. There may not be time for lengthy or involved explanations and discussions, but simple answers can always be given. If this is not the case, then keep on asking until it is.

When you report to the admission desk it will be very helpful if you have a card showing your hospital number. This will enable the admissions' clerk to find your hospital notes quickly. Next you will be taken, probably on a trolley or in a wheelchair, from the admission desk to the obstetric department where you will be seen by a midwife. She will enquire about your contractions, whether or not you have had a show of blood and whether or not the membranes have ruptured (waters broken). She will also take your temperature and blood pressure, feel your tummy and listen to the foetal heart.

Most hospitals no longer shave off all pubic hair, but many do a mini-shave to remove the hair around the vaginal opening. (This helps the doctor or midwife to see this area of skin more clearly in labour, especially at the time of the baby's birth). Likewise, the bad old days of large soapy water enemas are fortunately gone. Instead, a small enema or a suppository is given on admission to enable you to go to the lavatory and empty the bowel normally. (A full bowel may temporarily hold up progress during labour and may then empty itself just before or at the time of birth).

In hospital, cleanliness remains next to godliness, so unless you have had a bath immediately before coming into hospital you will probably be asked to have one on admission. If your membranes have ruptured, you will be asked to take a shower instead.

As soon as the admission procedures are complete, the midwife or doctor will carry out a vaginal examination to see how labour is progressing. For this, one or two of the examiner's fingers will be lubricated with antiseptic cream and will be gently inserted into the vagina. By this means, the degree of dilatation of the cervix and the amount of descent of the foetal head through the pelvis will be determined. Nowadays, dilatation of the cervix is measured in centimetres although some older doctors and midwives still use the traditional 'fingers breadth'. The dilatation of the cervix will be described in terms of one to ten centimetres dilated, or one to five

It is sensible to make sure that your suitcase is packed and ready for you to take to the hospital a few weeks before the baby is due.

fingers breadth dilated. Every time you are examined, ask the midwife or doctor how far dilated you are. It is good to know that one is making progress.

The descent of the baby's head is usually described in relation to the two bony points (ischial spines) in your pelvis. In early labour, the top of the baby's head will be above the level of the spines; later on it will descend to the same level and, later still, shortly before delivery, will be below their levels. In many hospitals, nowadays, the progress in labour will be marked on a partograph (see page 92). If you ask, you can see your own partograph and get a good idea of how things are progressing.

In normal labour a vaginal examination will be needed every two or three hours to assess the progress. One will also be done when the membranes rupture or when it is thought that you are fully dilated, which is ten centimetres or five fingers breadth—enough to allow the foetal head to come through.

AFTER THE ADMISSION PROCEDURES

In most hospitals you go from the admission room to a first-stage labour ward. You stay here until ready for delivery when you go to a delivery room where the actual birth will take place. In some hospitals you go straight to a room which serves for both first-stage labour and delivery. In either place you will sit up or lie in bed, whichever is the most comfortable, and will have a midwife with you or will be able to call one by means of a call bell. At this stage of labour the presence of your husband may be very comforting. He can be with you constantly, whereas your midwife will have to come and go depending upon how busy the labour ward is at the time. If your husband cannot be present, if you have both decided that you prefer him not to be there, or if the midwife has to go out, do not worry: she will be within easy reach. Togetherness certainly helps in labour, but whether or not other members of the family should be around at this time is debatable. Most hospitals find it hard to cope with family parties in the labour ward and most mothers-to-be prefer to be alone or with their husbands in this situation.

During the first stage of labour you can get up and walk about if you wish. You will probably not be offered anything to eat since there is a tendency to vomit later in labour and an empty stomach helps to avoid this. There is no objection to the drinking of fluids, such as water, fruit juice, tea or coffee, in reasonable amounts, but, here again, you may not be allowed to do so if there is any suggestion that you may require an anaesthetic at a later stage.

Modern Obstetric Care

The purpose of modern obstetric care in labour is to keep a regular check that the process is progressing normally. By such checks, any difficulties and problems, such as foetal distress, can be detected at an early stage.

FOETAL HEART MONITORS

One of the best ways of telling whether the foetus is coping with the strain of labour is to listen to its heart beat. Traditionally, this is done with a foetal stethoscope—a hollow metal tube, wider at one end than the other, which is placed on the mother's abdomen over the position of the foetal back. When the midwife places her ear against the other end she can hear the foetal heart, can count its rate and check that the beat is regular.

The modern foetal heart monitor 'listens' to the baby's heart either by means of an ultrasound head placed on the mother's abdomen, or by means of a tiny wire clip attached through the cervix on to the foetal scalp. This picks up electrical impulses from the foetal heart through the scalp skin. The sound waves or electrical impulses are then fed into the monitor which automatically records the heart rate and displays it as a flashing light, or beating sound or by writing a continuous record on a moving reel of paper. This latter method of continuous foetal heart recording is the most popular because it enables the obstetrician to see how the heart rate varies during labour and especially during and after contractions. The contractions themselves can be recorded through a simple pressure recorder strapped on to the mother's abdomen and printed out on to the same sheet of paper.

Normally the baby's heart rate is between 110 and 180 beats per minute. There is a constant small variation in rate, called beat-to-beat variation, and the rate reacts only slightly or not at all to the uterine contractions. A slow rate, below 110 beats a minute, or a high rate, above 180 beats per minute, a loss of beat-to-beat variation which gives a rather flat trace, or a sharp and prolonged drop in rate during and after a contraction, may all indicate foetal distress (see page 100).

Foetal monitoring is particularly valuable in monitoring foetal well-being in 'at risk' cases, such as when the mother has toxaemia. With the object of making labour as safe as possible for the foetus, many obstetric units monitor most cases, including normal cases. Apart from the inconvenience of the abdominal belt and the wires which are attached to the machine, the mother

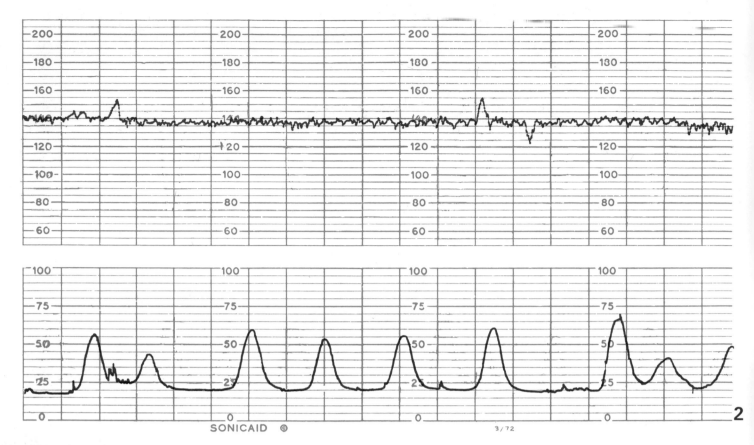

SONICAID ©   3/72   **2**

suffers no discomfort. The sight of the trace of the baby's heart, printed out by the monitor by the side of her bed, is very reassuring.

INTRAVENOUS DRIPS

An intravenous drip, for feeding liquid into the mother's vein, is often used in labour. It provides a way of giving the mother fluid if she is unable to drink and glucose if she is unable to eat. (Fluids and food are often restricted in labour to avoid nausea and vomiting). The other use for the drip is to give drugs to the mother. Oxytocin, also called Syntocinon, is a preparation of a natural hormone which makes the uterus contract. It may be given by drip for this purpose if labour is slow, or during or following an induction. Prostaglandins are sometimes used for the same purpose. Sometimes, too, a small attachment is put on to the drip. This counts the rate of the drops given **1** per minute and automatically adjusts the rate to keep it constant.

FOETAL BLOOD SAMPLES

Occasionally when it is thought that the foetus is becoming distressed through lack of oxygen, a sample of blood may be taken from its scalp. In order to do this, a hollow tube—an amnioscope— is passed into the vagina, through the cervix and placed against the baby's head. By passing a special instrument down this tube, a very small quantity of the baby's blood can be obtained and tested. The actual measurement that is made is that of the acidity (pH) of the blood because this gives a good indication of the actual blood oxygen level. The procedure does not harm the foetus in any way and is not uncomfortable for the mother. It provides valuable information about the baby's well-being and is very important in the diagnosis of foetal distress.

PARTOGRAPH

This is a simple chart that is used in many labour wards to show the progress of labour. The dilatation of the cervix and the descent of the foetal head are recorded on the chart after each examination. By comparing the rate of dilatation of the cervix with a normal graph, the patient's progress can be assessed and a rough estimate made about when delivery is likely to take place.

1 The partograph is used to record the progress of labour. The heavy line is the expected rate of opening of the cervix. The line joining the circles shows how quickly the cervix went from being 2cm open at the first examination to 10cm at the last (fully dilated). The dotted line joining the crosses shows the descent of the foetal head through the pelvis.

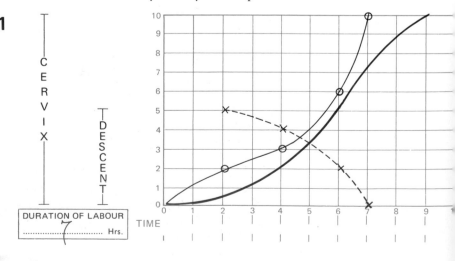

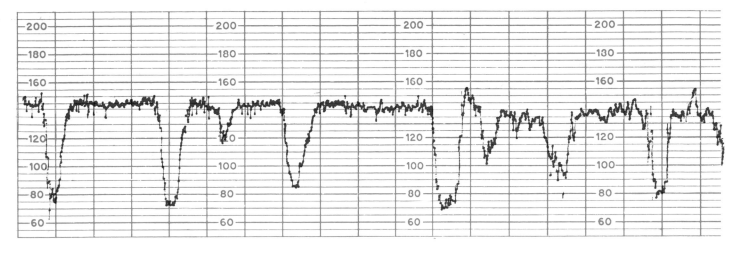

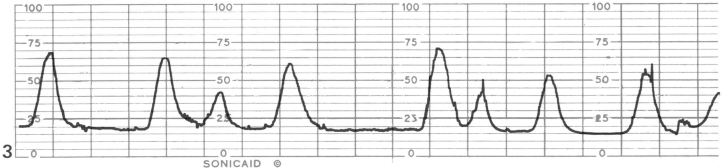

3

SONICAID ©

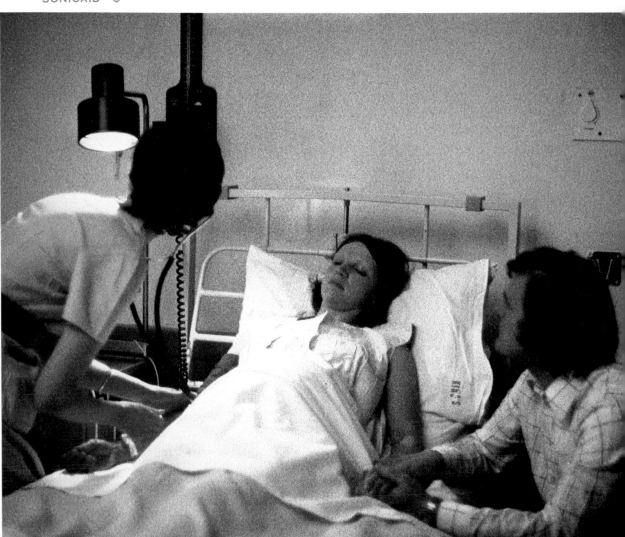

2 The foetal heart monitor print out: the top line shows the heart rate. The bottom line indicates when contractions occur. In this normal trace the heart rate remains steady even during contractions.

3 This trace indicates that the foetus is becoming distressed. When the contractions occur (bottom line), the heart rate (top line) slows and takes a little while to recover. Decelerations or 'dips' of this type call for rapid delivery of the distressed foetus.

4 A complete check is kept on blood pressure during labour to see that it does not become too high or too low.

4

How to Cope with Labour Pains

Uterine contractions, the squeezing action of the uterine muscle, which occur every few minutes in labour and eventually bring about the delivery of the child, last up to a minute at a time and are usually painful. The pain at the start of labour is no more than a discomfort and for some women labour never becomes more than that. For most women, however, the stronger contractions of late labour become distinctly painful. For this reason, some form of pain relief will usually be needed. The controlled breathing techniques of natural childbirth (see page 85) and firm rubbing of the back by your husband or midwife during the contractions help most women to some degree and for some women are all that is needed. Others, however, need more specific pain relief (see page 83). When you feel you need help, ask for it. If you are offered pain relief when you do not feel you need it, tell the midwife. No-one wants you have an injection or any other form of analgesic if you do not want it, but, equally, the midwife will be anxious to see that you do not have to suffer more discomfort than is necessary. Thus, by whatever means you wish, you will progress through the first stage, and become fully dilated and enter the second stage of labour.

HOW TO TELL WHEN YOU ARE FULLY DILATED

After the first stage has been going for some hours and during the thirty minutes or so before the cervix becomes fully dilated, contractions reach their strongest and most painful. Full dilatation changes the character of the contractions and, with each contraction, you will get a feeling of pressure on the back passage (rectum) and will experience a desire to strain down in the same way that you do when having your bowels open. About this time, too, there is often a little fresh vaginal bleeding. This is quite normal. To start with, the urge to push is not very strong, but as the baby's head begins to stretch the lower vagina it will become almost irresistible. You will now be sitting up in the bed, well supported by pillows. During contractions grasp your thighs and let your chin rest on your chest. As soon as the contraction starts, take in a long deep breath, then shut your mouth, hold your breath, and push down as strongly and for as long as you can. When you can no longer hold your breath, let it out and take in another deep one. If you still have a contraction, push again. Do not push if you do not have a contraction. (Pushing is hard work and you need a rest between contractions to regain your strength). This is the time when your midwife will give you lots of encouragement and praise as well as any extra instructions that are needed about when to push. Your husband will become very involved and will almost certainly be

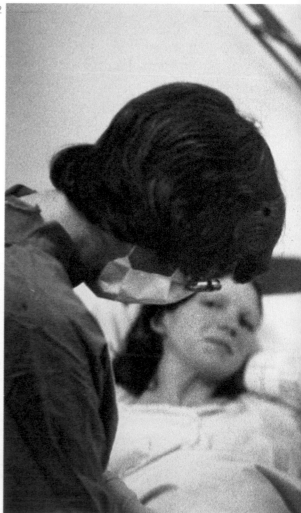

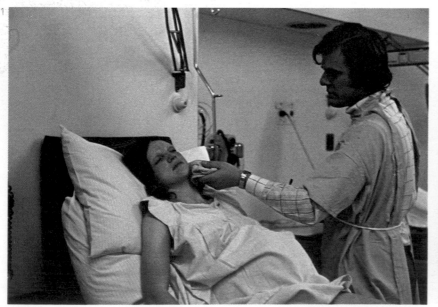

holding his own breath when you do, willing you to make good progress.

During the second stage, the midwife will frequently listen to the foetal heart, or check the trace if a monitor is being used. This is not a cause for alarm. She is merely checking to see that all is well with the baby.

1 Labour is very hard work and a loving hand to sponge your face can be very comforting.

2 Towards the end of the first stage of labour, the midwife looks for signs that the second stage is beginning.

3 When the foetal heart monitor is not being used the midwife listens to the heart with the traditional foetal stethoscope.

4 The birth of their child is one of the closest moments in any couple's life together. A husband's encouragement and affection are very comforting to the expectant mother.

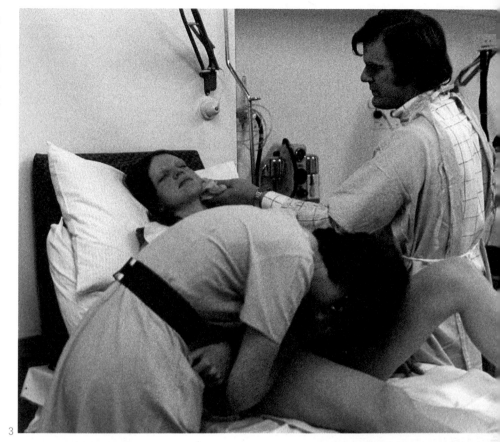

3

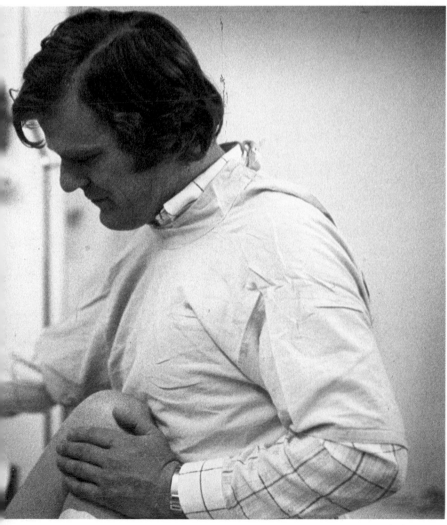

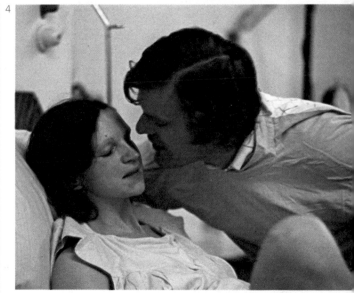

4

The Birth

Towards the end of the second stage of labour, you will feel the baby's head stretching your lower vagina and especially the skin between the back of the vaginal opening and the anus (perineum). Although the perineum becomes very elastic in labour it usually tears with the birth of the first baby (see page 89). The tear involves the perineal skin and the skin of the back of the lower vagina and underlying muscle tissues. The baby's head stretches the perineum most, so it is important that the head should be born gently and slowly. Slow delivery of the head is achieved by pushing gently at this time. The midwife will tell you when to stop pushing hard and will often tell you to pant quickly in and out so that the final push comes from the uterine contractions alone. Sometimes you will be asked to push gently at this stage, or asked to push gently and pant at the same time. At the same time the midwife will gently restrain the baby from 'popping out' and will ensure that it eases its way gently into the world.

As soon as the head is delivered, the mouth and nose will be gently cleaned. If there is much mucus present this will be sucked out with a soft plastic tube.

With the next contraction you will be asked to push gently again and this will bring about the birth of the shoulders and the rest of the baby's body. Your beautiful newborn baby will now be lying between your legs on the bed. You will want to know if it is perfect and if it is a boy or girl: don't worry—everyone will be telling you the good news.

Early bodily contact between you and the baby is important; the baby is usually lifted gently up on to your tummy. You may not be able to get the baby up to your breasts at this stage because the cord is still attached. As soon as the baby has cried and established regular breathing, the cord will be cut and you can cuddle the baby more easily. Quite often, some more cleaning of the baby's air passages will be necessary. For this, the baby will be placed on a small tilted table which has special suction apparatus and a supply of oxygen in case the baby is a little blue, as is often the case immediately after birth. Do not worry if your baby needs this kind of attention. It is all part of the normal procedure to ensure that normal breathing is established.

THE BIRTH OF THE PLACENTA

With the excitement of the baby's birth you may not notice an injection being given into your thigh muscles to make your uterus contract more

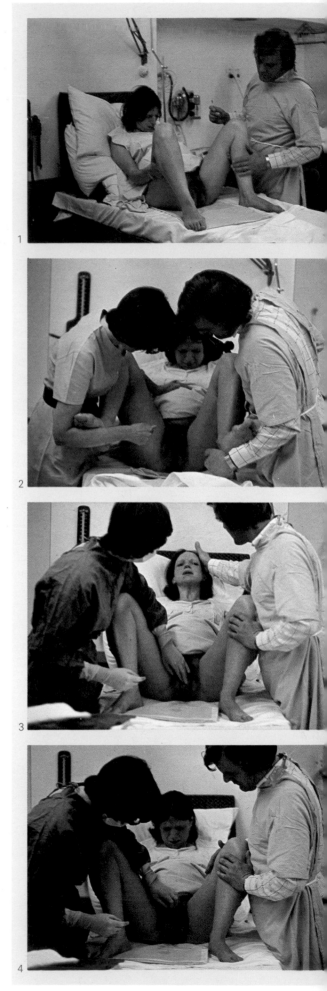

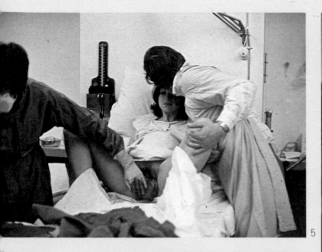

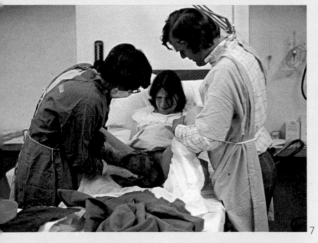

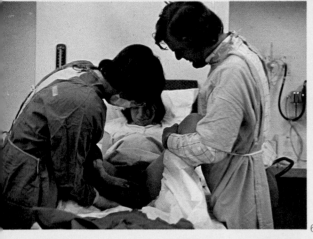

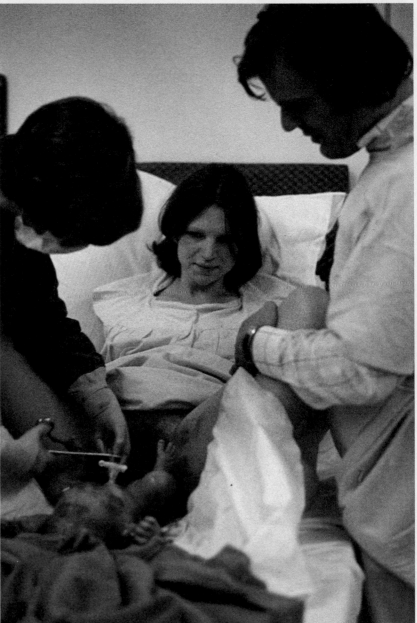

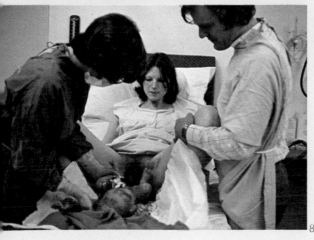

1 The ideal position for pushing in the second stage is propped up by pillows to support the back and with the knees bent.

2-6 When the baby's head becomes visible, the mother is usually asked to stop pushing and to pant instead, so that the birth of the head is brought about by the uterine contractions only. The midwife controls the birth of the head to prevent it from 'popping out'. In this way, it is eased gently into the world.

7 Once the head is born, the shoulders are eased gently out.

8 The baby's body quickly and easily follows the birth of the head and shoulders. The birth is now complete.

9 Once the baby is breathing independently, the cord is clamped and then cut.

strongly and squeeze the placenta out of the uterus and into the upper part of the vagina. From there is it usually delivered by the midwife who draws the cord and, therefore, the placenta down into the vagina and out into a bowl. Sometimes you will be asked to help by giving a final push down. The placenta is quite soft and slips out quite painlessly.

☐ **Finishing Touches** Once the third stage of labour, the delivery of the placenta, is complete, all that remains is a general clean up. Liquor amnii and a certain amount of blood can certainly spread quite a long way! Once cleaned up, your temperature and blood pressure will be checked. You are now ready to go to the lying-in ward where you will spend the next few days accustoming yourself to the idea of being a mother and getting to know your baby.

For the first twenty-four hours after delivery you will probably feel tired and excited. Visitors, at this time, should be kept to a minimum and should not stay long. Once you have had a good night's sleep, however, you will enjoy receiving visitors and their congratulations. Remember to give your husband his fair share of attention and credit!

BREAST MILK

About forty-eight hours after the birth, the breasts will fill with milk and become obviously bigger and often tender. The baby's sucking helps to bring the milk into the breasts. Do not expect your tummy to flatten and return to its normal shape at once. You will still be quite big to start with, but as the uterus contracts down and you do your post-natal exercises your figure will return. Much will, of course, depend on weight. If you have not gained an excessive amount of weight during pregnancy you should get back to normal quite quickly. Apart from the weight of the baby and the placenta, the retained fluids will be disposed within a few days of birth. By the end of the first week there should be no more than a fourteen-to-sixteen pound gain over your pre-pregnancy weight. Aim to be back to your ideal weight by three months from the birth. To do this you will need to eat sensibly and, perhaps, diet gently. Sensible dieting and breastfeeding are perfectly compatible and the baby will not suffer.

GETTING BACK TO NORMAL

After the birth your perineum will be rather numb—and if you have had stitches it will feel distinctly sore. The soreness can be relieved by sitting in a warm bath, by using a rubber ring to sit on when not in the bath and by taking a small dose of pain-killing tablets. The soreness may make it difficult to pass urine for the first few

hours after birth. You will usually manage this, but occasionally the midwife will need to help you to empty the bladder with the aid of a small soft plastic tube called a catheter.

The thought of having your bowels open, with the stitches in place, may worry you. If so, remember that you will probably not empty your bowels for two or three days after the birth and by then the tissues will be well on the way to being healed and will certainly be much less painful. An aperient or a simple suppository is often needed to get things on the move again.

After delivery, vaginal bleeding continues for two or three weeks or sometimes longer. The blood becomes darker and darker and finally brown before drying up completely. The first period will occur towards the end of breast-feeding or in four to six weeks after the birth if you do not breastfeed at all. In the first six weeks after delivery your uterus will return to its normal non-pregnant size. You may feel it contracting for some days after delivery, especially when the baby is feeding at the breast. These after-pains are most likely to be noticed by women who have had second or subsequent babies.

1

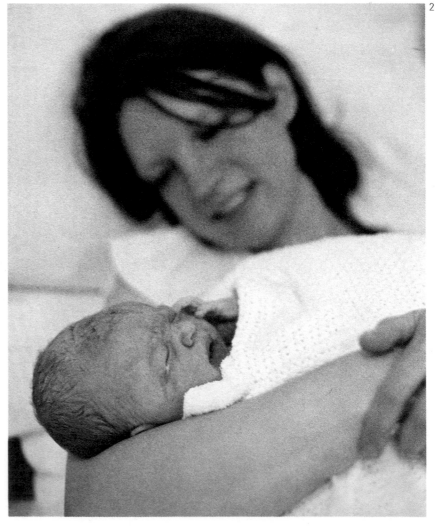

2

98

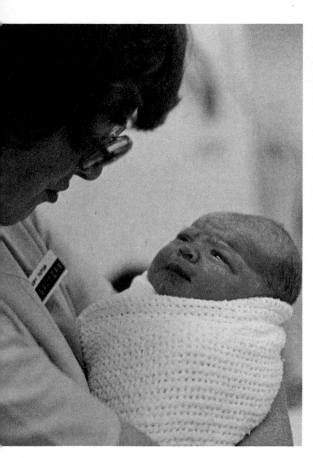

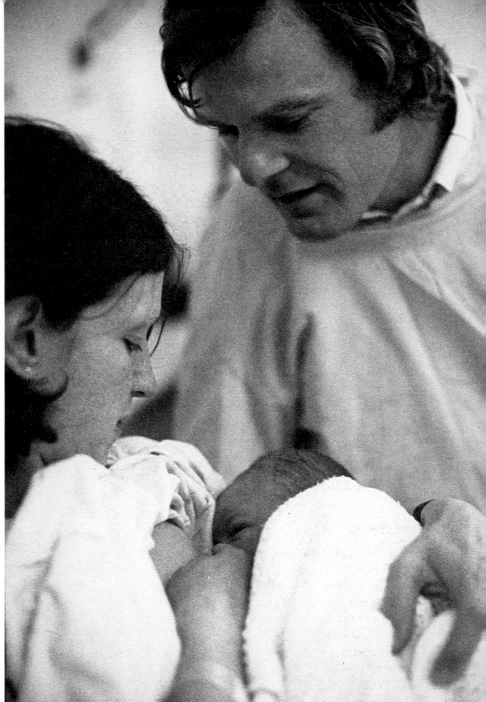

1 The midwife will clear any mucus from the baby's nasal passages and wrap him in a shawl.

2 He is then given to his mother to cuddle. The close bond built between mother and child is begun immediately following the birth.

3 After the long wait and the exertions of of labour and delivery, husband and wife can share together the first moments of being a father and mother.

4 Birth is exhausting for the baby as well as for his mother and both of them need to rest.

3

4

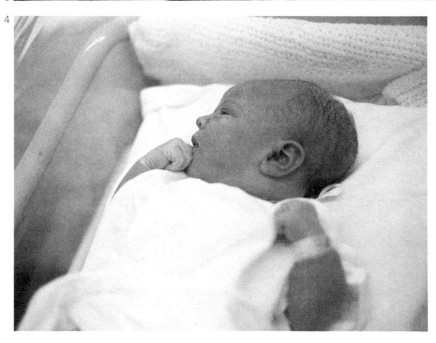

BIRTH BLUES

Birth is such a happy event that it is hard to understand why some mothers become depressed afterwards. However, nervous strain coupled with anxiety about the ability to cope with the new problems presented by the baby, result in some women becoming depressed two or three days after delivery. This reaction is quite normal and in the great majority of cases passes quickly. Too many visitors and overtiredness from lack of sleep make the situation worse, but for most women any slight depression goes within a day or two without treatment. If it persists beyond this time expert medical help will be needed. In hospital, doctors will be on the lookout for any prolonged unhappiness. If when you get home you, or your husband, or any member of your family, think you are depressed go and see your general practitioner.

Complications in Labour

DELAY IN LABOUR

An abnormally prolonged labour is very trying for the mother and may be dangerous for the foetus. For this reason, modern obstetrics pays great attention to assessing progress. If steady progress is being made and both mother and foetus are well, no action is needed. If progress is poor, careful assessment will be made by the obstetrician to decide why the delay is occurring and what needs to be done. Delay is most often due to poor uterine contractions. If this is so an oxytocin drip (see page 92) will be started to try to improve matters. If this does not work, or is considered inadvisable because the baby is too big to pass through the mother's pelvis, a Caesarean section (see page 101) will be necessary.

Delay in the second stage of labour may need forceps' delivery or Ventouse extraction.

MALPOSITION

The normal presentation of a baby at birth is called a vertex presentation.

The position of the head is quite difficult to determine, but by feeling the join between the two main bones of the foetal skull, this can usually be done. Sometimes when the foetal head is in the occipito posterior position, i.e. facing forwards, the baby is born this way, face to pubis. Sometimes, too, in this position or in the transverse position, the head is held up and can only be born with the assistance of forceps or Ventouse method. Before applying the forceps, the obstetrician will have to turn the head the right way around. He may do this with his hand, which is known as manual rotation, or with special forceps, known as forceps rotation. As rotation is uncomfortable for the mother, either a local anaesthetic, or an epidural block, or on rare occasions, a general anaesthetic, is needed before it can be attempted. The manoeuvre can only be carried out when the cervix is fully dilated and the foetus ready to be born.

MALPRESENTATION

Malpresentation is when some part of the baby, other than the head, presents. The commonest and most important malpresentation is a breech presentation.

Labour progresses normally with a breech presentation, but care is needed during the second stage when the arms and the after coming head are being delivered. Forceps will often be used for the head and local anaesthetic or an epidural block is essential. On rare occasions, a general anaesthetic is needed.

FOETAL DISTRESS

During labour the foetus may suffer from lack of oxygen. This happens when the contractions of the uterus squeeze the blood vessels to the placenta so tightly that they are unable to carry enough oxygen-rich blood and the foetus suffers. In normal circumstances, any deficiency in oxygen supply is quickly made up when the uterus relaxes between contractions and the blood vessels open up again. Sometimes, however, this does not occur to a sufficient extent and then the lack of oxygen causes foetal distress.

Diagnosis is made by listening to the foetal heart or by looking at the trace made by the foetal heart monitor (see page 92). When foetal distress is present, the foetal heart becomes abnormally slow, or sometimes abnormally fast, and irregular. Characteristic changes are seen on the foetal heart trace and if a foetal scalp blood sample is taken, it shows a high acidity which means a low oxygen content. Sometimes a distressed foetus passes meconium from its bowel into the amniotic sac and stains the amniotic fluid. Meconium staining of the fluid is not invariably a sign of foetal distress, but its appearance warns the obstetrician to be extra vigilant.

If foetal distress is diagnosed, the foetus must be delivered as quickly as possible. This may mean an emergency Caesarean section; or if the cervix is fully dilated a forceps' delivery. Fortunately, in the great majority of cases, the diagnosis is made early and the baby, once delivered, does not suffer from any permanent disability.

FORCEPS' DELIVERY

Modern obstetric forceps are light and designed to fit snugly around the baby's head. The use of forceps allows the doctor to gently lift out a baby who has failed to be born normally. This may arise either because the uterine contractions are not strong enough or because the mother cannot push sufficiently hard at the right moment to deliver her baby. Sometimes when foetal distress develops, delivery has to be speeded up and, in this situation, forceps are used to save the baby from suffering unnecessarily.

Forceps can only be applied in the second stage of labour when the cervix is fully dilated and when there is adequate room for the baby to be born through the vagina. Local anaesthesia is essential. On rare occasions a general anaesthetic is necessary. When forceps are used, the perineum is likely to be stretched more than usual, so an episiotomy is often needed to prevent the skin tearing. Because the forceps' blades fit closely around the baby's head to protect it during delivery, red marks where the blades make contact, often appear on the baby's face. These marks, and the occasional mild bruising of the face which often results from forceps' delivery, quickly fade and usually disappear completely forty-eight to seventy-two hours after the birth. Forceps' delivery is more common in women having a first baby and in women who have an epidural block. If complications develop any woman may need forceps.

VACUUM EXTRACTION

Vacuum extraction (Ventouse) is an alternative to forceps' delivery and is a means of assisting the delivery when the mother's efforts fail to achieve it. A small metal suction cap, attached to a pump, is applied to the baby's head. By drawing the suction cap gently downwards, the baby's head can now be delivered through the entrance to the vagina and the delivery thereafter completed normally.

The vacuum extraction is much favoured in some maternity units and, indeed, in some European hospitals it has completely replaced forceps. It does, however, have one slight disadvantage in that the application of the suction cup to the baby's scalp produces a localized circular bruise. This is a little unsightly to start with, but it quickly fades within forty-eight hours of delivery. Like forceps, the vacuum extractor is only used during the second stage of labour to help complete the delivery after the cervix has become fully dilated.

POST-PARTUM HAEMORRHAGE AND RETAINED PLACENTA

The third stage of labour, during which the placenta is delivered, can occasionally cause problems. Usually, as soon as the baby is born, the uterus contracts, separates the placenta from its attachment and pushes it down through the cervix into the upper part of the vagina from which it can be easily delivered. This contraction is important because when the placenta separates it leaves a raw surface in the uterus from which bleeding, sometimes severe, can occur. A strong contraction will, however, squeeze the blood vessels shut and stop the bleeding. If the contraction is not strong enough to control the bleeding, the doctor will take immediate steps to deliver the placenta manually and will then give a further injection into a vein in the arm. Occasion-ally a blood transfusion is needed.

The danger of port-partum haemorrhage is well-recognized by doctors and midwives. They will quickly give the correct treatment since, in this situation, speedy action is needed to stop too much blood being lost.

CAESAREAN SECTION

Caesarean section is the extraction of the baby through an incision that is made through the mother's abdomen and into the uterus. It is either decided for medical reasons before the onset of labour or as an emergency procedure during the course of labour. A woman, for example, with a small pelvis and a big baby or a woman with a severe degree of placenta praevia would be likely cases for a pre-decided Caesarean section. Foetal distress in the first stage of labour, or a failure to progress towards vaginal delivery after a reasonable period of time, are typical indications for emergency Caesarean sections.

Caesarean section is almost always performed under a general anaesthetic in an operating theatre. Local anaesthetic blocks are occasionally used, but are not favoured because the operation is made more difficult and the woman might suffer more discomfort.

The incision is made across the lower part of the abdomen, just above the pubis (below the bikini line!). The incision in the uterus is made into its lowest part, which explains why the operation is called 'lower segment Caesarean section'. In the classical 'upper segment' oper-ation, the incision is made into the upper part of the uterus, but this procedure is only rarely employed nowadays. The baby is delivered through the incision and the placenta is then removed before sewing up the uterus and the abdominal wall.

The operation usually takes about forty min-utes, from start to finish, and the mother should be awake and able to hear the good news about her baby almost as soon as the final stitches are put in.

Apart from the discomfort of the incision, a mother who has had a Caesarean section can expect to recover from the birth of her baby in the same way as a mother who has had a vaginal delivery. She will, however, stay in hospital a little longer—for about seven to ten days—and will have the skin stitches or clips removed about six days after the operation. The skin incision usually heals very well, only leaving an un-obtrusive scar. A woman who has had one Caesarean may need to be delivered this way in subsequent pregnancies. In many cases, however, normal delivery after a previous Caesarean section will be perfectly possible and safe.

The Newborn Baby

A New Way of Life
How a Baby Adapts Outside the Womb

Before birth a baby leads a somewhat sheltered life but, from the moment he is born, a new phase in his development starts. He has to adjust to a completely new environment. Some things like breathing, for example, he can do instantaneously without any help, but in many other ways he is entirely helpless and dependent on his mother's assistance.

FIRST BREATHS

Watching a baby take his first breath is, perhaps, the most dramatic and exciting event at birth. Some babies howl loudly for several minutes; others emit only one or two cries and then immediately settle down to quiet breathing. Nature leaves nothing to chance, and you will not be surprised to hear that babies practise breathing movements in the womb from a very early age. Some mothers feel these movements as rapid pulsations over the lower part of the abdomen.

Most babies breathe spontaneously and normally at birth, although it is customary for the midwife gently to clear the baby's nose and mouth, and to note the breathing pattern, heart rate, skin colour, muscle tone and general activity. Babies are usually blue at the moment of birth, but this is quickly followed by a healthy pink colour which spreads over the face, trunk and limbs. It usually takes a little longer for the fingers and toes to become pink.

Occasionally, there might be a slight delay before breathing begins. In this instance, the midwife encourages the baby by gently rubbing or pinching his toes. Sometimes there is a longer delay before the baby begins to breathe. There are several reasons why a baby may get off to a slow start. The 'breathing centre' in the brain, for example, is sometimes a little depressed following a difficult labour or delivery. Likewise, large doses of pain-killing drugs given to the mother during labour might also depress a baby's 'breathing centre' for a short while. Medical staff can often predict when a baby is likely to be slow to breathe, and arrangements can be made for a paediatrician to be present at the birth.

A CHANGE OF TEMPERATURE

In the womb, a baby is to some extent protected from extremes of temperature because of the warm amniotic fluid (waters) which surround him. He is, in fact, about 1°C warmer than his mother. Immediately after birth a baby's temperature falls a little before becoming stable. Anybody who has stepped out of a warm bath on a winter's morning will understand this! We can avoid a baby becoming too chilled by making sure that the delivery room is warm and by drying and wrapping the baby in a soft towel, and sheltering the cot from draughts.

Before leaving the delivery room the midwife usually takes the baby's temperature by placing a thermometer under the baby's armpit or gently into his rectum (back passage). The baby's temperature will subsequently remain stable if he is lightly clothed, the cot covered by one or two light blankets, and the room ketp at about 20°C to 22°C (68°F to 71.5°F). After a few weeks, if he wears an extra woolly and has another blanket on the cot, he will tolerate a room temperature of 16°C (60.8°F).

GETTING USED TO GERMS

Although certain maternal infections, such as German measles, can affect the unborn baby, he is to a large extent protected from germs by the membrane which encloses him. As pregnancy advances, special proteins, called 'antibodies' build up in baby's blood and, as a result, his white blood cells become skilled at mopping up any dangerous germs that dare to invade his territory. A baby is, therefore, born with the ability to ward off certain types of infection that might threaten him. Not all germs are harmful, however, and by the third day of life, a baby's breathing passages, bowel and skin become inhabited by different bacteria, many of which serve a useful purpose. Just the same, it is only common sense not to rely on a very young baby's defences to ward off every dangerous germ, and you will notice that the staff of the maternity ward, who handle many different babies, wash their hands carefully each time before doing so.

Eye infections, commonly called 'sticky eyes', are quite common in newborn babies. If you notice any discharge coming from the eye, mention it to the Sister or health visitor. It is very easily treated by a short course of eye drops. Not all 'sticky eyes' are caused by infection. Sometimes the eyelashes get stuck together by a temporary accumulation of mucus. This can be removed by gently wiping the eyelid and surrounding area with damp cotton wool.

FIRST FEEDS

Babies do, in fact, swallow in the womb, and ingest large amounts of amniotic fluid. This is not, however, important in helping growth, because all a baby's nutritional needs are met from the mother's blood stream. At birth, when the umbilical cord is cut, this important source of nutrition is also severed. A baby then becomes totally dependent on his mother to feed him. Breast milk takes a few days to come in but, during this time, a baby is not concerned with feeding. He is much more interested in sucking and sleeping.

Nearly all babies lose weight during the first few days of life, and do not regain their birth weight until the second week. Nature usually arranges things according to a well thought-out plan, and feeding is a really good example of this. At birth, a baby's gastro-intestinal tract, for example is already equipped to digest and absorb the foodstuffs that are present in human milk, but when he cries from time to time before the breast

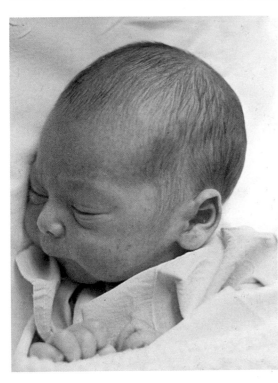

milk has come in, it is not because he is hungry—he is simply showing an instinctive and overwhelming desire to suck. When you put him to the breast at these times, you not only relieve his natural urge, but also stimulate the production of milk.

At first, only a small amount of fluid called 'colostrum' is formed in the breast. This, however, contains substances that help to protect a baby against infection. Gradually, as you allow your baby to suckle, more milk accumulates until he realizes that sucking can also provide him with a tasty drink.

Babies vary greatly in their sucking antics during the first few days of life. Some like to suck for a minute or two and then fall asleep, only to cry an hour or so later, when a further brief period at the breast relieves them. Others enjoy sucking for a longer time. Unfortunately, some mothers stop breastfeeding their baby after a few days because they think that they cannot produce enough milk. This is sad because it is sucking time not milk that a baby is after.

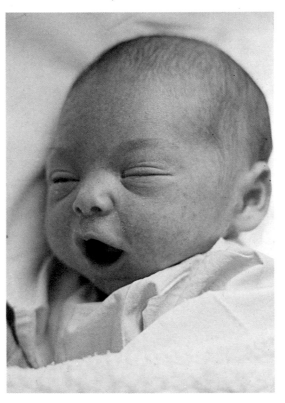

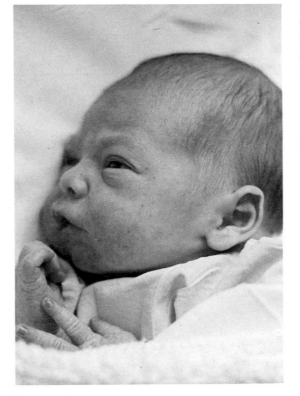

Perhaps the most dramatic way a baby adapts to life outside the womb is the sudden onset of regular breathing. Most babies, like this one, get through that hurdle without difficulty but the outside world challenges a baby with many other stresses. He now needs clothes and blankets to keep him warm. He doesn't need to be cosseted in a near-sterile environment but he does need, for example, sensible protection from germs carried by dirty hands. Soon he will need to have his hunger satisfied.

Those First Few Days Together

The relationship between a mother and her baby begins before birth—usually during the twentieth week of pregnancy when the baby begins to kick and the mother becomes aware of him as a living moving person. From the moment of birth, however, this relationship suddenly blossoms and takes on the completely new dimension of the mother caring for the baby as a separate individual. There is no doubt that maternal instinct is a very powerful force which determines how a mother will care for her baby. There will, of course be many occasions when a mother feels completely devoid of this very special instinct and wonders how on earth she will manage to get her baby off to a good start. The very fact that she wonders about such things is a sure sign that she will hit it off with her baby!

The basis, in fact, of getting a baby off to a good start lies with the interaction that occurs between a mother and her baby during the very first days of the baby's life. Interaction, at this stage, is not so dependent on the language of words, which comes much later, but with a 'language' that allows a mother and baby to 'converse' with each other by sight, touch, hearing and even smell and taste—a conversation without words. A mother and baby, in fact, have a rich 'vocabulary' that allows them to interact in a very subtle way. If, for example, a mother positions her face so that her eyes are level with her baby's eyes, he will focus and look at her, often within minutes of being born. If she talks to him softly when he cries, he will usually stop his antics for a while and listen. He enjoys being touched and cuddled and soon learns to recognize his mother's touch and smell. His capacity to learn and remember is, in fact, quite remarkable.

The most obvious example of mother and baby interaction during the first few days is the way in which the mother offers her baby the opportunity to suck when he cries. Soon she recognizes the different types of crying—the cry of real hunger, of pain, of anger, of tiredness—and responds in the appropriate way. A baby, of course, makes all sorts of sounds, including ones like burps which are usually regarded as socially unacceptable! It is easy to see how a baby's behaviour influences his mother, evokes responses and causes her to modify her style of mothering. Likewise it is easy to see how a mother influences her baby. From birth the baby sends out signals to his mother and, from that time forth, his development will depend on his mother's responses to his signals. The more responses he gets, the more signals he will send out. It is during the first precious days of interaction that the foundations for a happy relationship are laid down.

BEING AT HOME IN HOSPITAL

In many countries, it has become routine practice for mothers to have their babies in hospitals rather than at home. Although this policy has, undoubtedly, made childbirth much safer for mothers, it does mean that the initial interaction between mother and baby, which naturally flourishes best in a familiar home setting, now has to occur in an environment which is as strange for the mother as it is for the baby. In the past, obstetricians, paediatricians and midwives were quite rightly preoccupied with the physical safety of mothers and babies. Today, however, they are increasingly aware of the emotional aspects—of the importance, for example, of mother and baby interaction. One result is that hospitals are no longer thought of simply as places where ill people go to get cured, but as places where perfectly healthy women go to experience one of the most important events of their lives—the birth of a baby. Part and parcel of this new thinking is the need to try and make the maternity hospital feel more like home. This can be done by encouraging, within the hospital, contact between mother, baby, father and other family members. In order for this to happen, it is recognized that mothers need privacy and the freedom to care for and interact with their babies without being unduly hindered by regimented hospital policies. This is not always easy to arrange because, in the larger maternity hospitals, there may be as many as sixty to seventy mothers and babies in residence at any one time. Policy varies in different maternity hospitals and even between different wards, but many hospitals have adopted modern policies that cater for the individual needs of mothers and babies and this attitude is, undoubtedly, spreading.

Immediately after the birth, the most natural thing in the world is for a mother to wish to hold her baby close. The midwife, however, may be so preoccupied with other things, such as documenting the birth or making routine medical observations of pulse or blood pressure that she fails to recognize this urge. If this is the case, do not be shy. Let the midwife know that you want to hold your baby. In fact, have a clean dry towel standing by so that you can receive the baby as soon as he is born. It is a good idea to put him to the breast at this time because, apart from feeling nice, the

The foundation for a normal and happy mother-child relationship commenced when the baby was still in the uterus. But now there is much more scope for him to interact with his mother. During the first few weeks of a baby's life a mother starts to understand his needs; she begins to recognize and distinguish one type of cry from another. Often a baby is comforted only when he is allowed to suck; yet at other times the reassuring touch of his mother's hand is all that is needed. If a baby is separated from his mother for much of the day it is more difficult for the pair to tune into each other.

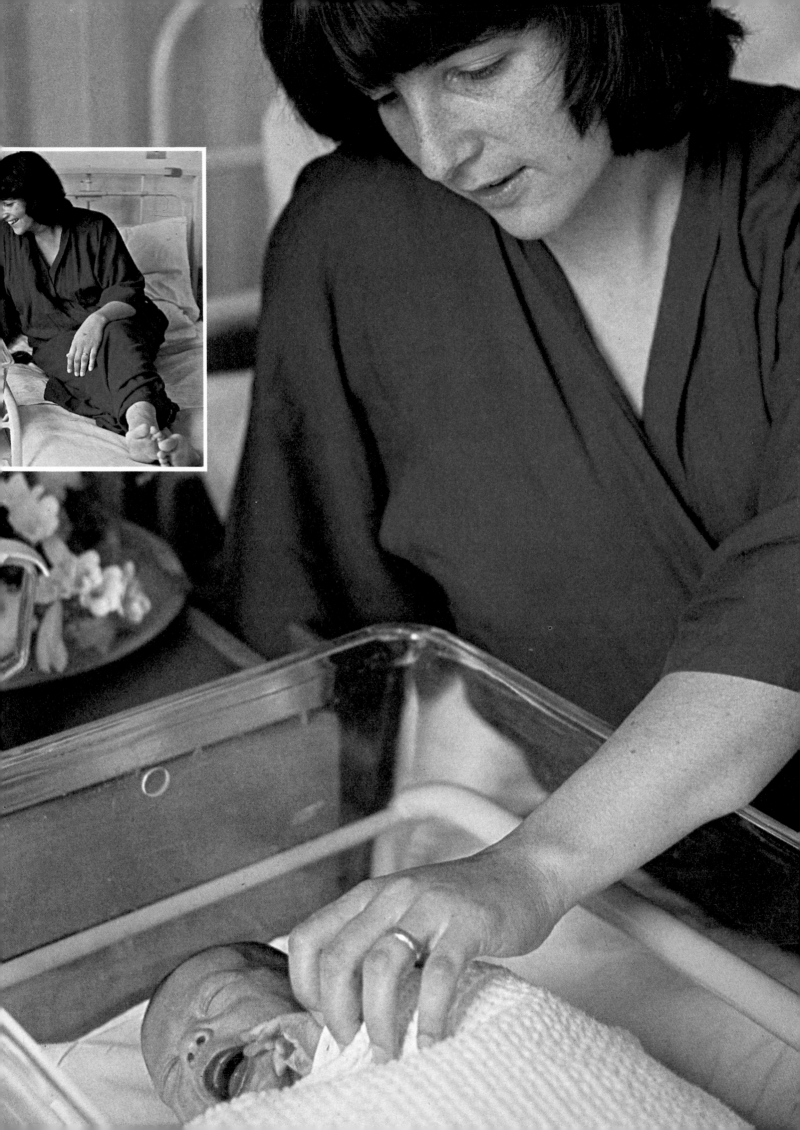

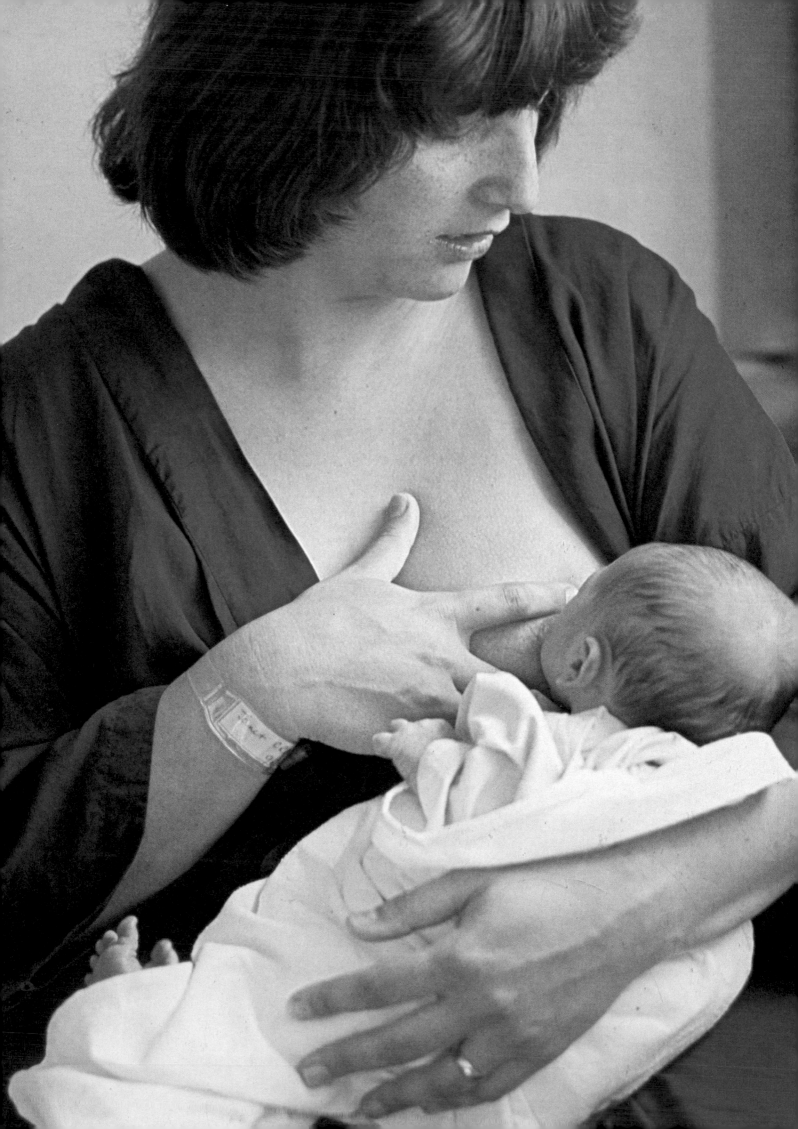

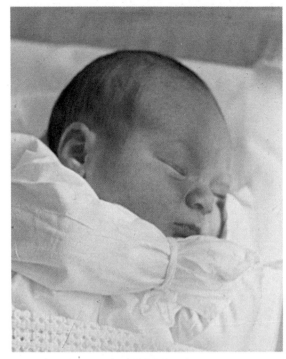

Breastfeeding has many advantages and is more likely to be a success when the baby is fed on demand rather than 'by the clock'. Some babies need to suck every hour or so, whereas others may sleep for six or seven hours between feeds. Some are satisfied after a few minutes of sucking but others need a much longer time at the breast. If you let the baby decide when he needs each feed, he soon settles into a regular feeding pattern. It is common to get conflicting advice about breastfeeding.

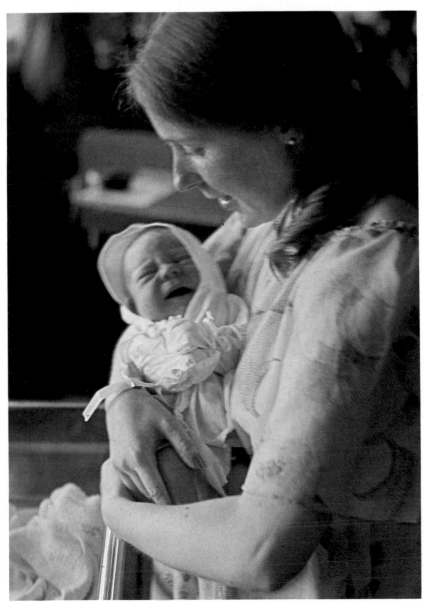

baby's sucking helps the uterus to contract down.

In some maternity hospitals it is still common practice, during the first day or so, for babies to spend a long time in the nursery, away from their mothers. This is done to give the mothers an opportunity to rest, but most mothers find it difficult to rest when their baby is not close to them. Closeness, which allows a mother to respond to her baby's cry, is, of course, an important part of the initial mother and baby interaction process. During your stay in the maternity ward, arrange for your baby's cot to be beside your bed at least throughout the day.

In many hospitals, it is also standard practice for babies to be removed to the nursery at night in order to allow mothers a full night's sleep. This usually means that the nursing staff will take care of the baby's night feed. Whilst this is acceptable to some mothers, many, particularly those who are breastfeeding their baby, prefer to have their baby by their side. Arranging for a baby to be with you throughout the night might pose problems if there are other mothers sharing your room who wish to have an uninterrupted night's sleep. If this is the case, ask the staff if there is a single room available. When this is not possible try to negotiate a compromise. For example, ask the night nurse to wake you when your baby cries. Remember that if you are going to be roused to feed your baby there is little point in accepting the sleeping tablet which is commonly offered.

DEMAND FEEDING

Many maternity hospitals advise that a baby should be fed 'by the clock', at certain intervals, but this imposes restraints on the natural interaction of mother and baby. There is no doubt that it is much easier to offer feeds to a baby on demand if you are breastfeeding. In this instance you do not have to keep asking the staff to let you have a bottle each time your baby wishes to suck.

Whichever way you choose to feed your baby, you may be given conflicting advice about certain details. This is because there is more than one way of doing things! Do not be afraid of trying different feeding positions until you discover the way that is most comfortable for you and your baby. If you are bottle-feeding, remember that milk is not a medicine to be given in a measured dose. It is best to let the baby decide how much to take. Let your baby enjoy sucking until he loses interest. This may be after a minute or two or after twenty to thirty minutes. Different babies also demand to suck at different intervals of time. Your baby may be ready to suck again one hour or four hours later. Rest assured that a regular feeding pattern will soon evolve if you let your baby, rather than the clock, decide.

Babies who need Special Care

A brief glance around a maternity ward is enough to convince anyone that babies come in all shapes and sizes. For example, about one in fourteen babies weigh less than 2.5 kg (5½ lb) and are called low birthweight babies. Some babies are small because they are born prematurely; others are mature, that is full-term, but have not grown very well in the womb. The word 'premature' is only used for babies who are born more than three weeks before the expected time.

Babies born just one or two weeks early generally behave normally, and, in fact, most who reach thirty-five weeks do well and rarely run into difficulty. The earlier a baby is born, the greater the risk. The medical profession is especially concerned about the few who may be born as much as three months before their time because they are obviously not yet ready for life outside the womb. Such babies are less active than full-term babies. It is as if they save all their energy in order to grow, but it may be several weeks before they are strong enough to suck. Some degree of jaundice is common between the third and fifth day, especially if the baby's delicate skin suffered a few bruises at birth.

Premature babies find it difficult to keep themselves warm at first because the insulating layer of fat under the skin is very thin. Compared to a mature baby, the premature baby's skin is also thin and has quite a red tinge to it. The fine downy hair ('lanugo hair') seen on the sides of a premature baby's face, shoulders and back soon disappears as the baby gets older. With very premature babies, breathing is the main concern. Some have brief spells, medically termed 'apnoeic attacks', when they forget to breathe. In this instance the baby is reminded to breathe by a nurse firmly stroking the skin of the baby's arms or legs. Other babies, with very immature lungs, labour over breathing for several days after birth. During this time they may well need oxygen.

The medical profession now knows a lot about how best to care for premature babies. For the first weeks the baby is nursed in a warm incubator, with his chest unclothed so that a watch may be kept on his breathing. Usually a special mattress is used which picks up a baby's breathing movements and sets off a 'bleep' if he forgets to breathe for a few seconds.

Babies who are small because they have not grown very well in the uterus are quite different from premature babies. They are much more active and can usually suck very well. Some, in fact, feed hungrily as if they are making up for lost time.

For low birthweight babies a close watch must be kept on the level of sugar in the blood during the first week. In some, it can become quite low

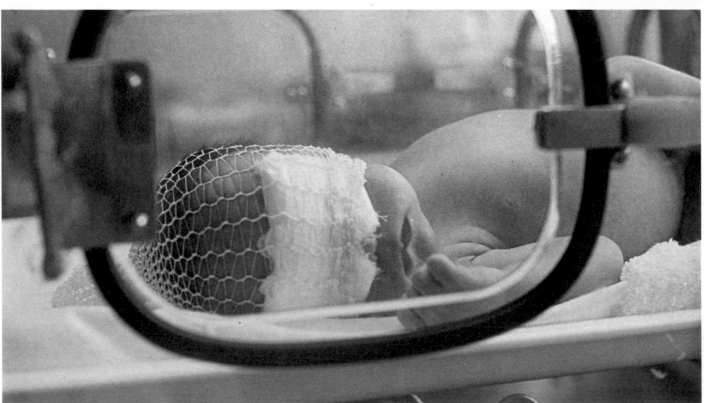

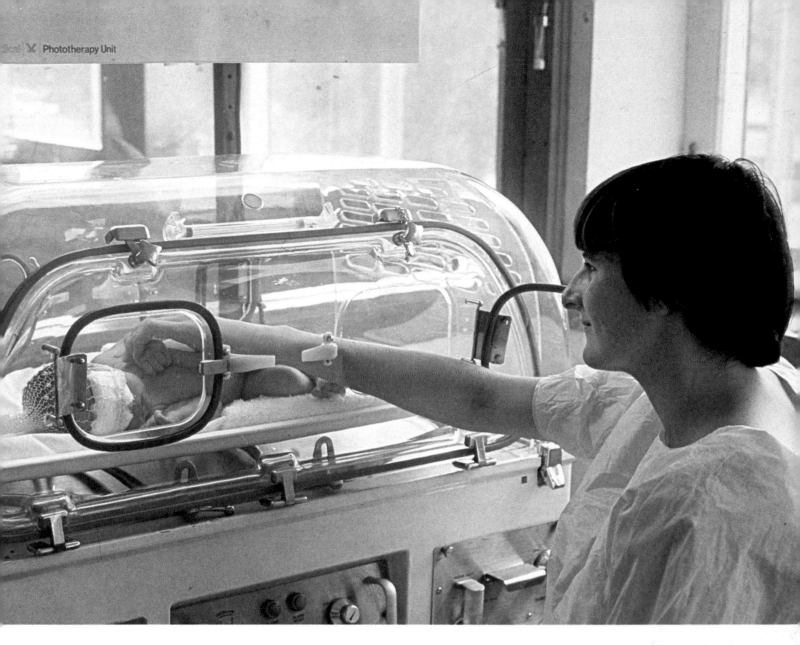

and cause the baby to be unwell. Midwives can measure the blood sugar very simply on a single drop of blood. If the level is low it is sometimes necessary to 'feed' a sugar solution into a small vein.

We can now be much more optimistic about the future for premature and small babies because, with modern methods of care, most survive and grow up as normal children. However, we look forward to discovering more about the prevention of premature birth and the causes of poor growth in the uterus.

JAUNDICED BABIES

Many normal babies develop a slight yellow discoloration of the skin, particularly on the face, between the third and fifth days of life. This is caused by a pigment in the blood known as bilirubin which is formed from the normal breakdown of red blood cells. Normally the liver clears bilirubin from the blood, but, in some babies, particularly if they are premature, it takes a little while for the liver to do this job properly. Usually the jaundice is so mild that it may go

unnoticed and it does not affect the baby's health in any way. This type of jaundice is called 'physiological' because it is a feature of normal babies.

Occasionally the jaundice becomes quite pronounced and the more intense it is, the longer it usually takes to fade completely. In this instance, instead of disappearing by the fifth day, it can last into the second week. Often it is not clear why jaundice becomes so exaggerated, but it does seem to occur in babies who are bruised at birth, those who do not take very much fluid in the first few days and those who are born after an induced labour. Sometimes we have to do blood tests so that we can keep an eye on the precise level of bilirubin in baby's blood.

It is unusual for jaundice to develop during the first day of life. When this does occur it is usually a sign that the baby's red blood cells are being broken down very rapidly, perhaps because, as in the Rhesus disease, the mother's and baby's blood are not compatible.

Some breastfed babies develop quite an intense degree of jaundice during the first week of life

Some jaundiced babies require light treatment (phototherapy). The bright light which is emitted from the phototherapy unit shines on to the baby's skin and breaks down the jaundice pigment in the blood capillaries. It is common sense to protect the baby's eyes from the bright light. Some small babies receive phototherapy while being nursed in an incubator; others can be nursed in a cot. There is no reason why a mother should not see, touch and talk to her baby from time to time during treatment. At feeding times the eye shields should be removed.

111

and this may persist for several weeks before fading spontaneously. In nearly all cases breast-feeding can be safely continued but, occasionally, if the blood tests show a very high level of bili-rubin, mothers are advised to stop breastfeeding temporarily until the jaundice starts to fade.

Physiological jaundice requires no treatment and many mothers are proud of their baby's tan. Jaundice is not, however, desirable. If the blood bilirubin level becomes too high and if your baby becomes deeply jaundiced, you will probably be advised to offer him extra fluids, perhaps in the form of sugar water. The difficulty here is that jaundiced babies are sometimes rather sleepy and you may feel frustrated having to work so hard to get him interested in the extra fluids. There is no reason to stir up trouble between you for a few extra ounces of fluid. It is best to compromise with the baby and, for the time being, to offer feeds at two- or three-hourly intervals instead of on demand and be prepared to spend a little longer at each feed.

PHOTOTHERAPY

Phototherapy—'light treatment'—is generally reserved for babies with deep jaundice. In some maternity hospitals, however, it is used quite freely even for milder degrees of jaundice. For this treatment, the baby is unclothed down to the nappy and his cot is positioned under a bright source of light which shines on to his skin. The light breaks down the bilirubin that is circulating in the tiny blood vessels in the skin. It is not ultra-violet light, of course, so there is no fear of the baby getting sunburnt. A soft shield is placed over the baby's eyes. Several days' treatment may be needed, punctuated, perhaps, by breaks of several hours each day. The amount of exposure that a baby requires depends on the blood level of bilirubin. This is checked daily and it can be frustrating if the treatment involves you being separated from your baby for prolonged periods. Normally phototherapy is given in the ward nursery but, as the apparatus is mobile, you could ask the staff if your baby can be kept by your bed during treatment. If so, your room will need to be warm and draught-free as the baby has to be unclothed for the treatment. If you cannot have your baby by your side, spend as much time with him as possible in the nursery. Remember that although the eye shields prevent him from seeing you, he will respond to your voice and enjoy your touch.

Treatment will, of course, be stopped tempor-arily during feeds so take this opportunity to spend a little extra time cuddling your baby. Ensure, too, that the eye shields are removed so that he can see you. Phototherapy causes most babies to lose a little extra fluid in the stools and, as a result, you may notice that these become quite loose.

The baby's skin may also become a little blotchy under the lights, but this is harmless and will disappear once the treatment is stopped.

BLOOD TRANSFUSION

Sometimes the bilirubin level rises rapidly in spite of phototherapy, especially when there is a definite cause for the jaundice such as Rhesus incompatibility. In these cases it may be necessary for the baby to have his blood changed by an 'exchange transfusion'. This is a simple procedure that involves using a syringe to remove a small amount of blood and immediately replacing it with fresh blood from a healthy donor. This is repeated many times over the course of an hour or so and, as a result, the bilirubin is washed out of the baby's blood stream. It is quite common for babies who are severely jaundiced from Rhesus disease to require several exchange transfusions. If so, do not worry. The technique has been in practice for many years now and paediatricians are very skilled at exchange transfusions.

1 Some small babies are nursed in incubators in a Special Care Baby Unit. It is easy for a mother to feel isolated from her baby, especially if he has to remain in the unit when she has gone home. Some units have rooms where mothers may stay but this may not be convenient if there are other children to be cared for at home. When visiting the unit it is important to establish proper contact with the baby. Ask the staff to let you put your hands inside the incubator and touch the baby. Sit on a chair beside the incubator and try to get the baby to focus on your eyes when he is awake.

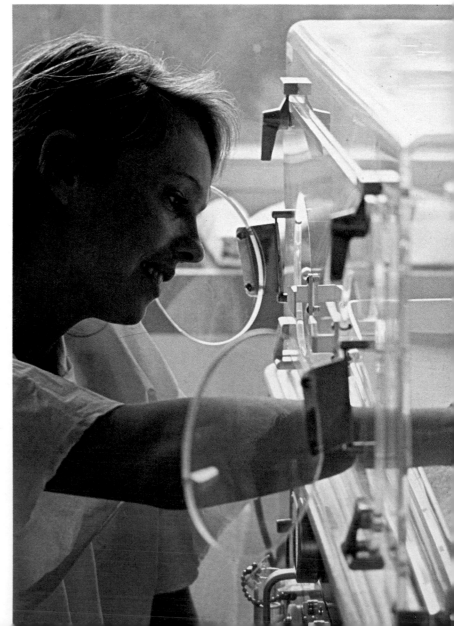

The Special Care Baby Unit

Most maternity hospitals have a special care baby unit. This is a ward where unwell babies or those needing close supervision, such as a premature baby, are nursed. Paediatricians have different ideas about which babies require the special observation of the units. In some hospitals, babies born by forceps or Caesarean section, and those who are a little slow to breathe after birth, are routinely admitted to the special care unit the first day of their life. Nearly all these babies turn out to be perfectly normal and, happily, this routine practice is on the way out.

If your baby is admitted to the special care baby unit for any reason, remember that he needs you around. However skilled doctors and nurses are, they cannot take over your special role of interacting with your baby. You can, in fact, do much to foster a good relationship with your baby while he is in the special care baby unit.

There is rarely any need for a baby to be whisked away from his mother straight after birth. So, before he is transferred to the unit, make sure that you have had the opportunity to see, touch and hold him. (This is not always possible if a mother has been given a general anaesthetic and is still asleep when the baby is transferred.) Remember to ask the staff precisely where the unit is within the hospital. You will find out later, of course, when you go to visit baby but, in the meantime, it is no fun lying there wondering where your baby is. You will feel happier if you know on what floor the unit is and how far it is from your own ward. Mothers naturally like to know exactly where their child is at any time. This is a need that usually remains with mothers even when their children have become adults! Some special care baby units have bedrooms where mothers can sleep so that they need never be far away from their baby. It is a good idea to ask the staff if there is such a room.

One of the most important periods of contact with a newborn baby is during feeding times. For this reason you should try to make an arrangement with the staff about feeding. If your baby

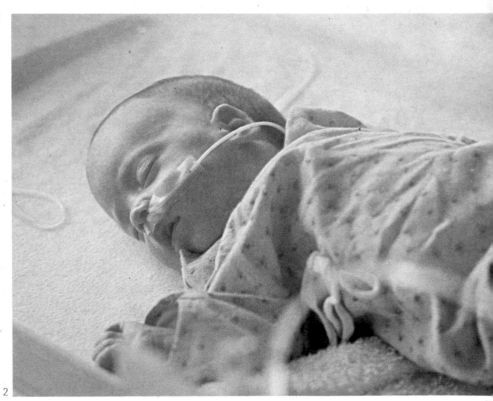

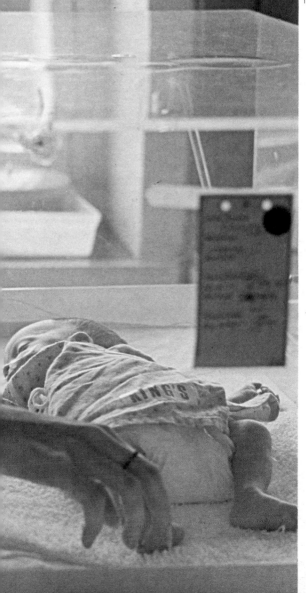

2 It takes a little while for some small babies to learn how to suck and swallow properly. A safe way of feeding is to give milk through a tube that has been passed via the nose, down the gullet and into the stomach. Babies get used to the tube as soon as it is in place; it certainly doesn't stop them sleeping. Small amounts of milk are fed at frequent intervals. A mother can provide breast milk for her baby by expressing her breast. If a baby learns to suck fairly quickly there is no reason why he shouldn't eventually breastfeed.

has no special feeding problem you give him his feeds. If you are not able to stay alongside the actual unit, remember to let the staff know when you are coming to see your baby so that they can leave the feed to you. It is disappointing to arrive at the unit all prepared to feed your baby, only to find him fast asleep having just been fed by someone else.

Some babies who need special care cannot be relied upon to feed by demand. If you are bottle-feeding you will probably be advised about the amount of milk to offer your baby. When your baby has taken the required amount it does not mean that you have to put him straight back in to his cot. If your contact with him is limited to feed times, he will enjoy staying with you a little longer and will feel reassured if he is allowed to fall asleep in your arms. If deprived of this extended contact, he will feel rather like the way we feel when the waiter puts the chairs on the tables just when we are relaxing after a meal!

Some babies who cannot suck adequately at first need to be fed through a small tube that is passed through the nose or mouth into the stomach. If your baby is being nursed in a cot you should pick him up and cuddle him from time to time so that he does not miss out on the physical contact he would normally receive at feed times. Once the tube is in position it does not irritate the baby in any way and causes no discomfort. If you are planning to breastfeed your baby after he has left the special unit, you can still supply him with breast milk by expressing your breast.

If your baby is unduly small, or needs close observation for some other reason, he may be nursed in an incubator instead of a cot. Many mothers feel isolated from their babies in this situation and, at first, tend to stand away from the incubator straining to catch a glimpse of baby. It is much better to sit on a chair beside the incubator because then it is easier for you to put your face at the same level as your baby's so that he can see you. There is no reason why, having washed your hands, you should not put your hands inside the portholes of the incubator and touch your baby. This is positively encouraged by many units but, sometimes, because of work pressures, the staff may not approach you about this and you may need to remind them about your wishes.

Arrangements for family visiting vary in different units, but nearly all allow free access at any time to fathers. If you have older children ask the staff about the visiting arrangements for them. Unfortunately, in many hospitals children are not allowed into the special care baby unit. You can, however, usually arrange for them to get a view of their new baby brother or sister if you make your wishes known to the staff.

First Medical Check-ups

A baby is usually examined on the first day of life and again just before discharge from hospital. The initial examination is to detect any obvious abnormality that might require early treatment. The second examination is done in more detail and gives you an opportunity to ask the paediatrician any questions that you may have about your baby's progress. It is a good idea to ask the sister to let you know when the paediatrician is coming so that you can be present at the examination. Even at this early age a baby will probably feel more secure if he knows that you are there.

What does the paediatrician do? He watches a baby's activity and the different postures that are adopted. You will already have noticed how the activity varies at different times of the day and that, for most of the time, a baby sleeps with his arms and legs partially flexed. Sometimes, especially when being undressed, he gets very cross, cries in rage and shows you just how strong his arms and legs are. Allowances are made for a baby's mood during the examination, so do not be disappointed if you think your baby has not performed at his best for the paediatrician!

SPOTS AND BLEMISHES

Most mothers are very conscious of the appearance of their baby's skin. A mild degree of jaundice, however, is very common between the third and fifth day and certain rashes or spots are also very common. 'Stork bites' are small pink blemishes found on the eyelids and nape of the neck. Do not worry, they will soon fade. Many normal babies come out in red blotches during the first few days of life. These can affect any part of the baby's skin, can be quite widespread and can cause mothers a lot of anxiety. We do not know why this rash, which is called *Erythema toxicum*, occurs but it never affects a baby's health and it fades in a few days.

A 'Mongolian blue spot' is a harmless blue-grey discoloration in the buttock region. This occurs in most negro and oriental babies and occasionally in white-skinned babies. It disappears during the first two years of life.

You will probably have noticed lots of tiny white spots over the baby's nose and, perhaps, cheeks and forehead. These are caused by a temporary blockage of glands in the skin and disappear in a few weeks. Ask the paediatrician about any blemishes that are causing you concern, then you can leave the maternity hospital re-assured about your baby's skin.

THE BABY'S HEAD

Having made his general observations, the paediatrician will examine the baby in some detail, perhaps starting with the head and face. A baby's head is not as delicate as you might think. It is built to withstand the pressures of being squeezed through the birth canal and, after this, your gentle touches are light relief! The skull of a young baby is made up of eight bones which are not yet fused into one and, during birth, the bones overlap each other a little to allow the head to mould as it comes through the birth canal. If you run your finger gently across your baby's head soon after birth you can often feel several ridges where the bones have overlapped. The moulding may persist for a day or two after birth and that is why the shape of a newborn baby's head is rarely perfectly round.

You may wonder why the paediatrician runs a tape measure around the baby's head. Before his first birthday the baby will probably have other routine medical check-ups. If the head size is measured again at these times, the paediatrician will know how well the head has grown from birth.

☐ **The fontanelle** On the top of the head, towards the front, is a diamond shaped area which is called the "anterior fontanelle'. It feels rather soft because four of the skull bones in this area have not yet fused together. It is quite normal to see or feel pulsations here. This so-called soft spot is not as soft as you might think because under the skin there is a tough membrane.

☐ **Bruising and swelling** A little bruising and swelling over the part of the baby's head which presented itself at birth, is common. This will subside in a few days. A somewhat larger firm swelling, called a 'cephalhaematoma', however, often causes parents concern. It is caused by a little bleeding around one of the skull bones and is harmless, although it is usually several weeks before it subsides.

Bruising of the face is quite common especially after a forceps' delivery, and the eye lids and cheeks often appear a little swollen at first. You may have noticed that the whites of the baby's eyes are somewhat bloodshot, but this will clear completely in a week or two.

THE BABY'S MOUTH

The paediatrician will carefully inspect the baby's mouth, usually shining a torch inside to get a better view. White blisters in the centre of the lips are caused by sucking and always clear up spontaneously. White patches on the tongue are usually caused by milk staining, but are some-times confused with a fairly common mouth infection called 'thrush'. If a baby has thrush his mouth is usually a little sore and the white patches are somewhat thicker and difficult to wipe off. The condition is not dangerous and soon clears with some medicine drops.

THE BABY'S BREASTS

Baby boys and girls often have slightly swollen breasts which discharge a little milk for several weeks after birth. Some mothers are tempted to get rid of the swelling by squeezing the milk out. This should never be done. It can cause the breasts to become infected.

HEART AND LUNGS

Before using the stethoscope, the paediatrician watches how the baby is breathing. Babies breathe more quickly than adults and you have probably noticed that, when a baby is falling asleep after a feed, his breathing becomes quite jerky and irregular. It soon settles down, how-ever, when he is sound asleep. A baby usually gets very cross when the stethoscope is put on his chest, especially if the instrument feels cold. If you watch carefully, you may see him try to push it away with his hands, showing you that he has a mind of his own! It is helpful if you can pacify him, perhaps by letting him suck at your finger.

1 Tiny, white spots on and around the baby's nose are caused by a temporary blockage of glands in the skin.

2 'Stork bites' are small pink blemishes which sometimes appear on the skin of a newborn baby. They will soon fade.

3 'Strawberry marks' are quite common. They gradually fade and disappear during the first few years of life, so do not be distressed if they seem a little unsightly or obvious at first.

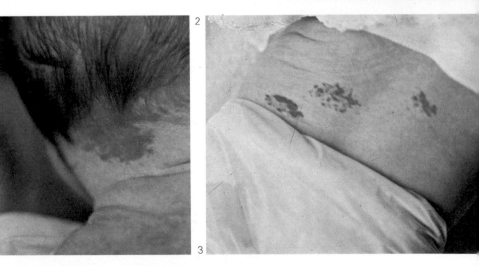

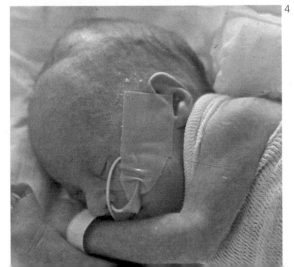

4 Cephalhaematoma is the name given to a large, firm swelling on the head of a newborn baby. It is caused by a slight bleeding around one of the bones of the skull. It is not a cause for anxiety and will disappear within several weeks.

Heart murmurs are quite commonly heard in newborn babies and do not necessarily mean that there is something wrong with the heart. In fact, most newborn babies who have something seriously wrong with their heart are obviously ill. A paediatrician will suspect a heart problem long before he has listened with a stethoscope from the baby's general appearance, his behaviour and response to his surroundings.

THE UMBILICAL CORD

It usually takes about a week for the stump of the umbilical cord to come off. If you notice any bleeding from it, or if the skin surrounding it becomes unduly red or inflamed, mention it to the nursing staff or to the paediatrician when he is making his routine check-ups.

TUMMY CHECKS

A baby's tummy usually looks rather large. When the paediatrician feels it he is making sure that there is no enlargement of the internal organs and that everything is present and is located in the right place.

THE BABY'S BOWELS

Most babies have their bowels open by the end of the first day. When this happens immediately after birth in the delivery room it can be easily overlooked. During the first few days a baby passes a greeny-black, sticky substance called meconium. If he has not presented you with a dirty nappy by the end of the second day, mention it to the nursing staff. After a few days the stools will gradually become yellow, but their colour is not all that important. You will notice that it varies a little from time to time, as does the consistency.

THE NAPPY AREA

During the check-up the baby's nappy is taken off as there are a number of things to be checked in this area. The paediatrician will, for example, look at the baby's groins for signs of a hernia and

1 Babies are generally given a check-up during the first day of life and again just before they are discharged from the maternity hospital. If possible, you should watch the baby being examined, and, when the paediatrician has finished, ask about anything that may be worrying you.

2 The main reason for measuring the circumference of a baby's head is to obtain a base line against which subsequent growth of the head may be assessed.

3 Careful examination of the hip joints is a very important part of the check-up. The paediatrician will detect any dislocation or instability of the joints.

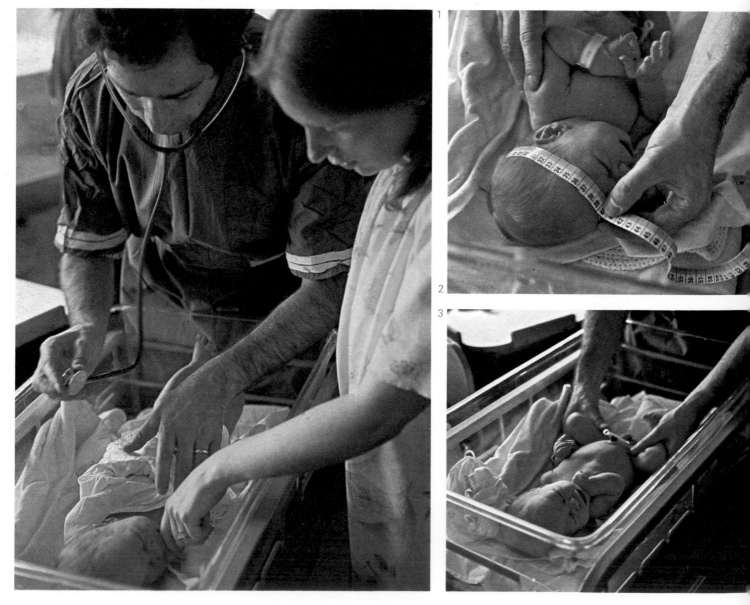

4 The back is carefully examined from the neck down to the base of the spine.

5,6 All babies have a soft spot towards the front of the skull in the centre. Its size doesn't really matter. It is quite safe to touch and the paediatrician feels it when the baby is settled to make sure it is not under pressure. It does feel rather tense when the baby cries.

7 Although it is traditional for the paediatrician to sound the chest with a stethoscope, he is unlikely to diagnose anything of importance in a baby who is well. Occasionally, a heart murmur may be heard, but often this is benign.

will feel for the pulse in the arteries that carry blood to the legs.

In boys, the opening at the tip of the penis (urethral meatus) is usually tiny and sometimes cannot be seen at all as it is covered by the foreskin (prepuce). Usually both testicles can be felt in the scrotum, but sometimes fluid accumulates there causing a swelling known as a hydrocele. This nearly always disappears as the baby gets older. There is often some bruising of the scrotum if the baby is born by the breech—the buttocks—and although this may look sore it does not seem to worry the baby.

Baby girls often have a vaginal discharge and, between five and ten days old, there may also be a little bleeding caused by temporary hormonal changes. This is quite normal and should not cause any anxiety.

SPINE, HIPS AND FEET

The paediatrician is especially interested in the baby's spine, hips and feet. A skin dimple or tiny

pit at the base of the spine, just where the buttocks begin, is common and quite harmless. Many years ago, it was not a rare sight to see older children walking with a limp because of dislocated hips. Things are different now because the hips are examined most carefully after birth to spot early signs of dislocation and, if necessary, treatment is commenced right away.

Sometimes a baby's feet tend to 'turn in' or 'turn out' a little after birth. This usually becomes less noticeable as the baby gets older but, occasionally, it is necessary to put some strapping around the ankles until the position of the feet improves.

MOST BABIES ARE NORMAL

It is natural for a mother to compare her baby with others in the maternity ward, but remember that no two babies are quite the same. Nearly all babies are normal, so the paediatrician is most unlikely to find anything wrong. If you have any worries about your baby's health, do ask.

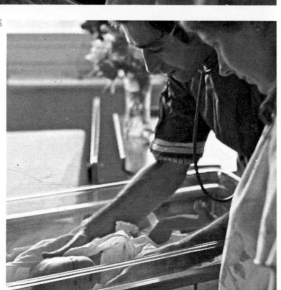

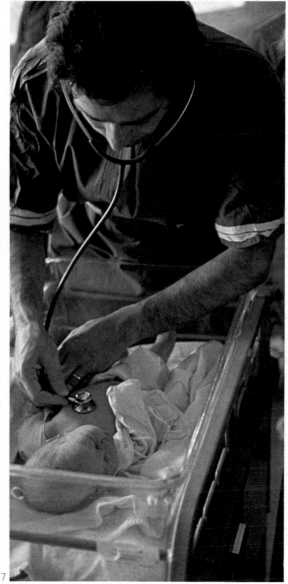

The Stay in Hospital

Not surprisingly, perhaps, few mothers sleep well immediately after all the hard work and excitement of labour. Rest is, however, very important. However excited and elated a mother may feel, she should resist the temptation to over-tax her energy so that, in the end, nature takes its course and she collapses into tears of exhaustion. Even when the labour has been straightforward, a new mother needs time to replenish her energy and her body needs time to adjust from pregnancy, labour and the confinement. Time is always well spent in hospital when a mother allows herself, within the limitations of the hospital routine, to make the most of the opportunity to relax and rest and to quietly get to know her baby.

Apart from visits to the lavatory, you should spend most of the first day resting in bed. From the second day onwards, you will probably want to get up for meals but, even then, you should spend a reasonable amount of each day resting in bed, building up energy for the time when you will need as much energy as you can muster to look after the baby and the home. The more relaxed and rested the mother is, the happier and more secure the baby will feel.

Many new mothers find it difficult to think about anything other than the baby, and the books that they planned to read in hospital remain unopened. This is a natural sequence following a nine-month build-up to one event. The important thing is to relax the mind as well as the body. Indeed, the body cannot relax if the mind is running round and round in circles.

Although the day begins very early in hospital, it also passes very quickly. Some mothers reach the end of their stay in hospital without even having completed their 'announcing a new arrival' cards! It does, however, help to write these while in hospital—time will be at an even higher premium when the mother goes home and has an entirely new routine to adjust to.

The stay in hospital is an excellent time for you to examine your baby minutely, to reassure yourself that all his or her various parts are present and correct and functioning as they should, and to raise any queries and anxieties that you may have. It is also an excellent opportunity to observe how the professionals handle infants; the way that they support the baby's head, for example, when bathing him so that he feels comfortable and secure; the ease and speed with which they change nappies or raise tiny arms and legs for dressing. It can be very reassuring for a new mother to realize that newborn babies are not nearly as fragile as she may fear and that they can withstand firm handling; that, indeed, they respond well and feel more secure when handled confidently and firmly.

It is also a very good time to raise any feeding queries or anxieties about the colour of a baby's motions, etc. A new mother should never suffer in silence, whether the anxiety is concerned with a personal discomfort, such as soreness of the nipples when breastfeeding, constipation, or whatever, or concern about one or other aspect of the baby's physical well-being or behaviour. However busy any maternity ward is, the staff will understand that you need guidance and reassurance on many points.

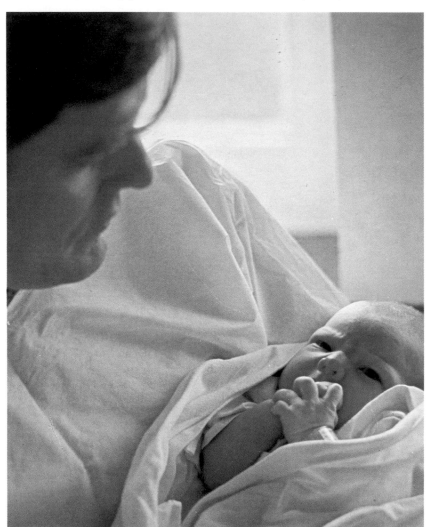

Attitudes have changed tremendously in hospitals during recent years. The need for mothers and babies to spend time together so that the mother/infant relationship can bond—become established—from the earliest possible moment is now widely recognized. Babies being whisked off to nurseries and left almost entirely to the care of the medical staff throughout the early days of life, is increasingly becoming a thing of the past. These days the baby usually lies in a cot beside your bed, and you are encouraged to handle and to tend its needs from the onset of life.

1 Nowadays, most hospitals recognize the importance of the new father and allow him plenty of opportunities to see his wife and their new baby. It is never too soon to establish a relationship between father and son or daughter—with lots of cuddling, love and eye-to-eye contact.

2,3 The way to make the most of your stay in hospital is to take every opportunity to relax, rest and get to know your baby. The more relaxed and rested a mother is, the happier and more secure her baby. In hospital, a new mother can learn a great deal by watching how the professionals handle newborn infants. It is very reassuring to learn to handle, bath and feed a new baby with the helpful guidance of experienced people on hand if you need it. It is also a wonderful chance to voice any doubts, fears and anxieties concerning yourself, your baby or your ability to cope. The sooner a mother begins to handle her baby and care for his everyday needs, the better it is for both mother and child. Modern medical staff understand this and will do everything they can to help you. Thus, the transition period from life in hospital to life at home with a newborn baby, is so much easier and smoother than it was in the past.

The open-visiting system that is now practised by most hospitals has disadvantages as well as advantages. A new mother will welcome the opportunity to see her husband as often as he is able to visit and will, doubtless, welcome parents and parents-in-law, but this is probably more than enough excitement during the early days after the birth. For this reason, it is sensible to restrict visiting to one's nearest and dearest relatives and not to encourage the attentions of friends and neighbours however pleased one usually is to see them.

Visiting time, as any one who has ever been in hospital knows, is a very concentrated period and can be very taxing for a newly delivered mother. There is always the temptation to 'put on a good act' however weary or weepy one may be feeling, just to reassure the family that all is well and that you are delighted to be the mother of a new son or daughter. There is always less risk of hurting anybody's feelings if you make the arrangement in advance to restrict visiting to close family only. Then, if you subsequently discover that you would like to see a particular person, arrangements can always be made at that point.

However busy the hospital routine, take time to care for your skin, hair and nails and to make yourself feel and look presentable. It is only too easy, when you have a new baby to care for, to forget that you also need to care for yourself. If you begin in hospital, you are much more likely to continue when you get home.

3

2

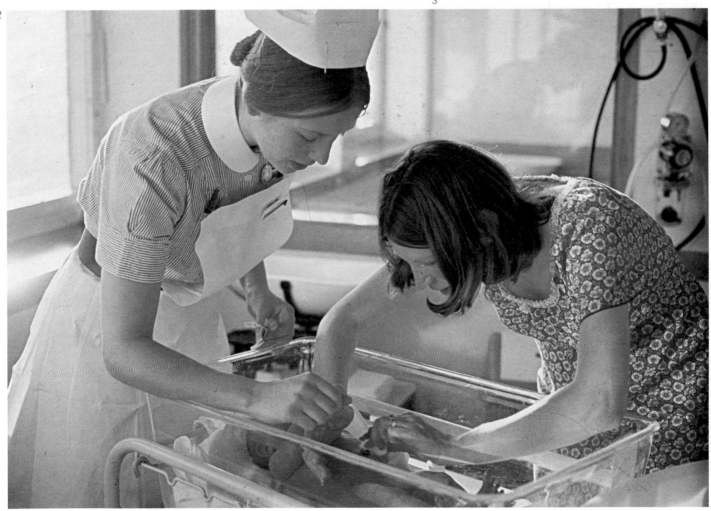

At Home with Your Baby
Finding the Right Balance

It is only too easy when you have a new baby, a husband, possibly other children and a house to care for, to forget that this is only possible if you take care of yourself, too. Output, in other words, is dependent on input! However good your intention to put child, husband and home first, as a new mother you are courting trouble if you forget that you, too, have needs; and that all these other areas of your life are dependent upon being in first-class physical, mental and emotional condition.

The more you understand about the puerperium, for example, which is the medical term for the first four weeks after the delivery of a baby, the more you will know what to expect and the more competent you will be at coping with the waves of physical tiredness and emotional turmoil that often arise during the early weeks of motherhood. The process of readjustment cannot and, indeed, should not be hurried. It is far healthier to accept that it will be several months before the body returns to a so-called normal state—the state which preceded pregnancy and childbirth. Never feel distressed because some compromises are necessary in relation to organizing the home.

The first few weeks at home can be the most difficult time of a mother's maternal life; but if you observe your baby carefully he will tell you all you need to know. In fact, during these early weeks, it is the baby who provides the measure and the order of the day. A tiny new baby, for example, may need feeding every three to three-and-a-half hours in the early weeks; another, weighing over 3.20 kg (7 lb) will, perhaps, feed every four hours. A baby who is breastfed will need feeding more often than one who is bottle-fed.

No two babies are alike: some are quiet and placid; others are lively and continually demand attention. Some babies cry when their nappy is soiled, others do not; some like drinks of boiled water between meals; some are quietened by being cradled; others by being held upright; some will sleep all through the night and others will not. It is only by observing your baby in all his moods that you will begin to recognize his own particular needs and rhythm.

Between feeding, changing and enjoying the miracle that is your baby, there will be housework, cooking, attending to friends or relatives

and vital rest periods when you should sit with your feet up or lie flat on the floor or bed. Of all these activities, the rest periods are of paramount importance, especially in the first four weeks after the birth. Without them, a mother cannot cope with the thousand and one demands upon her attention. This means having enough sleep; sitting down for meals at regular times and sitting down for five to ten minutes before you feed, change or bath your baby, so that you can attend to him in a quiet, collected, happy state. The relaxation exercises learned at antenatal preparation classes are invaluable at this time; so is any other form of relaxation that enables you to fall still and experience rest.

Adequate rest of the mind means learning to centre your attention on whatever is in front of you; tackling each task and day as it presents itself, and not churning over the things that should or ought not to have been done. A very wise man once said that 'There is only one choice in life. To be happy with what we have chosen to do.'

ORGANIZING THE HOUSEHOLD

Countless things present themselves to a new mother in the course of a day. They can only be approached one by one and not, by any stretch of imagination, can they all be dealt with. So, if the garden cries out to be weeded and you long to attend to it, forget the washing or ironing for a couple of hours, do it and enjoy it.

It is useful to remember that a new day is governed by the way in which a mother and father spend the previous evening—what your state of heart and mind is when you go to bed, even what time you ate your evening meal, plays its part. A popular time for bathing babies is in the evening, largely because this is a soothing experience for a baby. It also means that many fathers are home at that time, and it gives them an opportunity to get to know their baby. For bathing a baby, you will need to allow about an hour. This will be followed by an evening meal for you and your husband. Research shows quite clearly that a light evening meal, taken about three hours before bed, is most easily digested and allows the natural pattern of sleep to proceed most easily. A meal consisting of soup, salad, wholewheat bread, and fresh fruit, would be appetizing, delicious and nourishing. It would also be easy to prepare and not require a lot of

Not surprisingly, the first few weeks at home can be the most difficult time of a mother's life. It is very important to remember that the process of adjustment should not and, indeed, cannot be hurried. Waves of physical tiredness and a certain amount of emotional changeability are natural reactions after all the excitement and stimulation of the delivery. Be patient with yourself and be patient with your baby. Remember that no two people are alike and it is only through observation and experience that you can begin to recognize your baby's particular needs and rhythm, and establish a routine which allows both of you to thrive.

During your first few weeks together, do only those things which are absolutely necessary and firmly ignore the others. What really matters is that both you and the baby should be in a quiet, collected, happy state of mind and have time to get

cooking or last-minute attention.

Before you go to bed, allow a reasonable time to attend to dishes and other little chores, so that everything presents a tidy, orderly appearance first thing in the morning. Then you will not have to cope with 'last-night' next morning and this, in itself, is very refreshing.

Wake your baby for a feed before you go to bed and then, with luck, you may have five or six hours before another feed is needed. Do not feel that your baby *has* to have a 2 a.m. feed. Let him sleep if he wants and let him wake you if he needs it. So, with luck, the next feed will not take place until the early morning. It will probably be possible, then, to sleep for a few more hours.

When it is time to get up, bath or shower, and dress immediately, rather than give way to the temptation to struggle into a dressing gown. This routine will help wake you up, will make you feel good and prepared to face the day. Have a good nutritious breakfast with your husband, rather than a cup of coffee and a cigarette!

Follow this with feeding, changing, playing with your baby and putting him in his bed to sleep. During the morning, do those things which are absolutely essential and firmly ignore the others. Prepare the ingredients for lunch and your evening meal, so that there will be no rush later in the day. In the first weeks, pin a notice to your front door at 2 p.m., saying 'no callers till three-thirty' and take a rest period. However much there seems to do, make a practice of this. It will make a lot of difference to how you feel later in the day. Use what time is left in the afternoon

wisely, so that you are not too tired when your husband comes home.

Here are some suggestions for cutting corners in housework:

1: A house that is basically tidy needs only a dust and carpet sweep in the main rooms. Never go up or down stairs empty-handed.

2: It is much easier to sweep a kitchen floor and wipe it over with a damp cloth, than to struggle with the thought of getting down on hands and knees to do a thorough scrub.

3: When preparing meals, lay the table *first*. This will avoid a last-minute scramble, and suggest that things are well on their way, even if they are not!

4: Finely slice vegetables, Chinese-style, then cook in the minimum amount of water. They will take hardly any time to cook and will retain more goodness. Prepare them early in the day and refrigerate until you need to cook them.

5: When changing clothes, put them straight on hangers. Creases will drop out more quickly and the knowledge that they are in order is restful in itself.

6: Do nappies each day, and the laundry before there is so much that it becomes a pressure that takes several days to clear!

7: Do not iron bed linen. A neatly folded sheet that is placed on the top of a pile will be pressed by the time it is needed, if fresh sheets are always taken from the bottom. Do not iron kitchen towels or underwear. If your husband is agreeable, iron only the parts of his shirts that show!

8: Plan your shopping so that you do not have to

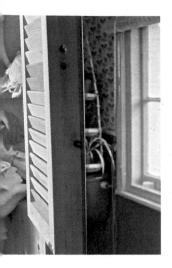

rush to the shops just as they are closing.

9: Do not be afraid to ask for help from others. A neighbour might be only too happy to prepare lunch for you when she cooks her own. A 'grandmother' may be delighted to look after a small baby when her own grandchildren are hundreds of miles away. If your income is low, and you do not have the money to pay for help, then consider other ways in which you or your husband may return kindness.

10: Team up with other mothers, so that you can help each other with shopping, baby-sitting, pursuing hobbies or courses of study. In this way, you can continue to play a part in the community and horizons will remain wide.

11: Know your limitations, never criticize yourself; and if you do not think you have any virtues, assume them!

GETTING DOWN TO THE MECHANICS

A mother's most useful basic aids are a refrigerator, vacuum cleaner and fully automatic washing machine. If the budget does not stretch to an automatic machine, try to afford a spin drier and a tumble drier. A tumble drier takes over where the spin-drier finishes. It avoids the necessity of finding somewhere to dry nappies and stretchsuits in wet weather, and will help to keep the home looking tidier.

In these days of high fuel bills, a pressure cooker is becoming an almost essential part of kitchen equipment. You can use a pressure cooker to prepare a wide variety of dishes very rapidly. For example, soups and stocks, vegetarian dishes, classic meat and fish recipes, cereals, stews and desserts. It is safer to use than a frying pan or deep fat fryer. A pressure cooker is marvellous for preparing meals quickly.

For preparing solid foods for your baby, you will need a small heavy saucepan with a close-fitting lid; a small deep casserole with a lid for baking and steaming (you can use a heat-proof cup for this); a small nylon sieve with a fine mesh; a hand blender for puréeing thick foods and a small electric blender for liquid purées. It is better to use a hand blender for thick purées. If you use an electric blender for food such as this, you will spend all your time scraping it off the blades.

to know each other—time to establish a really close and loving relationship. Usually, by trial and error, you find the right balance and get the priorities sorted out.

Babies who cry a lot

CRYING IS A LANGUAGE

If there is one sound in the world that is designed to make parents take action, it is a baby's crying. As this is the only way in which an infant can communicate his needs, it is just as well it is a compelling sound.

Advice such as it is better to leave a baby to cry rather than spoil him, or that a baby needs to cry to exercise his lungs, is unworthy of consideration. Babies never cry for nothing—and will go on crying until their needs are understood.

Hunger is the most common reason for crying, but what is often overlooked is that a baby also gets thirsty. If this need is misinterpreted, he may accept food in an attempt to quench his thirst, but, having failed to do so, will often begin to cry again.

Misinterpretation is, in fact, a common cause of prolonged crying. A baby, for example, who begins to cry because he is tired or overstimulated, is often jogged up and down or handed even more toys. What he really needs is peace and moments of being held lovingly close.

Likewise, a baby who is left unoccupied for too long in his cot or pram will express his boredom by crying. He will soon cheer up if he is placed so that he can watch his mother or other members of the family, or even just leaves wafting in a breeze. Baby-carrying slings are certainly a useful way of including a baby who is feeling excluded or deprived of bodily contact.

Rhythmical movements, such as those supplied by baby slings, rocking cradles or a pair of arms, are very soothing when a baby is distressed. So are rhythmical sounds, such as a soothing voice, lullaby or musical box.

Being over-dressed and, therefore, over-heated —or under-dressed and cold—are common causes of crying. Likewise, some babies have sensitive skins and will react to the scratchiness of a woollen garment or the suffocating cling of nylon and other man-made fibres.

Many babies also dislike being undressed. The sudden lack of contact with the clothing, and the sense of air playing on the skin, distresses them. If this is the case, the baby will appreciate a soft towel or shawl draped around his body whilst mother sorts out the various garments. Other babies startle easily and will protest at a sudden sound or react to the unexpected—especially if it is a stranger's face. Others rightly object to sudden movements, such as being jerked into a sitting up position without the warning of a gentle voice or touch. Babies also protest at being handled inattentively or hurriedly. They all are sensitive to their parents' moods and will respond with tears to their parents' agitation, whether this is expressed or unexpressed.

None of this is surprising when it is remembered that a young baby has been used to the total security and instant service of life in the uterus. After this, any delay between expressing a need and having it answered can seem like an eternity.

Whether a baby is 'saying' I am tired, hungry, thirsty, hot, cold, lonely, bored, frightened, uncomfortable or in pain, is not always easy for a mother or father to interpret. What matters is that the baby should be allowed to know, by the parent's loving and reassuring presence, that whilst all may not be well now, it soon will be.

Crying is a baby's first language. Like all languages, it is spoken in a very individual way. It takes time, patience and perseverance before one can truly say one has mastered the steps and can understand precisely what is being said.

Sometimes nothing seems to stop your baby crying. The noise and strain are intolerable, especially as this always happens on a very busy day or when you are already under the weather. Anyone, however calm normally, can suddenly feel real anger and resentment at her baby's apparently perverse behaviour. Get in touch with a neighbour or friend who can come immediately and look after the baby while you go out or keep you company to help things into perspective. If no-one is available, put the baby in his pram and go for a long walk. The fresh air will calm you down and the noise will immediately seem less. When you are feeling better, don't feel guilty.

After the instant service of life in the womb, it is not surprising that any delay between expressing a need and having it answered can seem like an eternity for a young baby. Whether a baby is crying because he is hungry, thirsty, cold, lonely, bored, frightened, uncomfortable or in pain, what really matters is that he should be allowed to know by his parent's loving responses that, whilst all may not be well now, it soon will be. Crying is a language and, like all languages, it takes time for parents to feel completely confident that they can interpret it correctly.

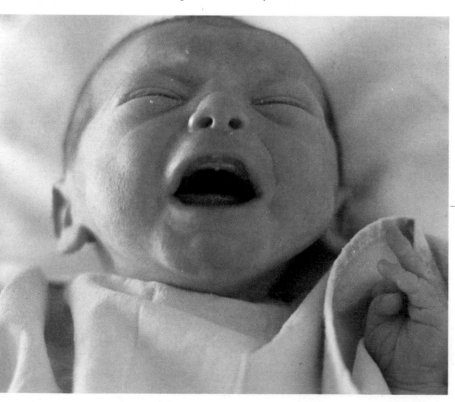

Feeding Methods
Breastfeeding

The question of whether or not to breastfeed a baby is one that can occupy a good deal of a mother-to-be's thoughts during pregnancy. It is essential to make the decision during pregnancy rather than when your hungry infant is already in your arms.

INFLUENTIAL FACTORS

From the medical angle, there are very few reasons for advising against breastfeeding. If the mother has a severe heart or kidney disease, or active tuberculosis, her obstetrician will advise her to bottle-feed.

A severe degree of inversion (or indrawing) of the nipples is likely to make breastfeeding difficult. It is to be hoped, however, that treatment during pregnancy for this condition will have done much to correct the problem. There are no conditions in a baby that preclude breastfeeding. Even the smallest and most immature babies, and those with a congenital defect affecting the lips and mouth, will benefit from breast milk. If a baby is unable to suck, the milk can be expressed manually from the breast and given to him in other ways.

ADVANTAGES AND DISADVANTAGES

Breastfeeding has several very important advantages for a baby. The milk is one hundred per cent suitable and also has the bonus value of containing antibodies to various diseases which the mother has had in the past. Breastfed babies are also far less likely to suffer from gastro-enteritis (a serious condition in young babies) and rarely get nappy-rash. From the mother's viewpoint, breastfeeding is a natural conclusion to pregnancy and delivery and helps with the involution (returning to normal) of the uterus. In addition there are no frequent and time-consuming milk-preparing sessions—the baby's food is always available at the right time, consistency and temperature.

Finally, there is that indefinable, but vital, bonding between mother and baby which arises so much more readily and quickly within the intimacy of breastfeeding.

The disadvantages of breastfeeding are all on the mother's side. Distaste for the whole process, together with, perhaps, a certain degree of embarrassment, or even revulsion, can be a potent reason for bottle-feeding. Fortunately, with today's excellent artificial milks, a baby will not go hungry if his mother decides against breastfeeding. One advantage that is commonly mentioned in relation to bottle-feeding, is that it can seem so much more scientific because the mother knows exactly how much milk the baby is taking. With breastfeeding, of course, a contented baby is the mother's only guide to a satisfactory intake.

HOW COW'S MILK AND HUMAN MILK VARY

A most important factor when deciding whether or not to breastfeed must be the understanding of how breast milk and cow's milk differ, and why breast milk is more suitable for a baby in the early days of life. (Even a short time—two to three weeks—of breastfeeding will be beneficial to a baby).

Milk, in common with other foods, is made up of three main constituents: protein, fat and carbohydrate. Cow's milk contains over twice the amount of protein found in breast milk. The main protein in cow's milk is casein, and there is more than five times the amount of this substance in cow's milk than in human milk. From the point of view of the baby's digestive system, casein, which forms curds in the tummy, is relatively indigestible.

Although the fat content of cow's milk is similar to that of human milk, the actual fat droplets in human milk are smaller. Once again, this part of breast milk is more easily digested by the baby. Breast milk contains a higher proportion of carbohydrate than does cow's milk. This is mainly in the form of lactose, which is easily assimilitated by a baby's immature digestive system. Cow's milk also differs in the amount of vitamins and minerals, and, lastly, completely lacks those important antibodies found solely in human milk. Much work has been done in trying to render artificial milks as similar to human milk as possible. The resulting milks are excellent, but they can never completely and satisfactorily replace the human breast as a source of ideal food for a baby.

THE HUMAN BREAST

The human breast, like most other parts of the human body, is a miracle of adaptation to a specific purpose. At puberty, around ten to fourteen years old, the breasts enlarge and

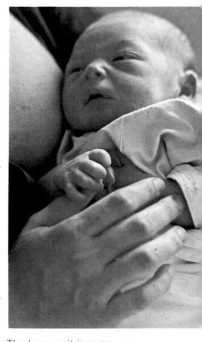

The long wait is over. Your baby is here, snuggled close to your breast. Your decision to breastfeed him is already forging those vital bonding links between you both which will last a lifetime.

Making yourself comfortable is an important part of the process of breastfeeding. Support for your back, arms and feet all go towards making feeding an enjoyable time for you both—one from which you, too, obtain strength and rest. The choice of a suitable nursing bra also adds to the comfort for you at each feed.

The inborn 'rooting' reflex ensures that your baby knows instinctively where to turn for the source of his food. Once he has found the nipple, he will settle hungrily to his feed. Now is the time for you to relax and let the worries of the day slip away for a few minutes. What a great feeling to be satisfied, warm and sleepy! You, too, are serene and happy knowing that you have supplied your new son or daughter with the best possible food for healthy growth and development right from the start.

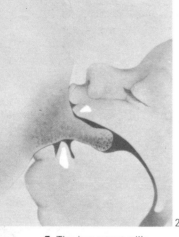

1 The important milk-secreting glands are embedded in the fatty tissue of the breast. The milk secreted is passed into the lactiferous ducts which open out on to the nipple.

2 The baby's lips and gums should press against the areola during feeding to empty the sacs formed at the end of the tubes which bring milk to the nipple.

grow into their adult size and shape. The size is very dependent on the amount of fatty tissue in the breast. Embedded in this fatty tissue are the milk-secreting glands. It is untrue that small breasts (which merely have less fatty tissue) preclude the ability to breastfeed. The ducts from the glands join together to form the lactiferous (milk-bearing) ducts which then open on to the surface of the nipple. The size and shape of the nipple is of great importance to the success of breastfeeding. Ideally the nipple should be long and erect enough to reach to the back of the roof of the baby's mouth. The nipple itself is surrounded by a darker area of specialized tissue, known as the areola. The pressure of the baby's lips on this areola squeezes the milk into his mouth from the lactiferous ducts just under the areola.

During pregnancy the breasts enlarge and may become a little tender, and the areola darkens. These changes occur under the influence of various hormones. A well-supporting bra is essential at this stage, and you may find that you need a larger size than usual. Towards the end of pregnancy a thin, yellowish, sticky fluid called colostrum is secreted by the breast. Some hospitals will advise you to express colostrum from your breasts during pregnancy by massaging with your fingers. Manual expression of the breasts is a useful art to master as you may need to do it after the baby is born, if for example he or she is in a special care unit and cannot be put to the breast. During pregnancy, however, it is not strictly necessary, and many mothers think it better to save the colostrum for the baby. Do not attempt manual expression of the breasts without first being shown how to do it by the midwife.

□ **Colostrum** continues to be secreted during the first day or two following a baby's birth. It has a high protein content, and also supplies the baby with valuable antibodies to any disease which the mother and baby begin a life-long acquaintance, this reason many doctors and midwives encourage mothers to put their babies briefly to the breast soon after birth. At the same time the mother and baby begin a life-long acquantance, and the essential bonding gets off to a good start. A mother's breasts continue to secrete colostrum for forty-eight to seventy-two hours after the birth. Then, under the action of hormonal changes in the body, the milk begins to come in.

□ **Milk Production** Quite unlike the yellowish, creamy colour of cow's milk, breast milk is rather watery looking and of a bluish colour. It is, however, exactly tailored to a baby's needs.

□ **'Draught reflex'** As the milk comes into the breasts before each feed you will often be aware of a tingling sensation around the areola, and milk will sometimes leak from the breasts. This is a reflex action—under the influence of a hormone—known as the 'draught' or 'let-down' reflex.

□ **'After Pains'** As the baby settles at the breast for his feed in the early days after his birth, you may be aware of cramping pains in the lower part of your tummy. These are known as 'after pains' and are due to a further action of the hormone, oxytocin, which causes the draught reflex. Under the action of oxytocin, the womb contracts down to its normal pre-pregnancy size.

THE TECHNIQUE OF BREASTFEEDING

□ **Timing of Feeds** With the advent of the civilized society of the Western world, many mothers now have to learn again the natural art of breastfeeding their babies. Perhaps one of the most vexing questions to new mothers, is how often should their babies be fed. Ideas have fluctuated over the years from the rigid timetable advocated by Truby King to complete demand-feeding whenever the baby cries. A compromise between the two extremes is probably the best approach.

In the early days following the birth, a baby is put to the breast frequently, about every two hours. But as the days go by, he sleeps longer and longer between feeds, until he and his mother work out a routine that suits them both. Usually, this routine settles down to feeding approximately every four hours—making a total of six feeds in all during the twenty-four hours.

□ **Surroundings and Position for Feeding** Ideally, the room in which a baby is fed should be quiet and warm. The mother should make herself as comfortable and relaxed as possible. A low armless chair is ideal. A cushion or pillow to support the elbow of the arm holding the baby certainly helps to ease any strain and a footstool puts the finishing touch to comfort.

□ **Nursing Bra** A nursing bra is highly recommended for breastfeeding and there are several good ones available. They mainly fall into two types—the type that has a front opening and the type with a flap over the nipple. Both are satisfactory.

□ **'Rooting' Reflex** When you pick up your restless hungry baby for his feed, you will feel the milk rushing into both breasts. As your finger touches baby's cheek, or as his face brushes your nipple, you will notice that his mouth opens and his face turns towards the source of the food. This process, known as the 'rooting' reflex, is present in all mature newborn babies.

□ **Length of Feed** Most babies are satisfied with approximately ten minutes at each breast, although there is a good deal of individual variation in this. After ten minutes at the first breast, the

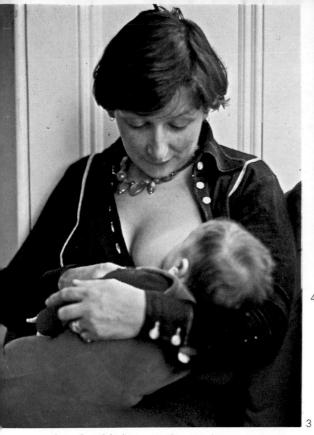

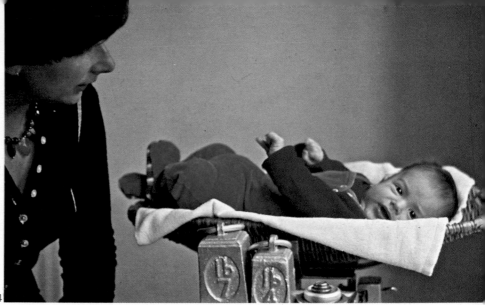

mother should change sides. Sucking at an empty breast can frustrate a baby and cause sore cracked nipples.

☐ **Excess Milk** Some mothers, who have an excess of milk, may find it helpful to express a little of the milk before putting their baby to the breast. This will ensure that a baby does not splutter and choke on a too rapid flow of milk. Remember that in order to maintain a good supply of milk, the breasts should be completely emptied at the end of each feed. If you feel that there is still some milk left after your baby has sucked for ten minutes on each side and appears contented, you should express the remaining milk by hand as shown by the midwife. The two great stimuli to the continuation of a good milk supply are complete emptying of the breasts at each feed, and the baby's sucking.

☐ **Complementary Feeding** An occasional bottle-feed given to a breastfed baby—either when you especially want to be out when one of his feeds is due, or when you find that your milk supply is low—will do no harm at all. Keep at least one packet of baby-milk in the store cupboard, in case this situation arises.

☐ **Changing Breasts** Occasionally, mothers may find it difficult to persuade their babies that it is time to change to the other breast. By sliding a little finger gently in between the corner of his mouth and the nipple, the air-tight seal around his lips can be broken.

IS THE MILK SUITABLE?

If a baby is gaining weight slowly but steadily, is contented and developing well, you can be sure that however thin and watery-looking your milk is, it is adequate. The quantity may be small, but the quality is always right for each individual baby. It is obviously more difficult with breast-feeding than with bottle-feeding, to determine the amount of milk that the baby takes at each feed. One way of establishing this is to test-weigh the baby before and after each feed.

☐ **Test-weighing** Test-weighing is a useful procedure if there is any doubt or anxiety about how much milk the baby is receiving. The principle of test-weighing is very simple—all that is required is an accurate set of scales (which you do not need to buy—they can be hired). The baby is weighed immediately before a feed and then immediately after he has finished the feed. If he soils or wets his nappy during the feed, this must not be changed until after he has been weighed for the second time. The difference between the before and after weights will show the amount of breast milk he has taken.

SUPPLEMENTS

From the time they are one month old, breastfed babies need vitamin A, D and C supplements. Dried milk supplements may also be necessary for one reason or another if the mother's milk supply is slightly insufficient—perhaps after a bout of influenza, for example.

CARE OF THE BREASTS

A little lanolin cream applied to the nipple area will help to keep this soft and supple. A well-fitting bra should be worn both night and day during the whole period of breastfeeding.

GENERAL HEALTH

Breastfeeding does not necessitate drinking vast quantities of fluid, neither does it preclude a mother from eating her favourite foods, although some foods, such as onions or prunes, for example, may make a baby restless. Alcohol in moderation does no harm. The doctor will ensure that the mother is not given any drugs which may be absorbed into the breast milk and thus affect the baby. The one thing that a mother

3,4 Test-weighing is a useful procedure, telling both mothers and nurses exactly how much milk the baby is receiving at each feed. Weigh before and after a feed, remembering not to change the nappy until the second weighing.

must ensure is plenty of rest—and this means rest from mental and emotional anxieties as well.

BREASTFEEDING PROBLEMS

The most common time for breastfeeding problems is immediately after the return home from hospital. This is when the world—in the shape of cooking, housework and, perhaps, other children—rushes in. Your rest periods are eroded, and you feel tired and tense when the time comes to feed the baby. It needs a determined effort to ignore all the interruptions and relax at feed-times, but this is really essential.

☐ **Engorgement of Breasts** Engorged breasts are enlarged, swollen and hot and tender to the touch. This condition most commonly occurs in the first day or two after the milk comes in. Frequent sucking, or expressing the milk, will do much to relieve this. If the engorgement becomes severe, the doctor will prescribe small amounts of oestrogen to reduce the milk supply a little.

☐ **Cracked Nipples** The cause of this painful condition can be an over-eager baby who chews on the nipple instead of grasping it properly around the areola. The treatment for a cracked nipple is rest for that breast for at least twenty-four hours, plus expressing the milk in order to ensure a continuation of the supply. If the condition is allowed to worsen it may cause a breast abscess.

☐ **Breast Abscess** This occurs when an infection creeps in through a cracked nipple and affects a section of the breast. The breast then becomes swollen, red and painful. Urgent medical attention is necessary. With rapid antibiotic treatment the condition can be resolved, without the necessity for discontinuing breastfeeding.

☐ **Inverted Nipples** Inverted nipples can cause difficulties at the onset of breastfeeding as the baby is unable to grasp the nipple firmly. Treatment during pregnancy by easing the nipple out with the fingers and by wearing plastic breast shields under a bra will correct all but the most inverted nipples.

MENSTRUATION

The time of return of monthly periods is very variable after the birth of a baby, and can be anything from three weeks to six months. Breastfeeding usually inhibits the menstrual flow, but successful breastfeeding can, and does, take place with normal menstruation. Do remember that 'menstruation' means 'ovulation', and that breastfeeding is no bar to pregnancy. Adequate pregnancy precautions are, therefore, necessary. If you want to use a contraceptive pill whilst breastfeeding, you will need medical advice as to which one is the most suitable.

Bottle-feeding

Perhaps one of the biggest disappointments that can afflict a new mother is if she finds that she is unable to breastfeed her baby. She may have been looking forward to this all through pregnancy and, if, for one reason or another, it proves impossible, the let-down can cause unhappiness and feelings of guilt and frustration.

If this happens to you, console yourself with the thought that tests have shown that bottle-fed babies develop as quickly as breastfed babies. If in addition you hold your baby lovingly close as you give him his bottle this will be a good substitute for breastfeeding.

Much work has been done, particularly over the last few years, to ensure that artificial milks are as like human milk as possible. The protein content has been reduced, and the carbohydrate, vitamin and mineral content made as similar as possible.

DRIED MILK

There are several well-known brands of dried milk, and your midwife, doctor or health visitor will be able to help you to decide which one to choose. Basically, all dried milks are cow's milk which has been passed through various processes to alter its constituents and to add the correct quantities of vitamins and minerals. The process of drying the milk has the benefit of ensuring that milk can be bought in quantity, and that it will store for several months.

The majority of babies are started straight away on to full-cream milk, but half-cream milks are available for very small babies who have difficulty in digesting fats. Tinned evaporated milk was given to babies in the past, but this is now considered unwise as it is not possible to adjust the proportions of the constituent parts.

Ordinary cow's milk straight from the bottle can be used to feed babies, but storage problems make this an unpopular choice.

Whatever type of milk you decide on, do keep to it. Chopping and changing the brand of milk is never necessary. If your baby does not seem to be thriving or settling well after his feeds, you will need expert help to find the cause.

TYPE OF BOTTLE

After deciding which milk your baby should have, you will then need to buy bottles, teats and sterilizing equipment.

Nowadays all baby bottles are upright ones, made of both plastic and glass. They come in two sizes, the 200 ml (8 fl oz) size and the 100 ml (4 fl oz) size. The latter size is useful for small babies, or for giving extra drinks of water or unsweetened fruit juice.

Most bottles have a wide neck for easy cleaning, and a teat that can be inverted inside the bottle and covered with a cap for storage and travelling.

TYPES OF TEAT

When choosing a bottle, be sure that you buy a teat that will fit it! The most important thing to check is the size of the hole, as this will determine the rate at which the milk flows out. The milk should fall out in a succession of rapid drops— approximately one drop per second. If you feel that the hole in the teat you have bought is too small, you can easily enlarge this with a red-hot needle. Before each feed, when you check the temperature of the milk on the back of your hand, check that the rate of flow is still satisfactory. Teat holes do enlarge with use.

CLEANING AND STERILIZATION OF BOTTLES AND TEATS

Cleaning and sterilizing is a vital part of the bottle-feeding routine. Without very great attention to this aspect of care, a baby risks contracting gastro-enteritis—a dangerous, and sometimes fatal, condition in young babies.

There are two main ways of sterilizing a baby's feeding utensils—the boiling method and the chemical method. Before you embark on either, there are three important tasks to be done.

☐ **Preliminary steps**

1: Wash your hands thoroughly. Hands can carry the germs which cause disease.

2: Clean the bottle, first with cold water to remove as much milk as possible. Then wash with hot soapy water, using a special bottle-brush to get into all the awkward places. Finally rinse thoroughly with cold water.

3: The teat needs special care to remove all the deposit of milk. Rubbing with salt, both inside and out, ensures maximum cleanliness. Rinse out afterwards with cold water.

☐ **Boiling Method** Remember that it is not enough to boil bottles and teats once a day. They must be boiled after every feed. After cleaning thoroughly, put both bottle and teat in a clean pan, cover completely with cold water and bring to the boil. Boil rapidly for at least ten minutes.

There are some disadvantages to the boiling method. Teats spoil rapidly and, therefore, need to be replaced frequently. Also, glass bottles do occasionally break. For these reasons many mothers prefer the chemical method.

☐ **The Chemical Method** After thorough cleaning, place the bottles and teats in a container of chemical solution. The solution should be made up according to the manufacturer's instructions. The feeding utensils must be left fully submerged in this solution for at least three hours, so it will be necessary for you to have other bottles and teats available for use. Before the next feed re-

Keep all your equipment for sterilizing and making up feeds together in a special part of the kitchen. Buy two or three bottles and teats so that you always have a sterilized set ready for the next feed. Remember to wash your hands thoroughly before preparing a feed. Keep a special knife handy to level off the scoop of dried milk powder. A heaped scoop will make the milk too concentrated which can upset your baby's delicate digestive system.

1 Always wash your
hands thoroughly
before cleaning the bottles
and teats after a feed.

2 Wide-necked bottles
are easier to clean but
do remember to clean the
awkward places
thoroughly with a bottle
brush.

3 Rinse the bottle under
plenty of cold, running
water to ensure that all
traces of soap are gone.

4 Milk deposits must be
removed from the
teat. Rub salt on both
inside and out and then
rinse.

5 Finally, leave every-
thing clean and tidy.
When it is time for the
next feed it will all be
ready for you.

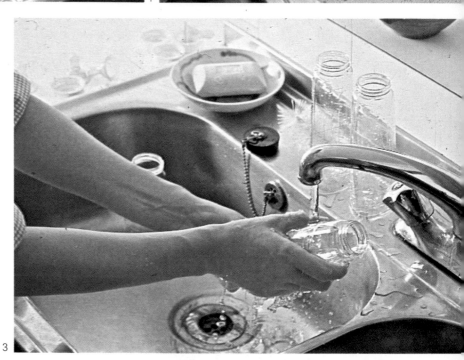

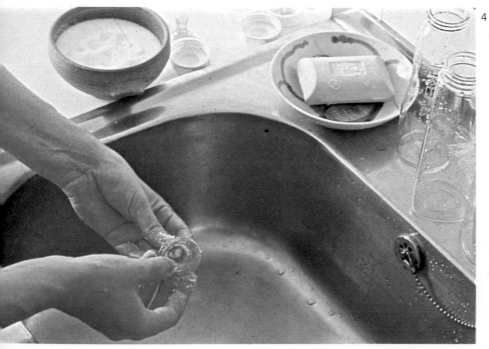

move the bottle, allow it to drain for a short while and then put the feed straight into the bottle.

PREPARING FEEDS

The vast majority of mothers who decide to bottle-feed their babies choose one of the proprietary dried milks. The instructions on how to make up these feeds are given on the packet, and should be followed to the letter. There are, however, a few guide-lines to remember when making up a feed.

1: Cleanliness. Hands must be thoroughly washed before being brought into contact with bottle, teat, scoop or milk powder.

2: Adding the Water. The water you add to the dried milk powder must be boiled and then cooled to just above blood-heat. Too hot water will cause the fat content of the milk to separate. If it is too cold, the powder will be difficult to dissolve. Add the water gradually, stirring all the time.

3: Amount of Powder in the Scoop. The correct amount is vitally important, so do not be tempted to heap the powder on the scoop, to press it down hard. Similarly, never add extra scoopfuls of powder.

4: Correct Amount of Water. Be sure to add the correct amount of water. When you have done this, hold the bottle upside down to make sure that the teat is not blocked. The milk should drip out at the rate of approximately one drop per second.

TEMPERATURE OF FEED

Most feeds are given to babies at about blood heat, but they will come to no harm if their milk is given cold. Always judge the temperature of a warm feed on the back of your hand before giving it to him. Never keep milk warm for a long period of time—warm milk is an ideal breeding ground for germs. For this reason, bottle-warmers are not recommended.

Many mothers prefer to make up a day's feeds in bulk, and this is perfectly all right if you have a large enough refrigerator for storage.

AMOUNT OF MILK NEEDED

Remember that over a twenty-four hour period the average baby needs 70 ml (2½ fl oz) of milk for every pound he weighs. This is given in divided amounts approximately every four hours. For example, a 4.5 kg (ten-pound) baby, being fed five times a day, will need 710 ml (25 fl oz) in twenty-four hours. Each feed will, therefore, consist of 142 ml (5 fl oz).

A baby may, however, vary in his needs from day to day. Always make up a little more milk mixture than you think he will need, and always

throw away any that is left over from each feed.

The actual feed should last for no longer than half-an-hour. If your baby has not taken the full amount by this time, put him down to sleep, but be prepared to feed him a little earlier next time. (If you are worried about this aspect of caring for your baby, ask your health visitor for advice.)

Your best guide to the adequacy of your baby's intake is a steady weight gain over the weeks.

☐ **Possetting** All babies return a little of their milk after a feed. If you are worried about the amount he is possetting, ask your health visitor's advice.

WATER

Remember that babies get thirsty, particularly in hot weather, and may need a drink of cooled boiled water between feeds. Alternatively, you can give him his vitamin C—in the form of unsweetened orange juice or rose hip syrup.

THE TECHNIQUE OF BOTTLE-FEEDING

Bottle-feeding your baby can be made as satisfying as breastfeeding. Allow feed-times to be relaxed and peaceful—and use them as an opportunity to get to know each other.

Make yourself comfortable in the same way that you would if you were breastfeeding. Likewise, cuddle your baby close, as you would if breastfeeding. As with breastfeeding, the baby must get a firm grip on the teat, although the actual mechanism of obtaining the milk is slightly different. More sucking is needed with a bottle, and less gripping with the jaws to force the milk out.

First test the temperature of the milk, then tip the bottle so that your baby will not be sucking air, and gently touch the side of his mouth with the teat. You will find that he will 'root' for the teat as he would for the nipple.

During a bottle-feed it is necessary, at intervals, to gently move the teat away from the side of his mouth to break the vacuum. You will be able to see when this needs to be done by the flattening of the teat, the level of the milk remaining static—and, of course, a frustrated baby!

TIMING OF FEEDS

Newborn babies are given their first bottle-feed any time between four and eight hours after birth. Only a little milk will be taken at first. This is a direct parallel with breastfed babies who are only able to take the small amount of colostrum that is secreted during the first two days after birth. As the baby becomes hungry, you and he, together, will evolve a routine that suits you both. Most babies settle quite happily into a routine of approximately four-hourly feeds.

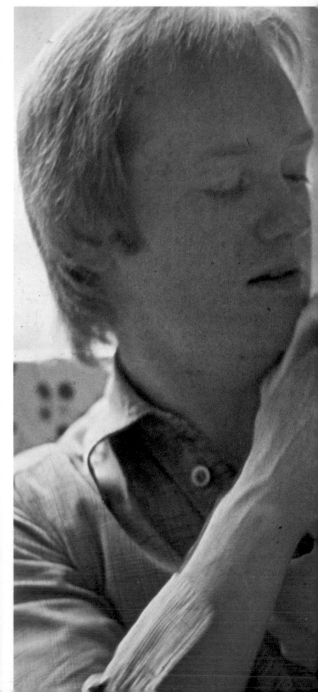

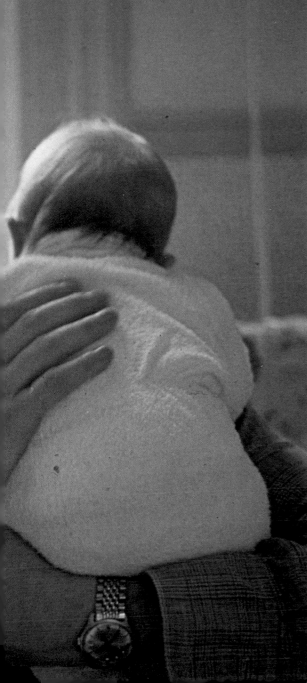

Let father take his share in caring for his child. He, too, may find feeding a time of rest and tranquility, as well as a convenient time for getting to know his new son or daughter better. Eye-to-eye contact forms a special part in building the relationship.

At first, your husband may need a little guidance in the technique of breaking the vacuum inside the bottle, which can arise with a hungry baby sucking hard on the teat and flattening it.

After the feed is finished, the winding process — only necessary for a couple of minutes — is a time for a quiet social 'chat' with all members of the family.

1 Older brothers and sisters can also take a share in caring for the new baby. Summer time on the lawn can make a drink of fruit juice for the baby into a lesson for his brother.

than this he will tire anyway. Put him down to sleep, but be prepared to feed him earlier the next time round.

With bottle-fed babies you can at least be sure of how much he has taken at each feed. By adding up the amounts, you can also arrive at the total for twenty-four hours.

WAYWARD FEEDERS!

Some babies gulp the first few mouthfuls down, then lose interest and start playing with the teat or nipple. These babies need firm but gentle handling to get them to concentrate on their feeds. A little time can be allowed for play but, after a few minutes, remind them of the business in hand. Giving the feed a little earlier, before a lively baby is awake and crying, can often settle him into a more satisfactory routine.

WIND

In the modern world, we have become obsessed with the necessity of bringing up a baby's wind, and no baby is allowed to sleep until he has made the requisite noise! All babies—whether bottle- or breastfed—swallow air as they feed. If your baby is sucking happily at the bottle, there is absolutely no need to distract him by breaking off to 'wind' him. This will only irritate him, make him cry, and swallow yet more air. If he is willing to suck his feed all in one go, by all means let him.

At the end of the feed, cuddle him close for a while—over your shoulder or propped in the crook of your arm. He may then reward you with a sleepy 'burp'. If this does not happen don't worry, there is probably no air that needs to come up. Prolonged winding will only make him miserable and irritable.

WHAT TO AVOID WHEN BOTTLE-FEEDING

Never leave your baby alone with his bottle. This is a cruel deprivation which can also prove to be physically dangerous. A baby cannot manage to hold the bottle in a way that allows him to suck, and he will, therefore, get very frustrated. More importantly, he can choke on the milk. Alternatively, if he regurgitates some of the milk, this can pass into his lungs and suffocate him. Milk can also readily pass into his middle ear, via the small tubes from the back of his throat, and set up an inflammation. For a baby feeding is not just the physical fact of sucking milk, but a time for love, comfort and security.

One further hazard that must be avoided when bottle-feeding is the giving of more milk from a bottle that has been left standing for any length of time. Germs breed rapidly in warm milk. If a baby does not finish all his feed, it should be thrown away.

Initially, perhaps, and especially if your baby is small at birth, he may need to be fed every three hours. Within reason, be guided by his appetite.

VITAMIN SUPPLEMENTS

Bottle-fed babies need supplements of vitamins A, D and C, as insufficient amounts of these vitamins are present in cow's milk. The easiest way to give these vital substances is to add concentrated drops daily to one of your baby's feeds.

Vitamin C can be given as rose-hip syrup, orange or blackcurrant juice, and is usually given, diluted with water, as a drink once a day between feeds. Vitamin C cannot be stored in the body, and so must be topped up daily.

Do not be tempted to give extra vitamin A and D, as these substances must not be given in excess. Many dried milks are fortified with vitamin A and D, so it is wise to check with your health visitor before giving concentrated drops.

THE SLOW FEEDER

Some babies do seem more difficult than others to wake and get started on their feed. This is particularly true of small and premature babies who, for obvious reasons, need their food regularly and in full measure.

If your baby is very slow, try to limit the time you spend feeding him to around half to three-quarters of an hour. If your baby sucks for longer

Weaning

Weaning is the rather old-fashioned term for the start of mixed-feeding. In our great-grandmother's days, babies had to be gradually weaned from the breast straight on to adult food. Nowadays, with an enormous range of milk products and strained and mashed baby foods available, this process is certainly easier. Weaning can be looked at from the viewpoint of a gradual development change in the baby as he grows up.

STARTING MIXED-FEEDING

The timing of the introduction of new tastes varies from baby to baby. There is no set rule. The best approach is to go along with your baby's tastes and to note when he is ready for a change from his milk-only diet.

☐ **Breastfed Babies** If breastfeeding is going well, breast milk (with the addition of vitamins C and D) is the only food that your baby will need until he is six months old. After this age, breast milk does not contain sufficient iron for his needs, so you will need to start giving him tastes of new foods.

☐ **Bottle-fed Babies** The general rule of milk being sufficient until six months old is as true of bottle-fed babies as it is of breastfed babies. In practice, most babies are started on mixed-feeding at around three to four months old. Mixed-feeding before the age of six weeks (except in very special cases) is unwise, as this can cause strain on baby's immature kidneys.

HOW TO START

If your baby is three months old and has been showing signs of restlessness long before his feed is due, the time has come to start mixed-feeding. Do not be tempted to thicken a bottle-feed with cereal; it is more satisfactory to start spoon-feeding straight away.

Begin by experimenting with one new food at one of his feeds—the 10 a.m. is the most suitable. It is unimportant which new taste you offer him first. It can be a cereal or a strained broth. Most mothers, however, find a cereal feed the most convenient to start with as it is easier to make up in tiny amounts. A teaspoonful made up into a runny solid with some of the milk mixture (or boiled and then cooled cow's milk if you are breastfeeding) is quite sufficient. Offer this to your baby before he has his bottle. Do not be surprised if he pushes it away with his tongue at first. Taking food from a spoon is quite a different experience and involves a different technique from sucking at a bottle or the breast.

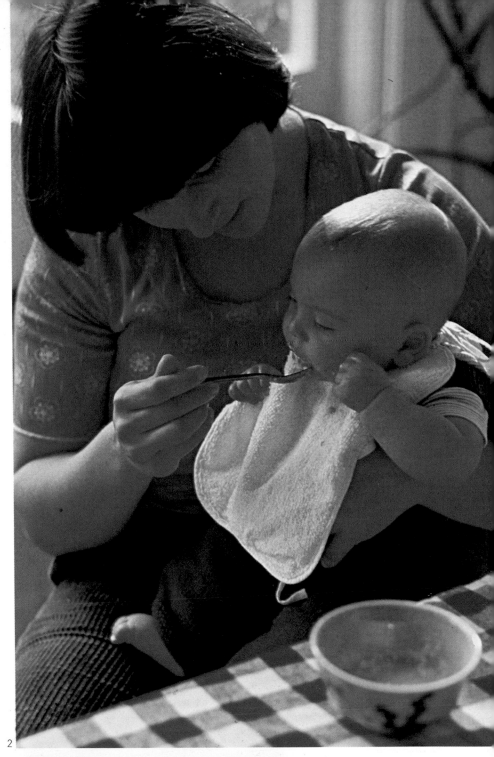

2

3

2 Mixed feeding is a totally new experience, and one which needs a good deal of concentration on the baby's part. Hold him comfortably upright and only give him a little off the spoon at first.

3 A sieve of some kind is a valuable asset to any kitchen where baby foods are prepared. He can then share in the ordinary family foods.

Feeding yourself is a pleasant, although messy, pastime. Before frustration at not being able to get sufficient food quickly enough into his mouth sets in, be ready to help him with that extra spoonful. Finger feeding is a good start. All babies should be allowed to do this for themselves in the early stages of self-feeding and the spoon should be introduced gradually.
Drinking from a mug is also something which has to be learned.

If he takes the first taste happily, introduce other tastes gradually. By introducing the foods one by one, you can find out with certainty which tastes agree or, perhaps, disagree with him. A good starter for the protein foods is either a home-made or powdered broth. As your baby gets more competent with spoon-feeding, introduce him to a wider range of foods. Gradually, over the weeks, he will work his way towards a three-meal-a-day timetable with just the addition of an early morning and bedtime drink.

☐ **Starting Cow's Milk** By the time a bottle-fed baby is six months old, he is ready to change from the proprietary dried milks to ordinary bottled cow's milk. Boil this for him until he is one year old, taking care to cool it sufficiently before offering it to your baby.

☐ **Types of Food** Day by day, the variety of your baby's diet increases. Ensure, however, that he does not get a liking for sweet foods. Sweet, starchy foods prepare the ground for overweight —both now and in later life. Educate his developing taste-buds with savoury tastes of cheese, fish, meat and vegetables with fresh fruit to follow.

He can now eat much of the family food, provided it is suitably strained or mashed. Remember that highly spiced or fried foods are unsuitable for a young baby but he will enjoy most other new tastes.

☐ **Finger-feeding** From the age of six months on, your baby will be becoming increasingly keen to feed himself—and the results will be rather messy. Self-feeding is best started by allowing him to hold a rusk, toast-crust or section of peeled apple. As there is a risk of his swallowing a large piece and choking, always stay near when he is feeding himself.

☐ **Spoon-feeding** Babies love to spoon-feed themselves. Sit by your baby whilst he does this and have another spoon at the ready to pop in the extra mouthful of food when his own efforts become too wild!

HYGIENE IN PREPARING FOODS

At the mixed-feeding stages, it is not now necessary to sterilize all the utensils you use to prepare your baby's food, but remember that good hygiene is always vital. Hands must always be washed before preparing food for any member of the family, and food must not be left uncovered, particularly in hot weather. Food that is reheated is a potential source of danger, as bacteria can multiply under these circumstances. If re-serving food, cook it again very thoroughly. It is worth remembering that babies, unlike adults, often prefer cold food and this will do them no harm.

THE MAIN FOOD GROUPS

The food we need can be divided into six main headings. For health, growth and development, a baby should have one or more daily portions of each.

☐ **Protein** Protein foods are the body-builders. They are complex chemical compounds which contain nitrogen and phosphorus in addition to carbon, hydrogen and oxygen.

Meat, fish, cheese and eggs are all excellent sources of first-class protein. Other foods, such as peas, lentils, beans and wheat also contain protein, but of not such a high standard as the first-class protein foods. This is why they are termed second-class protein foods.

☐ **Carbohydrates** Carbohydrates are energy producers. They are built up from carbon, hydrogen and oxygen, and are found, in abundance, in bread, sugar, potatoes, jam and biscuits—to mention just a few.

Growing children need carbohydrates every day to replenish their energy, but take care they do not eat carbohydrate foods to the exclusion of other foods. Taken in excess carbohydrates will put on unwanted pounds and inches.

☐ **Fats** Fats are the warming foods. These can be given as animal fats, such as those found in fat meat, butter and cream, or as vegetable fats, such as those found in margarine, olive and nut oils. They are also made up of carbon, hydrogen and oxygen, but in a different chemical combination from carbohydrates. Small quantities are needed daily by growing children.

☐ **Vitamins** Vitamins are needed in very small quantities every day to ensure normal growth and health. Each vitamin is found in one or other of the three main food groups, and also in fresh fruit or vegetables. The main vitamins are vitamins A, B, C and D.

Vitamin A, which is necessary for healthy bone development in children, is found in milk, butter, egg-yolk and cod liver oil.

Vitamin B group (several substances) is found in peas, beans, wholemeal bread, raw carrots and

1 The first class protein foods—meat, fish, eggs, cheese and milk—are the body builders and repairers. At least two helpings a day of a protein food is vital for health.

2 Fats are the warming food foods which also supply other substances vital to growth and health. Milk, butter and fat meat are all needed in small quantities daily for health.

3 The various vitamins and minerals are found in a wide variety of foods. A good mixed diet will automatically supply adequate quantities of the substances.

cabbage. It is important for the healthy growth of nervous tissue, and for red blood cell formation. *Vitamin C* is the vitamin that prevents scurvy. It is found in all citrus fruits and tomatoes. As it cannot be stored in the body, it must be taken every day.

Vitamin D is unusual inasmuch as it can be produced by the action of sunlight on the skin, as well as being found in eggs, milk, butter and cod liver oil.

All these vitamins (with the exception of the B group of vitamins) can be given to your baby or toddler in the form of drops or bottled fruit-juices. As your toddler eats more and more of a mixed diet, he should obtain sufficient vitamins from this.

☐ **Minerals** Certain minerals—iron, calcium, sodium and potassium—are also necessary for health and growth, but a normal mixed diet will contain adequate amounts.

☐ **Roughage and Water** Roughage in the form of green vegetables, salads, wholemeal bread and fruit is also necessary for healthy bowel functioning. Water, too, whether it is in the form of fruit juice, milk or straight out of the tap, must be taken in adequate quantities every day.

These, then, are the foods that everyone needs daily—a daunting list, perhaps, when viewed on paper! But just think how naturally most meals fit the pattern.

From a baby's point of view the tastes of carbohydrate and protein in cereal and broth, together

with vitamin drops of A, B and D and drinks of vitamin C will come first. Then, as he gains the skills of chewing, more variety and roughage can be added in the form of bread, rusks, pieces of apple and carrot as well as milk to top up his needs. Tastes of your own home-cooked food will follow, until by the time he is two years old, he will be eating almost the same diet as you are, with the exception of highly spiced or very fatty foods. Drinks, too, will have progressed from milk only to a variety of fruit juices and, perhaps, even weak tea. All these steps will follow logically and simply.

MENU FOR A SIX MONTH-OLD BABY

When your baby wakes, probably around six-thirty, you can give him a drink of orange juice or rose-hip syrup. He will still need a daily intake of about 120 to 150 mls (6 to 8 fl oz) of milk to drink. For breakfast: cereal and milk feed. For lunch: choose from meat, fish, cheese or egg, plus vegetables, plus milk feed. A pudding is not recommended since a baby may develop a preference for this and refuse meat, vegetables or milk. If puddings are given, they should consist of plain yoghurt, mashed banana or stewed or puréed apple. Raisins, sultanas, dates and currants should not be given until the baby is eighteen to twenty-four months old. Ideally fruit should be served at breakfast or teatime rather than as a second course for lunch, when meat, vegetables and milk are sufficient. At tea-time, he will need either a rusk or bread and butter and fruit juice. At six p.m., fruit purée and milk feed. At ten p.m. he may require a milk feed.

A baby has a good idea of how much food he needs. Provided he is not given too much cereal or cakes or sweet things, he should not be overweight with this kind of diet.

4

5

6

4 Roughage in the form of green vegetables, salads, fruit and wholemeal bread is important for healthy bowel function.

5 Carbohydrates are the energy producing foods and are found in bread, potatoes and sugars of all kinds. They should not be taken in amounts in excess of the energy expended.

6 Blenders and other such aids have pride of place in preparing meals for a six month old baby
A variety of foods can be easily prepared to a texture especially geared to his requirements.

☐ **Vegetables** Begin with cauliflower, parsnips, carrot and Jerusalem artichokes. Follow these with French beans, lentils, and peas. Finally, introduce spinach, cabbage, onions, sprouts, swede, turnip and potato. (Never give potatoes which show any trace of green to babies). Boil all the vegetables in the minimum amount of unsalted water and, for maximum nutrition, purée with the vegetable water. (A baby's kidneys cannot dispose of salt in the body until he is about eight months old).

☐ **Eggs** At four to five months old, give yolk of egg only. Soft boiled eggs can be mixed into cereal or vegetables. Next give scrambled egg and egg custards.

☐ **Cheese** Cottage cheese is excellent because it has a low fat content. This can be followed by Cheddar, Edam and other hard cheeses melted into hot vegetables and purées.

☐ **Fish** Only white fish should be offered at first. Cook in a little milk, or place a small piece on a plate and steam over boiling water or vegetables. Cover with a lid and cook for ten to fifteen minutes until cooked.

☐ **Yoghurt** Bought fruit yoghurts usually contain a lot of sugar, and yoghurt containing fruit seeds must be strained. It is far better to give plain yoghurt.

☐ **Meat** Fresh chicken, rabbit, beef, lamb, sweetbread, kidney and liver are all suitable if combined with equal quantities of vegetables. (Do not cook frozen food such as poultry for a baby. Unless well-thawed and really thoroughly cooked, it can cause gastro-enteritis).

☐ **Cereals** Puréed cereals are a valuable part of a baby's diet, but less than a third of a baby's solid intake should be of cereal. Begin by serving rice, then slowly introduce other cereals such as wholewheat, semolina, maize, rye and oats.

☐ **Fruits** Ripe mashed bananas are a good first choice; so are apples stewed in a little water. If tinned fruits are used, the sweet syrup should be strained off before they are puréed. Raisins, sultanas and dates should not be given until a baby is about eighteen to twenty-four months old.

HOLIDAY FOODS

A toddler is rather conservative where food is concerned. For this reason it is wise to ensure that some of his familiar foods will be available on holiday. The slightly older child of two or three years will probably enjoy new tastes and textures as much as you will. Give these in moderation, and avoid food that is too greasy or too highly seasoned. Children are adaptable little people. By allowing them to sample all kinds of foods early on, you will be laying the foundation for a healthy and unprejudiced palate in later life

Teething

Cutting teeth is a normal physiological function, which in large numbers of babies causes no problem whatsoever. Teething is, however, often blamed for a variety of symptoms which are totally unrelated. It never, for example, causes a fever, diarrhoea or a continually miserable, crying baby.

So, do not dread the arrival of your baby's teeth—regard teething as one more important developmental step.

NUMBER OF TEETH

Everyone has two sets of teeth throughout their lives. The baby, or milk, teeth are twenty in number and are already present in the gums at birth. The permanent teeth are thirty-two in number and develop deep in the gums throughout the first years of life.

ONSET OF TEETHING AND THEIR ORDER OF APPEARANCE

Babies vary a good deal as to when they start the teething process. Some babies are born with an erupted tooth already present. At the other end of the scale, some babies are toothless at one year old.

Teething, as so many other characteristics, is determined by the genes, and whatever you do, or do not do, cannot make any difference to the early or late teething pattern that your baby has inherited. As with most physical things, there is an average time for the eruption of the teeth.

The pattern of the order of appearance of the teeth can vary. Sometimes the upper side incisors erupt before the lower incisors. This is of no lasting importance—merely a variation of the normal.

The most usual order for the teeth to appear is for the two lower central incisors to arrive first, and to be closely followed a month or two later by the two upper central incisors. Then, by one year old, the two lateral incisors in each jaw are present, so that by his first birthday a baby can usually show you eight teeth.

By eighteen months a baby has cut four of his molar (or chewing) teeth. The bigger canine teeth, in between the incisor (or cutting teeth), appear around the eighteen-month to twenty-month-old mark. A brief pause of a few months is followed by the eruption of the four back molars to complete the set of twenty milk teeth.

SIGNS ASSOCIATED WITH TEETHING

Not all babies show that their teeth are erupting. The first hint you may have is when a spoon

1

1 Tooth brushing can be fun when you join in and show him how. An up-and-down motion will dislodge the tiniest crumbs from between the teeth which, if left, will contribute towards decay.

2 Toddlers show off their new teeth with pride. Help to keep them in this pristine state by healthy eating and regular brushing.

3 Diagram to show the usual order in which the teeth appear.

chinks on a brand-new tooth. Other babies do, however, exhibit certain signs that their teeth are on the way.

☐ **Dribbling** All babies dribble—but some do so more than others. This is a phase of development which normally ceases when the baby is around one year old. There is often an increase in the amount of dribble when the eruption of a tooth is imminent.

☐ **Fist-Chewing** All babies chew their fists, and take any objects they are given straight to their mouths. They do this because it gives them pleasure. Some babies may seem to chew more during teething.

☐ **Pink Cheeks** Occasionally one sees a baby with one bright red cheek. Often this flushing is associated with a tooth erupting.

HELP FOR TEETHING BABIES

Although most babies cut their teeth with a minimum of fuss, a few babies do seem to need extra comfort at this time. Crisp crusts and rusks to chew on at mealtimes can satisfy a baby's need to have something in his mouth. Between meals, a hard clean teething ring will help.

☐ **Analgesics** Occasionally, when they are teething, babies can be fretful at bedtime. If he is still miserable after you have done your best to comfort him with a drink and a cuddle, give him the prescribed dose of junior aspirin, or one of the paracetamol mixtures. Beware that he does not get into the habit of crying just to get you upstairs for an extra cuddle.

NOT DUE TO TEETHING

There are certain conditions which are traditionally ascribed to the eruption of a tooth, but which, in fact, are not due to this cause and should never be ignored.

Convulsions are never due to teething. If your baby has a convulsion, always contact your doctor. The commonest cause for convulsions in this age group is a high fever which, in turn, is due to an infection somewhere in the body. It will need the skilled attention of your doctor to find and treat the cause.

Bronchitis is never caused by teething, although, of course, a baby may suffer from bronchitis whilst his teeth are erupting. Again, a doctor must be consulted.

Lack of appetite does not occur with teething either. You may notice, however, that your baby is a little wary of the spoon during the days immediately prior to the eruption of a tooth. The hardness of the spoon may be too much for a tender gum. He will not, however, refuse fluids at this time, so give him extra drinks and soft foods.

If his lack of appetite extends to fluids as well as food, contact your doctor. This symptom may be the first sign of a throat, ear or urinary infection.

Remember that the teething process takes many months and that it is, therefore, possible that your baby will suffer from one form of illness or another during this time which has nothing to do with the eruption of his teeth.

TOOTH-BRUSHING

As soon as a child has ten-to-twelve teeth, buy him a small toothbrush and start to teach him how to brush correctly with up-and-down movements, gently massaging the gums. Help him with tooth-brushing after each main meal and make it part of the regular bedtime routine. This is a good habit to develop when young.

DIET

Avoid sticky, sweet foods which will damage the teeth and cause obesity. It is particularly harmful for teeth to be subjected to a prolonged concentration of sweet substances. Dinky feeders filled with sweet fluid, for example, cause decay in a very short time. They will also establish a permanent liking for sugary, tooth-damaging foods.

Encouraging a child to chew on hard foods will ensure that his gums and teeth are kept in tip-top condition and able to perform the function for which they are made.

First teeth are important. The removal of even one or two for reasons of decay, will alter the shape of your toddler's mouth and, perhaps, interfere with the correct eruption of his second set of teeth.

Bathing and Nappies
Bathing Routines

When a baby is tiny, he can, provided you are careful with taps, be bathed in a washing-up bowl in the kitchen sink; a bidet is another possibility or a hand washbasin. What matters, is that the room is warm. The temperature should be about 18° to 21°C (65° to 70°F).

A room thermometer will tell you the temperature. It is also a good idea to have one in the baby's bedroom. What seems warm to an adult can be cold to a baby, and temperature can drop rapidly in the evening.

Observation of your baby will tell you whether he is happier being bathed before or after a feed. Bathed before a feed, he may be hungry and bathed too soon after a feed he may feel sick or resent being kept awake. Often, a bath can soothe a restless baby.

Before beginning the bath-time routine, sit down for a few minutes rest, so that you feel calm and confident. Collect everything you need—soap or specially prepared bath liquid, cotton-wool,

warm towels, hooded nappy pins, creams, nappy and clean clothes. Put cold water into the bath, then add hot water. Always make this a practice in order to avoid the possibility of scalding the baby or child. When the water is ready, it will need to be about 29.4°C (85°F). Test it with your elbow rather than your hand. It should feel comfortably warm.

The following method of bathing a baby is good because it introduces a baby to water slowly, and you will not have to cope with the difficulties of an extremely slippery crying infant in the water for too long a period!

Undress the baby and lay him wrapped in a warm towel on your lap. Wash his face with water only for the first few weeks, using cotton-wool or a muslin square. Wipe from the middle of his face outwards towards the sides. Use a clean piece of damp cotton-wool for each eye. Blot dry with cotton-wool.

Then wash the scalp; use soap or shampoo

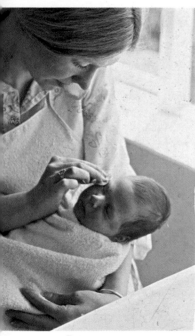

1 Undress the baby and wrap him in a warm towel on your lap. Wash his face with water, using cotton-wool or a muslin square, wiping from the middle of his face outwards.

2 Then wash the scalp, supporting his back and head by placing your arm under his body and your hand at the nape of his neck. Next, unwrap the towel and wet and soap his body.

3 When you have washed from top to toe, lift—supporting his head on your wrist and arm—and place him in the water.

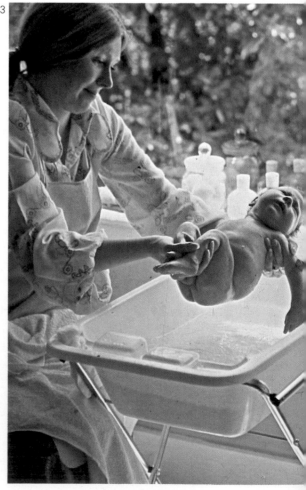

once or twice a week only. Hold the baby over the bath, with your hand at the nape of his neck, supporting his head with your arm under his body. Wet his scalp, including the fontanelle, with your free hand. Thoroughly rinse away all traces of soap or shampoo, and dry his head gently with a soft towel.

Next wet and soap his body, neck, arms and legs. Begin with his neck, running a soapy finger in all the creases. Wash under the arms by gently flexing his elbow and moving it backwards, then the groin and thigh. Turn him over and wash his back and bottom. Lift the baby, supporting his head on your wrist and arm, and place him in the water.

Continue to support his head on your wrist and hold him securely under the armpit with your hand. Rinse off the water with your free hand. Lift him out of the water on to a towel on your lap and blot him thoroughly dry. Make sure that all his creases are well-dried, using a second towel if necessary.

Dress him in a vest to keep him warm while you put on a new nappy. Talcum powder is not essential. It can, in fact, cause dry skin and may become caked in skin creases and cause irritation. The dry powder may also irritate his nose and throat. Zinc and castor oil cream can be applied

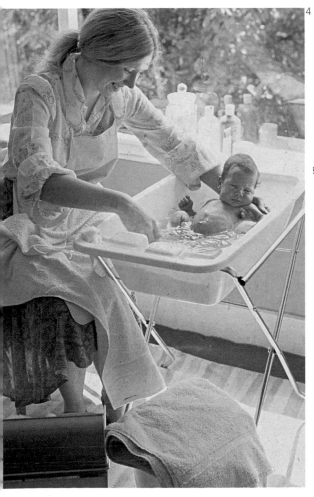

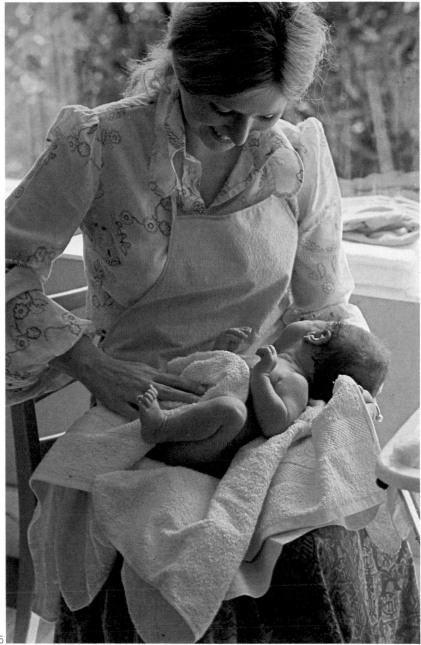

to the nappy area to avoid or ease any soreness.

Once your baby can sit up he can be bathed in the family bath. Never leave him alone in a bath, even when he can sit unaided. Put a towel or non-slip mat in the bottom of the bath to prevent him slipping over.

Do not attempt to clean a baby's nose or ears with an orange stick. The nose is kept clean by sneezing; and wax in the ears will move out to the ear canal. Once it has done so, it can be easily removed. Cut a baby's nails straight across, with scissors, when he is asleep.

For a baby girl, wash the genitals from the front towards the anus; do not wash inside the vulva. For a baby boy, do not pull back the foreskin when washing the penis. Just wash the genitals gently and dry throughly between the folds to prevent any soreness.

4 Hold him securely under his armpit and rinse off the soap with your free hand.

5 Lift him out of the water on to a towel on your lap and blot him dry. Make sure that all his creases are well dried. Once he can sit up you can use the family bath. Never leave a baby, toddler or young child alone in the bath. Young children can drown in a couple of inches of water.

Nappies

Nappies are available in a bewildering variety of materials, shapes and sizes, but this does mean that there is a kind to suit every mother's particular requirements for her baby. Whatever kind you choose, make sure that they fit firmly. However, no baby should be trussed up, nor should there be too much pressure on the genitals.

WASHABLE NAPPIES

☐ **Terry towelling** nappies are available in various qualities; at one time they were always made of one hundred per cent cotton—now they are often mixed with a small quantity of man-made fibre. Thin nappies are less bulky to wear, are easier to wash and dry quickly, but are less absorbent. Thick towelling is more absorbent and is, therefore, especially suitable for older babies and for wearing at night time. Hemmed nappies are best because they do not fray after a few washes. All towelling nappies should be washed before being used for the first time. You will need at least two dozen and, considering that they will be in use for at least two or three years, it is often cheaper to buy the best quality.

☐ **Muslin** nappies, which are very soft, can be worn during the day by a tiny baby or placed as a nappy-liner inside terry nappies. Muslin squares can also be used as bibs, draw sheets and face cloths.

☐ **Shaped** nappies take longer to dry than square ones and removing stains from them can be difficult. They are sometimes too big for young babies. They do, however, make nappy changing easy and quick. A shaped nappy can be worn under or over another nappy. Because they fit so neatly they are particularly good for toddlers.

☐ **One-way nappy liners** are worn inside a nappy and help to keep a baby's skin dry. Because they are made of a non-absorbent material, the urine passes right through them. They do not need replacing at each nappy change, but should be washed regularly. They may help to discourage a tendency to nappy rash.

☐ **Disposable nappy liners** save a great deal of work and are especially useful for young babies who soil often. With care they can be washed two or three times before disintegrating. Wet strength paper tissues can also be used for the same purpose.

CLEANING AND STERILIZING NAPPIES

You will need two lidded plastic buckets—one for soiled nappies and the other for wet nappies; used nappies should be washed daily. Shake faeces into the lavatory bowl and hold the nappy under the flushing water before placing in the sanitizing solution. Rinse wet nappies in running water and remove excess moisture before sanitizing. Nappies should be soaked for at least two hours in the sanitizing solution in a bucket with the lid on. This process sterilizes and cleans. They should then be rinsed thoroughly—several times, in fresh water.

When a baby has nappy rash—ammonia dermatitis is the most common kind and is recognized by the strong smell of ammonia—the final rinsing water should contain vinegar (acetic acid) to the proportion of 28 ml (1 fl. oz) of vinegar to 4.5 litres (1 gallon) of water. Wring only a little water from the nappy and hang it out to dry. This will leave sufficient acetic acid in the nappy to counteract the ammonia.

Fabric softeners can be added to the final rinse, but are not necessary unless the nappy has become stiff. Nappies dried outdoors will feel soft and smell fresh.

Nappies washed in special nappy cleaning solutions need also to be washed in a hot soapy solution from time to time. This will help to keep them white and soft and prolong their life. Do not use household bleach to remove stains, as this can discolour the nappy if it is not made from pure

1 The first few times a mother changes a nappy she may well feel all fingers and thumbs, but, in no time at all, she becomes very adept and discovers that it is something she can —and often does—do with her eyes closed. It helps to remember that, in the early weeks, a baby is likely to wet and possibly soil his nappy before the end of a feed and, therefore, it is wiser to change him after rather than before a feed. A baby should not, of course, be left for hours on end in a wet or soiled nappy.

cotton. Also, if a household bleach is not made up precisely following the manufacturer's instructions and the nappy is not well-washed and thoroughly rinsed, the solution could cause irritation of a baby's skin.

WASHING NAPPIES

Never use detergent or enzyme powders for washing a baby's nappies or clothes. It is extremely difficult to rinse detergents from fabrics and they commonly cause skin rashes and irritations in babies and children. Always use soap flakes or soap powders for hand-washing and washing machines. Nappies do not need to be boiled each time they are used.

Soiled nappies which are placed in water the moment they are removed will remain soft and white for longer. Before washing, rinse them thoroughly and remove excess water. Wash in hot soapy water; badly stained nappies will need to be soaked in a soapy water, or rubbed with soap before being boiled. Thorough rinsing of nappies is of vital importance to remove all traces of soap.

NAPPY SERVICES

If you can afford it, a nappy service which collects, launders and returns nappies will be well worthwhile, as it saves you a great deal of time and energy. The availability of such services differs widely from area to area. When they do exist, the laundry will generally mark the nappies for you and often you can buy new nappies direct from them.

DISPOSABLE NAPPIES

These save time and money spent in nappy laundering; but for each terry towelling nappy you will probably need two disposable nappies. Because disposable nappies need changing more often, it is better to use towelling nappies at night-time. There are many different kinds of disposable nappies available. The best way to make a choice is to ask other mothers for their opinions then try the various kinds until you find one you prefer. Disposable nappies are not suitable for very young or very small babies.

Nappies of this kind can often be bought in bulk which is very useful if you have a lot of storage space. They are invaluable when travelling, on holidays, when the washing machine breaks down, or if you are tired. Unless you are quite sure that the plumbing can cope with the disposal of nappies, it is better to incinerate them, or put them in a plastic bag in the refuse bin. Disposable nappies are best torn up before attempting to flush them away; they should break up and disappear within three flushings.

☐ **Nappy holders** are used with disposable

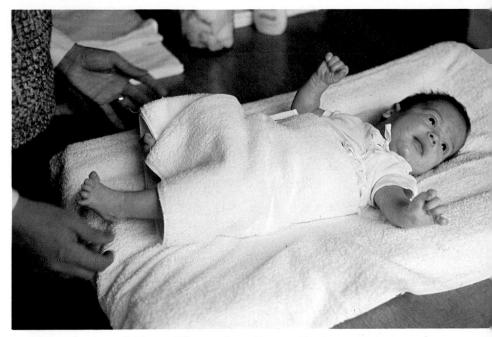

nappies and are available in different sizes. Your baby will need several because they will need to be washed regularly. Buy one pair at a time until you find the right fit. It is sensible to buy packs of the cheapest varieties rather than a couple of expensive ones.

☐ **Plastic pants** are here to stay, but need to be used with care and discrimination. The temptation is to leave them on too long and, as the urine cannot evaporate—as it would if the baby just wore a nappy—this encourages the development of nappy rash. Leave the plastic pants off whenever you can, and do not use them if the baby has a rash. Plastic pants should not fit tightly round a baby's waist or legs. Look for those with soft edges; and avoid any with ridges that will trap dirt. Wash them frequently and pat dry before hanging in the fresh air. Never dry by direct heat and do not use them when they become hard and brittle. Newborn babies do not need plastic pants.

FOLDING NAPPIES

It is wise when folding nappies to avoid a great deal of material between the baby's legs. This is especially important when toddlers are learning to walk, as bulky nappies can encourage a baby to walk bow-legged.

☐ **1: For young babies,** use the following method with terry towelling and muslin squares.
Fold the muslin into a triangle, and place under the baby with the centre of the triangle pointing down between his legs. Bring this up between his legs, fold the other two corners across his stomach and, slipping your fingers between the baby and nappy, pin all three together. Fold the terry towelling into an oblong and pin like a skirt around the baby's waist.

2 The new baby is wearing a muslin square and terry towelling nappy wrapped skirt-like round his waist. Fold the muslin into a triangle and place the baby so that the triangle is pointing towards his feet. Bring the point up between his legs, fold the other two corners across his stomach and pin all three together. Fold the terry towelling into an oblong and pin, like a skirt, around the baby's waist.

Always wash nappies with soap flakes or soap powders —never use detergents—and rinse them thoroughly with clean water before hanging them out to dry in the fresh air.

□ **2: For older babies,** fold a terry towelling nappy into a triangle (as above) and pin in the same way. Do not use a second nappy as a skirt.

□ **3: For boys (and girls who sleep on their tummies),** fold the nappy in half to form a rectangle, then fold over one third. Place the baby on the thinnest part of the folded nappy, with his waist level with the top. Bring the rest of the folded nappy up between his legs and spread over the abdomen. Pin in place.

□ **4: For toddlers,** the kite method. Arrange the nappy to represent a diamond shape. Fold the left and right hand corners into the centre, then fold the top and bottom points to meet in the centre. Place the baby's buttocks on the nappy with his legs towards the shortest fold and his waist on the opposite, wider fold. Lift one corner over the baby's body, take the nappy up between his legs and pin together. Lift the other corner over his body and place it underneath the rest of the nappy. Pin the fold together.

Always use hooded nappy pins; when you remove one, close it before putting it down.

TIMING THE CHANGE

In the early weeks a young baby is likely to wet and possibly soil by the end of a feed. It is, therefore, better to change him after rather than before a feed. Babies will usually sleep in a wet or soiled nappy so there is no need to wake them for a change. A baby should never, however, be left to lie for hours on end in a wet nappy. Sometimes a baby's crying will indicate that a nappy needs to be changed.

At changing time, you will need cotton-wool, tissues, baby lotion or oil. Remove the nappy and gently wipe away soiling with a tissue. Clean the baby's bottom with cotton-wool and baby lotion, or oil, or soak the cotton-wool in warm water. Provided your baby is topped and tailed or

1 Wipe a baby girl's bottom away from the vagina towards the anus.

2·5 For boys (and girls who sleep on their tummies) fold the nappy in this way. Fold it in half and then fold over one third. Place the baby on the thinnest part of the nappy, his waist level with the top edge, and bring the rest of the nappy up between his legs and spread it over his abdomen. Pin in place. This method of folding a nappy allows the baby to move his legs easily.

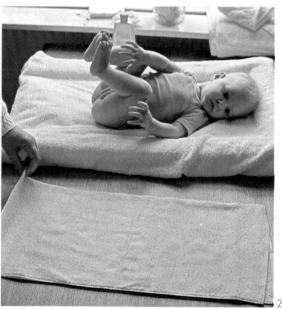

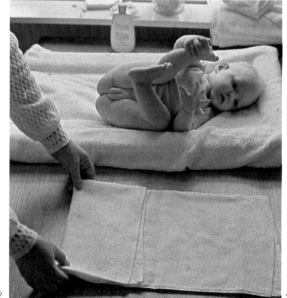

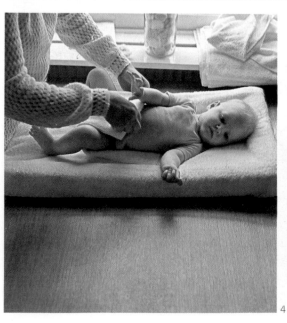

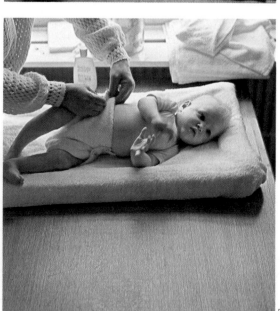

bathed each day, you will not need to use soap when you change his nappy. Wipe a baby girl's bottom away from the vagina and towards the anus. This prevents any germs or infection from the bowels reaching the vagina or bladder. Wash the groin and fold of flesh between the thighs and dry thoroughly. Petroleum jelly or zinc and castor oil creams can be used for most babies. These give a protective film to the skin, but do not need to be used at each nappy change. They are often prescribed by doctors to ease soreness.

NAPPY RASH

If your baby's bottom begins to look sore, ask yourself the following questions. Are the nappies thoroughly clean, with all the soap rinsed out of them? Am I using plastic pants too often and for too long periods? Does the baby lie for too long in a soiled or drenched nappy?

Nappy rash is experienced by most babies at some time; but the answers to the questions will give you a clue to the cause and treatment of the soreness. Leave the nappies off as often as possible, so that the baby's bottom is exposed to the air which will help the skin to recover. If the soreness persists, then visit your doctor. Any rash that is not treated can lead to severe irritation. Ammonia dermatitis is the most common kind of rash. This starts round the genitals and is distinguished by the strong smell of ammonia present when the baby's nappy is changed. Rinsing nappies in a solution of vinegar and water will help to prevent this. (See *Cleaning and Sterilizing Nappies* – page 146.)

A rash that begins on the buttocks could be caused by thrush, a fungal infection; if so, your doctor will probably treat it with gentian violet or Nystatin ointment. Do not diagnose the condition yourself; always take the baby to a doctor to ensure that it is completely cleared up.

6-11 Here the kite method of folding nappies is demonstrated. This method is ideal for toddlers as it allows greater freedom of movement. Always try to pin nappies in a way which minimizes the bulk of material between the legs. Too much bulk not only makes a child look bow-legged, but also encourages him to be bow-legged.

A New Mother
Around and About

During the first few months after the birth many mothers find that a sling is very useful for carrying their baby whilst doing simple household tasks or shopping. Babies are calmed by the movement of their mother's body and there is no doubt that sling-carrying does bring a special closeness between parent and child. In the early days, when a baby's head is very floppy, a sling will need to be strong enough to support him. For walking excursions with older babies, a proper carrying frame will be necessary.

TRAVELLING

Babies find movement soothing and will sleep in a car or stay peacefully awake. Whether awake or asleep, it is essential for safety reasons for a baby to travel in the back of the car in a carrycot that has been secured by a harness. When a baby is too big for a carrycot, he will need to be secured in an approved safety seat and, later, as a child, in a seat harness. Either you or your husband may need to travel in the back with him. Never give way to the temptation to sit in the front with your baby on your lap. If an accident should take place, even at a very low speed, a baby could be hurled against the fascia or through the window.

When travelling long distances with young children, plan the journey in advance, so that you can work out appropriate stops for letting off steam, picnicking, and nappy-changing. Start the journey, if possible, a little before the children's bedtime so that they will, with any luck, sleep on the way. If you are going by air, check what facilities are available so that you will know what you need to provide. Check the length of time that it takes to get to the airport.

HOLIDAYS

If you are going abroad, check what immunization is needed. Prepare a first-aid kit to take with you and include scissors, bandage, sticky plaster, antiseptic cream, pain killers, insect repellant, calamine lotion and sun-tan and sun-screen creams. Choose cotton clothes for warm climates. Cotton is cooler and more comfortable to wear than man-made fibres. Remember to include long-sleeved tops and trousers to ward off insects and a light but warm sweater for evenings.

When you are travelling with a child, be prepared for travel sickness. A slow rolling movement upsets the balance mechanism in the middle ear more than a jerky up-and-down movement. Before setting out, do not give your child a large, greasy meal. Instead offer a light, simple meal about one hour before the start of the journey. Whilst travelling, avoid things like crisps and chocolate which cause thirst. Choose dry biscuits and glucose sweets instead. Take the wise precaution of having some plastic bags in a readily accessible place, plus a damp flannel, but do not put any ideas in the child's head!

You will need to have a good stock of suitable amusements to keep your child happy during the journey. Puzzles, pads and crayons, jigsaws, hand puppets and games that can be played on laps are all ideal and will help to pass the time. When boredom sets in, introduce songs, stories, jokes and I-spy games.

SENSIBLE PRECAUTIONS

When abroad, take care about the choice of food; however exotic it may look, avoid foods sold in street markets and ice-cream, too, if you are at all doubtful. If your child has diarrhoea, encourage him to drink plenty of fluids and add a *little* salt to the drinks. If the attack lasts longer than twelve hours, or if your child is obviously unwell, take him to a doctor. Take water-sterilizing tablets with you or drink only bottled water.

Fair-skinned children need sun-screen creams for protection against sunburn; they should also wear a sun hat. Keep out of strong sunlight, and allow your suntanning programme to proceed very slowly. If children are bitten by mosquitoes, try to stop them scratching, for this will only infect the bite. The prevention and cure of prickly heat (distinguished by itching red spots and minute blisters on the face, neck, back and chest) is to bath or shower frequently and change one's clothes often.

If your baby is at the mixed feeding stage, take some of his favourite foods with you. If he is given mashed portions of adult meals, avoid pre-prepared or reheated dishes and custards, cream and cold meats. All these are likely sources of food poisoning.

THE WALKING STAGE

Once a baby is up and about on his feet, let him roam around barefooted as often as it is practical and safe to do so. When he does need shoes, make sure that they are comfortably lightweight, that

1 Babies find rhythmical movements very soothing and, for this reason, often make very happy travellers. Safety should, of course, be a priority consideration on any journey and, however tempting it may be to cuddle him on your lap, a baby or child should never be allowed to travel in the front of a car.

2 For short periods at home and particularly for shopping, many mothers enjoy carrying their babies close to their bodies in a sling. There is no doubt that a baby finds this soothing.

they have flexible leather uppers and that they fit well. A toddler will quickly outgrow his shoes so do not be tempted to keep them until they are worn out. Keep a careful check on sock sizes, too. Tight socks are as harmful to feet as tight shoes.

Once your baby can walk, harness reins are an essential accessory for outings. Never rely on holding a child's hand—he can pull free from your grasp in a second. A toddler should always be strapped when in a pushchair or highchair. At this age a playpen ceases to be useful in terms of keeping a child out of harm's way. It will, however, make a useful base for a blanket house! An enterprising toddler will be up and out of a playpen as fast as you put him in. Now is the time to have safety gates positioned at the top and bottom of stairs and to keep the garden gates locked.

A highchair will be coming into its own now. Choose one that has a good-sized tray, so that a two-year-old can use it as a desk when drawing or moulding dough. It should be easy to clean and sturdily made. A highchair that comes apart to form a low chair and feeding table is a good idea if you have enough room in the kitchen to accommodate it.

A LITTLE HELPING HAND

By the time a child is about eighteen months old, he will be ready and willing to help you in the home. Encourage him in little tasks—collecting newspapers and mail from the front door and unpacking groceries. Then move on to more ambitious jobs. Teach him to carry things in both hands, clasping his thumbs over them so that he will not drop anything.

Give him child-sized mops, brooms and dustpans, and let him use suitable adult-size tools. Introduce each one slowly so that by about five or six a child can handle a vacuum cleaner and even an iron responsibly. Remember that a child will not maintain attention for long periods, so change the activities frequently. Speak slowly, and explain each step carefully. Inspect and praise his work.

A two-year-old to three-year-old will empty wastepaper baskets, wipe off fingermarks and dust quite competently. Do not be tempted to give money for the jobs done. The joy of helping you in the home and being praised for a task well done is satisfaction enough. A three-year-old can be introduced to cooking—breadmaking, for example, is a delight at this age.

This is also a good time to consolidate hygiene —hands to be washed after visiting the lavatory, before cooking, eating, and so on; teeth to be brushed last thing at night, first thing in the morning and after meals; hair to be brushed and shoes to be cleaned.

2

Physical Health

Pregnancy and delivery are normal physiological functions, but no one can ever pretend that they feel the same after their baby's birth as they did before their baby was conceived—better, maybe, but not the same!

GETTING BACK TO NORMAL

Your body has gone through a good deal of change during the past nine months. It will take time for the purely physical processes to settle down into the pre-pregnancy routine again—as long as six months. Whilst there is no need to become obsessed with your health, a little extra care will speed the physiological processes back to normal.

REST

Remember that you are busier now than you were during the last weeks of your pregnancy—and, perhaps, busier than you have ever been before. You and your baby may not yet have evolved a routine that suits you both, and the sheer volume of extra work can be both time-consuming and tiring.

An early bedtime is a good idea during the first few weeks, even if this means getting up again to give your new son or daughter a last feed. A rest, if not actually in bed, at least with your feet up, during the afternoon is also advisable for the first few weeks. Settle your baby down after his lunch-time feed. Ignore the housework whilst you relax with a good book, or take time off to catch up on your favourite hobby. Rest is particularly important if you are breastfeeding. Tiredness is one of the commonest causes of failure to continue breastfeeding.

DIET

You will be paying a good deal of attention to your baby's diet in the early days, and it is also important to consider your own. A full, mixed diet, with no crash slimming course, must be the rule of the day. Naturally you will be anxious for your figure to return to normal as soon as possible, but do not let this wish over-ride health factors. Simply reduce carbohydrate foods—biscuits, sweets, bread and cakes—and concentrate on the protein foods—meat, fish, eggs and cheese—with good helpings of fresh fruit and vegetables. The more nutritious the food, the less you will need. Sweet, starchy carbohydrate foods may give a quick burst of energy, but they also leave you hungry again after an hour or so. Nibbling between meals is bad for health.

Never skip a meal because you are too busy—a ten-minute sit-down with some scrambled egg, a glass of milk and some fresh fruit, or a cheese salad and a glass of milk, will make very little difference to what you get done in a day, but all the difference to how you will feel.

Do not believe the old wives' tale that if your body craves for sweet sugary foods or lashings of cream cakes, it is because you need these foods. This is quite untrue! Cheese or fruit will take the edge off a nagging appetite for longer, and will also do you far more good.

Iron and vitamins, in tablet form, will be an essential part of your dietary intake for three months after your baby's birth. Do not forget to obtain these, either from your own doctor or from the hospital before you leave.

Breastfeeding mothers are often concerned about the effect that their diet will have on their babies. Within reason, however, there is no need to eat any differently. Trial alone will tell a mother if certain foods she has been eating have a detrimental effect on the baby. Sometimes, for example, an excess of fresh fruit or spicy foods can upset a baby's tummy. Even this will resolve itself as he becomes more mature.

Alcohol in moderation can do no harm, but in excess neither you nor your baby will benefit.

If you are breastfeeding there is no need to force yourself to drink vast quantities of fluid. Simply drink to quench your thirst. Two and a quarter litres (4 pints) is the average amount of fluids needed during each twenty-four hours.

As it is possible for some drugs to be absorbed in breast milk, always check with your doctor first before taking any medicines, including contraceptive pills.

BOWELS

Eating the right type of food—fruit, vegetables, stoneground wholemeal bread—will avoid constipation as well as toning up your body generally. The avoidance of constipation is particularly important following the birth of a baby. The muscles of the pelvis have been stretched by the birth process, and any excessive straining can predispose a mother to prolapse of the vaginal walls.

EXERCISE

The need for exercise to keep your body in trim and your mind alert goes hand-in-hand with adequate rest and a nutritious diet.

☐ **Walking** a baby in the pram is a new experience for the first-time mother. Weather permitting, you should try to slot half an hour's walk into your day.

☐ **Lifting** is the one everyday activity around the house that should be avoided. Husbands should be pressed into service to carry heavy loads of shopping for their wives at this time—even if they have been unaccustomed to doing this before!

□ **Post-natal exercises** These are just as important—if not more important—as the antenatal exercise that you practised so conscientiously every day before the birth of your baby. You will have been shown the basic post-natal exercises whilst in hospital, and you will have practised them during your stay. Now, at home, beginning two or three weeks after the baby's birth, you will have to make a determined effort to fit the exercises into your tight daily schedule of caring for your baby, husband and home. But do try; efforts will be rewarded by a speedy return to a trim figure and a general feeling of well-being. The exercises shown take only ten minutes. If you can do these twice every day your muscles will soon tone up again.

LOCHIA

Lochia is the term that is applied to vaginal discharge following delivery. Immediately after the birth the discharge is bright-red in colour and may contain a few blood clots. Gradually, over the succeeding days, the loss becomes less and of a brownish or pinkish colour. This shows that the uterus is involuting (returning to normal) satisfactorily. In hospital the midwife will record the amount and colour of the lochia and the height of the uterus on your temperature/pulse chart.

The bright-red discharge may return for a few hours or days when you start getting back into your normal routine again at home. This should not, however, persist for long. If it does, seek medical advice.

The total duration of the Lochia varies from two to six weeks. It tends to cease earlier in women who are breastfeeding their babies. This is due to the effect that a sucking baby has on the uterus.

RETURN OF PERIODS

Again this is very variable, and is often postponed for longer in women who are breastfeeding. The only clue that you may get as to the return of the periods is when the vaginal discharge becomes red and more profuse for a few days.

INFECTIONS AND OTHER COMPLICATIONS

Infection of the uterus is very rare these days. When an infection is present the lochia will become bright red and offensive, and there will be abdominal discomfort. Antibiotics will quickly clear the infection.

Occasionally a minute piece of tissue from the placenta is left inside the uterus. When this happens there will be a return of red discharge, usually about ten days after the delivery. An

injection of a substance to make the uterus contract will control the bleeding. A subsequent D and C (dilation and curettage) will be necessary to remove the piece of tissue. This will be done under a general anaesthetic.

RESUMPTION OF SEX

Not surprisingly, many new mothers find themselves tired to the point of exhaustion at the end of the day and, therefore, disinclined to resume sexual intercourse. Physically there is no reason why lovemaking should not be resumed as soon as the discomfort and soreness following delivery have worn off, but the vaginal discharge makes some couples aesthetically unwilling.

By the time the post-natal check is due, the vaginal discharge will probably have cleared, and, provided all is declared well from the physical point of view, sex can be resumed. There is, however, far more to harmonious sex relationships than mere physical factors. If a mother is tired and feeling disinclined neither she or her husband will enjoy making love. She, who has borne her husband's child—with no small degree of effort—should set the pace for the timing of the return to sex. An understanding husband will show his love for his wife at this time by an increasing tenderness and awareness of the emotional and physical help that she needs. By helping with the care of their baby and sharing everyday household tasks, he can see that she avoids becoming overtired. A full participation in the pleasures and pressures of everyday life will contribute to a richer relationship in every way.

When sex is resumed, contraceptive precautions are necessary. The type of protection can be discussed with the doctor at the post-natal 'check. Until the mother's body has had time to return fully to its normal state (usually about six months after the baby's birth) it is more satisfactory if the husband is the partner to take contraceptive precautions.

It is not lazy to put your feet up for an hour in the afternoon.
    Looking after a new baby and a toddler is enough to tax the resources of the strongest. A quiet time with a favourite book will work wonders for both you and your toddler

Post-natal Exercises

If you want to get your figure back after the birth of your baby, then practise some post-natal exercises for a few minutes, twice per day—taking it gently at first. You will soon regain your former slim figure and feel fitter as well. Don't regard the exercises as a chore. Enjoy performing them and they will do you twice as much good.

1 Lie flat on your back, with your feet together and your legs straight. Keep your arms by your sides. Raise your head to look at your toes but without straining your shoulders. Relax and then repeat the sequence six times.

2 Lie flat on your back, with your feet together and your legs straight. Keep your arms by your sides. Draw your right leg up at the waist, making it shorter than the left. Then stretch it down from the waist, making it longer than the left. Return to the starting position and relax. Repeat the sequence using the left leg. Return to the starting position and relax. Repeat the sequence with each leg, three times.

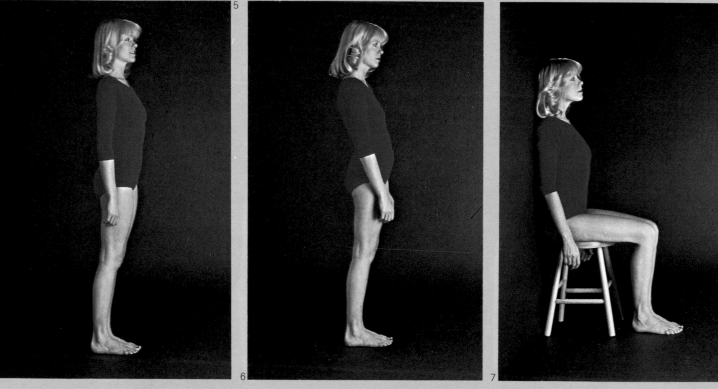

5,6 Every now and then during the day, check that your posture is upright and correct. Your weight should be placed slightly on the front of your foot. Keep your knees straight. Raise your rib cage and pull in the muscles of your abdomen. Raise your head towards the ceiling but keep your shoulders relaxed.

This exercise can be practised at frequent intervals during the day when you are standing still for a moment.

7,8 Sit on a stool, with your back straight against a wall. Keep your feet flat on the floor, directly under your knees.

Bend forward and touch your toes. Then slowly uncurl from the base of your spine to your head and neck. Relax, still sitting up straight, and then repeat the sequence three times.

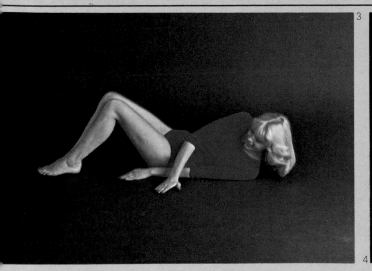

3 Lie flat on your back, with your feet together and your knees bent. Keep your arms by your sides. Tighten the muscles in your abdomen. Reach across your body with your right arm and place your right hand flat beside your left hip. Return to your starting position and relax. Repeat the sequence using the left arm and the left hand. Return to the starting position and relax. Repeat with each hand three times.

4 Lie flat on your back, with your feet together and your knees bent. Tighten the muscles in the lower abdomen and in the buttocks so that the small of your back is flat against the floor. Keeping these muscles tight, tighten the muscles of the back passage and the vagina. Slowly, relax all the muscles. Repeat the sequence three times.

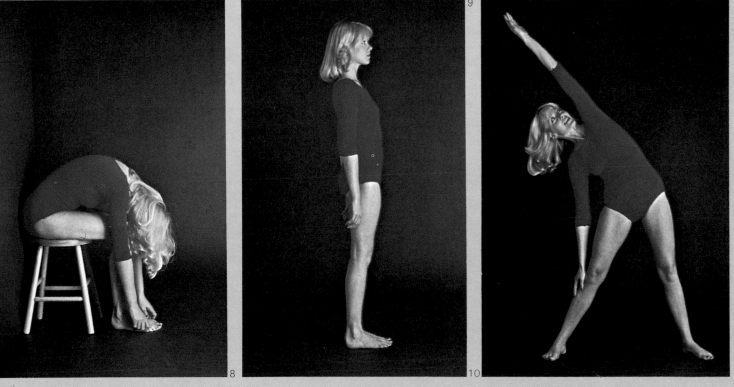

9 At frequent intervals during the day, tighten the muscles of the pelvic floor — as if you are trying to hold back a motion or the passage of urine. Relax and repeat whenever you are standing still for a moment.

It is helpful if you can ask a physiotherapist to assist you when you first do this, so that you understand which are the proper muscles to contract.

10 Stand up straight, with your feet slightly apart and your weight evenly balanced between them. Keep your arms by your sides. Raise your left arm in a half-circle and, at the same time, stretch over to the right. Slide your right hand down the side of your right leg. Make sure that you keep your back straight and your bottom tucked in, so that you can feel a gentle pull on the muscles on the left side of your waist. Repeat, using the right arm. Repeat the sequence with each arm, three times.

Mental Health

Body and mind are, of course, inextricably interwoven, and a mother's mental and emotional reactions will be different following the birth of a baby.

Immediately after delivery, she will feel overjoyed, stimulated, excited—and probably very relieved! Within the next three or four days, however, she may experience post-natal depression, and feel acutely miserable. The slightest criticism will upset her and she will be liable to burst into tears for no apparent reason.

All these feelings are common reactions, and doctors recognize them for what they are—a relief from the tension and effort of delivery.

In hospital the mother will have the support of the nursing staff and other mothers. On arrival home, however, there is often no-one around to talk to, except the baby! Insight into one's own problems is half the battle won. As long as you are aware that the depression may persist even after you get home, you can do much to help yourself.

THE POSITIVE APPROACH

☐ **Friends** Contact your friends again as soon as you can, and make an effort to arrange a meeting —a coffee morning, for example. Your baby should sleep well after his bath and breakfast. He will also sleep quite happily in his carry-cot in a friend's house. In this way you will be picking up the threads of life again, and will have someone with whom you can share your joys and tribulations.

☐ **Hobbies** A little later on, perhaps, you could begin—or recommence—your favourite hobby— perhaps enrolling for an evening class in a subject that interests you. Evening classes are ideal because husbands can be available to 'babysit'. This will widen your horizons and ease any sense of isolation.

☐ **Evenings Out** Make an effort to go out with your husband at least once a fortnight to a theatre, cinema, meal or whatever interests you both. If you have no nearby relatives available for baby-sitting, make enquiries to see if there is a local group of mothers who are working a baby-sitting rota system. If there is nothing like this available in your locality, perhaps you could start one? Above all, when you do go out, relax and enjoy yourself. Leave a telephone number and then forget everyday tensions for a few hours.

☐ **Accepting help** For day-to-day management problems that you may have with your baby, do make full use of the help available from your health visitor, clinic or mother-and-baby club.

MATERNAL FEELINGS

A patent source of worry to many new mothers is a lack of immediate overwhelming love for their babies. They have been led to expect that as soon as their baby is born they will instantly adore him or her. This does, indeed, happen in a small percentage of births, but more commonly the love emerges and grows gradually as you feed your baby and tend to his needs.

Do not be afraid to admit that strong and immediate maternal feelings have passed you by. You are by no means alone in this, and the lack of 'instant love' does not mean that you will be anything other than a good mother.

DEALING WITH DEPRESSION

Unfortunately, even with the best intentions to try to keep post partum depression at bay, some women do become depressed to a degree which needs expert help.

It used to be thought that depression, following the birth of a baby, was a condition specific to pregnancy. Post partum depression is now considered to be the reaction of a vulnerable personality to the stress of pregnancy and delivery, followed by the responsibilities of a new baby.

Some degree of depression is probably present in every woman who has just had a baby. This ranges from the sensitive emotional reactions of the first few days to the deep depression of the mother who is urgently in need of medical help.

SIGNS AND SYMPTOMS

If the depression continues, the sufferer feels continually tired with a persistent headache, and aches and pains all over the body. She becomes increasingly prone to feelings of inadequacy and tears and loses interest in her appearance, food and, eventually, even the care of her baby.

A physical examination reveals nothing abnormal to account for her symptoms.

WHAT TO DO

If you feel everything is getting on top of you and that life is becoming hopelessly difficult, contact your health visitor or doctor. There are ways in which depressive illnesses can be tackled, but in addition to your immediate family, you will need the regular and frequent support of an understanding professional.

☐ **Insight into the problem** This is the biggest step along the road to recovery. When you understand what is happening and why, you will be better able to cope and to try to organize your mind along constructive lines.

For example, take one small task at a time, give

it your full attention, do it to the best of your ability, and congratulate yourself on the outcome. Bring order into your day by keeping a routine. A disciplined time-table, that must be adhered to, is invaluable for preventing thoughts from running round in circles about your own imagined inefficiency. There will be setbacks, but refuse to be discouraged. Each time you succeed, you will be one step nearer to recovery.

☐ **Physical fitness** Check that your physical health is being properly attended to. Adequate rest periods with a good, nutritious diet and at least one part of the day devoted to taking your baby out in the fresh air—preferably in congenial company—will help. Your doctor, too, will want to be sure that you are not anaemic or lacking in nutrition.

☐ **Drugs** If all these comparatively simple—but effective—measures fail, your doctor will be able to prescribe anti-depressant drugs. These do not get to the root of the problem, but they can help to ease the problem during the worst few weeks.

However impossible it may seem to you in the lowest trough of depression, the cure can be complete and permanent. Making the right efforts and accepting the right kind of help will enable you to enjoy your baby again, and the depression will seem like a bad dream.

Outside Help

Whilst in hospital, all the necessary help and facilities were immediately available. But when you get home, life can seem strange, bewildering and friendless at times. Fortunately, there is much outside help available, both from a financial and personnel point of view.

PERSONNEL

If you are discharged from hospital forty-eight hours after the birth of your baby, the district midwife will visit you daily to make sure that all is well with both of you.

Following on from her visits, which will normally cease when your baby is ten days old, the health visitor, attached to your doctor's practice, will start to pay you regular visits.

Your general practitioner, is, of course, always on call should either you or your baby be in need of medical treatment. Through him, the range of hospital specialists are also available.

In addition, all towns and many villages have a weekly, or monthly, child health clinic to which all mothers are welcome. Here, advice on general baby care and feeding, together with development assessments and immunization procedures, are readily available, from health visitors and a community doctor especially trained in the care of babies and young children.

In many areas home helps can also be organized to assist with the everyday household work of a mother who has had an early discharge from hospital. Ask your health visitor (preferably prior to your baby's birth) if there are any arrangements regarding this service in your locality. Payment is made by you—either at the current rate for domestic help, or at a reduced rate if you are in a low-income bracket.

FINANCIAL HELP

In Britain you are entitled to free dentistry and free prescriptions until your baby is one year old. The child health clinic will sell vitamins A, C and D drops and tablets at a reduced rate for both you and your baby; many clinics also sell baby milks at a reduced rate. Some of these dietary items are free for mothers in a low-income bracket. The health visitor will give details.

Family allowances have been paid for the second child in the past and are now available for the first child.

FAMILY PLANNING

Expert advice regarding family planning can be obtained either from a general practitioner, or from the Family Planning Association which has numerous clinics in every part of the country.

POST-NATAL CHECKS

When your baby is six weeks old you will have an important date in your diary—an appointment for a post-natal check. This check should be regarded as essential and as the logical end to the care which was first started at the beginning of pregnancy. Primarily, the obstetrician will want to ensure that the reproductive organs are well on the way to returning to their normal state.

Children will gain much from playing together while you and a friend chat over a cup of coffee. Isolation can be a very real hazard to mental health. So get out to meet your friends and pick up old interests again.

be started on anti-hypertensive drugs.

MEDICAL HISTORY

On meeting the obstetrician, you will be asked how you are feeling generally, how you are coping with your baby and how the feeding is going. Now is the time to ask all those questions that pass through your mind day by day.

The doctor will enquire about the lochia, and whether the discharge is red or brown or has ceased altogether. He will also ask if you have had a period since the birth of your baby. Any discomfort from stitches will be enquired about.

It is important to mention any pain around the back passage. Occasionally, after childbirth, a small crack in the delicate skin around the anus can occur. This is due to haemorrhoids (piles) and can be extremely painful. Do not be too embarrassed to mention this problem.

The obstetrician will also want to know if you are having any stress incontinence—an embarrassing and uncomfortable condition in which one involuntarily passes a small amount of urine when coughing, sneezing or laughing. This is common after childbirth and is due to the stretching of the muscles around the outlet of the bladder. Treatment is an increase in the post-natal exercises designed to strengthen the muscles of the pelvic floor. (See page 156.)

THE POST-NATAL EXAMINATION

The obstetrician will examine your tummy to make sure that the muscles are regaining their normal tone. At the same time he will feel to make sure that your uterus is involuting well.

Legs will be examined to see if there are any varicose veins resulting from pregnancy.

Finally, the doctor will need to perform an internal examination.

FINAL CHECKS

☐ **Family Planning Advice** If advice is required the doctor will discuss contraceptive measures and the spacing of a family. There are also special family planning clinics to which a mother can go for further advice later.

☐ **Genetic Counselling** If the mother has, unfortunately, given birth to a child who has a defect or deformity of any kind, the obstetrician will briefly discuss the possibility of similar defects occurring in future children. Often, however, this genetic counselling is time-consuming, and extremely specialized, so further visits are arranged.

☐ **Baby Check-Ups** Sometimes, under the same roof, at the same time, a paediatrician will also be holding a clinic and will give your baby his six-week development check-up.

If the need is imperative, for any reason, for you to return to work, your child will come to no harm if he has a reliable, constant mother-substitute to whom he can turn while you are away. Continuity of care, either in his own home, or in other familiar surroundings, will ensure that he will not miss out on all the day-to-day learning situations.

THE POST-NATAL APPOINTMENT

If your baby has been born in hospital, you will have been given the date and time of your post-natal appointment before you leave. For several reasons, six weeks after the birth is chosen as the most suitable time. By this time the uterus should be involuting well and be virtually its normal size again.

ROUTINE TESTS

Before seeing the doctor the mother is weighed by a nurse. By six weeks, her weight ideally should be back to, or near, her pre-pregnancy weight.

The urine is also tested routinely by the nurse to ensure that kidney function is normal.

Blood-pressure is also measured. This reading is especially important if the mother has suffered from toxaemia (in which the blood-pressure is raised) during pregnancy. The blood-pressure usually returns to normal within hours of the birth of the baby. Very occasionally it remains high. Under these circumstances the mother will

Working Mothers

DO YOU NEED TO WORK?

There is a saying: 'If you educate a man you educate a person, but if you educate a woman you educate a family.' All babycare and childcare experts know that this is true and that a child needs his mother because, however incompetent she may believe she is, she is her child's first and most important teacher. Sadly, there is an idea in circulation at the moment that to be a mother and a housewife is to be a second-rate citizen; that worthwhile work and opportunities to use education and talent only exist outside the home, away from the family. Nothing, however, is further from the truth. The better educated and more talented the mother, the more fortunate the child.

A mother who appreciates that her child has five senses, and a mind that needs stimulation, and who makes a point of showing and naming everything for him, speaking to him, singing to him, reading to him and generally teaching him and bringing the world to him while he cannot go to the world, is performing the most marvellous and worthwhile job that life has to offer. Such babies become the brightest and most alert.

The first essential, then, when considering whether or not to work, is to pause for reflection. If, having reflected, the need remains imperative for economic, psychological or personal reasons, a first-class mother-substitute will need to be found.

☐ **Nannies** Nannies are the ideal choice because the child will, at least, be guaranteed the individual attention that is so vital to his development. Nannies, if they are happy in their work, also stay in one person's employment for as long as they are needed. This protects the child from being handed to one person after another. Nannies are, however, expensive and many homes are not large enough, either literally or psychologically, to accommodate another person.

☐ **Au pairs** This system fluctuates between being very successful and disastrously unsuccessful, depending, of course, on the family concerned and the individual *au pair*. Some *au pairs* have a natural interest in children; others are totally uninterested.

The first essential is to plan, in advance, exactly what is expected from an *au pair*. In general, the girls are paid by arrangement for a maximum five-hour day, have a room of their own and live as one of the family; they require at least one and a half free days a week and time for language tuition.

☐ **Child-minders** Some registered child-minders make truly excellent mother-substitutes; others— usually unregistered—are totally unsuitable and cause a child irreparable psychological harm. A parent needs to exercise extreme caution when making a choice. Good physical care is not enough. A child who is expected to sit quiet and still, in order to keep clean and tidy and not disturb the minder or her house is in grave danger of being mentally and emotionally starved. An essential safeguard is to call unexpectedly on a few occasions.

DAY NURSERIES

These do not have an educational function and do not, therefore, have trained teachers on their staff. Staff usually consists of trained nursery nurses or untrained assistants. There is usually a long waiting list which is limited to priority cases, such as mothers with psychological problems, or one-parent families. Fees are charged according to circumstances.

Some employers provide day nurseries, in order to encourage female employees to work for them or to remain working for them. These are usually financed by management, plus a small contribution from the mothers. The kind of care which can be expected varies tremendously.

NURSERY SCHOOLS

These provide an educational as well as a child-minding service. Staff usually consists of at least one specially trained teacher. They offer long hours—usually between seven-thirty a.m. and six p.m. They do, of course vary tremendously and private ones in particular should be visited and decided upon with care.

☐ **Playgroups** These are usually run by groups of mothers and offer first-class facilities for helping children to develop, to make the most of their pre-school years and to become adjusted to social groups. They have the advantage of involving parents from the same community. Their hours are, however, usually short.

THE MOTHER'S FEELINGS

No mother finds it easy to hand over her child to another woman. Feelings of insecurity and jealousy are common. A child becomes very confused when he is resented for protesting when his mother leaves him; and resented for *not* protesting when his mother leaves him! Parents should *never* burden a child with their emotional reactions—he simply does not have the mental or emotional maturity to cope with their problems.

The First Three Years

Development in Infancy

A baby's capacity to learn is probably greater during the first year of life than at any other time. By his first birthday he is skilful at using his hands, can say a few words, understand the meaning of simple phrases, and, perhaps, walk a few steps. A baby is a very well-organized being and there is a definite and natural order in the way in which he learns to do things. He must, for example, be able to hold his head steady before he can sit unaided, and must know how to sit before he can stand. The various stages in a baby's development are called milestones, and one of the most rewarding aspects of parenthood is to observe the remarkable sequence of the developmental steps that a baby takes from birth towards maturity.

You can learn a lot about your baby's development by keeping a note book to record the age at which he first performs each new skill. Although the *order* in which babies learn things is similar, the precise age at which they first carry out a skill varies a lot from baby to baby. Parents should not be anxious simply because their baby does not follow a text book. One often, for example, sees babies who are late in learning one skill, but who are perfectly normal in all other respects and it is surprising how quickly such babies can 'catch up'. You may know, for example, of a baby who was not talking by his second birthday, but who, six months later, was chatting incessantly.

Paediatricians are more concerned about babies who are late in learning several different skills or who lack general understanding and interest in their surroundings. Just as some normal babies may be a little late in learning a particular skill, so there are babies whose development appears advanced in some way. Some babies can sit without support or walk several months early, but this does not mean that they are intellectually superior. Hereditary factors have some influence on development. For example, several members of one family may have been 'slow walkers' or 'slow talkers'. However, the environment is also very important. A baby who is frequently left in his cot to gaze at the ceiling for most of the day is likely to be a late developer, whereas a stimulating environment will encourage a baby to learn and develop skills early.

Most babies who are normal at birth, or soon after birth, usually continue to develop normally. Nevertheless, nearly all mothers welcome the opportunity of being reassured about their baby's development from time to time. Medical policy, regarding the timing of the developmental examinations, varies considerably but, generally, a baby will be examined in the infant clinic once or twice between his discharge from the maternity hospital and his first birthday.

Confirmation that a baby's hearing and vision are normal is especially important because prompt recognition and treatment of any problems may prevent further handicap. The paediatrician will enquire about the baby's general health and will ask the age at which the baby achieved certain milestones, such as smiling, sitting without support, reaching out and grasping objects, etc. If you have kept a notebook you will find it very useful, but do not worry if you have not and cannot remember your baby's various milestones. There is no need to feel disappointed if your baby cries a lot and does not perform as well in the clinic as he usually does at home. The paediatrician will make allowances for the unfamiliar surroundings and also knows that sleepy babies rarely perform at their best.

The speed with which a baby develops during the first year of life is truly breathtaking. In the course of a few months he changes from being a totally dependent helpless being into a person who smiles, sits up, plays, grasps objects and raises spoons and cups to his lips. These various stages of development are known as milestones. Every child is, of course, an individual and it is very important not to become over-concerned if a baby does not follow a particular sequence or pattern of behaviour. The staff at the infant clinic will certainly keep an eye on his progress during the first year of life and, if for any reason, development is considered to be unusually slow, appropriate steps will be taken to encourage normal healthy development. There is no doubt that stimulating playthings and a lively companionable home life are invaluable in helping a baby to master the various milestones of development. It is, however, equally important not to over-excite or exhaust a baby or child and to remember that 'peace' times are as important as play and conversation times.

164

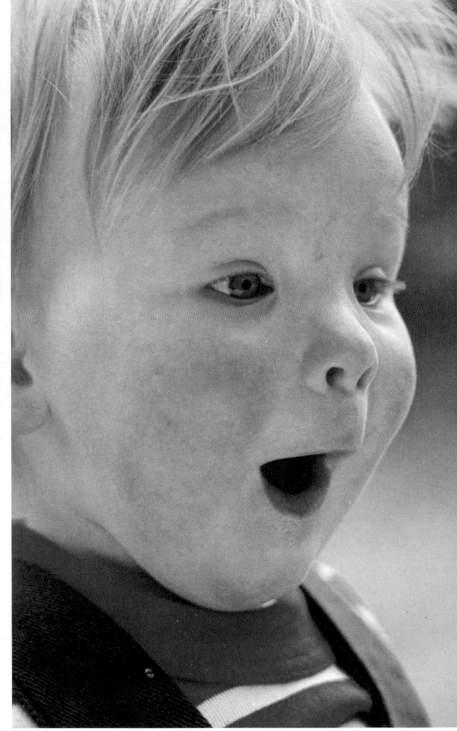

If their were any complications during pregnancy or at delivery, if your baby was ill after birth or if another member of the family had a developmental problem, the paediatrician may wish to see your baby rather more frequently during the first year. This is a precaution so that if the baby's development is slow, it can be spotted early and the appropriate help given. It is a fact that most babies born in the above circumstances develop entirely normally. If your baby was born prematurely, remember that he will reach his milestones rather later than a full-term baby of the same age. A baby aged six months, who was born two months prematurely, behaves like a four-month-old. By two years old, however, he has generally caught up with his full-term counterpart in every possible way.

How a Baby uses his Hands

The hands of a newly born baby are held closed for most of the time. If your baby happens to open his hands, place your finger against his palm. He will immediately grip your finger tightly. Try to pull away and his grip becomes stronger. Although it is a delightful sensation to feel that baby will not let you go, he is not consciously holding on to you. He is simply showing that he has a strong 'grasp reflex'. This reflex is one of many that a baby is born with. It usually disappears by the age of three months, by which time the baby's hands are held open for most of the time. At this stage when you put a small toy, such as a rattle, in his hand, he will deliberately hold it. It is a good idea to have brightly coloured shapes threaded on a string across the baby's cot or pram because this will stimulate him to reach out and touch. He will not, however, take an object, such as a small brick from you, until he is five months old. His first attempts will be very clumsy. His hand will wander here and there before coming to rest on the brick. Watch how he grips; at first he will grasp the object awkwardly between the palm of his hand and the fourth or fifth finger, but as he gets older the grip becomes more mature. At six months he will transfer objects from hand to hand and will, of course, take everything to his mouth. For this reason, he should not be left unsupervised with small toys. He usually stops mouthing objects when he is about one year old. By ten or eleven months a baby's grip is really quite advanced. He will pick up very small objects between his finger and thumb. The kind of objects that might accidentally find their way to the floor and be a source of danger for a baby at this age include beads, peanuts and tablets. If you want to see how a baby gradually develops a mature finger-thumb grip, sit him on your lap when he is about eight months old and let him reach for a small pledget of cotton-wool placed on a table in front of him. He will usually release whatever he is holding and offer it to you by about eleven months old. Before this age he goes through a stage of resolutely refusing to give things to you, however nicely you ask. At thirteen months he can place two small bricks (one-inch cubes) one on top of the other. At fifteen months or earlier he can use his hands sufficiently well to be able to feed himself with a spoon, and can pick up a tumbler of milk without upsetting it.

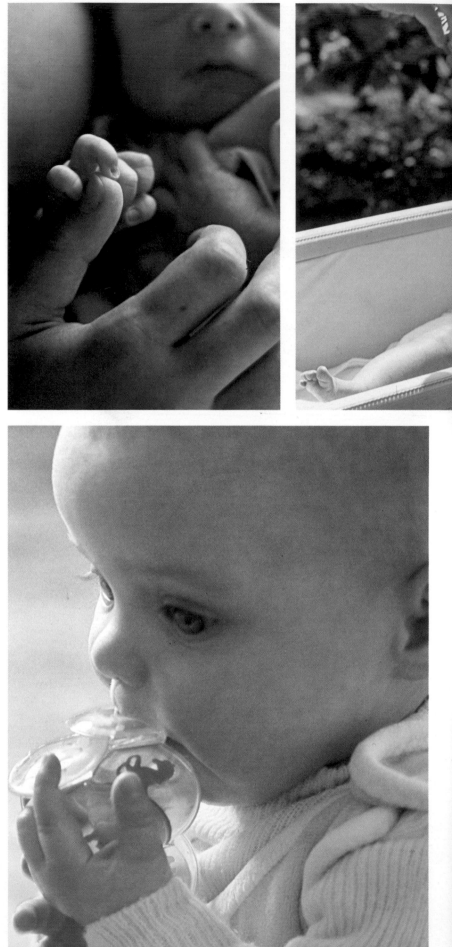

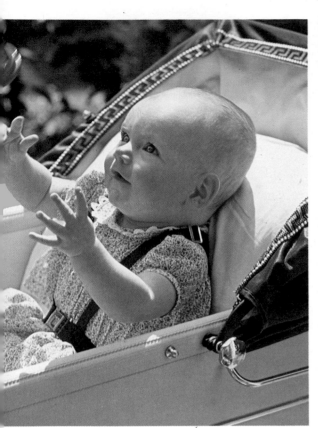

The strength with which a newborn baby can grasp a person's finger is a source of constant amazement and wonder for parents. There is nothing more thrilling than watching a baby make progress each day. What he could not do yesterday, he can do today. The natural awkwardness of grasping rattles and other objects between the palm of his hand and the fourth and fifth fingers will slowly but surely give way to a co-ordinated handling of anything and everything that is given. By about three years old, a child will be able and will want to cope with such complicated things as fastening buttons and building towers of bricks. While a young baby and toddler are mastering all these early hand movements and practising co-ordination, it is important to keep any small object that might be mouthed and swallowed or pushed into ears and nostrils well out of reach.

Learning to Sit

Before a baby can sit firmly without support he must be able to hold his head up and keep his back straight. If you gently pull a very young baby up from a lying to a sitting position you will see how his head falls back and lags behind his shoulders. When held in a sitting position his head slumps forward on to his chest and his back is very round. The head lag that is seen when a baby is pulled up becomes much less obvious by the age of three months and disappears by five months. Round about this time he can sit propped up in a pram. Mothers worry sometimes about sitting a baby propped up. They fear that this will damage the baby's back. From about three or four months it is, in fact, a perfectly safe thing to do, provided the baby is well supported. It does at least give him a good opportunity to see what is going on around his pram.

From time to time the baby will lean forward, supporting himself with his hands outstretched in front of him. Then, at seven months, an important milestone is reached—he sits for a few seconds without any support. A baby's confidence rapidly increases and soon he plays with a toy in his hands without toppling over. By ten or eleven months he can twist round to pick up a toy behind him without over-balancing.

Life becomes very much more interesting for a baby when he can sit up, unsupported, and see what is going on around him. The age at which babies can achieve this varies from individual to individual, but seven months is average. At first he will only be able to sit up, unsupported, for a few seconds at a time. But slowly his ability and his confidence increases and soon he is able to play with his toys without toppling over. By ten or eleven months, he is becoming really confident and can twist round and reach for a toy.

On the Move

Not all babies go through a crawling stage, but it is the most common form of getting around before walking. It is a good idea to let a baby spend some of his 'play time' lying on his tummy. In this position he will go through various stages of development. A newborn baby, for example, will lie with his legs tucked under his tummy and his head held to one side. By three months old he can lift his face up and straighten his legs. A month or so later he will lift his chest up and make swimming movements with his arms and legs. At about six months old he can support himself on his hands with his arms outstretched in front of him. A baby usually crawls by nine or ten months, but he may use a variety of other methods for moving around. He may roll over on the floor or shuffle along on his bottom. His newly developed mobility makes him vulnerable to accidents in the home unless sensible precautions are taken. (See page 193.) Babies should be discouraged from crawling towards doors that might suddenly be opened. Other 'danger' zones include fires, staircases, electrical fitments, sharp instruments such as table knives, drawers and cupboards. All these suddenly become within the reach of exploring fingers once the baby is mobile and are of great interest to his developing and inquiring mind. During busy times when you cannot closely supervise your baby's activities, let him play with a favourite toy inside a play pen.

It is an exciting and somewhat busy and harrassing time for parents when a baby who has been happy just to sit and coo and observe life suddenly rolls over on to his side, then on to his tummy and begins to make the 'swimming' movements that

usually precede the first attempts to crawl. Of course, some babies never crawl, but go instead from the sitting position straight into the standing position; others find out they can get around just as quickly by sitting on their bottoms and shuffling along. Once a baby is mobile, be it on his bottom, tummy, hands and knees or feet, safety becomes a prime consideration for the entire family.

Learning to Walk

When you hold a newborn baby upright and allow his feet to come into contact with a firm surface, such as a table top, he will lift each leg up in turn and place it in front of the other, just as if he is going for a stroll. This automatic reaction, called the 'walking reflex', disappears by the age of one month. At five or six months a baby has a steady head and a straight back and, when you hold him upright, he will take most of his weight on his legs. At nine or ten months he will stand holding on to furniture. At about eleven to twelve months he will walk, still clinging to the furniture or using your hand for support. A baby's first steps by himself usually happen at about thirteen months and always cause excitement. At first, in order to balance himself, he walks with his legs spaced quite widely apart and with his elbows held out on each side. By about fifteen months he can often crawl upstairs, but it is not until about eighteen months to two years that he can go up and down the stairs without help. Slowly but surely he gains confidence in walking and by eighteen months he can pull a toy on wheels along the ground. Remember that as his mobility and confidence increases, he will start to explore more and more things in and around the house. Accidents to toddlers in the home are very common and their effects can be most serious. Once a baby has learnt to walk confidently, his agility far exceeds his ability to recognize danger. It is, therefore, your responsibility to see that he is protected from danger. (See page 193.)

After all those months of being on his back, tummy, bottom and knees, imagine a child's delight when he discovers that he can stand on his own two feet. He's a bit wobbly, of course, when back, leg and feet muscles are unused to such antics and it certainly helps to have an adult to cling to or a surface to lean against. But every day muscles grow firmer and stronger and limbs which, at first seemed to have a mind of their own, begin to come under their owner's control. Suddenly a baby finds that not only can he stand—he can walk, and what's more, he can walk with a purpose. Gradually, day by day, he becomes more confident. However many times he lands on his well-padded bottom, or more painfully, on his chin, he gets up again. What are a few tumbles compared with the delight of being able to move around, peep into all those mysterious corners and investigate what the world is made of?

6

7

1-5 When babies are still somewhat unsteady, a babywalker is a marvellous aid. At first, it is fun and games and trial and error all the way. It takes time, for example, for an infant to learn that when she pushes the walker forward she must remember to move her feet forward, too. If she does not, she has her first lesson in the law of gravity. Once the basic idea is mastered, however, it's child's play. Push and move becomes the order of the day and, soon, babywalker and baby walk simultaneously together. When the baby can manage to walk without the walker, it will be used as a marvellous transporter for toys.

6-9 Going upstairs is one thing, coming down is another. For some weeks, most young children go up and come down facing the same way. Then, slowly, as confidence increases, they learn to turn around at the top and come down facing the way that they are going. It now becomes more important than ever to ensure that there are no treacherous holes or frays in the stair carpet and that it is very firmly tackled.

How a Baby uses his Eyes

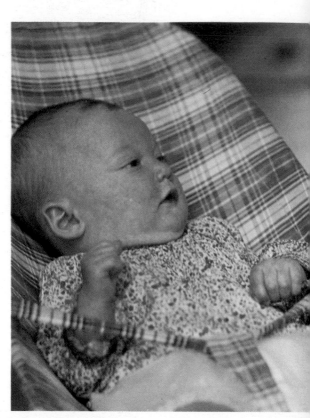

A newborn baby will turn his head towards a bright source of light and if his mother holds her face in line with his, about twelve inches away, he will briefly focus his eyes on her. Eye-to-eye contact is, in fact, an important form of inter-action between a mother and her newborn baby.

A baby also likes to fix his eyes on bright red toys and, by the time he is one month old, he will follow a moving brightly coloured object for several inches. At about three months he will follow a moving object fully from side to side and, by this time, will gaze attentively around the room. Between three and six months he goes through a stage of scrutinizing his hands as he lies on his back. By six months he 'searches' for objects with his eyes and will, for example, turn his head to catch sight of a toy that interests him.

1

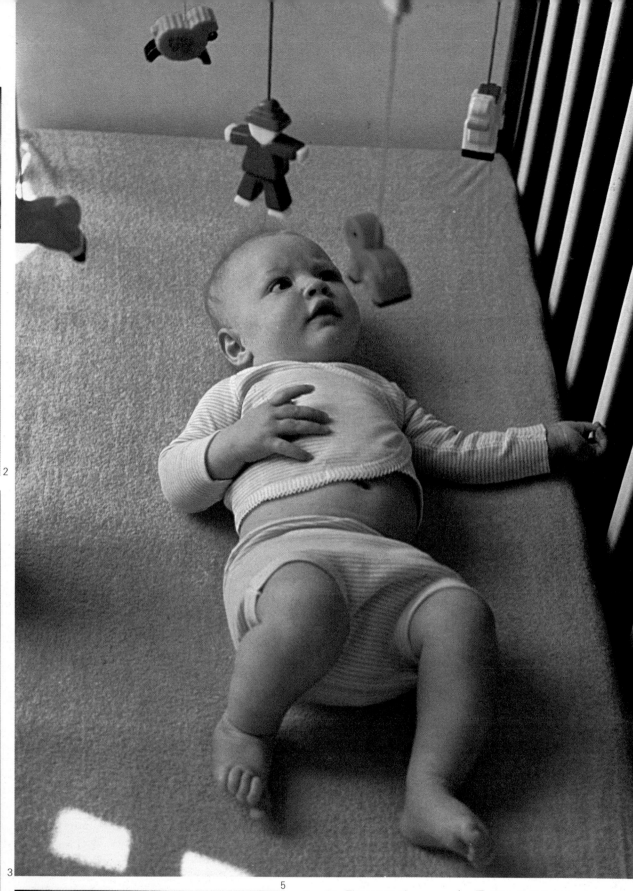

1-3 The sense of sight is a wonderful gift and the youngest baby will welcome opportunities to use it. Colourful mobiles suspended above a cot are ideal for stimulating a baby to use his eyes and focus clearly.

4,5 One need that is commonly overlooked is the need for simple eye-to-eye contact with mother and father and other human beings. Early inter-reaction of this kind is vital to a parent's and a baby's relationship.

Hearing and Speech

Hearing and speech are, of course, related. (See page 204.) A newborn baby's hearing is sensitive and, from birth, he will cry, startle or grimace in response to a sudden loud noise. This is a natural reflex reaction, but by the age of three or four months a baby will turn his head towards a sound made within eighteen inches of either ear. He gradually learns the *meaning* of familiar sounds and by the age of five or six months he will become very excited when he hears his food being prepared, and will quieten at the sound of approaching footsteps. It is not surprising that if a baby is deaf his mother is usually the first person to suspect it. Any doubts about a baby's hearing should be mentioned to a doctor promptly because the early recognition and treatment of deafness improves the outlook for a baby's speech development.

A baby usually starts to make speech sounds at the age of two months, using vowels like 'a' and 'ee'. (See page 204.) By ten or eleven months he will understand the meaning of 'No!', will obey simple requests, and may know how to say one word with meaning. He gradually increases his vocabulary thereafter.

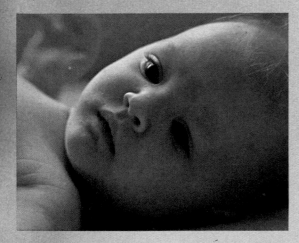

Opportunities to use the sense of hearing are, of course, very necessary when developing a child's sensitivity to sound. But, as in all things, the right measure is all-important. Today's world abounds in harsh discordant sounds. One of the most effective ways to help develop a child's sense of hearing is to reduce unnecessary distractions and avoid excessive exposure to sound. Many mothers have noticed that the sounds generated by ordinary household gadgets and machines contribute very directly to a build-up of irritation both in themselves and their children.

Social Behaviour

1 That babies are sociable beings, who enjoy interacting with

The development of social responses and the general understanding of situations is a measure of a baby's intellect. Mentally retarded infants, for example, are usually so slow to learn skills that all their milestones are generally delayed. By about six weeks a normal baby smiles in response to his mother. Long before this, however, he will smile fleetingly in his sleep. There is no doubt that some babies do smile socially long before six weeks. It is not usually until five months old, however, that a baby will smile at his own image in a mirror and reach out to touch it.

At three months a baby will show much interest in his surroundings. He gazes around the room attentively and is delighted when offered a toy. At four months he will usually show understanding by opening his mouth when he sees the approach of the breast or bottle at feed time. It is quite remarkable that, by five or six months, a baby will hear a sound such as dishes rattling, will *recognize* what this means and will *react* by showing pleasure and excitement. A delightful example of a baby's general understanding of situations occurs between six to seven months when he stretches out his arms as you are about to pick him up from the cot. At about this time he also begins to imitate simple acts and becomes increasingly more skilful at this game as his first birthday approaches. At ten to eleven months he will help when being dressed by holding out his arm for a sleeve. After his first birthday his general understanding increases rapidly hand in hand with the development of language.

parents, other people, objects and surroundings in general, becomes apparent at a very early age. The first smile is, of course, very special and most parents watch eagerly for it and express great delight the first time their baby grins.

2 A baby who is given an opportunity to look at himself in a mirror will express great pleasure and interest in his reflection and try to puzzle out the mystery by reaching for himself.

3-5 Soon, he begins to interact in many other ways —he will, for example hold out his arms and, therefore, make the work of dressing and undressing him so much easier. Slowly, but surely, he begins to interact and express greater interest in a variety of objects—he takes great delight in discovering what a thing will and will not do and begins to imitate all the actions that his parents and other people make. Long before he can truly co-ordinate his fingers and hands, he will attempt to dress and undress himself and try to fasten and unfasten shoe laces.

6 Later other children become important and he will find special joy in interacting with and sharing social moments with brothers and sisters and other children.

6

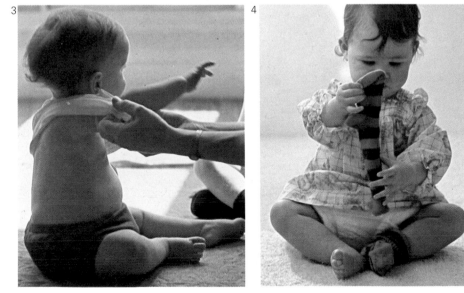

3

4

5

Common Health Problems

Unlike adults, the bodily functions of babies and children are concerned with growth and development. Indeed, when growth and development are normal it is an important sign of good health. Nowadays the emphasis is on the prevention and early detection of ill health. Parents take their young children to local clinics where growth and development are assessed and immunization against certain infective diseases is offered. This approach is much better than attempting to treat ill health once it has taken hold.

Much of a family doctor's time is taken up with attending to childhood complaints. The most common childhood illnesses are infections, usually involving the breathing passages. Fortunately most of these illnesses clear up by themselves after a few days. Indeed, the majority of childhood ailments can be managed safely at home. If hospital admission is necessary, arrangements should be made for mother and child to be admitted together whenever possible in order to avoid the puzzlement and distress a small child can feel at the separation from his parents.

Weight Gain

No two babies gain precisely the same amount of weight from week to week, and some have spells when they gain weight irregularly. For several weeks a baby's progress may disappoint you, and then quite suddenly without reason he gains weight rapidly. In spite of these fluctuations, weight gain is greatest during the first month or two after birth and gradually becomes less as a baby gets older.

As a general guide, a baby gains about 198g (7oz) per week in the first three months, and 155g (5½oz) per week in the second three months. During the second year the weekly weight gain is about 43g (1½oz). Some healthy babies who were lightweight at birth remain below average size, whereas others who were equally small at birth seem to catch up. If a healthy small baby does not 'catch up', it does not mean that something is wrong; it is perfectly possible, of course, to be small and healthy, just as it is possible to be large and unhealthy.

If for some reason you think that your baby is not gaining enough weight, you should discuss the matter with your doctor. He will want to know about the baby's general health, the type and amount of food eaten, and, if available, some previous measurements of the baby's weight. After examining the baby, and, perhaps, reviewing his weight gain during the course of several weeks, it usually becomes apparent that the baby is thriving normally. The usual problem is the conflict between the amount of weight the mother wants the baby to put on, and the weight gain that nature decides is appropriate.

Some babies do gain weight poorly and the most common cause of this is underfeeding. Whilst it is true that nearly all women can breast-feed their baby satisfactorily given the proper conditions, it has to be admitted that if conditions are wrong the milk supply may not be enough to satisfy the baby's needs. If the mother misses meals and does not take enough calories and liquids for example, or if she cannot take an adequate amount of rest and becomes tired or run down, the milk supply is liable to diminish. Occasionally, too, bottle-fed babies are underfed. This might come about when a mother does not know and has not been taught how to feed her baby. Poverty and wilful neglect are other notable causes of underfeeding.

Only occasionally is there a medical reason for poor weight gain, and usually in these cases the baby or child shows other signs of ill health, such as poor appetite, lethargy, anaemia, vomiting, diarrhoea, chronic cough, etc. There are many different medical causes of failure to thrive and investigations are generally necessary so that a proper diagnosis can be made.

It is possible, of course, for a baby to gain an excess amount of weight and if this pattern persists for several months he becomes visibly fat and develops characteristic 'bracelets' of fat around the arms and legs. Large babies are not healthier than small babies. Many doctors, in fact, think that fat babies are at a disadvantage compared with babies of a normal weight; overweight babies are probably more prone to suffer from colds and coughs.

If your baby happens to be overweight you may meet doctors or nurses who have very strong views on the matter and who suggest that you cut down the amount of food you are giving the baby. Certainly, before the age of three months, when a baby should be on an entirely milk diet, it is useless to try and restrict milk intake in any way. Babies of this age generally know when they have had enough. Thickening bottle-feeds by adding cereals or rusks is not a good idea and is certainly one cause of excess weight gain.

Once solids have been established you may inadvertently encourage a baby to become overweight by getting him used to cereals and sweet-tasting purées rather than meat and vegetables. Another situation that can lead to overweight is when baby is established on solids and yet clings to a late night (10 p.m.) and early morning (6 a.m.) milk feed. In this case, you should gradually dilute the milk feed or replace it with fruit juice. A baby may be thirsty rather than hungry at these times, or he may merely enjoy the comfort of sucking.

VOMITING

Many babies bring back a little milk each time they burp and although this may cause anxiety if the milk comes back with force, it really is quite harmless. Some young babies have a 'weak valve' at the point where the gullet joins the stomach and a little of the milk feed tends to be ejected back up the gullet, especially when the baby is put down in his cot after the feed. It may help to sit him propped up for an hour or so after the feed, but whatever you do the vomiting will gradually become less during the first year, particularly when solids are introduced. If the vomiting is particularly troublesome and if a baby is still too young to have solids, your doctor may advise adding a special thickener to the milk feeds.

Another cause for vomiting is excessive handling during or after a feed. For example, mother may worry if she cannot get the baby to burp during the feed. She may continually change his position in the hope of getting him to part with some wind, first putting him over one shoulder, then over the other, then sitting him on her lap. It is not surprising in these circumstances that the baby vomits.

The different types of vomiting described so far are all examples of 'nuisance vomiting'. The baby's health is not affected; he continues to look well, to have a good appetite and to gain weight. The vomiting is a nuisance because it dirties baby's clothes (and yours) and the smell lingers.

There are, however, more serious causes of vomiting in a young baby and you should tell your doctor immediately if vomiting occurs in association with any change in the baby's behaviour, such as a sudden reluctance to feed and lethargy. Other signs that indicate the need for a doctor's opinion include fever, a change in bowel habit, blood in stools, blood or bile in the vomit, a swollen tummy and weight loss.

Vomiting should never be treated lightly in an older baby or child because so-called 'nuisance vomiting' does not occur at this age. Often the cause is merely a dietary indiscretion or a minor infection, but the doctor should always be consulted so that a proper diagnosis can be made.

ABNORMAL STOOLS

The stools (faeces) of babies and children come in all sorts of shapes, sizes, colours, consistencies and frequencies. Fully breastfed babies usually have frequent loose stools during the first few weeks of life. Sometimes the stools are so loose they are like water and merely stain the napkin. You can tell that this is not diarrhoea, associated with some sort of illness, because the baby looks well and there are no other symptoms.

The bowel action generally becomes infrequent by the time the baby is one to three months old and then he may go several days without passing a stool. This is not constipation because the motions remain soft. As this is normal, it is quite wrong to give a laxative medicine to make him open his bowels more frequently. If a baby appears unwell, vomits, develops a swollen tummy or passes blood in the stools, you should always consult your doctor.

The stools of a bottle-fed baby are much firmer than a breastfed baby's because of differences in the chemical make up of human and cow's milk. A young baby fed on cow's milk may have his bowels open four to six times each day, but after several months this generally settles to one to two motions each day. Constipation is quite common in bottle-fed babies and the stools may become so hard that they are difficult to pass. They may even cause a little bleeding from the inside of the anal canal. You may, for example, notice a small streak or two of fresh blood on the surface of the stool. If the baby has insufficient fluids, or sweats a lot because of hot weather or overclothing, this can cause or aggravate constipation. If you are using a milk powder that requires the addition of sugar, use brown sugar instead of white. Another simple approach is to give the baby a few extra small drinks of orange juice. If these measures fail, give him two or three spoonfuls of prune juice, or puréed prunes, once or twice daily. It is best not to use laxative medicines without consulting your doctor.

Constipation in a toddler is usually caused by the child deliberately refusing to have his bowels open, especially if he has been potty trained too early and too forcefully. As a result, he refuses to go until eventually the stools become quite hard and difficult to pass. A child should never be forced into using a potty. The use of laxatives or suppositories often makes matters worse by focusing undue attention on the child's bowels. A toddler can become an expert at using his bowels to completely disrupt family life. Try to vary his diet by introducing more fruit and vegetables. If this doesn't help, consult your doctor before using any medicine. Constipation does not lead to the absorption of poisons or toxins from the bowel.

Infectious Fevers

MUMPS

Mumps is an infectious disease of the salivary glands which is caused by a virus. Usually the first thing that is noticed is a soft swelling at the side of the neck just below the lobe of the ear. This gradually gets larger and pushes the ear lobe forward until the whole side of the face looks swollen. The swelling is tender and painful and the other side of the face is usually affected after a day or two. Most children have a slight fever during the first few days of an attack, and for some the pain gets worse when they taste sour liquids, such as lemon juice or vinegar. The swelling generally lasts for three to seven days.

If you suspect that your child has mumps, you should tell your doctor. There are other causes of swelling at the side of the neck, such as enlarged lymph glands. In boys, mumps can cause pain and swelling of the testicles, but this complication hardly ever occurs before a boy has reached puberty. Occasionally a young child gets a high fever, headache, vomiting and a stiff neck caused by mumps meningitis, but he usually recovers rapidly and completely.

There is no special treatment for mumps and the child is usually infectious until the swelling subsides. It is very unusual to get a second attack. If a child who is susceptible to mumps comes into contact with the infection, he runs the risk of developing the condition between two and three weeks after contact with it.

MEASLES

Measles is a highly contagious infection that is caused by a virus. It generally starts off as a bad cold, but you can usually suspect that something is not quite right because the child's eyes become bloodshot and watery, and a dry, irritating cough develops. A fever also develops which may also be intermittent.

The rash comes out around the fourth day and consists of pink spots situated behind the ears and close to the hair line. Within twenty-four hours, it spreads over the face, trunk, arms, abdomen and legs. Spots appear on the feet a day later. By this time the rash on the face is fading. The child then improves rapidly, but as the spots fade from the body and limbs during the next two days they leave behind a harmless brownish discoloration which clears up in a week or two.

As soon as you suspect that your child has measles, you should let your doctor know. Complications include ear infection, bronchitis and pneumonia. You should certainly call the doctor if the child still has a fever two days or more after the rash has come out, or if the fever settles for a day and then comes back. The common complications of measles are usually caused by bacteria. Antibiotics are, therefore, an important form of treatment. There is, however, no special medicinal treatment for an uncomplicated attack of measles. The child will not feel like eating anything at the height of the illness. Instead you should offer him his favourite cool drink at frequent intervals. Most children want to be in bed whilst they are feverish. Although some seem to experience discomfort from too much light in a room, there is no special need to darken the room unless the child is happier with it that way. He can get up when the fever has gone, and provided there are no signs of a cold or cough, can go out and play about a week after the rash started.

Measles is infectious five or six days before the rash appears and for four or five days after the temperature has become normal. A susceptible child who comes into contact with measles runs the risk of developing the illness ten to fifteen days later; a second attack is rare.

CHICKEN POX

The first thing that is usually noticed in this viral infection is a crop of pimples on the trunk, but occasionally a child may feel generally unwell or feverish a day before the rash comes out. Whether or not you are sure that the rash is chicken pox, you should let your doctor know. The pimples rapidly develop into small 'water blisters' which break, and as they dry up a crust or scab is formed. Fresh crops come out over the face, scalp. abdomen and limbs, each spot going through the 'water blister' and scab stage, but after about four days, no new spots appear. The spots are usually very itchy and if the child scratches them they may become infected and turn into small boils. The itching can be eased by the use of calamine lotion or by letting the child take a warm bath to which bicarbonate of soda has been added. Pat him dry afterwards.

A child who has had chicken pox is no longer infectious seven days after the rash started, and he may return to school even though he usually still has scabs at this stage. A susceptible child who comes into contact with chicken pox runs the risk of developing the disease fifteen to eighteen days later. An attack of chicken pox confers life-long immunity against a second attack. If the mother has had chicken pox as a child she passes her immunity to her baby who is generally protected from the disease for the first three to four months of his life. After this the immunity generally wears off.

GERMAN MEASLES

The virus that causes German measles is quite different from the one that causes real measles. German measles does not usually begin with a cold or cough, although there is occasionally a slight fever or sore throat a day or two before the rash comes out. The rash consists of small pink spots which first appear on the face and then spread to the rest of the body within a day. On the second day the rash starts to fade, but as it does so the spots merge together giving the skin a diffuse flushed appearance; by the third day the rash has often gone.

German measles may be confused with other conditions that cause a pink rash, so you should contact your doctor for a proper diagnosis. He will carefully examine the back of the head and neck because German measles usually causes swelling of the glands in this region. No special treatment is required for the swelling.

The child is infectious from one day before until two days after the start of the rash. A susceptible child who comes into contact with German measles runs the risk of developing the illness ten to twenty-one days later. Although the condition is harmless for children, it can cause abnormalities in foetuses during the first three months of pregnancy. Obviously a woman in early pregnancy should avoid catching German measles, but in practice this is not always possible. Any woman in early pregnancy who thinks that she may have German measles should see a doctor promptly so that the diagnosis can be confirmed by a blood test and the appropriate action taken. German measles vaccine is now available and should be given, before puberty, to girls who have not acquired natural immunity by this time.

SCARLET FEVER

Sometimes tonsillitis occurs together with a generalized rash. In this event, the condition is called Scarlet Fever. It is unusual for this illness to occur under the age of three years. It is no more serious than tonsillitis itself and in some children the rash is so mild that it is not noticed. The germ is spread by droplets from the nose and throat, but it is not highly infectious. In susceptible children, signs of tonsillitis, such as sore throat, fever, headache and vomiting, develop three to five days after contact and the rash appears a day or two later. It involves the whole of the body including the face, and often looks more like a red flush than a proper rash because the tiny red spots are so close together. The skin around the lips does not usually develop the flush and looks pale in contrast to the rest of the face. The tongue, at one stage, appears quite red and angry-looking ('red strawberry tongue').

It is easy for a new parent to become over-anxious about every aspect of a baby or young child's health and development. The human body is a collection of near-miracles, and most infants, however vulnerable and frail we may think they are, have great reserves and powers of self-regulation and self-repair.

When ailments do arise, there is, of course never any need to worry alone. If a baby's or child's behaviour is giving rise to anxiety, a consultation with the family doctor or a visit to the health clinic will help to allay any unnecessary fears. The majority of childhood ailments can be safely taken care of at home by parents and will clear up within a few days.

The doctor will generally prescribe a course of penicillin and the child generally feels a lot better after five to seven days.

During the illness it is not feasible to stop the patient coming into contact with other members of the family, nor should you try. However, the doctor may wish to take a throat swab to see if the germ has disappeared from the throat before allowing the child to mix freely outside the home.

Immunization

The medical care of babies and children involves the *prevention* of diseases as well as their *treatment*. One of the most remarkable achievements in child care has been the prevention of certain infectious diseases by the use of immunization.

Antibodies are complex chemicals that circulate in the blood and kill many different viruses and bacteria. Generally, each antibody attacks a specific type of germ. For example, the antibody against measles kills the measles virus, but not the chicken pox virus. Immunization is a way of building up antibody levels in the blood.

In 'passive immunization' the child is given the antibody to a particular disease, but although this sounds sensible it does not give protection for very long because the antibody soon wears off leaving the child without protection again. Usually 'active immunization' is used, and here the child is inoculated with a small dose of either killed germs or live germs that have been inactivated and made harmless. Following active immunization, antibodies are produced that stay for a long time in the blood stream, giving a good degree of protection against the disease.

During the first year of life a basic course of immunization is given against diphtheria (D), tetanus (T), whooping cough (P) and poliomyelitis. Incidentally, 'P' stands for the scientific name for whooping cough, pertussis. The DTP vaccines are combined in one injection, known as the 'triple vaccine', and poliomyelitis vaccine is given by mouth at the same time.

The triple vaccine and the poliomyelitis vaccine are given three times during the first year so that the baby's antibodies are built up to a high level. The age of baby, when the first dose is given, varies in different countries from as early as one month to as late as six months. Another thing that varies is the time interval between the three doses.

During the second year, measles vaccine is given. At school entry, booster doses of diphtheria and tetanus vaccine are given along with oral poliomyelitis vaccine. At school leaving, booster doses of tetanus vaccine and oral poliomyelitis vaccine are given.

In some places, immunization against tuberculosis (BCG vaccine) is offered to babies during the first few weeks of life. The vaccine should certainly be given to all susceptible children, regardless of their age or local policy, if there is another member of the family with tuberculosis. This applies even if the tuberculosis is said to be 'healed' or 'inactive'. The doctor can tell whether a child is susceptible by doing a simple skin test. The fact that a child is susceptible merely means that he has not yet built up any natural immunity to the disease.

Vaccination against German measles is now available. In the United Kingdom it is offered to all girls between ten and fourteen years who have not already had the infection.

Smallpox vaccination used to be given routinely in infancy, but this is no longer recommended.

An example of a suitable immunization schedule is illustrated, but do not be surprised if the scheme carried out in your own clinic is a little different. It is important that the full course of three injections is given in the first year because an incomplete course leads to incomplete immunity. You should keep your own record of the dates and type of immunization given, so that if you change your doctor or move into a different area it will be clear to others precisely where your child is in the immunization schedule.

Serious complications, occurring as a result of immunization procedures, are very rare indeed and it is also true that serious complications, occurring as a result of the common infectious diseases, are very rare. However, one of the reasons for immunization is to reduce the number of cases of infection in the community; obviously if there are fewer cases of, say, whooping cough occurring in the community then your child will stand less chance of catching the disease. If you have reservations or anxieties about immunization, perhaps because of something you have read or heard from friends, you should discuss the matter with your doctor. Doctors who are interested in the welfare of children also understand the feelings of parents and are usually pleased to answer your questions.

Immunization Schedule

Age	Type of vaccine
During 1st year	1: First dose of D/T/P* and oral polio
	2: Four to eight weeks later: D/T/P and oral polio
	3: Two to six months later: D/T/P and oral polio
During 2nd year	Measles
5 years (or school entry)	Booster dose of D/T** and oral polio
10–13 years (if not naturally immune)	BCG (tuberculosis)
10–14 years (girls, if not naturally immune)	German measles
15–19 years (or school leaving)	Tetanus and oral polio

* D/T/P: diphtheria, tetanus and whooping cough vaccine ("triple")
** D/T: diphtheria and tetanus vaccine

Respiratory Infections

The nasal passages and the mouth are in direct communication with the air outside and also lead down to the bronchial tubes. It is, therefore, not surprising that children, particularly between the ages of two and six years, get frequent colds and coughs. This is part of normal growing up and does not cause any damage to the lungs. In most cases the germ that starts off the infection is called a virus. This is so minute that it can only be seen with the help of a very powerful microscope. Antibiotics have no effect on viruses, so your doctor may not wish to prescribe anything at the start of a cold. Occasionally larger germs, called bacteria, come on to the scene and antibiotics may help then.

There is very little you can do to prevent a child catching a cold or cough. If he is having a reasonable diet, tonics and extra vitamins are of no help, and keeping him indoors when it is wet or cold outside will not prevent him from catching colds. If you have more than one child, colds will quickly pass from one member of the family to another and there is no point in preventing contact between the children.

Respiratory infections can involve any part of the breathing passages and the child's symptoms and the treatment will, to some extent, depend on the site affected. It is not necessary to nurse the child in his cot or bed if he feels more at ease on the sofa in the living room. There is no point in making a toddler rest if he does not want to; if he prefers to walk about it nearly always means that he is well enough to do so. If he loses his appetite, do not force him to eat because it will probably make him sick; instead offer him his favourite drink at frequent intervals.

If he has a fever, the room where he is nursed should not be at a temperature higher than 21°C and he should be lightly clothed. It is dangerous to wrap a feverish child in warm blankets because his temperature will rise even higher. Junior aspirin tablets are helpful in reducing the fever. One or two tablets may be given safely to toddlers and repeated in four hours if the temperature is still raised.

COLDS

A cold generally lasts a few days and the usual sign is a runny nose. The nasal discharge is thin and clear at first, but it may turn green later on. Young babies may not have a fever or lose their appetite; in fact, they get thirsty and may demand more milk than usual. You must, however, be prepared for the baby to take longer over feeds because it is difficult for him to suck properly when his nose is blocked. He snorts and gets restless, frequently stops to remove his mouth from the teat or nipple and cries in frustration. A good sneeze temporarily relieves the nasal obstruction. If your doctor has prescribed nose drops, use them gently; if you cannot get the drops into baby's nose without a battle it is best not to use them at all. There is no point in being obsessional about wiping the baby's nose. This will only make it sore. Mucus frequently trickles down the back of his throat and causes him to wake up coughing. This is not serious and does not mean that the cold has 'settled on his chest'. In fact, young babies rarely suffer complications from a cold and it is not necessary to call the doctor unless the baby develops a fever, persistent coughing, vomiting, loss of interest in feeds or laboured breathing.

In toddlers, a cold may begin with quite a high fever and the child may look flushed and take to lying down on the sofa. He may get obstreperous and miserable even when you try and comfort him. You usually suspect that he is sickening for something, but you cannot be sure what it is going to be. At this stage, it is a good idea to call the doctor. When it is clear from the outset that the child has a cold there is no need to ask for a doctor, unless a fever develops several days *after* the start of the cold, or if there is a persistent cough, wheezing or laboured breathing, earache or discharge from an ear.

COUGHS

A really troublesome cough usually means bronchitis, which is an infection of the bronchial tubes. *All young babies with a troublesome cough should be seen by a doctor.* When a toddler has a cough, but is generally well and is up playing with his toys there is no need to call the doctor. If the child is feverish, lethargic and off his food, he should be examined by a doctor. If the breathing is laboured, particularly if grunting ocurs, this may mean pneumonia and the doctor should be called promptly.

Sometimes a lot of phlegm builds up in the bronchial tubes and you may actually feel a 'rattling' in the chest when the child breathes. Although this may worry you. it is not a serious sign unless the breathing is laboured. Toddlers often wheeze with each attack of bronchitis and this does not mean that they have asthma. Your doctor may not wish to prescribe a medicine to stop the cough because coughing helps to clear the bronchial tubes. Most cough medicines for young children do not work very well and the cough gets better in a few days without them. The doctor may, however, prescribe an antibiotic.

when a cough is taking a long time to clear up. Children who have been immunized against whooping cough may get the condition in a mild form and, in this instance, it is not easy to be certain of the diagnosis. It is always a worry when a young baby gets whooping cough because he can become ill and exhausted very quickly. The treatment that your doctor suggests will depend very much on the age of the child and the severity of the condition, but cough medicines do not help very much.

Remember that whooping cough is easily spread from one child to another. It is highly infectious for the first two weeks of the illness, but then gradually becomes less infectious. Five weeks after the start, there is little chance of passing it on. It is practically impossible to prevent spread between family members, so there is no point in keeping brothers and sisters apart. Visitors, however, should not be allowed in the house if they have a troublesome cough, especially when young babies are present.

If your child has been in contact with whooping cough and is going to develop the disease, then he will do so between five and fourteen days after contact. This length of time is called the 'incubation period'.

WHEEZINESS

A wheeze is a high-pitched musical noise which comes from the chest when the child breathes out. It usually means that there is some narrowing or obstruction of the bronchial tubes. Toddlers may get wheezy each time they have an attack of bronchitis because the bronchial tubes get partially blocked by phlegm. This type of bronchitis, which starts off as an ordinary cold and is usually associated with a fever, is very common, especially during the winter. The attacks stop by the age of five or six years.

Toddlers with wheezy bronchitis are not usually wheezy between attacks. You should contact your doctor when your child has his first attack of wheezing. Wheezy bronchitis will take its own course, generally lasting several days, with the wheeziness coming and going at short intervals during the day. Unfortunately medicines are not much help in controlling the wheezing, but your doctor may prescribe an antibiotic. Once you have got used to your child having these attacks there is no need to call the doctor if the wheeziness is mild and the child is not really ill.

Asthma is quite a different condition that affects older children and adults. The wheezing in this case is mainly caused by spasm in the muscle of the bronchial tubes. Attacks usually start quite suddenly without a preceding cold or fever and the child is often wheezy from time to time

Between the ages of two and six years, children frequently get colds and coughs. A cold generally lasts a few days and the usual sign is a runny nose. In toddlers a cold may begin with quite a high fever and the child may look flushed and want to lie down. He may get obstreperous and miserable even when you try to comfort him.

If a fever develops several days after the start of a cold, or if there is persistent coughing or wheezing, call a doctor.

WHOOPING COUGH

Whooping cough starts off as an ordinary cold with, perhaps, a slight cough. If the child has not had whooping cough before and has recently been in contact with a case you may suspect the diagnosis. One clue is that the cough comes in attacks that last several minutes; between spells there is no cough. Each attack consists of a series of coughs, in rapid succession, during which the child's face usually looks congested. You may wish that he would stop coughing and take a deep breath in; eventually he does of course, but then he starts another bout of coughing. The coughing attacks usually happen more frequently during the night, and retching or vomiting may occur soon after an attack. You may hear a whoop or crowing noise when the child stops to catch his breath, but this is not always present.

Whooping cough generally lasts four weeks or even longer. Doctors usually suspect the diagnosis between attacks. Only a few children with asthma know what brings on an attack; it might be something they are allergic to, or an emotional stress, or strenuous physical exercise.

Children with asthma often have relatives with the same condition or with other allergic problems, such as hay fever or eczema. It is also common for children with asthma to have hay fever or eczema as well. Fortunately, there are many different kinds of medicine that can be used to treat and, to some extent, prevent attacks. Affected children must be closely supervised by a doctor.

Another cause of wheezing is the accidental inhalation of a foreign body, such as a peanut or bead. This can be when a young child who is perfectly well and playing with a small object, suddenly has a coughing or choking attack which leaves him with noisy wheezy breathing. The doctor should be called at once if this is suspected.

Wheezing in young babies is generally caused by an inflammation of the very small bronchial tubes. This is called 'acute bronchiolitis'. Coughing and laboured breathing also occur and a doctor should be contacted whenever a baby becomes wheezy.

CROUP

Croup is an inflammation of the vocal cords and windpipe. It gives the child a barking cough, difficulty in breathing and causes a crowing noise in the throat each time he breathes in. There are several kinds of croup. A typical case is that of a child who has been well during the day, or who has a slight cold, and who wakes up with a hoarse cough and noisy breathing, sometimes struggling to catch his breath. There is no fever and the symptoms are usually relieved by breathing moist air. This kind of croup, which is called spasmodic croup, often starts up again after several hours and it may occur several nights in succession. There are more severe kinds of croup where the child has a high fever and is generally ill as well as having severe difficulty in breathing.

You should always call your doctor if you suspect croup. Close medical supervision is often required. Whilst waiting for the doctor to come, you can moisten the air the child breathes by taking him into the kitchen whilst you boil several pans of water on the cooker. There are special 'steam kettles' available for the relief of croup in children and it is sensible to have one in the house if you know your child is prone to spasmodic croup. Another alternative, if you have running hot water, is to take the child into the bathroom whilst you run a bath.

Although croup sounds very distressing, it is important to remain calm and avoid panic.

SORE THROAT

A sore throat may occur in association with a cold or bronchitis. The child may complain of pain or you may suspect the problem when you notice his difficulty in swallowing or a drooling of saliva. You should call the doctor. He will inspect the tonsils, but even if they are inflamed there is rarely any need to have them removed. Even repeated attacks of tonsillitis usually cease to occur spontaneously as the child gets older. Do not forget to tell the doctor if other members of the family have a sore throat.

Repeated attacks of tonsillitis in a child are sometimes caused by a germ being passed round the family; certain members of the family may 'carry' the germ in their throat without being unwell. If the doctor suspects this, he can gently swab the throat of all members of the family and then see if the swab grows any germs. He may wish to treat all the family simultaneously with the same antibiotic to destroy the germs and avoid the risk of re-infection.

EAR INFECTIONS

The middle ear chamber, which is made up of the ear drum and three tiny bones, often gets infected in babies and children. The infection usually starts off as a cold or bronchitis, but after a day or two the child either complains of earache or frequently puts his hand up to the affected ear. He usually has a high fever. In severe cases, or when treatment is delayed, the ear drum may perforate and a greeny-yellow or cream discharge comes from the ear. This should not be confused with the slight, light brown, thin ear wax that can be seen in any child with a fever. *A child with earache should be seen by a doctor within twenty-four hours; you should not give any form of ear drops whilst waiting for the doctor to come.* He will normally prescribe an antibiotic. Aspirin is helpful in relieving the pain and some children find that holding a warm flannel against the affected ear gives some relief. If your child gets an ear infection each time he has a cold, it is important that treatment is given promptly at each attack. There is a risk otherwise that the delicate sound conducting mechanisms of the middle ear will become damaged and cause a degree of permanent deafness.

An ear infection in a young baby can be hard to diagnose because it can occur without a fever. You might suspect the problem when a baby, who has had a cold for a day or two, cries in a shrill tone, refuses to be comforted, and frequently reaches out to touch one or both ears. The doctor can only be sure of the diagnosis by looking at the eardrum with a special torch. Suitable treatment can then be given.

Miscellaneous Childhood Ailments

CONVULSIONS

About one in fourteen of all children has at least one convulsion or fit. The usual kind is known as a 'febrile convulsion' and it is caused by the high temperature that sometimes occurs in infections such as colds or bronchitis. This sort of convulsion is prone to happen in children between one and three years old. The usual story is that the child is noted to be off colour and feverish, as though he is sickening for something, when suddenly his eyes roll upwards, he loses consciousness and makes jerking movements of all limbs which generally last a minute or so. He may pass urine or evacuate his bowels during the fit and is usually drowsy for several hours afterwards. You cannot do anything to stop the convulsion once it is happening, but you can turn the child on to his side and put a soft cushion under his hips. In this position he is less likely to inhale vomit. The convulsion will send his temperature up still higher and it is important to keep him cool whilst waiting for the doctor to arrive; never wrap the child in blankets, instead remove his top clothes and if he has a really high fever (above, say, 38.5°C (101°F)) sponge him down with lukewarm water. However, do not soak him with water or leave him in a draught.

Some toddlers are prone to convulsions each time they have a fever. In this instance, it is a good idea to let them have two junior aspirin tablets at the first sign of an infection. The doctor may suggest giving anti-convulsant medicine between attacks. He may also suggest an EEG test (electro-encephalogram). This is a harmless investigation that measures and records the brain's electrical activity. It is not to be confused with 'ECT', which is electric shock treatment used for treating some adults with severe depression. Febrile convulsions have nothing to do with epilepsy and they cease to occur after the age of five years. Convulsions that occur in very young babies are not usually caused by fever, but may be related to problems that occurred at birth, such as slowness in starting to breathe. Young babies may not have typical jerky movements; instead they may merely turn pale, roll their eyes upwards, and become generally stiff. These attacks can generally be controlled by anti-convulsant medicine. However, before your doctor prescribes any form of treatment for these repeated attacks. It is necessary to carry out a number of investigations to find the precise cause.

BREATH-HOLDING ATTACKS

These attacks, which are related to temper tantrums, usually start between twelve and eighteen months and stop by the age of five years. The child bursts out crying when he has hurt himself, or when he has been punished, or perhaps, when he has not got his own way over something. During the crying spell he holds his breath for about ten seconds and goes blue. Sometimes he holds his breath for a little longer, loses consciousness and goes limp and pale, but recovers after a few moments. Occasionally a convulsion occurs during the attack, and it is not surprising that these episodes cause parents a lot of anxiety. Unfortunately, they are difficult to prevent and medicines are of no help at all.

If an attack is precipitated by a child not getting his own way, it is useless giving in to him. If one does, he will merely repeat the performance when the next opportunity arises. There is also no point in scolding him or doing anything which shows him how concerned you are because then he will realize that he has a very powerful weapon. The time during which he holds his breath seems an eternity to most parents. Some say that they can bring an attack to a finish by giving the child a firm slap on the bottom.

You should, of course, let your doctor know if your child starts to have attacks of any kind that cause him to stop breathing, change colour in any way or lose consciousness, even if you are convinced that it is the child's temper that is at the root of the problem.

BOW LEGS, KNOCK KNEES AND FOOT PROBLEMS

It is normal for a baby to have some degree of bowing of the legs during the first year or so of life. This is particularly noticeable when he first starts to stand because he holds his feet apart, and his nappy fills out the space between the top of his thighs and makes him look more bow-legged than he really is. During the second year, the bowing corrects itself and he generally develops knock-knees which is another normal phase of development. Nearly eighty per cent of three year olds have some degree of knock-knees and, in nearly all cases, the condition corrects itself by the age of seven years.

When starting to walk, many children tend to turn their toes inwards. Usually this is caused by the whole leg being rotated slightly inwards. In these cases no treatment is required because the condition corrects itself by the time the child is six years old. Sometimes in-toeing is caused by a mild foot deformity which usually improves without treatment, but your doctor may advise that simple foot exercises are carried out.

All children have flat feet when they first stand and start to walk, but this generally improves as the small muscles in the feet become stronger. It is quite common for a toddler to have flat feet when he is standing relaxed, but when he lifts his heels off the ground and rises on his toes, the flattening of the feet disappears.

SQUINT

When the eyes are not in line with each other, either when at rest or when moving, the term 'squint' or 'strabismus' is used. During the first month or two of life it is quite common for babies to have a mild squint from time to time when they are trying to focus on a close object. However, if a young baby has a persistent squint the doctor should be told so that the eyes can be properly examined as soon as possible. A baby with a persistent squint is never 'too young to have his eyes examined'. After two months you should always report a squint to your doctor, even if it is only intermittent. There are many different causes of squint, and as a general rule early treatment is important. One problem is that if the eyes are not properly lined up, the child learns to cope in a manner which impairs the vision of the squinting eye. This is what is meant by a 'lazy eye', and it is the end result of neglecting a squint.

WORMS

Threadworms are by far the most common worms to infect children and nearly all children get infected at some time; so there is no cause for alarm if you see what looks like little white threads, 3 to 6.5 mm ($\frac{1}{4}$ to $\frac{3}{8}$ inch) long, in the child's stools. They do not affect the appetite, nor do they cause tummyache, anaemia or nose-picking; usually they cause no symptoms whatsoever. During the night the female worms crawl out of the bowel to lay their eggs and this might cause itching around the anus. Very occasionally, in girls, the worms' nocturnal activities lead to an irritation of the urethra (the canal through which urine is passed from the bladder) and an urgent desire to pass urine when there is very little or no urine to pass. Similar urinary symptoms can be caused by a bacterial infection of the kidney and bladder, so you should not put the trouble down to the worms without taking the child to the doctor.

In most cases, threadworm infection burns itself out in time and no treatment is recommended unless there are symptoms. The problem is that the eggs that are laid on the skin around the anus soon find their way into clothes and dust. They are then picked up on the child's fingers, passed into the mouth and swallowed. The worms hatch out inside the bowel and the cycle repeats itself.

When a child has threadworms, other members of the family are almost certain to have them as well. If symptoms are present your doctor will suggest the appropriate medicine which should be prescribed for all members of the family at the same time.

NAPPY RASH

Red discoloration around the anus and in the buttock cleft is common, especially in babies who have frequent loose motions. It generally improves by itself, especially if you take care not to leave soiled nappies in contact with the baby's skin for any length of time. There is, however, no need to disturb a baby's sleep by frequently looking to see if the nappy is soiled.

The whole nappy area may become red, sore and spotty and this is known as 'nappy rash' or 'ammoniacal dermatitis'. It is likely to occur when wet nappies are left in contact with the skin for long periods. In this situation, germs from the bowel have time to break down the urine in the nappy to release ammonia which inflames the skin. Changing a baby's milk or giving him some kind of medicine will not of course, get rid of the rash.

Detergents and soap may aggravate the condition, so you must rinse the nappies out properly after they have been washed. It is best not to use rubber pants over the nappy. This traps warmth and moisture and prevents the skin from healing. If the room is not too cold, it helps if you let the baby spend some of the day without a nappy. This will, however, probably, involve extra washing because of soiled sheets. Prolonged exposure to air is probably the quickest cure for nappy rash. You can purchase a simple 'barrier cream' from the chemist. This should be applied liberally each time the nappy is changed; many mothers use the traditional 'zinc and castor oil' cream and claim good results.

If the rash is extensive or oozing, or if you can see definite red pimples, you should seek your doctor's advice. Red pimples, with scaliness of the surrounding skin, may mean that the nappy rash has become infected with thrush (see below) and a special antibiotic ointment, called Nystatin, should be used for this. Thrush infection is one reason why a nappy rash takes a long time to clear up. Once thrush is recognized and treated, the skin usually clears up rapidly.

THRUSH

Thrush is the name given to a fungal infection that commonly involves the inside of the mouth of young babies. When the mother's vagina is infected by thrush the baby may pick it up during birth. It shows after several days as white patches on the tongue and inside the cheeks that look rather like milk stains. Unlike milk stains, however, the patches are difficult to rub off and they usually leave a raw bleeding surface underneath. A baby's mouth can get quite sore and he may become fretful at feed times. The infection should be promptly treated and your doctor will generally prescribe some mouth drops (Nystatin Drops). Sometimes a nappy rash gets infected by thrush (see above) and this generally shows as red pimples with some scaliness of the surrounding skin. The infection responds rapidly to Nystatin ointment.

CRADLE CAP

Crusts on the scalp, called Cradle Cap, is common during the first few months of life and generally clears up by itself. You should not pick at the scaly areas.

ECZEMA

Eczema is a skin reaction that occurs in susceptible children, in response to many different factors. In most cases it is not possible to know precisely what the skin is reacting to; an emotional state might trigger it off, or a chemical or material that comes in contact with the skin, or something eaten or inhaled. Eczema tends to occur in children where other members of the family also suffer from allergic conditions, such as hay fever, asthma or eczema itself. A child with eczema may also have hay fever or asthma.

Very severe eczema may involve the skin over the entire body. In less severe cases, the usual sites, are behind the ears, over the elbows and behind the knees. It is common for the face to be involved in young babies. The rash is red and usually itches a lot; the skin feels rough and scaly. During a flare-up the skin may look really angry and constant scratching causes patches to become weepy. As these dry up, scabs or crusts are formed. The inflamed skin can easily become infected when the scabs are scratched. Eczema is noted for its tendency to flare-up and improve in bouts but, even during a good phase, it is usual for the skin to feel coarse and dry.

It is easy to confuse eczema with other rashes. If you suspect that your baby or child has eczema, consult your doctor. Even if your child really has the complaint it is likely that he will outgrow the condition. Eczema is less common in babies who have been breastfed, so if there is a history of any allergic disorder in your family that is a special reason for you to breastfeed your baby.

There are many different approaches to treatment and your doctor will advise you what to do. Unfortunately, many parents become obsessed with trying to find something that their child is allergic to. If you are convinced, for example, that a particular sort of food causes the eczema to get worse, then by all means withdraw it from the diet. Only use ointments or creams that your doctor has prescribed.

A child with eczema must not be vaccinated against smallpox, nor should any of the family living with him be vaccinated. This is because it is dangerous for the smallpox vaccine to contaminate eczematous skin. Other immunizations are safe and should be carried out.

HERNIA

An umbilical hernia is very common in young babies and consists of a round swelling at the navel, anything in size from that of a pea to that of a plum. It is caused by a weakness in the muscle at the base of the navel, so that a small part of the bowel pushes through and causes the navel to bulge, especially when the baby cries. This type of hernia is harmless, does not require treatment, and becomes smaller as the baby gets older.

An inguinal hernia is much more common in boys and is caused by a weakness of the muscles in the lower part of the abdomen. A piece of bowel squeezes out between the layers of muscle and causes a swelling in the groin that sometimes reaches down into the scrotum. When a girl has an inguinal hernia, there is also a swelling in the groin. In this case it may spread down to the labia. An inguinal hernia may not be visible when the baby is lying down quietly, but appears when he is held upright, especially when crying.

An inguinal hernia does not go away by itself, but it is easily treated by a small operation. If you suspect that your baby has an inguinal hernia, he must be seen by a doctor promptly because there is a risk that the part of the bowel that has herniated will become obstructed.

Toys are just as important to a child who is unwell as they are when he is fit and active, and they have to be chosen with particular care. A sick child often needs toys for a slightly younger age group—toys that can be easily managed without requiring too much effort. If buying new toys, introduce a small toy daily rather than one big one which has to last through the whole illness. A very large tray or flat surface which stretches across the bed is important. When you spend time with the child, or when friends come in, have a jigsaw, paper and crayons and a selection of good reading matter at the ready.

Accidents in the Home
Make the House a Safe Place

If babies, toddlers and children could be said to be experts in any one thing—keeping parents on their toes would win the vote. A child does not give much advance warning that what he could not do yesterday he can do today. The only way to avoid being taken by unpleasant surprises is to remain at least one jump ahead. Preferably, start making your home child-proof in pregnancy so that you can remain many jumps ahead. Being wise after an event is easy; being wise before an event can also be easy if one plans ahead.

Begin by taking a good look around the house. Make sure that all pills and medicines, which children often mistake for sweets and delectable drinks, are placed in lockable child-proof medicine cabinets which are placed out of reach. Household cleaners can also look very appetizing. Do not store these under the sink where they are accessible to children. Place them out of reach. Stairs are perfect practising areas for young commandoes—place a safety gate at the top and bottom and make sure that the carpet is properly secured and not a good alternative for a deadly trip-wire. Wobbly items of heavy furniture, which have stayed put with the help of pieces of paper, may be safe for 'knowing' adults, but they will not stand up to young children's antics. Some privacy may be necessary in bathrooms and lavatories, but locks will need to be raised so that children do not lock themselves in, howl to get out or retire into a mischievous and potentially dangerous silence. Slippery customers will need protection against slippery surfaces.

Take a stroll around the garden. Laburnum and laurel, for example, are lovely plants but, along with others of their companions, they are also deadly poisonous. A parent will either need to replan certain areas of the garden or be prepared to make sure that children do not make a picnic of poisonous seeds and berries or, indeed, the compost heap. Lucky owners of garden ponds, streams, lakes or swimming pools will only remain lucky if these are made child-proof, or if babies are taught to swim. Toddlers and young children have been known to drown in a couple of inches of water. Marble-topped tables or wrought iron accessories have a habit of getting into children's flight paths; plastic accessories may be a come-down, but they are far safer. Patios, which are mounted by concrete steps, or which have a drop to anything but a soft landing will need some safety revision for young tumblers and divers. Garden gates in general, particularly those leading on to roads, will need to be fastened by unreachable locks. Tool sheds are a child's paradise—unfortunately, they contain many things, such as poisonous weedkillers and sharp-edged tools, that are likely to hasten the child's passage to the real place! Keep him on earth by *always,* even when you are working in the garden, locking the door. The real thing, like the garage and the car, are far more exciting than toy replicas. Keep young mechanics at bay by always locking the door. A child can discover how to release a handbrake and service himself with interesting-looking tools and oils and brake and clutch fluids in a second. Never allow a toddler to run and greet the car; one day you may not see him. Never allow him to stand nearby when you are reversing or to imitate mechanics or do-it-yourself dads by lying under the car.

ROOM BY ROOM CHECKS

Toddlers and young children are taught peek-a-boo and waving games from their earliest days. Ensure that they do not practise these at upstairs' windows. Secure all upstairs' windows with child-proof safety catches. Remember that a toddler quickly learns how to move chairs and other pieces of furniture so that he can stand on windowsills to look out. The same applies, of course, to reaching any tantalizing object which has been placed out of his reach. Heavy or valuable ornaments are best put into storage until the child is less at the mercy of his own whims and fancies.

☐ **Electrical Equipment** Electric plugs fascinate toddlers and young children. For them holes are meant for probing. The only way to ensure safety is to invest in safety shutters for every socket. Trailing flexes are an obvious danger—a child will keep pulling to discover what is on the other end of them. If they are placed, for safety, under carpets, they can become frayed without your knowledge and cause a fire. All wires must be properly insulated and secured. It is wise to check safety factors with your local electricity board and, of course, to have all electrical circuits inspected regularly for safety.

Toddlers love switches, particularly ones that hiss and make an interesting smell. Gas plugs will either need to be sealed off, or heavily disguised with a heavy piece of furniture. Matches and lighters are also a source of endless fascination and should always be kept out of reach. When a child is old enough to understand the danger, he should be taught how to use them safely. A child who is shown how to use matches is less likely to become obsessed by them, and light them in a secret and dangerous place like a cupboard or tent.

☐ **Danger from Fires** All fires will need fireguards. These will need to be child-proof, i.e., made of fine mesh so that a child cannot poke his fingers through or use them as a post box. They will also need safety fasteners so that they can be secured against the interest of young weightlifters. Modern oil fires and gas fires are certainly safer, but they are never an ideal choice when there is a toddler or young child in the house. Barbecues and bonfires are always potentially lethal; and, pretty though they are, there is no such thing as a safe firework for any age group.

☐ **Kitchen care** The kitchen is the chief disaster zone. Cooker guards are essential, so are saucepans with two little side handles, rather than one long handle which can be pulled and tilted with disastrous results. The only way for a child to be completely safe is to be kept out of the kitchen, well away from the temptation of countless dangerous gadgets. Most parents, however, indulge their children's desire to be with them, where the action is going on, so, at least, ensure that the action is as safe as possible by strapping the child into a highchair or restraining him in a playpen.

☐ **Dining safely** Important though it is for children to dine in style, tablecloths should never be used for babies, toddlers and young children. One enthusiastic tug can cause serious burns, scalds, cuts and bruises. Children are also safer confined in playpens if one is serving tea or coffee from low tables. A parent's or visitor's lap is no place for a child when the adult is enjoying a hot cup of anything. Unless children are restrained safely in highchairs, oven-to-tableware dishes and bowls should never be used in their presence. They should, for obvious reasons, be in a playpen or highchair when adults are bringing hot food in from the kitchen to the dining-room.

☐ **Sleeping and playing safely** Cats and some small dogs love sleeping on babies and this can cause suffocation. A cat net is essential for the pram, and bedroom doors should be closed. Babies do not need pillows—these can cause suffocation; and the pram or cot mattress should never be protected by thin polythene covers which can cling to their mouths and noses and cause suffocation. For the same reason, children should never be allowed to play with polythene bags.

Young spacemen and girls will put these over their heads and risk death from suffocation. Children should always wear day and night-clothes made from non-flammable materials. A minimum requirement is natural fabrics. These burn far less quickly and fiercely than man-made fibres.

All toys must suit the age and temperament of the child. What is right for one age group will be dangerous for another. Toys should be painted with lead-free paint and be free of sharp jagged edges or small parts which can be dismantled and swallowed or pushed up noses and in to ears. Babies, in particular, need to be protected from the habit of 'mouthing' and, therefore, possibly swallowing small play items, or, indeed, any kind of item. (See Suitable Toys page 220.)

FIRST-AID

However many precautions you take, you will need a first-aid box (which is kept safely out of children's reach) and a first-aid manual. Take time to study the manual and to attend a first-aid course. There is nothing like a little knowledge for minimizing everybody's suffering when an accident occurs.

☐ **Word of warning** Do not frighten or worry yourself to death by becoming over-obsessed with all the possible paradise-capers that your child may indulge in. Having taken all reasonable precautions to safeguard him, just stay reasonably vigilant and comfort yourself with the thought that an over-protected child is far more accident-prone than a child who is, within reason, allowed to learn to live and *survive* by trial and error!

1 The kitchen is the most accident-prone zone in any house. Cooker guards are essential, so are saucepans with two little side handles, rather than one long handle, which can be pulled and tilted by young children with disastrous results. The only way to keep a child completely safe when you are working in the kitchen, is to keep him well away from the temptation of countless dangerous gadgets. If parents do indulge their toddler's or young child's desire to be with them, the child should be kept safely restrained.

How to Cope with Emergencies

Emergencies occur with babies and young children commonly as a result of accidents in the home. Indeed, accidental injury or poisoning is one of the most common reasons for children attending hospital. It is remarkable that a child's home, which is generally considered to be a place of security and safety, may also be one of danger. We all know of children who suffer more than their fair share of accidents and who are labelled 'accident prone'. A child may be especially explorative and adventuresome, and it is a necessary part of his development to be exposed to *known* risks. Most accidents, however, are preventable and parents must ensure that they do not *unwittingly* expose their child to dangers.

If an emergency arises, whether as the result of an accident or illness, prompt and sensible handling of the situation may greatly improve the child's outcome. Keep in a safe place the telephone number of your doctor and nearest hospital. If you do not have a telephone make sure that you know of *several* nearby telephones which can be reached in the event of an emergency. Do not rely on one such telephone—if public, it may be out of order; if private, your friend may not be in.

BURNS AND SCALDS

If the child's clothes are on fire, he should be rolled into a blanket or overcoat to smother the flames. A child with an extensive burn or scald should be rushed to the nearest hospital by the fastest means available. Do not remove his clothing, do not apply anything to the burnt or scalded area, and do not give him anything to drink.

The severity of a burn or scald largely depends on the *amount* of skin involved. Plasma—the fluid part of blood—oozes from the affected part and a serious state of shock occurs if a lot of plasma is lost. In general, if more than ten per cent of the body surface is involved it is necessary to replace the lost plasma with a transfusion. As a rough guide, the skin covering the whole of a limb is equivalent to ten per cent of the body surface.

If the burn or scald is only slight, immerse the affected part in cold water and cover it with a clean dry dressing. Ointments and creams should not be used. Take the child to your doctor or hospital casualty department for advice about further care.

CUTS AND GRAZES

The most important thing is to stop any bleeding that might be coming from a cut by firmly pressing a dry dressing or suitable clean cloth over the source of bleeding. Keep pressure on the dressing for several minutes and avoid the temptation of releasing your finger every few seconds to see if the bleeding has stopped. Do not apply any form of tourniquet. In untrained hands, a tourniquet could totally stop the circulation to the affected limb.

A gaping wound will need careful cleaning and stitching. It is best not to give the child anything to eat or drink before taking him to the hospital casualty department in case a general anaesthetic is required.

Any puncture wound should be regarded as serious and should be seen by a doctor. Although the mark on the skin may be tiny, the internal damage may be severe.

For certain injuries, the doctor may think it advisable for the child to have a booster dose of tetanus toxoid. A booster injection works only if the child has previously been immunized against tetanus according to one of the schedules, so remember to have him immunized at the appropriate times.

Minor cuts and grazes should be cleaned with soap and water, dried with a clean cloth and dabbed with a mild antiseptic solution. It is best not to use iodine because it stings badly. The wound should be covered with a dry dressing and left undisturbed for five to seven days. If necessary it may then be re-dressed.

HEAD INJURY

A baby or child who suffers a knock on the head that causes him to lose consciousness must be examined by a doctor as soon as possible. In most

2 However safety-minded parents are, minor accidents such as cuts and bruises, are an inevitable part of family life. For this reason, a medicine cabinet is an essential piece of equipment in any home. When there are young children in the house, the cabinet must, of course, be kept out of reach and locked at all times. It is advisable to study a first-aid manual and, if possible, to attend a first-aid course. There is nothing like a little knowledge for minimizing everybody's suffering when an accident occurs.

cases observation in hospital for a day or two is needed. A skull X-ray is usually taken, although skull fractures heal up quickly and are not important in themselves. The matter for concern is the possibility of underlying brain injury, but this complication cannot be diagnosed by conventional X-rays. A period of close observation in hospital helps the doctor to assess whether there has been any significant brain injury.

After a serious knock on the head, even if there has been no loss of consciousness, a child is apt to complain of headache, looks rather pale and perhaps vomits once or twice. He may even feel a little sleepy. If so, put him to bed, ask your doctor to see him and do not be afraid to waken the child every few hours to make sure that he is conscious.

NOSE BLEEDS

Occasional nose bleeds are very common and are generally associated with colds, nose-picking or a knock on the nose. If a child seems especially prone to nose bleeds he should be seen by a doctor just in case there is a more serious underlying cause. This is, however, most unlikely. Although a profuse nose bleed can be frightening, it generally stops by itself and there are a number of things you can do to help. Do not let the child blow his nose—this usually makes matters worse; instead, get him to sit down quietly and gently pinch the end of his nose for at least five minutes before slowly letting go.

CHOKING

If a child chokes on a lump of food or a small toy that has stuck in his throat, never push your fingers or any instrument into his throat to remove it. Hold the child upside down and slap him firmly on the back. If this does not help or if his breathing becomes distressed and he goes blue, he must be rushed to the nearest hospital.

If a sharp piece of food, such as a fishbone, becomes stuck in his throat he should be taken to the nearest Casualty Department.

SWALLOWED OBJECTS

Babies and small children will swallow anything that can be put into their mouths. Usually the object is passed in the faeces (waste matter excreted by the bowel) and no harm is done. You should not give the child a laxative, merely examine each motion carefully so that you know when the object is passed. Keep your doctor in touch with events. He will probably not wish to examine the child unless vomiting, abdominal pain, abdominal distortion or sudden alteration in bowel habit occurs.

Occasionally a child swallows a sharp object, such as an open safety-pin. In this event, the doctor should be consulted straight away.

OBJECTS STUCK IN EARS OR NOSTRILS

Small children sometimes push tiny round objects, like beads, into their ears or nostrils. Unless the object is virtually hanging out, do not try to retrieve it. Take the child to your doctor, who will arrange for it to be removed. Incidentally, a child may push something up his nostril without his mother realizing he has done so. After a few days a smelly bloody discharge from one nostril will alert parents to what has happened.

PARTICLES IN THE EYE

When a baby or young child gets something in his eye a lot of damage can be done during the struggle to remove the particle. He may allow you to irrigate the eye with water from an eye-dropper. Otherwise take him to a doctor or Casualty Department.

If chemicals have been accidentally splashed into the eyes, the child should be held firmly with his face upwards over a sink. Several glasses of water from the cold tap should be poured over both eyes. He should then be taken to hospital without delay. Take the container holding the chemical with you so that it can be identified.

POISONING

If your child has swallowed something that you think may be poisonous, telephone a doctor or hospital Casualty Department immediately and state the substance and amount taken. Ask if it is safe to make him vomit before bringing him to hospital and if there is anything else you should do. In most cases it is a good thing if he can be made to vomit soon after swallowing the poison, but certain chemicals—e.g. turpentine—can cause damage if aspirated into the lungs, and other poisons, such as lysol, used in household disinfectants, and caustic soda, burn the throat when vomited. The safest way to induce vomiting is to lay the child on a sofa or bed with his face downwards, projecting over the edge. Insert your fingers boldly into his throat and move them around until he vomits; as long as your fingers are inserted far enough into his throat he will not be able to bite you. If it has been a long time since he has had anything to eat or drink, let him have a drink before you make him vomit.

Remember to take the vomit and a sample of the poison with you to the hospital.

A child may not look ill soon after swallowing a poison, but you must still seek help immediately. Several hours later, when the poison may be showing its effects, it has usually been absorbed from the stomach and inducing vomiting at this stage is not much help.

The Psychology of Parenthood
The Birth of a Parent

The most important thing is to live and enjoy each moment fully. When parents attend to the actual moment they are living, they are able, one step at a time, to build a secure basis for each new development. A child's needs do not come in one overwhelming job-lot. Parents need only attend to each need as it arises. A secure baby becomes a secure child; a secure child becomes a secure teenager and adult. Parent and child grow together, step by step.

The fact that beginnings are important is never more obvious than when one holds a newborn baby. The feeling of responsibility and the desire to do the right thing can, as many new parents know, be almost overwhelming. A common reaction, in fact, when parents realize how important they are to their child's early development and education, is a feeling of inadequacy which gives rise to panic and a desire to pass on the responsibility to someone else—a health visitor, social worker, playgroup leader, teacher. It helps to remember that panic is a state of mind that never has anything to do with the moment one is living. In a true emergency, for example, one is much too busy coping to panic. Panic may arise before, or after an event, but (allowing for a person being of sound mind) it does not arise at the time.

When parents panic about parenthood, it is because they have temporarily forgotten that we are only asked and, indeed, are only able to cope with one thing in one moment. We are not, for example, asked to cope with a baby as a school-child and teenager as soon as he is born. His needs and questions do not come in one overwhelming job-lot. We need only attend, give attention to, each need as it arises.

If, while we are nursing a baby, we worry about what is in store for him and us when he is a schoolchild or a teenager, we deprive him and ourselves of the opportunity to enjoy and live that moment fully. The danger of panic, of running ahead of ourselves and the baby, is that we miss what is happening, what is needed now. When we attend to the moment we are actually living, we are able, one step at a time, to build a secure platform which serves as a spring-board to the next step, the next phase. A secure baby becomes a secure child; a secure child becomes a secure teenager and adult. Parent and child grow together, step by step.

To be a parent is to be doubly responsible

because the mind of the parent is the most powerful influence that a child meets in his formative years. He will absorb the 'food' of a parent's thoughts and beliefs as easily as, when a baby, he absorbed his mother's milk.

Parents who take their doubled responsibility seriously always find the strength available to take a detached look at themselves, at the ideas they hold, at the limitations and prejudices we gather over the years. Parents who then make a determined effort to root out any that they know will impede their child's physical, mental, emotional or spiritual growth, are the best that any child could hope for.

Fear of the future, then—what may or may not happen—and fear of the past—of distressing moments repeating themselves—are at the root of all unhappiness and feelings of inadequacy. Just consider, for a moment, what life would be like if parents began each day as a totally new and fresh experience, with none of yesterday's burdens or tomorrow's uncertainties impressed upon it. What a day that would be! To open one's eyes as if for the first time; to rise ahead of habitual anxieties and thoughts, and to conserve the energy that is usually drained by these for looking, listening, tasting, touching and smelling everything absolutely afresh.

If one is in any doubt that this is the way to successful parenting and also the richest, happiest and fullest way to live, one needs only to recall

one's own early childhood or to look at life through the eyes of a normal young child. The first thing that is evident is contentment; contentment which stems from a child's ability to make the most of whatever is presented in any one moment, whether it is a rattle to pat, a leaf to examine or a finger puppet to watch. The freedom from tension that arises from living the moment that is actually happening is wonderfully refreshing to experience. Likewise, if we could, just for a moment, look at the adult condition through our childhood or child's eyes, we would realize that most adults (parents) fail to live simply because they are always preparing to live, or because they spend the time re-living moments that have already been lived! What a waste of time, our child might be forgiven for thinking. Is life so long that it can bear so much shortening, so much hurrying? Why not follow my example—be born anew—share my beginning, begin life afresh?

When the answer to this invitation is yes, a parent is born and, from that time forth, every day presents infinite opportunities to experience life anew, in step with one's child. A child whose parents are willing to do this, who set aside all the trials and tribulations of yesterday, who meet him as if for the first time and begin each day afresh, is more than fortunate—he is blessed. Beginnings are indeed important and, what is more, whether we are parent or child, one day or one hundred years old, things are always beginning.

UNDERSTANDING YOUR CHILD

The art of understanding a child is to pause every now and again to remember that he has a body, mind and spirit; that to be truly happy and wholesome he needs to achieve his full potential physically, mentally, emotionally and spiritually. Parents who remember this cannot go far wrong because they will realize that all care and training, if it is to be useful, must always nourish the whole child; and that, for this reason, we need to avoid the temptation of limiting our care to a child's bodily needs. It is all too easy, as every parent knows, to become so absorbed in training—all aspects of hygiene and diet—that there is no time for the rest. When this happens, more time is spent fobbing off a child's questions and, therefore, slamming doors on his awakening mind, than on answering questions and leading him on to new horizons.

One of the finest aids that parents can draw upon when trying to understand a child, is to recall that, from a child's point of view, everything is difficult before it becomes easy; that a simple action like climbing stairs requires tremendous effort when every stair comes up to one's knees! That crossing a busy street can feel like

being submerged in a rough billowing sea of legs, skirts and trousers.

There is no doubt that children are subjected to many unnecessary pressures and stresses simply because the differences in their physical dimensions and abilities are overlooked. A moment's reflection, however, safeguards a child from this by revealing many things which he cannot take for granted. For this reason it is invaluable, on occasions, to review the home and everyday environment from a child's point of view. The easiest and most practical way is to kneel down occasionally and, literally, to look at life from a child's eye-view.

The simple answer if a child begins to display behaviour problems is to stop, look, listen and then return to the beginning. Childhood, like youth, maturity and life itself, is too important a span to be marred by deadlocks, frustration or hurry. When parents appreciate, as Robert Frost did, that:

Our life depends on everything's
Recurring till we answer from within.
The thousandth time may prove the charm . . .
Human development is seen in its true perspective and one begins to understand why childhood and parenthood often entails the restepping of steps until each one is consolidated for all time.

TIME TO GROW

The willingness to walk in step, in harmony with a child and to make the most of the present moment, is what determines how happy a mother, father and child are in each other's company. Indeed most of the problems which parents encounter with children stem from moments when this has been forgotten and when the parent's and child's view of life comes into conflict. It helps to remember that the only way out of any deadlock is to stop, to remember that the greater part of progress for a child (or parent) depends on a desire to progress; that enjoyment is essential to progress; and then to begin again by withdrawing one's attention from what happened yesterday or may happen tomorrow, and giving it instead to what is happening now.

When a child is hurried or pressurized, the natural sequence of events is interrupted and, not surprisingly, he begins to display behaviour problems simply because he cannot cope with the demands and pressures that are made upon him.

A simple way for new parents to appreciate this is for them to remember the events of their own life; to consider, for example, aspects of their own development which, having been left blank or unconsolidated in childhood, remain to this day to cause them difficulty. Many mothers, for example, who believe that they have a block

against adding up simple sums, are astonished when they realize that the cause of their difficulty is that they did not learn their multiplication tables when they were children. Once they fill in the missing steps, they discover that they can add up as competently as anyone else! This simple principle of allowing a child to proceed at a pace which is natural for him—true to his own nature at any given time—is a great avoider and healer of friction and one of the finest aids that a parent will ever have.

It is, of course, easy to understand how such principles are lost sight of. Parenthood, today, is crammed with 'experts' writing and talking about the various milestones which a parent can expect a child to achieve before he or she is this or that age. Generalizations do have a place and are very helpful, but it is essential to remember that every child is an individual. A parent should never

2 The art of understanding a child is to pause every now and again to remember that he has body, mind and spirit. To be truly happy and healthy he needs to achieve his full potential physically, mentally, emotionally and spiritually. Parents who remember this cannot go far wrong because they will realize that all care and training must nourish the whole child. For this reason, we must avoid limiting our care just to a child's bodily needs.

Parenthood and childhood can only be enjoyable when you accept that a child needs time to grow and that the process cannot be hurried without ill effect. When, in addition to understanding this, parents accept that they are their child's first and most important teacher, the true work of parenthood really begins. All that is then necessary for a perfect childhood is for parents to remain in step with their child, ready to offer new directions, stimulation and guidance when it is needed.

regard a child as backward or retarded simply because he does not smile, sit, crawl, or whatever, according to a textbook. Comparisons, in fact, whether they are made with one's friends' children or with textbooks, are rarely constructive and are responsible for much unnecessary tension.

Parents who are prepared to trust their own unique knowledge of a particular child, need not look far for guidance. They are the best experts their child will ever have! The joy is that when parents trust themselves to meet a child's physical, mental, emotional and spiritual needs, they can appreciate as William Shakespeare did, that: 'Every time serves for the matter born in 't . . . ' and that the most positive way to live for oneself, one's child, and everybody else, is to share the moment that the other person is living and never wish to be anywhere other than one is, doing anything other than one is!

Certainly, parenthood can only be enjoyable when one accepts that a child needs time to grow

and that the process cannot be hurried without ill effect. When, in addition to understanding this, parents accept that they are their child's first and most important teachers, the true work of parenthood really begins. All that is then necessary for a perfect situation is for parents to remain in step with their child, ready to offer new directions, stimulation and guidance as and when it is needed. This principle of watching, waiting and then acting at the right time, allows a child to master all the skills that parents desire for him. The knowledge that is confirmed every day is that 'Haste is ever the parent of failure'; and that anything that is rushed or missed at one stage remains as a blank to trouble a child—and parents!—in later life.

A MOTHER'S SPECIAL ROLE

Daily, mothers recognize the magnitude of a mother's role—so do others. Especially during the first few years of her child's life, a mother must perform a multitude of functions. She is her child's

first and most important contact with the world and through her he will learn about himself. In *What's Wrong With The World*, Gilbert K. Chesterton wrote that the career of a mother within the home is vaster than the career-seeking of a woman away from the home. It is, he said,

'To be Queen Elizabeth within a definite area, deciding sales, banquet, labors, and holidays; to be Whiteley within a certain area, providing toys, boots, sheets, cakes and books; to be Aristotle within a certain area, teaching morals, theology, and hygiene: I can understand how this might exhaust the mind, but I cannot imagine how it could narrow it. How can it be a large career to tell other people's children about the Rule of Three and a small career to tell one's own children about the universe? How can it be broad to be the same thing to everyone, and narrow to be everything to someone? No; a woman's function is laborious because it is gigantic, not because it is minute.'

Spending time with your child is not only a necessary, even vital, adjunct to his mental and emotional development, but the way to really happy and fulfilled parenthood. Helping a child to look at the world for the first time, to perceive clearly without preconceptions and prejudices as he does, is remarkably refreshing.

For a child, every day is full of surprises, discoveries, new games and pastimes, freshly acquired skills and little victories over the day before. Sharing these moments is one of the greatest treasures of parenthood.

Sharing a joke, learning a new game, working out a puzzle together, blowing bubbles— whatever the activity, the child is learning not only a particular skill, but about his relationship with you. Your encouragement and willingness to be there when he needs your help, daily builds his confidence and assurance, to enable him to tackle harder tasks.

It is just as important not to offer help before it is needed as it is to recognize when assistance is required. Allow the child to develop at his own pace—neither pressurizing him into tasks too hard for his abilities, nor doing everything for him. Show him, encourage him and then let him try himself.

Learning Basic Skills
First Steps to Language

The first step to language is the moment that your baby sounds his first 'Aa', for the gift of sound is inseparable from the gift of language. As it is natural for a bird to sing, so it is natural for a child to express himself in words. Each word is a note in a symphony that is language, and every child wants to join in the song, to express himself and to communicate with others. When a baby says 'Aa', he is expressing pure delight. Watch and listen: when your face appears, he says 'Aa'; he finds his hand and says 'Aa'; discovers his foot and says 'Aa'. Other sounds emerge. Soon he expresses his delight in 'Ee', 'Oo', 'O', 'Ai', and 'Aow'. Each of these sounds expresses delight: delight in creation, in discovery. A baby listens and, in listening, imitates. Soon he mirrors what he hears and changes the sound accordingly. When he bangs himself and you say 'Aa', he hears a different sound, a sound that registers concern. Next time he takes a tumble, he recalls that intonation and the 'Aa' that he sounds then will be of an entirely different nature from the 'Aa' he sounded when he first discovered his own hand. Thus it is with all language—we learn by imitation, not only learning new words, but discovering through listening that the same word can convey many meanings.

For one's child's sake it is worth remembering that the gift of language is a child's key to the whole universe; the gift of language is the gift of knowledge.

When your baby sounds 'Aa', sound it back; play with him; talk to him; sing to him. When he adds consonants to the vowels and begins to sound 'mmm', 'ddd', sound back. Play and offer others: 'kkk', chchch', 'ggg', 'jjj', 'bbb', 'ppp', 'ttt', 'yyy', 'www', 'hhh', 'rrr'. Back up these sounds with words—the *true* words that you would use in conversation with any intelligent being.

By about ten months old, your baby will start to respond with actions which show understanding of the spoken word. Soon, one word at a time, he will begin to respond to speech with recognizable sounds that are his first attempts at meaningful words. Share his delight; encourage him; talk to him and name things for him.

By about the third year, he will, with your help, have realized that everything has a name. So the language game develops until, by the beginning of the fifth year, with your help and encouragement,

your child will have a vocabulary of about two thousand words.

If when a baby first sounds 'Aa', parents remember that this is the first step to being able to express oneself in words, the magic journey will have begun. In a few short years the child will not only discover the joy of communication but will, with the parents' help, have received the tools that enable him to express himself truthfully and thus enrich and nourish not only his own life, but that of every person he meets, through spoken words.

SPEECH PROBLEMS

As a child learns to speak by imitation, the example he is given is obviously all important. If a parent slurs his words or leaves a word unfinished by not sounding the consonant at the end, for example, a child will imitate that pronunciation; if an adult runs words into each other, a child will not be able to distinguish between where one word ends and another begins, and he will jabber and not leave spaces between his own words. If a parent speaks very quickly, a child, in an effort to appear mature, will imitate the adult. The difficulty here is that, not having been given sufficient opportunities to

A baby listens and, in listening, imitates. Soon he begins to repeat the sounds that he hears.

When your baby sounds 'aa', sound it back; play with him, talk to him and sing to him. By about ten months old, he will start to respond with actions which show understanding of the spoken word. Soon, one word at a time, he begins to respond to speech with recognizable sounds that are his first attempts at meaningful words. Share his delight and encourage him by talking to him and naming things for him. By about the third year, he will, with your help, have realized that everything has a name. So the language game develops until, by the beginning of the fifth year he will have a vocabulary of about two thousand words.

practise and consolidate the pronunciation of individual words, the overall effect of speed renders the child's speech unintelligible.

It is also true that many children begin to develop speech problems, such as stammering and stuttering, because they fear that they will not be listened to unless they get the words out at break-neck speed.

A very effective way of helping a child who has a speech problem is to set as fine an example as possible by clearly enunciating the whole word, by leaving reasonable spaces between words and, generally, speaking at a speed which will leave the child in no doubt as to where each word begins and ends. Reading aloud to a child is particularly helpful in this respect, especially if one makes it an exercise of allowing him to hear each syllable which makes up the sound of one whole word. It is also useful, when reading, to leave a prolonged space between the words. At first this constant pausing between words may make the reading appear ridiculously slow but, in practice, it has a very restful, calming, soothing effect on a child and enables him to focus his attention and listen very precisely.

When one couples such practical help with a determination to stop and listen when a child speaks, many speech problems, however seemingly deep-seated, show a marked improvement.

There is no doubt that, in many instances, the problem of a child who is slow or reluctant to speak, originates in a parent's unwillingness to listen to him at an earlier stage. A child who is listened to from the moment he first sounds 'Aa', in babyhood, becomes a communicative child who is always interested in words and who takes every opportunity to extend his vocabulary. The ability to listen and, therefore, to speak and express oneself well, are the finest educational and social aids that all parents can, very easily give to their children.

The finest aid that parents can draw upon when encouraging a child to be more communicative, is the knowledge that every child will co-operate if he is given something that is worth listening to and talking about! Whilst it is always important to remember that every child is an individual with individual interests, parents can be certain that every child is primarily interested in discovering the truth about the universe. From a very early age a child will begin to ask questions—what, where, why, how? Some questions will be simple, some will, initially, seem difficult to answer, some questions like 'Why is rain wet?' 'Who gives God

1 Because a child learns to speak by imitation, the example he is given is all-important. If a parent slurs words or leaves a word unfinished by not sounding the final conso-nant, a child will imitate that pronunciation. If an adult runs words into each other, a child will not be able to distinguish when one word ends and another begins. When a child has a speech prob-lem reading aloud to him is a great help. It is of course, very important to speak each word slowly and clearly.

1

2

His super powers?' 'Where do dreams go in the morning?' may be impossible to answer.

The important thing about children's questions is to listen, to give them the respect that they deserve and to answer truthfully. Children are only discouraged from asking questions and communicating with their parents, when they learn, from experience, that they are going to be fobbed off with 'Not now, darling. Ask me later.' or a flat 'I don't know'. A child who knows, from experience, that he can trust a parent to answer him truthfully, who receives an 'I don't know, but we can try to find out,' will never switch off, withdraw into himself and become uncommunicative. He will remain alert and interested and will continue to regard life as a challenging adventure in which something new and interesting can be experienced and talked about every day. Children welcome new experiences but will only benefit if given the opportunity to ask questions.

☐ **Speech therapy** If, in spite of all normal efforts, support and encouragement on your part, a child does not begin to speak, or if his speech is seriously distorted, you will need to seek medical advice. There are probably as many causes for speech problems as there are children, but your doctor will probably begin by arranging for your child to have his hearing tested. He may also suggest that you seek the advice and help of a speech therapist.

First Steps to Writing

Just as it is natural for a child to express himself in speech, so it is natural for him to express himself in written words. Scribble-writing, having taught him how to hold a pencil and that it is he who directs the pencil, will give way to recognizable shapes and letters.

For a child's written work to develop, it is, of course, essential that he practises writing every day. At the scribble-writing stage, it is only necessary to give a child a pencil and paper and allow him to gain muscular control and make the glorious discovery that it is he who is responsible for the marks that appear. A watchful attentive parent will know the precise moment when a child has sufficient control to be shown how to draw a straight horizontal line and a straight vertical line and when he is ready to move on to a circle. All letters are composed of straight lines and circles or half circles.

When the child has had sufficient practice with straight lines and circles and half circles, he can then practise the small letters of the alphabet.

Once a child can control where he writes on the page he can be encouraged to arrange the words on the page with care and take pride in the presentation of written work. As he grows older,

3

2,3 Scribble-writing is essential phase for a child who is learning to write. It teaches him how to hold a pencil and draws his attention to the fact that it is he who directs the pencil. Slowly, but surely, he gains muscular control and makes the glorious discovery that he is responsible for the marks that appear.

the fine examples of calligraphy that can be found in museums will encourage this.

There is a school of thought that says careful writing inhibits a child's creative flow; there is also a school of thought that believes that untidy writing leads to confusion in the mind and, likewise, inhibits creative flow. It will not take a watchful parent long to decide which school of thought to follow! The same principle applies to pronunciation. Careful pronunciation equals good spelling; slovenly pronunciation equals careless spelling.

The young writer will flourish initially with pencils, thick crayons and felt-tip pens. Later a fountain pen will achieve better results than ball-point pens. If, however, ball points are used, a thick rather than a thin one is more comfortable for a child to hold. At an early stage, using a variety of different colours can encourage a child to practise writing. There is no reason for writing to become a chore. All skills are easier to learn when they seem to be fun.

Whatever the child's age, parents cannot fail to do their best for their child if they provide opportunities and experiences that will make the placing of pen to paper worthwhile. Every child has a need to express himself; every child can be helped to do so.

1 At the scribbling stage, a child does not think in terms of making letters or pictures. He is simply gaining better control of his movements by practising scribbles. The actual scribbles are as different as the children who make them—some are large and bold, some small and timid. Some children are happier with large sheets of paper others with small-size sheets. It does, however, help to vary the size, since this will determine to a large extent the way that a child scribbles. If, regardless of size, a child constantly uses only a small portion, do all you can to increase his confidence.

First Steps to Art

From the very first moment that a child picks up a pencil or a crayon and begins to scribble, he is creating. Just watch how his attention focuses and fuses.

The actual scribblings are as different as the children who make them—some are large and bold, some small and timid. Some children are happier with large sheets of paper, others with small-size sheets. It does, however, help to vary the size, since this will determine to a large extent the way that a child scribbles. If, regardless of size, a child constantly withdraws into a corner of the paper and uses only a small portion, do all you can to increase his confidence and sense of security. Apart from this, leave him quite free to express himself.

It does not help when a child is very young to ask: 'What are you drawing?' in the hope of encouraging him to make the next step to recognizable symbols. At the scribbling stage, the child is not thinking in terms of pictures. He is simply gaining better control of his movements by practising scribbles. Let him scribble to his heart's content, and only when he is clearly able to hold and guide the pencil or crayon and showing signs of discontent, gently lead him on to the next step by drawing for him, as perfectly as you can, a straight line, free-hand. Let him watch you do this, then let him practise. When he is able to draw a straight vertical line, try a horizontal. Later, add a circle, a triangle, an oblong and other simple geometric shapes.

When a child has mastered these simple exercises, he will have a range of useful skills that will one day help him to make patterns and, later, drawings of what he sees around him. In the meantime, keep his interest and enjoyment alive by giving him colours such as red, yellow and blue, and show him how red and yellow become orange; yellow and blue become green; red and blue become purple—and so on. When he has exhausted the possibilities of the first three colours, add new ones to the range.

ART MATERIALS

Materials for the two-to-four age group should, above all, be materials which help to satisfy the desire for movement and control. Crayons and poster paints are perfect for this. Water colours are not so useful, however, as they are inclined to run and create frustratingly blurred colours.

Always beware of poor-quality materials. A child who is constantly frustrated by poor 'tools' will soon tire of art.

Thick crayons, poster paints in powder form rather than liquid (these can be mixed to any desired consistency and give the child an opportunity to experiment); long-handled brushes: a flat bristle and one round hair brush; plus a very large pad, will set your child off to a good start.

Remember that the more ready-made colours you buy, the less incentive your child will have to mix and match and discover for himself. Care of tools is essential and this should be introduced right at the beginning: 'Is your pencil sharpened? Have you put your crayons back into the box? Have you washed your paint brushes?'

☐ **Colouring Books** There are two schools of thought about colouring books. Some people believe that colouring in pre-ordained areas helps to teach a child's control; others believe that they are positively harmful and inhibit a child's freedom of expression, either by discouraging him into believing that he cannot draw as well, or by making him so dependent on other people's outlines that he does not even bother to try.

☐ **Finger-Paints** There are also two schools of thought about finger-paints. Some people believe that they encourage a free-for-all mess that results in the child feeling confused and uncertain; others believe that they have a useful purpose for children who are tense, timid or fearful, or who, for some reason or another, missed out on the scribbling or water-play stage. The general belief is that it is possible that finger-painting may retard a child who is already able to control the movements of a pencil, crayon or brush.

FREEDOM OF EXPRESSION

It helps to remember that at the same time as a child is learning to scribble and control movement, he is also learning to express himself in words. Soon, drawing and speech begin to merge. For example, as he scribbles, he will say: 'This is a dog'. You look and can only see scribble but, for him, the marks are very significant. He is beginning to think in terms of pictures and naming things, whereas before he was not considering anything outside himself and the sheer joy of scribbling.

Do not correct his scribbling by showing him how to draw a dog; just accept that, for the moment, he is at an in-between stage when his thinking and his ability to express himself in words is ahead of his ability to draw. When he says, 'This is a dog', instead of imposing an adult's idea of how a dog should look, make the most of the moment to extend his awareness of dog. For example, listen to the story he is telling while scribbling, then ask questions, such as 'Is the dog wearing a collar? What colour is he? Does he have a patch? Long or short fur?' Listen to his

answers. All the while in his own way, he is beginning to connect the act of drawing with the picture of a dog—symbol and name are beginning to merge—and, slowly but surely, in his own good time, his scribbles will become more and more suggestive until, one day, round lines for the dog's head and lines for his legs will begin to emerge from the scribble to establish a relationship to dog not only through thought and speech, but through drawing also.

Once this stage is reached the child will move quite naturally out of the scribbling stage into the drawing. The big moment has arrived when in showing you a drawing, for example, of a house, you too can recognize the basic shape!

ATTENTION TO DETAIL

Once a child can draw and paint a recognizable shape, the best help you can give is daily to increase your child's sensitivity to his environment. For example, when out for a walk, make a point of looking at houses and gently draw his attention to the tiles on the roof, to the windows, the door, the garden path, the fences, the hedges and the flowers.

It is never helpful, at any stage, to show a child how to draw unless he specifically asks for help. A parent who constantly says: 'Draw it like this', is simply limiting a child's freedom of expression, dulling his joy in creating and encouraging him to imitate or make a poor copy of their creation. At worst, feeling unable to draw as well as the parent, the child gives up and loses all interest in trying.

The same principle applies to colour. If a child paints the sky yellow and the earth red, it is simply because, at this stage, he is so busy establishing a relationship between the object and his drawing that he is not relating to the 'right' colour. Colour, for the moment, is insignificant. Once again, let him go at his own pace and do not spoonfeed him colour by imposing a secondary

2 There are two schools of thought about finger-paints and paints that you squirt on to paper. Some people believe that they encourage a free-for-all mess that results in the child feeling confused and uncertain. Others believe that they have a useful purpose for children who are tense, timid or fearful, or who, for some reason or another, missed out on the scribbling or water play stage. A child who is able to control the movements of a pencil does not need finger-paints. He or she would be better off with thick crayons and poster paints and a variety of brushes.

stage while he is still trying to master an earlier one. Just as the move from scribble to drawing evolved naturally, so will the move from using any colour to true colour.

The same principle of non-interference applies to proportion. If the candles on the birthday cake your daughter has drawn are too large in proportion to the cake, this may well be because at the time of the drawing she was influenced by feelings about the candles—her difficulty, for example, when blowing them out. If you encourage her to tell you about her drawing, you may discover that the proportion is often right in relation to her feeling about a subject.

When, however, it is clear that she has reached a stage of wishing to express herself in proportion, encourage her to group objects, such as a melon, an apple, and a grape and let her make the discovery of proportion for herself. When she shows you the result, the right question at the right time is often all that is needed to encourage her to look again, to see if she has drawn the truth in relation to the size of the three objects.

Having shown her the way by presenting the first three objects, leave her to choose others, and help by giving her new opportunities to increase her sensitivity to size through shared experiences, such as a visit to the zoo: 'What was the largest animal we saw? Who had the longest neck? Longest ears? The shortest tail? The smallest face?'

Whatever problem arises in relation to your child's desire to express himself, always let his need, his age and stage of development be your guide. Never rush him; simply be there when he is ready to make the next move and provide him with the opportunities and materials.

EVERY CHILD IS AN ARTIST

All children are naturally creative, all have the potential, regardless of varying abilities, to find joy and delight in art. A parent's task, quite simply, is to provide the opportunities for a child to use his senses to the full. It is never too late or too early to start. A mother who places her baby's pram in a position where the baby can see leaves wafting in a breeze encourages her child to use his eyes. A father who hands a leaf to his child encourages him to look, touch, smell—to see the leaf and study it in ever greater detail.

Parents who continue to encourage their child to look, listen, touch, taste, smell, help their child in the most positive way possible to build the bridge between his inner world of experience and his outer world of expression. Thus they help him to discover that art need never be a poor copy, but a glorious reflection and confirmation of what is.

Every child is naturally creative and every child has the potential, regardless of varying abilities, to find joy and delight in art. A parent's task, quite simply, is to provide the opportunities for a child to use his senses to the full. Outings, for example, are rich in sensory experiences and will provide material for drawing and painting. Never rush a young artist, simply be there when he is ready to make the next move and provide him with the opportunities and materials that he needs to do so.

A Baby has a Mind
Developing the Five Senses

A child's five senses can easily be blunted and deadened either by lack of use or by over-use. A word of caution for the care of the senses is to stop using them before they tire. When they tire, impressions grow stale and harmful. This is particularly easily understood with the sense of taste. If, in a greedy moment, one eats to excess, taste tires and mind, body and spirit reap indigestion or sickness. All five senses should be used no more than is necessary at any one time to keep sight, hearing, taste, touch and smell fresh and alive.

Just as a child may have more or less air in the lungs according to the amount he breathes in, so he may have more or less wonderful moments in his life according to what use he makes of his five senses—hearing, sight, taste, touch and smell—and his mind. The senses are informers—the only direct way in which we may make contact with creation. Like any precision instrument they improve with use and become blunted by disuse or misuse.

What a child is—and what he will become—is determined, first by how he uses his senses and, second, by how his mind uses the information that they collect. The senses are like bees—they speed around creation collecting and registering a visual impression here, a sound impression there. The mind is the hive where the 'goods' are brought and the sifting work is done.

To set a child on the path to a wonderful way to grow up would first be to remind ourselves that *we* have five senses. The more parents are aware of the tremendous potency and range of sense, the more they are able to ensure—through every-day opportunities—that their child is also aware that he has five senses and that he uses the full range and does not limit himself to a dependence on one or two.

What commonly happens is that at an early age—three, four, five years—each of us chooses a certain sense which we come to rely on as our predominant informer. We back up this first choice with a close second, then allow all the others to fall into neglect. Slowly, over a period of time, the neglected senses cease to register on our consciousness and only the occasional shock or comment reminds us that they exist. This is very evident in any gathering of people. For example, when five mothers meet for coffee, one might say: 'What a lovely smell that plant has.' Another: 'Listen to that mistlethrush singing!' Another: 'This has a delicious flavour.' Another: 'This material has a beautiful feel.' Another: 'What a lovely view.' Each, in her own way, is registering the impression of the sense that she has chosen to rely on and, for that moment, is drawing another's attention to: smell, hearing, taste, touch or sight. If we could roll five mothers into one, we would have one very useful mother!

In reality, each person has the use of all five senses and there is no reason why we should not grow up experiencing the wealth of using them all to the full—bearing in mind, of course, that we can only use *one* sense fully in any one moment. How, then, in practical terms can parents discourage a child from settling for half measures and encourage his use of the full potential? A useful exercise would be for parents to reflect carefully on which of the five senses they neglect. If, for example, a parent always eats on-the-run, he or she clearly would not have a well-defined or refined sense of taste. If a parent relied on a constant background of half-heard music or talking from radio or television, he or she would not have an alive sense of hearing. The morning would pass without hearing the rain falling on nearly-dry washing or the beginnings of mischief in a toddler's laugh. If the parent constantly dwelled on what life was like before, or what it might be like tomorrow, seasons would come and go, moments would bloom and fade, toddlers would grow into children, without the parent having looked at and consciously registered anything *real* between the sunrise and sunset of any one day—or any one lifetime.

If it was the sense of smell that had been neglected, the parent would cease, in time, to register the sweet fragrance of newly-washed hair, a just-cleaned room—and other subtleties. If a parent never came into contact with the living warmth of natural substances such as wood, clay, cotton, silk, and wool and was constantly and instinctively withdrawing the skin from the suffocating cling of man-made fibres, the sense of touch would soon fade and not register the delight of the breeze in the hair, the sun on skin.

CARING FOR THE SENSES

A child's senses can be blunted and deadened in two ways. The first is when they are not used; the second is when they are over-used. A word of caution, then, for the care of the senses is to stop using them before they tire. When they tire, impressions grow stale and poisonous. This is very easily understood with the sense of taste. If, in a greedy moment, one eats to excess, taste tires and mind, body and spirit reap indigestion or sickness. All five senses should be used no more than is necessary at any one time to keep sight, hearing, taste, touch and smell fresh and alive.

Another way to care for the senses is to understand that whatever the sense is allowed to dwell on creates an attraction in the mind which then

What a child is —and what he will become —is determined first by how he uses his senses and, second, by how his mind uses the information that they collect. The five senses should be constantly alert collecting and registering a visual impression here, a sound impression there. The mind should be just as alert sifting the information it receives.

The more parents are aware of the tremendous potency and range of the senses, the more they are able to ensure — through everyday opportunities — that their child is also

aware of his senses and that he uses the full range. Most people limit themselves to appreciating one or two senses only, but there is no reason why a child should not grow up experiencing all five — bearing in mind, of course that only one sense can be used fully in one moment. Like any precision instrument, the senses improve with proper use and become blunted by disuse or misuse. Encourage your child to use his senses fully at every opportunity.

becomes a desire for fulfilment. If one desires to slim, for example, one needs to withdraw the senses from cream buns and bars of chocolate and put them to a more conducive-to-slimming use. The same principle applies to any 'infatuation' a child may suffer from!

STRENGTHENING THE SENSES

To sense anything fully and truly, one must first come to what T.S. Eliot described as 'the still point', 'the timeless moment'. This means that when one listens, one just listens; when one looks, one just looks; when one tastes, one just tastes; when one smells, one just smells; when one touches, one just touches.

What prevents us from using a sense fully most of the time is out-of-place thinking—the state when the mind is full of multifarious thoughts and impressions that jostle and clamour and make constant claims on our attention. To come to 'the still point' is simply a matter of not allowing the mind to be filled with anything other than the purpose in hand. What many mothers, fathers and teachers realize is that a child is never more receptive, intelligent and happy than when he is helped to a point of stillness and order so that he can listen, look, taste, touch or smell one thing fully at a time.

Avoiding Over-stimulation

There is no doubt that the world in which most children are born today abounds in harsh discordant sounds, sights, taste, touch and smells which do assault their senses. The age in which we live has been aptly christened the 'machine age'. Opportunities to escape from it are daily decreasing. Today's countryside, for example, is as likely to resound to a machine chorus as a dawn chorus; and town- and city-dwellers are awash, from morn to night, in a constant cacophony of sound-waves. It is not surprising in these circumstances that people speak of 'tensions', 'stresses', and being under 'pressure'.

One of the most effective ways to help a child's sense of hearing, for example, is to reduce the unnecessary sound effects and distractions, and avoid excessive exposure to sound. Many mothers have noticed that the sounds generated by ordinary household gadgets and machines contribute very directly to a build-up of irritation both in themselves and their children. The fact that the irritation can, in its turn, have a disastrous effect on listening, on the general humour of family life, relationships and a child's overall development, is widely acknowledged.

The answer for those who are aware of the effect that constant sound vibrations have on ear, nerves and mind, is resolutely to set about reducing the number of times in which machines and gadgets rule the roost. A child whose parents ensure that there is a space in each day when machines and gadgets are brought to rest, radio and television switched off, is a fortunate child indeed.

A good home, of course, will offer a variety of materials and activities which will encourage a child to look and touch but, even more important than providing the right equipment is the need to provide the space in which it may be enjoyed. A home that is overendowed with toys, furniture and amusements, creates a confusion of clamouring impressions that weary the senses and overexcite the mind. This is very evident when a child sits, surrounded by a clutter of every conceivable game and toy, and says bewildered: 'What can I play? What can I do now, mummy?'

The answer, as many parents have found, is to clear away the excess and create a space in which the child may rest his attention on one activity. Freed from the confusion of too many stimuli, the child will then come to that state of absorption which is natural to the young and concentrate his or her entire being on the challenge of moulding a piece of clay, or dressing and undressing a toy.

Children need space to breathe and move, space to rest their eyes, space for quiet reflection, space to consolidate what they are learning. A quiet uncluttered corner is as essential to inner growth as an activities' corner.

A WORD ABOUT TELEVISION

Television rarely helps to develop a child's senses for the simple reason that it makes life too easy. It spoon-feeds, serves everything up on a plate—in close-up, what's more. The absence of need to participate may blunt a child's senses and leave him with the impression that the real thing—the watching and waiting—is too much like hard work for him to bother.

A good home provides a variety of materials and activities which encourage a child to use his senses. But, even more important than providing the right equipment, is the need to provide the space in which it may be enjoyed. A home that is over-endowed with toys, furniture and amusements creates a confusion of impressions that weary a child's senses and over-excite his mind. Constant over-stimulation, produces a state in which the brain cannot cope. Then a cycle of over-stimulation, over-excitement, exhaustion and depression begins to run and has a disastrous effect on the child's over-all behaviour and development. Everybody, from the youngest to the oldest, needs a quiet period in the day. One way to safeguard a child from over-stimulation is to clear away the excess and create a space in which he may focus his attention on one activity. Freed from the confusion of too many stimuli, a child will then come to that state of quiet absorption which is natural to the young and concentrate his entire being on one toy.

Pre-school Play

Play is a child's work; the touching off point to learning about the universe. Its chief purpose is to enable a child to grow in understanding by using his five senses—hearing, sight, taste, touch and smell. The best way a parent can help is to play along with play. In doing so, they will be in excellent company: Plato is said to have recognized the practical value of play when he distributed miniature tools to three-year-olds who were later to become master builders. Aristotle also taught that children should be encouraged to play at what they would one day do seriously as adults. In more recent times, Froebel stated that the kind of play children enjoy and the toys they find most attractive can be used to gain their attention, and to develop their capacities and knowledge.

Playthings and toys provide the stimulus that will spur a child on to investigate the world around him and to apply his intelligence to understanding the true nature of what he experiences. A parent's part is to set the scene and provide the opportunities for a child to learn through play.

DEVELOPMENT OF PLAY

☐ **Play in babyhood** By about the fourth month of life, a baby's looking, listening, and touching become co-ordinated. He learns that if he uses his hand to bat the rattle in his cot, it will swing and make a sound. From that moment, he will repeat the action again and again. He does so because he has made the delightful discovery that he can cause something to happen: he bats, the rattle rattles! All playthings for this age group should be suitable for 'mouthing' and sucking; they should be small enough to be easily grasped, but *not* small enough to be swallowed. Mobiles, rattles, musical boxes, tambourines, floating bath toys, cotton-reels, 'rattle' boxes, a safely-fastened bunch of keys, are great fun for this age group. Favourite play is *peek-a-boo, ride-a-cock-horse, this little piggy,* and making a splash in the bath.

At about seven months, play is no longer mere repetition of the same action—it takes on interesting variations. *Now I see you; now I don't* becomes very popular, and learning about space relationships includes the delight of dropping and (with luck) retrieving objects. Nesting saucepans, hammer-and-peg blocks, wooden blocks, sound-effect toys, are ideal for this age group; so, too, are peek-a-boo games with finger puppets.

☐ **Experimental play** By twelve months to two years, life is full of exciting possibilities and the growing realization of what can be done with various objects. Grading play material, such as placing one brick on top of another and fitting easy objects into their right places, becomes great fun. So do pots, pans, saucepans, spoons and anything else that can be located in the kitchen. An essential at this age is to allow a child to experiment with natural substances such as earth, water and sand, however messy this is. It is true that, at this age, a child continues to put everything in his mouth as a chief way of 'knowing' something. It is a question of making sure that he will not come to physical harm, rather than inhibiting his need to explore.

☐ **Imaginative play** From the moment a child can speak, imaginative or make-believe play comes into being. It usually makes its entrance via a teddy bear or doll: the toy being made to do or say what the child wishes him to do or say. The next step is when something that is *not*, for example, a doll *becomes* a doll. A duster, for instance, may be nursed, spoken to, made to respond. The next step is when there is no visible symbol, like the duster, but an entirely imaginary 'person' who cannot be seen, but who can be trodden on, have his feelings hurt and express himself in no uncertain terms—frequently terms that the child would hesitate to use! Children mainly use imaginative play to further their understanding of the real world.

☐ **Real-life games** The two-to-four-year-old child masters, through play, all the skills he requires to take his place in the adult world. He learns about the function of things, and learns about natural law. From a very early age, the main motivating force in his life is to be grown up: to do as adults do. To help his natural ambition, provide the child with 'grown-up' playthings. Ideal items are pastry sets, kitchen scales, tea sets, carpentry sets, carpet sweepers, first-aid items for a doctor's bag.

☐ **Collective play** Learning how to play the game is the first essential for life, and the seeds are sown the moment a child begins to share himself with another. At this stage, play becomes a collective discipline with rules and codes of honour. Discipline, in this sense, means a child's willingness to share happily with others, to use persuasion rather than force and to acknowledge both his and other's rights.

☐ **The great outdoors** There is no better place than a garden or a park for a child to develop his five senses—hearing, sight, taste, touch and smell—and to kindle a life-long delight in trees, plants, insects, birds, animal life and how nature works. Blankets for 'houses', tents, hidey-holes are much appreciated; so is a magnifying glass; binoculars; equipment for pretend or real picnics; ropes for swinging and skipping.

Playthings and toys provide the stimulus that will spur a child on to investigate the world around him and to apply his intelligence to understanding the true nature of what he experiences. A parent's part is to set the scene and provide the opportunities for a child to learn about himself and the world around him through play.

A two-to-four year old child can master, through play, all the skills he will one day need to take his place in the adult world.

Toys

Toys are the tools of childhood. Through them children learn about the world around them—and how to co-ordinate fingers, hands, eyes, ears, limbs. They experiment and consolidate experience by repeating the same actions time and time again. Through toys and the way that a child plays, personality emerges and becomes recognizable. The way that a child plays with toys can, in fact, tell his parents a great deal; at one time it was thought that the preference shown by a child for particular toys foretold his later career. But, remember, there is no *right or wrong* way to play with a toy—give your child freedom to experiment, to innovate; and to explore all the possibilities—likely and unlikely! In the early years, the simplicity and joy with which a child plays with toys, adapting them to suit his own plan and purpose, with no regard for the designer's original intention, is delightful to watch.

A successful toy is one that a child returns to repeatedly; a 'bad' toy is one that does not work properly, or breaks the first time it is used. Children of all ages are frustrated and angered by poor-quality toys, but there is a place for throw-away toys—the paper streamers, windmills, balloons, whistles, that are not expected to last.

SAFETY FACTORS

Whatever kind of toys you choose, there are certain basic things to look for: baby toys must be washable, with safe eyes and stuffings, and paints should be non-toxic. There should be no sharp

A successful toy is one that a child returns to again and again. In the early years, the simplicity and joy with which a child innovates and adapts ordinary household materials and toys to suit his own plans and purpose, is delightful to watch. A good mixture of solo playthings, plus swings and climbing frames is perfect for children who are just learning to be social beings. Outdoor toys are a particular boon to busy mothers and always popular with children.

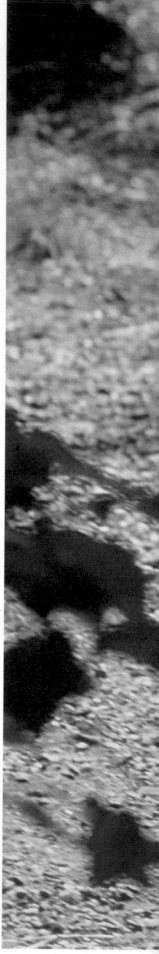

edges, or tiny bits that can be swallowed. This is especially important in a family where there are children of different ages. What is suitable for an older child (who would not dream of biting on a small piece of plastic) is not always right for a baby who is at the stage of putting everything into his mouth. A toy that is too advanced for a child's use can be dangerous if played with unsupervised.

Remember too, that it is sometimes important to show a child how a toy works, not by taking it over, so that the child has no chance to play (and that is all too easy) but just by being there and offering advice when needed. This may seem a bother to an adult who has 'things to get on with', but occasionally joining in a child's play forges an invaluable bond between parent and child. It is good for adults to forget life's pressing problems and often it takes only a short while for a child to master a particular toy and reach the stage where he no longer needs adult help.

SIMPLE PLAYTHINGS

It is not necessary to spend a great deal of money on toys. The best are often close at hand in your own kitchen—a wooden spoon and an old saucepan to beat, strong plastic containers filled with different shapes of pasta or beans, rice or large buttons, make marvellous rattling toys, as will a bunch of keys threaded on a short length of string. Large, strong cardboard boxes can be used to make houses; smaller boxes make good cars, boats, trains; smaller boxes still become the materials for suits of armour and tiny ones fit over fingers and turn into puppets.

The materials for sand and water play are all part of the household equipment. A child will be well away with a plastic bowl, spade, colander, fine sieve, an assortment of cardboard tubes, paper cups and plastic containers. The only extras you need to provide are plastic aprons, protection for the floor and good humour when it comes to clearing up.

A large roasting tray, covered with a generous layer of salt, forms a good surface for early writing practice, whether it be swirls or straight lines and circles and letters.

Empty plastic bottles of all shapes and sizes can be played with at bath time; measuring cups and kitchen scales will keep a child happy when you are cooking. Dough, which can easily be made at home and stores for weeks in the refrigerator, can be used by children to learn about cutting, mixing, rolling out and kneading. Bake your child's efforts in a moderate oven until lightly browned. The following recipe is edible (though not tasty!): to 1.3kg (3lb) flour, add 450g (1lb) salt, 142ml ($\frac{1}{4}$ pint) cooking oil and 284ml ($\frac{1}{2}$ pint) water to make a pliable mixture. Add the oil and water slowly to the flour and salt. A few drops of food colouring can be added if wished.

Early reading books can be made from pictures cut out from magazines, pasted on to cardboard, and bound together with plastic rings. Relate each book you make to a special subject.

HOME-MADE TOYS

It can be enormous fun to make your own toys, but the following safety measures need to be observed. Wooden toys must be strong enough to bear a child's weight, if that is what they are intended for—so test them by standing on the toys. Check to make quite sure there are no sharp edges, corners and splinters. Any nails that are used should be punched below the surface of the wood and the hole filled; screws should be counter-sunk or protected by cups. Any loose pieces should be large enough to prevent a child swallowing them or pushing them into ears or nose; all paint must be non-toxic.

If you make soft toys, remember that foam chips (and foam plastic) are flammable and give off extremely toxic fumes if burned or overheated. Use polyester fibre or kapok instead. Bells, beads and buttons should not be small enough to swallow and if used should be firmly attached with strong thread. Eyes for dolls and animals should be locked or sewn very firmly in position. Fabrics should not be loosely woven; the fluff of the pile of fur fabrics should not be easy to pull out, swallow or inhale. Make sure that the fabric is colour fast, and that all seams are strong enough to withstand play!

TOYS FOR THE FIRST THREE MONTHS

Flat on his back, a baby looks up at the world around him, peeps at the end of his cot, slowly learns how to turn his head and begins to move hands, arms and feet. This is the age when seeing, touching, hearing and smelling are being developed. For this period, choose simple, colourful mobiles to hang from the ceiling or attach to cot and pram. Rattles can be picked up, grasped at, chewed, investigated, and listened to; large colourful beads, (too large to swallow) threaded together, can be shaken, handled individually and rattled; animal shapes can be squeaked, grasped, squeezed and chewed; soft toys will be cuddled and sucked.

THREE MONTHS TO A YEAR

As the senses develop, so does curiosity. Choose toys for their range of textures, shapes, colours and sounds. Simple shapes and colours are best; avoid toys that are fussy or multi-coloured. Look for toys that are well-designed and versatile— some bath boats, for instance, can also be taken

It is not necessary to spend a great deal of money on toys and playthings. The best are often close at hand in your own home. The materials for sand and water play, for example, are all part of household equipment. Given bowls of water, collanders, sieves and an assortment of containers, children will be blissfully

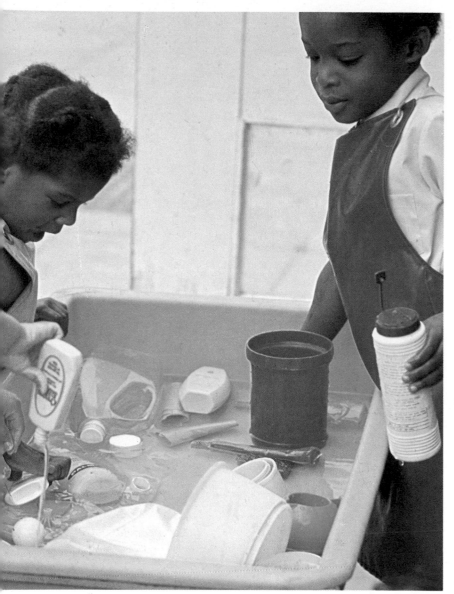

in later life! Have plenty of shelves, bags and storage containers to encourage him. Help him sort out the toys from time to time, so that he begins to understand how much easier it is to find something if it is in the right place!

In these early days, introduce one toy at a time, remembering that it will be played with for only a short period.

FROM ONE TO THREE YEARS

During this time, children need the space to move about and be active—pull-along toys and push-and-pull toys will be very popular. Bricks and building blocks are important and a child needs lots of them. Buy unpainted wooden bricks, beginning with rectangles and squares and adding other shapes as time goes on. Remember the younger the child, the simpler the shapes need to be. Now is the time when children lift things up, twist, turn, screw, open and close anything and enjoy sand and water play. So choose toys that fulfil these requirements, making sure that they have no sharp edges, or are small enough to be swallowed.

Chunky wax crayons and paints to use on rolls of lining paper will be popular. Soft toys, board books, posting boxes, more complicated stacking figures, nursery rhyme friezes and rag dolls and teddies to carry around will all be needed.

FROM THREE TO FIVE YEARS

Curiosity and boundless energy are the hallmarks of this period in a child's life. It is the time to introduce scaled-down models of the adult's world—transport toys, household equipment, prams, building materials, and so on, always making sure that they are strongly constructed and truly functional. Frustration at this age can be infuriating for a child. It is a time to learn about words with linking letters and numbers, to play imaginative games with theatres, to begin with first train sets, doll's houses, and village buildings. Playing with farm and zoo animals, telling the time and accomplishing tasks all belong to this period. It is a time when money spent on good outdoor play equipment—a swing with rubber 'safety seat' slide, climbing frame—will be well-invested.

WHEN CHILDREN ARE ILL

Toys are as important to a child who is unwell as they are when he or she is fit and active, and they have to be chosen with particular care. A sick child often needs toys for a slightly younger age group—toys that can be easily managed without requiring too much effort. Introduce a small new toy daily, rather than one big one which has to last through the whole illness!

happy. As well as providing entertainment, such games stimulate a basic understanding of sizes, textures, shapes, volumes, weights and measures. This familiarity with basic concepts will prove invaluable later.

Outdoors, barrels to crawl through and crates and cardboard boxes will provide hours of happy and inventive play.

apart and used as stacking toys. This age group loves stacking toys—they never tire of piling them up and knocking them down again. It is also the time for pull-along toys and, as a baby begins to stand and take those first few steps, the time for a good, strong baby-walker. This is an expensive item, so it is well worth looking for a second-hand version. It will need to be strongly constructed, with the wheels squarely set and the base firm, deep and able to take a good weight. Over the years, this will be used to carry bricks, animals, toys, people and garden weeds! Sit-and-push-along toys will be popular, so will rag books, threading beads, nesting beakers and boxes.

Keep your child's toys in the right place; for instance, store bath toys in the bathroom. Return them to the same place when they have been used, so that the child recognizes that is where the toys live. This is a simple and unobtrusive way of introducing the concept that 'there is a place for everything and everything has its place.' Started early, this will save much friction and aggravation

A Child's World of Imagination

From birth a child reaches out to learn. Events from that time onwards encourage or discourage this natural process. The quality of a child's imagination is determined, to a very large extent, by the quality of the images that he or she is exposed to. A child who grows in imagination is a child whose parents act from the knowledge that it is essential to present him with the finest possible influences, challenges and experiences from his earliest days. Such parents seek the best nursery rhymes, songs, poems, books, music, ballet, drama, paintings, sculpture and architecture to inspire the child's developing mind. Every child needs a parent whose mind will stir his own to positive action; and every child will turn first to his mother and father. They are in the unique position to develop his senses, mind and imagination.

A child needs a wealth of natural phenomena to stimulate his senses. He also needs a wealth of opportunities to ask questions, listen to answers and to share hopes, fears, thoughts and ideas. The most important thing is to remember that a child is always in a state of becoming—of continuous transformation of body and mind—and to watch and meet each new need as it arises.

Emerson, the writer, obviously wondered about imagination. He wrote: 'Imagination is not a talent of some men but is the health of every man.' Napoleon said: 'The human race is governed by its imagination'. Shelley and Wordsworth wrote poetical lines to the effect that 'The great instrument of moral good is the imagination.' Joubert wrote: "Imagination is the eye of the soul.'

Imagination is a creative faculty of mind. From the onset of life a child begins to store experiences in the form of images. These images are what is retained of any impression that is collected by our five senses—hearing, sight, taste, touch and smell. As a child's mind develops, he discovers, within him, the ability to reflect images from his store of images, and to form and re-form them into mental patterns. Imagination enables him to draw on the past to enrich the present and also to visualize the future.

Every child is an individual and will, therefore, react to experiences in an individual way. The kind of images that each child stores will largely depend on what sense he is using in any one moment and, in general, will be influenced by which sense a child chiefly favours (see **The Five Senses**—page 212). Some children will, therefore, collect mainly visual images, others auditory or tactile.

ENRICHING IMAGINATION

The quality of imagination is determined to a very large extent by the quality of the images that a child is exposed to. This is why it is essential to offer young children only the best. Everything he sees, hears, touches, tastes or smells will form memory 'material' in the form of images; the feelings that he has about what he sees, hears, touches, tastes or smells are an integral part of the memory material. When he begins to draw on this material to re-create experiences he has had, or would like to have now or in the future, he is using his imagination.

A child's imagination is enriched in two ways. The first is dependent on how effectively he uses, and continues to use, his senses; the second, on the quality of the environment in which his senses operate. In mental development, as in physical development, there is a sequence of stages through which a child's mind develops. These stages—from simply being able to look, to being able to describe in words what one is looking at— should be respected and allowed to unfold naturally in their own time.

A child needs a wealth of natural phenomena to stimulate his senses: pebbles on the beach; geese in flight; an ant hill viewed through a magnifying glass; the smell of new bread baking; morning dew; spiders' webs; the sun rising and setting; the touch of exotic materials passed on for dressing-up boxes. He needs all this plus a wealth of opportunities to be heard, to converse, to ask questions, listen to answers; to share hopes, fears, thoughts, ideas.

ENCOURAGEMENT

The way for parents to encourage a creative imagination is the same as for any mental process. First it is important to remember that a child is always in a state of becoming—of continuous transformation of body and mind; then to watch and meet each new need as it reveals itself.

From birth, a child reaches out to learn. Events from that time forth encourage or discourage this natural process. He will not, for instance, learn much strapped for hours in a pram or pushchair; or left alone for hours in front of a television set. Only the child who is encouraged by his parents' love and attention will retain that spirit of adventure which allows him to travel along both real and creatively imaginative paths. A child who grows in imagination is the child whose parents act from the knowledge that it is essential to present him with the finest influences, challenges and experiences from his earliest days. Such parents seek the best nursery rhymes, songs, poems, books, music, ballet, drama, paintings, sculpture, architecture to inspire the child's developing mind. Every child needs a parent whose mind will stir his own to positive action; and every child will turn first to his mother and father. They are in the unique position to develop his senses, his mind, his imagination.

MAKING A MARK

The simplest observation of a young child reveals that he is essentially a creative and imaginative being, a person with a function to fulfil. Every human being's desire to make his

mark is entirely natural, and is linked to the natural human desire to be happy, to know everything and to live forever.

It all begins in babyhood with playful exploratory movements; the discovery of natural substances: water, mud, clay, sand and wood; how to use them; how to make one's mark upon them! The child loves these substances because they are responsive. He can create on them his own imprint. Then, at about two years old, he discovers the concept of permanence and, therefore, another aspect of imagination. He begins to appreciate that objects hold their form and exist whether or not he is seeing, hearing, tasting, touching or smelling them in that moment. Through imagination, he can recall such things and reflect them in the mirror of his mind. Soon, through play, he uses his imagination to practise for the future. He will, for instance, act out a

grown-up role—be a fireman, a train driver.

SENSITIVE SEEKERS

The young child has much in common with the artist. The child, like the artist, seeks to understand what moves creation, himself and others, and what his rôle is in the ever-changing kaleidoscope. Both struggle to make fragments whole; to transform images, words and impressions into larger concepts in which ideas and knowledge can be formulated, expressed and shared with others. Sensitive parents do more than care physically for a child—they stimulate and inspire, both through the sharing of their experience and through introducing a child to the imaginative experience of others. One day, the child will spontaneously find his own unique way to express outwardly and share what is, quite naturally at first, an inward experience.

From Baby to Child
The Negative Phase

The small baby is very aware of unity—he does not recognize himself as a separate entity. Once he has the 'tools' of language, however, and can say: 'Me, I, myself', he discovers that he can use language to his own advantage—for getting things—and begins to assert himself. This phase, which usually arises between the age of eighteen months and two and a half years, is known as the negative phase.

It is a phase which parents find very distressing because it can appear that a child is deliberately doing everything in his power to upset as many people as he is able. He refuses to do anything he is told and responds to every request with a very definite and negative 'no!' In very simple terms, the child has discovered that he is a person in his own right, that words are powerful weapons and that he can make a very definite mark on others by refusing to respond to their requests and by resisting any instruction. If, in turn, his wishes are resisted, he will use everything in his power to get his own way. Temper tantrums, he discovers, are very alarming and embarrassing for parents, and he soon begins to use them to excellent effect. He will think nothing of throwing himself on the ground in the middle of a busy supermarket and screaming at the top of his voice. A common response on the part of the parent is to soothe and to pacify him at all costs—anything for a quiet life, anything to bring the embarrassing incident to a close and remove oneself from the public spotlight. Not surprisingly, the child learns, from these experiences, that thrashing the floor and screaming his head off brings him the desired result. The parent gives way, peace is temporarily restored. In a very short time, a pattern is formed and a young tyrant is born!

Many people, including many childcare experts, are convinced that the negative phase is inevitable and not something that it is possible to avoid. This is usually because one essential point is overlooked. The truth is that the moment a child has the 'tool' of language and is able to say 'me, I, myself', is also the moment when a child's access to the world of mind is expanding. In other words, the moment a child begins to assert his personality is the moment when his mind needs occupation. When this fact is overlooked and a child's mind is not given some real occupation, the child becomes frustrated and trouble, known as the negative phase, begins.

The way, then, to avoid the negative phase—and temper tantrums—is to give the child some real instruction: by teaching him the letters of the alphabet, taking him for walks and pointing things out, giving them their proper names, reading to him and passing on as much information as he needs without asserting any pressures. If this is done for about fifteen minutes, three times a day, then for the rest of the day the child will be as happy as a king playing. This is how the negative phase is avoided or transformed into the positive phase.

COPING WITH TEMPER TANTRUMS

If, in spite of all reasonable parental efforts to soothe, a child continues to thrash the air in a fury, or holds his breath until he turns blue and is on the verge of passing out, do not panic. He may look as if he is killing himself, but he will not. He may even lose consciousness but, if so, he will begin to breathe again! Simply withdraw, if you are at home, and pretend to give your attention to something else. Without an audience to perform to, a child recovers all the quicker. If the incident arises in a public place, do not be embarrassed by what other people may be thinking, or how they are rating you as a parent. Many of them will be parents themselves and will understand what the drama is about. Do not leave the child, but give your attention to something else. Look at the goods displayed in the shop, read an advertisement, watch a plane passing overhead. Sooner, or later, the child will come round! When he does so, welcome him back with open arms.

THE TWO FACES OF LOVE

The most important thing, perhaps, to keep in mind when conflicts arise is that love has two faces and both are equally essential for a child's well-being and development. Love may, for example, be soft, gentle, tender, mild as a mother's milk, but it may also be fierce, hard, penetrating, piercing. A child who is allowed to grow up believing that love is conveyed only in moments of sweet tenderness will not be a whole person. He will be a victim of sentimentality—of cloying sweetness—and this will pervert his judgement to the detriment of his own and other people's well-being and happiness.

One of the worst aspects, resulting from sentimental love, is the current idea that a loving parent allows a child to make its own choices. In truth, this is proof of neglect, if not hatred: that a child should be allowed to sink of his own choice. No truly loving parent expects a child to make a choice before reason and discrimination have been developed. Even when a child receives the best parental training and guidance during his early years, the ability to reason and to discriminate is really only beginning at the age of ten years upwards.

If, then, during moments of conflict, the parent, by applying the right discipline, cuts through a habit which is threatening to ruin a child's whole life, then that discipline is an act of love.

A child, to be whole, needs to experience the two faces of love. Provided parents remember that, whichever way they look at it, love causes one to act for the benefit of the loved one, and gives the strength to do so, they cannot go wrong. Slowly, but surely, a child begins to understand from his parents' example, that love may give rise to an embrace, a joy, a gentleness; or a reproach, reproof or punishment. Then he has understood for his own and other's benefit that love speaks through the word 'no' as well as 'yes'; and that its hard face is as essential as its soft.

Many people, including the majority of childcare experts, are convinced that the negative phase, when a child says no to everything and refuses to do anything he is told, is inevitable and cannot be avoided. This is usually because one essential point is overlooked. The truth is that the moment a child has the basic 'tools' of the language is also the moment when his mind is beginning to expand and, therefore, needs occupation. If this simple fact is overlooked, the child becomes bored and frustrated.

The way to avoid the negative phase is to give the child opportunities to develop his mind —teach him his alphabet, take him for walks, point things out, name things for him. In these simple ways, the negative phase can be transformed into a positive phase.

227

Potty Training

The first thing that parents usually decide is whether or not they are going to conduct a time and motion study on their child and, from the early months of his life, dangle him at appropriate moments over a pot in the hope that his natural reflexes will work and that he will oblige! Time and motion is fine as an approach, but it is important to realize that the child is totally oblivious of what is going on and that this method will not hasten the day when he achieves voluntary bowel and bladder control.

Any parent, in fact, who becomes too ambitious is much more likely to postpone rather than forward that happy day. Over-reacting and forcing a baby to sit on a pot is emotionally and psychologically harmful and will reap a variety of problems. The child will quickly echo a parent's tension and anxiety by becoming tense and anxious himself. A natural process which naturally takes a certain amount of time to become naturally controlled becomes, instead, an unnatural obsession which will take its toll on the mother and the child. The consequences may remain to trouble and affect a child's attitude towards natural functions, including the sexual act, for the rest of his life. Equally, the wear and tear you inflict on your own nerves will do nothing to enhance your relationship with him.

VARYING RATES OF PROGRESS

Whether or not one plays the time and motion game of trying to catch the child's urine and faeces at just the right moment, one needs to accept that most children are not able to control their bowels and bladders voluntarily until some time during the second year of life. Even then, it is rare for bowel and bladder control to come at the same time. The control usually begins with the bowels and is followed a few weeks or months later by bladder control. The actual timing does, of course, vary from child to child and it is essential not to make comparisons with friends' and neighbours' children. This usually achieves nothing but tension and a corresponding temptation to compete or lose patience and try to hurry the process in the child.

Even when a child does achieve daytime control during the second year of his life, he should not be expected to achieve night-time control and should not be chastised for this lack of control. With help, this will be achieved at some time during the third year of life. If he is still having difficulty at four years old, and if this is causing you concern or increasing anxiety, have a word with your doctor.

Parents who become over-ambitious about getting their baby to use his potty are more likely to postpone rather than forward that happy day. Making comparisons with other children is never helpful and over-reacting by trying to force a child to sit on a pot is psychologically harmful and will reap a variety of behaviour problems. Not surprisingly, a child soon echoes his parents' tensions by becoming tense and anxious himself.

BE PREPARED

Even during the second year of your child's life, be prepared for some trials and tribulations, and good and bad days. Above all, remain calm and unconcerned. Anything else invites trouble. Introduce your child to the pot, if you have not already done so, and time it as well as you are able to coincide with the time when he would normally pass a motion. The first time you succeed in having one for the pot, looked pleased, but do not over-play the scene with expressions of rapture and joy. This may create the wrong response in the child and he may, unconsciously, seek a variation on the theme by discovering what will happen if he does not oblige. He is not being wicked—just interested and observant!

Over-reacting by showering him with excessive interest or praise when he succeeds or, alternatively, with despondency or disappointment when he does not, are both potentially troublesome. A child may, for example, begin to reflect a parent's excesses by becoming over-interested himself. He may scoop out the faeces, offer them to the parent with great pride and then become confused because they show anger or distaste for his action. He may also be confused because, although his parents are pleased, they throw the results of his labours—his gift—down the lavatory!

A certain amount of handling and playing with faeces is inevitable. A child does not share the adult's distaste for certain substances and will quite naturally touch—and taste—anything. Again, it is important not to over-react. Make it clear that his behaviour is not acceptable without giving the child the idea that there is something shocking or disgusting about what he has done. A young child is sensitive to his parents' reactions and will not need strong responses in order to accept that certain behaviour is not acceptable.

Some parents recommend discarding nappies and putting a child into trainer pants during the day in the second year of life. The fact that the urine runs down the child's legs, instead of being soaked up by a nappy, is thought to encourage the child to use the pot. This does sometimes work. Other children, however, simply ignore or even enjoy the sensation. One can only experiment to see which category one's child fits into and not mind which one it is! Trainer pants are certainly less bulky than nappies and offer reasonable protection if used with an absorbent liner and cotton-wool or some towelling.

One consequence of over-reacting to successes and 'failures' is that, over a period of time, a child may realize that he has a handy new weapon with which he can assert his independence and he may begin to hold on even when there is a strong desire to evacuate a bowel. This stool-holding creates a lot of concern for parents, so do remember that often it can be avoided by not appearing over-concerned.

Keep a vigilant eye on your child during the day and offer him the pot at appropriate times. Even after he has achieved control, he will forget when he is involved in a particularly absorbing activity and will need a reminder when he begins to wriggle, etc. It also helps to offer the pot before going out or immediately on your return.

At night, pot your child before he goes to bed, just before you retire and first thing in the morning. It is not necessary to awaken him when you lift him before your own bedtime—his natural reflexes will work when his warm bottom comes into contact with the cold pot. A rubber sheet and nappies are necessary night-time accessories. Do not, as is sometimes suggested, refuse to give a child a drink before he goes to sleep in the hope that this will encourage him to stay dry. Thirst is uncomfortable and will probably delay sleep.

USING THE LAVATORY

A large lavatory seat can be an alarming experience for a child. Ease the adjustment from pot to lavatory by purchasing a child's seat. The child will also appreciate a platform, a footstool for example, to help him reach the seat and the lavatory chain. If the lavatory has a high-cistern chain, you will need to lengthen the chain with a piece of cord or rope.

Show your child how to use a toilet roll and then let him use it. Messy pants may be the price that you and he have to pay while he is mastering this skill. He will, however, never learn to be independent if he is not allowed to practise. Teach him, from his earliest days, that it is essential to wash hands after each visit, but do not over-emphasize germs. The idea that there is something nasty about the body and its functions always has unfortunate consequences.

A STEP BACK

If a child who has been dry during the night and day suddenly begins to bed-wet or soil his pants, do not be upset or angry. Occasional accidents are inevitable and often occur if a child is particularly excited about an event, outing or visitor. If the accidents become the rule rather than the exception, the child will need help and patient understanding. Such behaviour usually reflects a temporary physical disturbance following an illness, or an emotional disturbance. Opportunities to converse, plus extra love and attention will usually rectify the problem, but if it persists, ask your doctor's advice.

Comfort Habits

THE NEED FOR COMFORT

When you are a toddler or a young child and are left to your own devices for a few moments, you will look at, listen to, taste, touch or smell anything and everything. You will, as every mother knows, taste a worm as easily as a strawberry. Not surprisingly, in this situation, the word 'don't' becomes a very common experience.

Whilst it is understandable that parents need to resort to this word to protect their child from potentially dangerous situations, there are also many occasions when the word is used unnecessarily; when it is applied to save a parent the inconvenience of a child getting untidy or ruffling the surface-appearance of a house or garden. What is often overlooked is that, from a child's point of view, 'Don't . . .' is the equivalent of saying 'Don't learn'. If, in the course of discovering the world, a child finds himself constantly confronted with the word don't and is, therefore, constantly tantalized, frustrated, checked, he will begin to seek consolation in comfort habits such as cot-rocking, head-banging, thumb-sucking, blanket-sucking and playing with his own body—masturbation. This is a fairly inevitable sequence of events for a child who is over- or unnecessarily restricted, and underlies the importance of reserving the word 'don't' for dangerous situations.

A child who is allowed and encouraged to make maximum use of his senses, whose mind and hands are healthily occupied, will not be nearly so prone to seeking solace in comfort habits as a child who is constantly checked in his effort to comprehend, through his senses, the world in which he finds himself.

Another reason why a child seeks comfort is that the world, for him, can on occasions seem a very insecure place. When you are young and inexperienced, nothing can be taken for granted. People come and go, routines change, moods and environment alter—nothing seems permanent. It is not really surprising that, on occasions, a child feels overwhelmed and that, in seeking to reassure himself, he makes the discovery that his own thumb and other parts of his body are permanent, in that they are always present, or that he finds one thing, such as a nappy or piece of blanket, which he can wed himself to and never put down.

Another reason for comfort habits is that a child often finds himself, literally or metaphorically, in a situation where he is expected to run before he can walk—to display, in other words, a

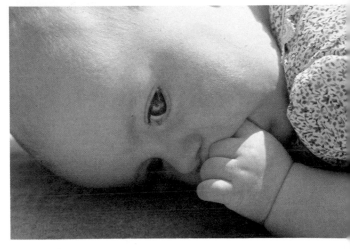

When you are very young and inexperienced nothing can be taken for granted. Sometimes, in seeking to reassure himself, he makes the delightful discovery that his own thumb is permanent, or finds one thing, such as a nappy or piece of blanket, which he can wed himself to and never put down.

The most effective remedy for all comfort habits is to resist saying: 'Don't do that' and to offer, instead, an alternative activity. This will immediately attract the child's attention and occupy his hands and mind in a more useful way. Parents can say, 'Don't do that', with no effect at all, but the moment they say, 'Let's do this', there is an immediate response. A child whose mind and hands are kept healthily occupied soon forgets undesirable occupations. A child who is given love and attention when he needs it is not compelled to seek compensations in a variety of comfort habits.

maturity which, for the moment, is beyond his scope. He reacts to this stress by taking a step back to the security of an earlier stage of his development and seeks comfort, for example, in sucking.

Three points to check, then, if a child seeks comfort in comfort habits are: Is he unnecessarily restricted? Is he feeling pressurized? Is he insecure? Having established the reason for the behaviour, it is, of course, essential to make the appropriate adjustments without expecting the habit to dissolve miraculously overnight.

☐ **Thumb-sucking** As a habit, thumb-sucking has the advantage over dummies in that the thumb is not so frequently dipped in sweet substances which ruin a child's teeth. A baby is naturally fascinated by his own hands and fingers and will suck his fingers and thumb for reasons of exploration as well as comfort.

If, however, an older child begins to suck his thumb, parents can be sure that he is in need of love and attention and that there is a reason which needs seeking out. The reasons are as many and varied as children themselves, but it is wise to check that the child is not feeling unwell, under emotional strain or stress or insecure. Jealousy of a younger brother or sister may, for example, cause an older child to resort to thumb-sucking.

Many parents fear that excessive thumb-sucking will distort the shape of a child's mouth and cause protruding teeth. This is, however, extremely rare.

☐ **Head-Banging and Cot-Rocking** Although these two habits are alarming and noisy from the parent's point of view, the child rarely comes to physical harm. A simple precaution, however, is to pad the head of the baby's cot or the wall around the cot, and to screw the legs of the cot to the floor.

The essential action, of course, is to discover why a child is driven to seek comfort in compulsive rocking and head-banging. If, having given

your child extra love and attention and having checked the points in *Need for Comfort*, page 231, the behaviour continues, consult your family doctor or health visitor.

☐ **Masturbation** Comfort habits are always a challenge. Some, like cot-rocking, head-banging, thumb- and rag-sucking, hair- and ear-pulling and tooth-grinding are comparatively easy to live with. Others such as masturbation are more painful because they stir up fears, distaste, or embarrassment. From a child's point of view, however, there is no difference between thumb-sucking and masturbation—both are comfort habits indulged for the benefit of consolation—compensation.

Difficult though it may be to appreciate, the time for concern is when a child ceases to masturbate openly and goes to the trouble of seeking out private places and furtively concealing himself. The reason is obvious—the secrecy and furtiveness imply knowledge of a more positive way to spend time and, therefore, implicate a deliberate decision on the child's part to withdraw from life in favour of a solitary negative indulgence.

Masturbation will *not* lead to insanity or an inability to experience a normal sexual life, but it is not to be encouraged for the simple reason that it can become a compulsive habit which interrupts healthier pursuits and whips the child into a state of feverish excitement. It can also incline a child to solitude and lessens his need of relationships with other people.

Compulsive masturbation is, in fact, always a symptom of distress which needs to be tackled positively. Certainly it should not be ignored because of a fear of making a child guilty or giving him the idea that there is something 'not nice' about his body and sex in general.

THE REMEDY

The most effective remedy for all comfort habits is to resist saying 'Don't do that' and to offer, instead, an alternative activity. This will immediately attract the child's attention and occupy hands and mind in a more useful way. Parents, in fact, can say 'Don't do that' until they are blue in the face, but the moment they say 'Let's do this', there is an immediate response. A child whose mind and hands are kept healthily occupied soon forgets undesirable occupations. A child who is given the love and attention that he needs is not compelled to seek consolation and compensation in a variety of comfort habits.

Behaviour is always an effect and never a cause. The positive approach is to look beyond the behaviour and consider why a child is behaving in the particular way—and then take the necessary action to meet his need.

Becoming Social Beings

Nobody who has ever sat two babies alongside each other would deny that babies are sociable beings who are interested in each other and that they do have their own mysterious way of communication. Do not, however, be surprised if, at this stage of your child's social development, curiosity overcomes the usual social niceties and results in one baby poking the other in the eye. If this happens, your baby is not displaying vicious anti-social tendencies—he is merely displaying a natural curiosity partnered by a natural ignorance of cause and effect!

Take comfort in the thought that social niceties will come with your gentle guidance, but that they will take time. Until that time, be prepared to keep a watchful eye on the proceedings. Remove all potentially dangerous weapons such as sharp-edged toys, go to the rescue whenever necessary and do not over-tax your child's or the other child's patience by leaving them too long in each other's company. Do not, of course, give way to the temptation to avoid social situations for your baby because they are such hard work. Practice will make perfect!

MAKING FRIENDS

A child who grows up alert and adventurous and never at a loss for impressions that interest himself and others, will never lack good friends because love of life attracts life.

The commonly held idea that friends are only true friends if they are indulgent and ready to make allowances for all the peculiarities and weaknesses which a person cares to display, is not to be encouraged. A true friend, a child needs to be taught, is a person who always has the friend's best interests in mind. For this reason, he is far more active in helping and encouraging his friend to overcome his fears and limitations than he is in turning a blind eye and ear to faults or weaknesses. A true friend is not a person one stagnates and hibernates with, but a person with whom one develops and grows mutually stronger.

☐ **Friendlessness** For some children: 'I want a friend,' becomes a constant plaintive cry. Such children need to be taught that the only way to have a friend is to be one. When a child is encouraged to notice that other people exist, to consider their needs before his own and to give the kind of attention which he, himself, enjoys receiving, he will not lack good friends or, in fact, the right kind of attention.

CLINGING

When a child clings like glue, as if his very life depends on it, to his mother, father or one particular friend, we can be sure that he is not feeling secure and able to cope with the world at large. Such a child will need infinite patience and gentle handling. If a child suddenly becomes very clinging and resists joining other children, it is important not to say: 'What's the matter, darling? You are becoming a mummy's boy.' Such responses, whether they are mocking or meant with the best intentions, all serve the same negative purpose which is to focus one's own and the child's attention on the deviation. Positive responses will vary according to the child's age and individual make-up, but the essence is always the same: that is to focus the child's attention on anything other than the deviation and allow him to take a step towards independence. At the same time, it is important to give him all the love and support that he needs and, if necessary, to remain near at hand or at his side until he is sufficiently reassured to take the next step on his own.

TOO SHY TO SPEAK

The first essential is not to draw the child's attention, through word or action, to his shyness. This will only make matters worse and prolong the problem. The second, is not to force the child into social situations. This will only confirm the idea and fear that he cannot cope. A small amount of socializing in a small group of people will gradually work wonders for a shy child's confidence. A child who is established in shyness will need generous support, and is often best helped by being given something specific to do such as taking coats or passing round the sandwiches.

If the shyness is caused by feeling different from other children—a speech impediment, perhaps, or a prominent birthmark or other physical (or social) handicap, find ways to focus the child's attention on his positive attributes and assets.

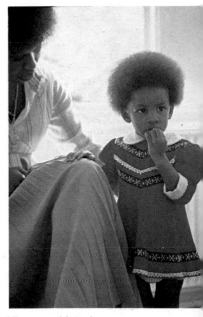

Like everything else, learning to become a sociable being, who is able to take other people's feelings and likes into account, takes time. Until that day arrives, keep a discreet and watchful eye on the proceedings and be prepared to go to the rescue as and when necessary. Never force a reluctant child into social situations. This will only confirm the idea and fear that she cannot cope. A little socializing in a small group of people will work wonders for a shy child's confidence.

The more unconcerned he becomes about an impediment, the less likely other children will be to notice it.

If a child, who has been previously happy socially, suddenly begins to hover on the fringes and does not appear to have much to contribute, it helps to remember that output is dependent on input. Is he, for example, being offered sufficient enrichment and stimulation in the form of interests, activities and outings?

The most helpful guidelines for any social situation is to teach a child, by example, that the only way to be truly at ease with others is to consider the other person and not oneself. A popular person is always the one who knows how to put others at their ease and does not expect to be the centre of attention.

TELEVISION

Today, one of the worst impediments to the development of children's relationships, is prolonged viewing of television. The first thing that is evident when a child is allowed to become addicted to television is that all his interests are planned around television programmes. Over a period of time, there is an inevitable and often total decline in other activities and in human relationships. For some children there is a danger that television will become the only 'friend' that they will ever want to know.

If a parent wants a child to be truly alive and happy and able to form real and lasting relationships, it is essential to ensure that television does not become the most important factor in a child's or parent's life.

Friendships, as parents quickly discover, are not easily encouraged or discouraged. The drawing together of two people or a group of people is usually a very personal matter. What is always evident is that attraction is a very powerful force which comes into being quite naturally when people of like-minds and mutual interests meet.

Parents naturally want their child to be popular and to have good friends, and there are many practical ways in which to help. A useful first step is to ensure that a child is a happy, likeable person whose companionship is of benefit to others. This is taken care of by giving the child as many opportunities as possible to develop his physical, mental, emotional and spiritual potential.

234

Discipline

A happy, healthy and balanced child is one whose parents define very clearly what is and what is not acceptable behaviour. Ultimately a child can only find the courage to be himself when he likes and respects what he knows of himself. Without discipline, a child will always be at the mercy of his own desires and, soon, adults and other children will begin to avoid him.

At certain times in a child's life it may seem that he is forever doing something that needs checking and on such occasions, the day can become one long miserable nag. Discipline will not take long to register on a child if parents ensure that what is on their tongues is also on their minds.

With discipline, as with everything else in the first seven years of a child's life, the mind of the parents is the most powerful influence. In practical terms right discipline is the framework which gives a child the security of a freedom of choice within clearly defined limits which he understands. True discipline enables a child to live happily with others and teaches unity, wholeness, fellowship, peace, integration; through it he learns to balance his own desire against the need of a group.

Inevitably there will be occasions when a child's will comes into conflict with an adult's will. The essential thing is for parents to ensure that what is on their tongue is also in their mind. A child can spot at once when a parent says one thing and means another. Choice of words is also important—some invite argument. Children are happier and less likely to make a fuss when told exactly what is expected of them.

THE RIGHT BALANCE

The words *discipline* and *disciple* are related. They come from two Latin roots which mean to learn/teach. In current language, however, the positive meaning of the word discipline is rarely mentioned or conveyed, and is now used in the negative sense of: instruction via rules, subjection, mortification, chastisement, penance or punishment. It is hardly surprising, in these circumstances, that it is unfashionable.

When the sound—and meaning—of a word is changed in this way, attitudes change with it and the issue becomes confused. One result of this confusion is that the word discipline is now associated with the word repression. The result of this is that many parents have become afraid of discipline and have dispensed with it for fear of crushing and damaging a child.

Whilst there is no evidence to suggest that the current fear of repression is justified, there is more than ample evidence that lack of discipline creates problems and that the increase in violence, mental ill health and other social disorders are closely related.

TO SMACK OR NOT TO SMACK

There is, as every parent is painfully aware, a school of thought that says 'to smack is to fail oneself and one's child,' that 'might is not right' and 'one must always reason with a child.' The truth is that a small child is not reasonable.

236

Reasoning can start when children are about eight, nine, ten years old. The ideal way to smack a child who is flouting discipline is to put on a good act of anger without really feeling it. But if a parent actually feels irritation, it is no good leaving the situation until his temper has died down—the moment for effective action will have passed. It is better to smack and be done with it, rather than clam up feelings until they rush out in an uncontrollable flood. It is also better to smack than to indulge in a whining nag all day whilst busily trying to keep tempers. The important thing to remember is that when smacking, aim for the bottom, legs or arms—never the head.

ESPECIALLY FOR MOTHERS

An important aspect of discipline is to remember that until the child is about seven or eight, it is the mother's territory. Do not give way to the temptation to abdicate responsibility to father—'Just wait until your father gets home . . . ' All that this succeeds in doing is to undermine the mother's authority and allow the child not to take her seriously. A happy child is a child whose mother defines very clearly the line between what is and what is not acceptable behaviour, and what will enable him to live in harmony with himself and others. A child can only find the courage to be himself when he likes and respects what he knows of himself. Without right discipline, a child will always be led by his nose, at the mercy of his own desires.

CHECK LIST

☐ Discipline, like love, is empty for a child unless it is accompanied by real attention.

☐ Change the activity frequently for the under-fives. Give the child something you know he can do; watch if there is difficulty and be ready to help. Ease the child's frustration and discipline will take care of itself.

☐ Children change in a few weeks. Change with them—the former discipline may not apply. Do not cosset a child—he needs to know how to cope with pain as well as pleasure.

☐ If one activity is stopped provide another—otherwise it is like holding a lid on a boiling saucepan. Parents may stop the steam escaping for a while, but not forever!

☐ Never let a child think that he is no good. There is a great difference between disapproval and saying: 'That's not what you should do'.

☐ Turn a blind eye nine times out of ten rather than nag, but when taking aim the tenth time do not miss.

☐ Remember to praise. Approval is a very subtle reward and a very effective discipline. An approving tone of voice and expression enables a child to achieve his full potential.

☐ Remember that self-confidence springs from experience—not always successful experience, but that which adds to a child's store of knowledge. Failure can make him angry and give up, or it can make him work harder. When he is hurt and cross, wait until his irritation subsides, then suggest a new way of approach. If he fails again, praise him for perseverance.

☐ Check that the expected standard of conduct is reasonable. Every child is different and confidence can be sapped by being rushed a stage or at another's pace. Choosing realistic goals that allow for more success than failure, while watching carefully for the next challenge, is a very effective discipline.

☐ Never discipline a child in a way that shames; or in a way that is designed to make him a credit to you, rather than true to himself.

☐ The golden rule is: always be simple and direct. Expect to be obeyed. Having punished, put the incident out of mind and see the child afresh.

Attention Seeking

Attention, because it is synonymous with love, is a very powerful substance—the most significant award—reward—that one person can give another person. Its effectiveness is determined by how aware we are at the moment of giving it, or receiving it. For example, if we are only half-attending to a child, he receives a half-measure; if our attention is focused fully on him, he receives a full measure. The width, breadth and depth of happiness is always determined by how successful a person is in giving or receiving single-minded and whole-hearted attention.

A young child is naturally generous with his attention. He will give it wholeheartedly, with or without invitation, to anything or anybody who attracts his interest! He soon learns, however, that attracting attention is more difficult, that this is dependent on another person's willingness or unwillingness to respond. Familiar cries are: 'Mummy. *Mummeee*. Are you listening?' 'Mummy. *Mummeeee*. Are you watching?' Mummy, taste . . . touch . . . smell. '*Mummeeeee*.' A familiar answer is: 'In a minute, darling.' Minutes, however, are so elusive and, as every child soon discovers, have a habit of growing into hours: after breakfast, after lunch, after tea, tomorrow—never. The baby is a boy; the boy, a man; the man, a father. The process begins again; 'Daddy. *Daddeeee*.'

When a child's interest in the natural world—the world of elements: fire, air, water, earth, and their corresponding senses: sight, hearing, taste, touch and smell—is undermined, he begins to seek compensations. If, at this stage, the balance is not restored by making sure that he receives the appropriate award of attention for normal behaviour, he makes good the loss by abnormal behaviour. If he then makes the discovery that attention is more forthcoming for this—and it usually is!—he continues to substitute unnatural behaviour for natural behaviour. This can become a vicious circle which is very difficult to stop. For this reason, it is important to avoid the bad behaviour, more attention spiral before it really becomes a serious problem. It is easier to prevent than cure it.

The guiding principle, then, when a child first starts to deviate from previously normal behaviour, is to remember that attention is a food; that whatever is fed with it will grow, will benefit from the nourishment. Likewise, anything that is starved of it will decrease in strength and, given time, will die of malnutrition.

Growing up is not rewarding for a child if it means being taken for granted, being noticed less and less—receiving less love and attention. When a child says: 'Mummy look'; 'Mummy' taste this'; 'Daddy, touch this'; 'Daddy, are you listening?' and the parent responds by giving his or her attention, a child knows that he counts.

When a parent backs up such responses by reaching out spontaneously to a child and saying: 'I love you', the moment conveys a depth of happiness, healing reassurance and self-confidence which will never be lost.

Unsolicited gifts of love and attention have a depth of penetration which solicited love and attention can never have. Wise parents know this in their own experience and ensure that it will not

be lacking in their child's experience.

To a certain extent, of course, children will always compete for attention and every child needs to be a favourite. A parent who extends an attentive welcome to each child fulfils this need.

GIVING PRAISE

Giving praise and a smile for a child's achievements, considerate behaviour, indeed all the efforts, large and small, is one of the most effective aids a parent will ever have. Sadly, some parents withhold praise because they fear their child will become a 'show-off', or because they are convinced that he is a show-off. Children, like adults, do need to be appreciated, to be encouraged with praise and voiced approval. If these are offered at the right moment, the child is not driven to swing from a chandelier to attract attention, or to be boastful. A generous measure of reassurance, of letting a child know that he can please, works

When a child says, 'Mummy look' or 'Daddy listen' and the parent responds by taking an affectionate interest in whatever the child is doing, the child knows that she counts.

It is no exaggeration to say that the breadth and depth of a child's happiness is determined by how successful he or she is in giving and receiving single-minded and whole-hearted attention.

wonders, even for a show-off! When parents transfer their attention from a child's weakness and give it, instead, to his strength, praise is always possible. The healing taste of such moments carries every child from strength to strength.

Just as praise will speed a child's progress and his determination to please his parents, so criticism will impede progress. If a child is displaying a fault, such as selfishness with toys, it is very important to correct the fault in such a way that the fault, *not* the child is blamed and censured. For example, if a child is bewailing the fact that nobody will play with him, instead of saying (or thinking!) 'that's hardly surprising when you are such a horrible child', one might say: 'People always back away from selfishness, but have you noticed how they always respond to generosity and kindness? Why not ask him if he would like to ride your bicycle?' In this way, a child is instructed about the effects of selfishness and the potential of generosity, and is left in a state where he can give his attention to solving his problem rather than to nursing his hurt feelings. The principle to remember is that it is always an act of love and friendship to censure the fault, and an act of an enemy to blame the person.

The same principle is true of praise. True praise is never flattery which puffs a child up for the wrong reason. Praise, properly applied, is an act of love. One need never fear spoiling a child, making him conceited, if one remembers to praise the virtue that he is displaying. The virtue may be truthfulness, for example; or perseverance in achieving a difficult feat of balance, such as a handstand; or determination to tie a shoelace; or enterprise in seeing a new possibility in a toy; or even just kindness in sharing.

239

There are endless permutations of how children will react to a new baby. The art of avoiding jealousy, or reassuring a child who is feeling jealous, is to ensure that your love for the newborn baby is inclusive not exclusive. A child who is assured of his mother's attention when he needs it, quickly learns not to begrudge others their turn. Such a child can afford to be generous because experience has taught him that he can afford to be.

When there is a defenceless baby in the home, it is important to remember that toddlers and young children are susceptible to sudden moods and may strike out at anything and anybody while under the influence of temporary anger. There is no certain way of protecting a baby from a child or a child from a baby every moment of the day. It is simply a matter of remaining vigilant and listening for warning signs and symptoms—a change of sound which foretells hostility or mischief which may get out of hand.

Jealousy and Favouritism

JEALOUSY

However confident a young child is that he is loved, a certain amount of jealousy is inevitable when the position of being the only child in his parents' lives changes to being one of two children in his parents' lives.

The first essential when introducing a child to a new baby, whether this is at home or in hospital, is to ensure that the baby is in the cot and not in your arms. A child who has been separated from his mother, while she is in labour, is much more likely to be reassured that she is pleased to see him if she has both arms free to greet and cuddle him. Do not be in too much of a hurry to draw the child's attention to the baby; take time to talk to him and to listen to him. When the excitement of the reunion has died down, introduce him to his brother or sister. Many babycare 'experts' are concerned that a child will be jealous of all the presents that a new baby receives and suggest that it is a good idea to have a present for the child, from the baby, in the cot. It is not, however, ever wise to deceive a child. By all means have a present or presents, but let him know who they are from!

☐ **Avoiding Jealousy** There are endless permutations as to how children will react to a new baby. The art of avoiding jealousy, or reassuring a child who is feeling jealous, is to ensure that the love that flows to the newborn baby is an inclusive and not exclusive love. For this reason, it is not advisable to settle the older child in another room whilst feeding the baby. It is far better to keep an open door, heart and mind; to have a picture book or other suitably quiet activity or game close at hand and allow the child to be present if he wishes. If the child expresses a wish to be fed in the same way as the baby, explain that when he was as small and as helpless as the baby is now, he was fed in this way. But that now he is grown up, you are very proud because he is able to eat from a spoon and drink from a mug, just like mummy and daddy. A child who is given sufficient praise for what he is able to achieve, is far less likely to feel that, in order to get his fair share of love and attention, he must cease to be himself and behave as the baby does.

☐ **The Guiding Principle** It is essential to appreciate that each child needs a fair portion of each day when he can be sure to receive his parents' undivided attention. A child who is confident that his time will come, quickly learns not to begrudge others their turn. Such a child can afford to be generous because experience has taught him that he can afford to be. A child, on the other hand, who habitually meets the reverse—who knows himself to be begrudged, usurped—learns to display the same kind of spitefulness with which he is met.

The guiding principle, then, for avoiding jealousy is to set aside a time each day when a child can be sure of receiving your whole-hearted and single-minded attention. A child who receives ten or so minutes of his parents' time when he needs it will often play happily for hours afterwards.

☐ **Protective Custody** It is important to remember that children are creatures of the weather and that they will strike out at anything and anybody under the influence of a temporary storm. With the best preparations in the world, feelings will sometimes get the better of an older child. There is no foolproof way of protecting a baby from the child and the child from himself every moment of the day. It is simply a matter of remaining attentively vigilant and listening for warning signs and symptoms—a change which foretells hostility or mischievousness which is likely to get out of hand.

If, in spite of careful vigilance, an accident does happen, remember that the child will be as frightened of what he has done as you are. Whilst making it perfectly clear that such behaviour is not acceptable and will be punished, do not over-burden the child with guilt by constantly referring

to the accident. This will only increase his hostility and make similar incidents more likely.

A young child is not responsible for his actions —parents can only do their best to ensure that he is not left at the mercy of temporary storms and their potentially dangerous consequences.

FAVOURITISM

Favouritism in families is a common situation. Indeed a mother or father who does not have some difference of affection for certain individuals is a rarity. It would, of course, be a very different and happier world if every child could be sure of an equal place in his mother's and father's heart, but this ideal is rarely realized. Given this situation, the least that can be done is to ensure that preferences are not backed up by preferential treatment. It is when a mother or father is seen by one child to bestow favours unequally on another that trouble sets in.

If a parent falls into the trap of regarding one child in a particularly favourable or unfavourable light, it is essential to look again afresh. Clearly no one child is all good and another all bad. The way out is to meet everybody, including one's not-so-dearest, as if one has never met him, or her, before. This is marvellously refreshing for oneself and the other person. It has the instant effect of enabling one to step free of habitual attitudes and see the person as he, or she, really is in that moment. An integral part of looking afresh is to put aside all likes and dislikes about a person and to remain open to whatever is presented. When feelings are

in sway, one never can be objective.

The way to avoid the pitfall of favouritism is to refuse to be led by likes and dislikes. These are always a hindrance, never a help, and have a disastrously limiting effect on a parent's relationship with a child. A guiding principle is that every child is different, and that it is fair, not identical treatment that is needed. The art is to see what a child needs in any one moment, meet the need with favour and then let the child move on and be ready to receive the next in the same spirit.

Questions about Sex

The most important factor to keep in mind when answering children's questions about sex or anything else is that the answer should always be truthful. Untruthful answers, such as 'Mummy is going to buy a baby at the supermarket,' cause a child to think twice before trusting that particular adult again. A serious result of this is that he either keeps the questions to himself or seeks the answers elsewhere.

THE BEST TIME

The best age to tell a child about sex is when the child asks a question. Having been asked a question, it is important to answer the question that is asked and not attempt to answer questions that have not yet been asked. For example, if a child asks: 'Did I live inside you, mummy?' that is the moment to explain about pregnancy. It is not, however, the moment to insist on telling the child everything that there is to be known about sex in one long-winded indigestible session!

The timing of answers and explanations is certainly important. Answers that are withheld for too long cause frustration, while answers given in advance of the questions can cause a negative reaction which only hinders the child from asking further questions.

SEX GAMES

'If one comes across children playing sex games and experimenting with each other,' a radio interviewer once asked, 'is that a good moment to tell them about sex?' The answer is only too obvious. A parent would only choose such a moment to tell the child about sex if he, or she, wished to add fuel to the fire and strength to their elbow!

The positive way to deal with such occasions is to offer a distraction—an alternative activity which immediately engages the children's minds and bodies in a more appropriate manner.

NUDITY

Parents often ask whether or not they should walk about naked in front of their children. If one could do this without any attachment to one's body, self-consciousness or inhibition, it would be harmless. It is, however, rare for adults to be so at ease with themselves physically that they are able to behave in a totally natural and asexual way when naked. More commonly, the situation carries an atmosphere of being contrived and the presence of inhibition communicates itself to the child. Contrived nudity in front of children can,

in fact, have a reverse effect from the one intended. The child either becomes obsessed with details concerning his own and other people's bodies, or he becomes more inhibited himself.

HOMOSEXUALITY

It is not only people with an 'innate tendency' who can be attracted to homosexual relationships. People with anything like an 'innate tendency' are extremely rare and, when this is the case, there is a definite physical aberration. Such aberrations are quite different from a slight tendency to effeminacy in boys, or masculinity in girls. These are superficial and borrowed characteristics which are, therefore, rectifiable at an early age.

Children, youngsters and adults who are attracted to homosexual relationships are usually the victim of a simple idea, which may have stemmed from a parent: 'I always wanted a son, not a daughter,' or an idea which arises from a passionate attachment to or antipathy to one or other parent.

There is no doubt that many boys do have a profound fear that they are incapable of becoming men. If, subsequently, anything in their upbringing convinces them of failure in their own eyes this can result in boys playing a woman's part in a homosexual relationship. Where girls are concerned, a dissatisfaction with their own bodies lies behind a desire for a homosexual relationship. This again is caused by a destructive idea, such as a fear of being considered inferior or of not being in control of events and natural physical functions, like menstruation. Left unchecked in childhood, such ideas may cause a girl to form a homosexual relationship.

WITNESSING THE SEXUAL ACT

The idea that it is healthy to allow a child to witness his parents during the sexual act, is dangerously misguided. A child subjected to such an experience, is either alarmed by the intensity of strange sights and sounds and the apparent loss of control of the two people he most depends upon, or he is forced into a sexual precocity which can only leave him feeling feverishly disturbed. Either way, only harm can result from his being subjected to experiences which he has not the physical, mental or emotional maturity to cope with.

THE GUIDING PRINCIPLES

When parents understand that it is natural for a child to want what he sees and hears about, they will also understand that the less that is said to a child about sex, the better it is for the child. This does not mean, of course, that a child's questions

The simple answer to the question of the best age to tell a child about sex is when he begins to ask.

It is important to answer the question that is asked and not attempt to answer questions which have not been asked. For example, if a child asks, 'Did I live inside you, mummy?', that is the moment to explain about pregnancy. It is not, however, the moment to insist on telling a child everything there is to be known about sex.

The most positive way to deal with children's sex games or such things as masturbation is to offer a distraction—an alternative activity which will engage the mind and body in a more appropriate manner.

should be fobbed off. A child's questions should always be answered. It simply means that one should take the lead from the child and not force an interest in sexual matters by being over-talkative about the subject or allowing him to be unnecessarily subjected to unsuitable television programmes, commercials, films, and so on.

The simple knowledge that talking about, or allowing the mind to dwell on anything—be it a toy car or bar of chocolate—creates an ever-increasing desire for it, can be an invaluable help for boys and girls. Then they can understand that the way out of any dangerously tempting situation is to give one's attention very firmly to something else. Parents who succeed in teaching their child this, and who never miss an opportunity to remind themselves and him that there are three sides to every question—body, mind and spirit—not only prepare the child for a balanced attitude towards sex, but to life itself.

Sleeping Habits

HOW MUCH SLEEP?

Nobody can decide how much sleep another person needs or *should* need! Individuals do, of course, vary and no two children are alike. Provided the baby or child is healthy and alert during the day, he is getting sufficient sleep, even if, from the parent's point of view, it seems insufficient.

Never try to force a wakeful baby to go to sleep by making the house as quiet as a grave and the room as dark as a tomb. It is far wiser to allow the baby to settle down naturally; to allow him, for example, to enjoy the movements of a mobile. A toddler or older child should, if he wishes, be allowed suitable toys, books or games in bed. He is much more likely to settle down to sleep if he is not left in a state of wakefulness with nothing to occupy his mind and hands. The same principle applies to the morning—bed is not the place for a child who is awake. Ideally, rather than be left in a state of wakeful idleness and boredom, the child should be encouraged to get up and get on with the adventure of a new day.

The brightest and happiest children are the ones whose parents resist the temptation to leave them lying abed and who are, instead, allowed to get up and make the maximum use of the wakeful hours of any one day. Lying in bed, when one is not tired, is exhausting rather than refreshing. Early to bed (i.e., before a child is over-tired and too excited) and early to rise (i.e., as soon as a child wakes up) is a wise maxim for parents to apply to a child's bedtime and morning routine.

For the first six weeks or so of life, babies are happier when swaddled for sleeping. This has the advantage of preventing them from rolling around and getting into uncomfortable positions in the cot. At the same time, it helps them to feel secure. However, once they become interested in looking at their own hands—finger-play—they usually prefer to remain unswaddled. The ideal and safest sleeping position for a new baby is on his tummy, with his head turned to one side. Then, if he is sick, there is much less risk of the milk running back down his throat to choke him.

Never tip-toe around the house from fear of disturbing a baby. Allow him to become accustomed to ordinary household sounds.

BEDTIME ROUTINES

The bedtime routine should never be rushed and should always consist of a quiet period spent together just before and during. It is always wise to start the bedtime routine earlier rather than to find yourself in a position where you must rush.

It is never too soon to begin the delightful routine of saying a prayer and singing a lullaby or reading a bedtime story to a child. Long before he can understand the meaning of the words, he will enjoy the soothing sound of his parent's voice.

☐ **Bedtime problems** Most children, at one time or another, either resist going to bed or become afraid of going to bed. If a child is displaying fear of the dark, it is important to ensure that his mind is not being over-stimulated before bedtime. Too much television, for example, can produce 'apparitions' in the mind which make it impossible for a child to get to sleep.

If a child is afraid of the dark, spend time with him in his darkened room and help him to realize that there is light in the darkest room; that if he looks he can see a great deal, and that even if he closes his eyes, he has four other senses to rely on: hearing, taste, touch and smell, to inform him that you are nearby. In extreme cases leave a nightlight for the child.

It is also wise to check that there is not a shape or shadow in the room, or a sound that is troubling and causing his imagination to run riot.

A frightened child will also appreciate a door being left ajar rather than closed. This enables familiar sounds to reach him and allay his fears.

☐ **Disturbed sleep** Nightmares, sleep-walking and compulsive bedtime rituals are very rare in a pre-school child. When they do arise, one can be sure that they are the product of an over-active mind or an emotional disturbance. Check that the child is not feeling under too much pressure and that he is not being expected to cope with things which are beyond his capabilities.

If a child wakes screaming in the night from a nightmare, stay with him until he returns to reality and give him the opportunity to discuss his fears. If a child walks in his sleep, gently lead him back to bed.

Compulsive bedtime rituals, such as insisting that twenty toys are arranged in a precise pattern, may seem amusing at first, but if the ritual begins to dominate a child's life and gives rise to hysterical tears when resisted, it is wise to seek a doctor's advice. Never ridicule a child's fears. For him the fear is real. Help him in as many simple ways as you know how, to understand that there is nothing to fear but fear itself.

☐ **Going out for the night** Never deceive a child by going out for the evening without telling him. He will be far less distressed if he knows that a babysitter is looking after him than if he wakes up to find that you are not there. The more information you give the babysitter about your child's preferences—nightlight, favourite toy, door ajar —the happier your child and the babysitter will be in your absence.

At one time or another, most children either resist going to bed or become afraid of going to bed. When this arises, it is important to ensure that the child's mind is not being over-stimulated before bedtime.

The bedtime routine should never be rushed and should always include a quiet period spent together. It is always wise to start bedtime preparations earlier rather than having to rush. It is never too soon to begin the delightful routine of saying a prayer, singing a lullaby or reading a bedtime story. Long before a child can understand the meaning of the words, she will enjoy the soothing sound of her parent's voice.

If a child is afraid, spend time with her in the darkened room. In extreme cases, leave a nightlight. A frightened child will also appreciate a door left ajar. This enables familiar sounds to reach her and allay her fears.

Never ridicule a child's fears —for him or her, they are very real. A child who regularly and frequently has nightmares or sleep-walks needs help.

Faddy Feeders

The question of now much food a child really needs and how to encourage a fussy feeder to eat, can only be asked in a country where people are in the very fortunate position of not only having sufficient or more than sufficient food to eat, but a bountiful variety. This offers them the chance to please themselves about what they enjoy and do not enjoy eating.

The truth is that a normal hungry child will eat something and a starving child will eat anything. If, therefore, a child refuses food simply because he has a preference for this or that, he can be regarded as a fortunate unfortunate in that he has been born into a country and a family who are in a position of not only having enough food, but a variety of food to offer him. The parents are also fortunate unfortunates because they can, at least, take comfort in the thought that no normal baby, toddler or child will deliberately starve himself to death and that, with careful handling, he can be coaxed from faddiness to normal eating.

A SENSE OF PROPORTION

Parents who are driven half out of their mind by worry about a child's eating habits do not make the best coaxers. For this reason it is best to allay fears by asking your doctor to examine your child to see if, in spite of his peculiar eating habits, he is in good sound physical condition. If, apart from displaying fads and fancies, a child is generally bright, alert and active at times other than mealtimes, you can be sure that there is little to worry about. However, reassuring yourself will take the 'heat' out of the situation and allow you to cope with the psychological aspects more rationally and tactfully.

The first essential is to remember that a child has a great love of drama. Life, for example is much more interesting if there is never a dull moment—if parents can be kept on the go, fetching and carrying, looking happy, sad, anxious, distressed, cross! Life is good when you can make your mark; and holding the reins for a change and directing events is sheer delight! When, in addition, a child discovers that he can dictate—get his own way by digging his heels in, or, rather, not digging his spoon in, life is perfect. The baby or child is not, of course, being deliberately heartless and unkind; he is merely expressing a natural interest in and delight in drama!

The parents' first defence, then, in lowering the temperature, if the temperature has been raised, is to appear unconcerned. If a child refuses one meal altogether, do not panic; just clear the meal away;

resist the temptation to offer in-between snacks and bide your time until the next mealtime. If there is a repeat performance, do not worry; the child's interest in how you will react may still be stronger than his appetite. Keep calm—he will eat when he is hungry. Be sure, however, to reserve this pleasure for the next mealtime. Giving way and gratefully offering tasty snacks will only prolong the problem. This eat-what-is-there-or-have-nothing, may sound like a heartless kill-or-cure approach, but with a normal healthy child a parent can be sure that it will cure and *not* kill.

However messy a child, table, indeed a room, may become during a meal, there is no doubt that a child does like his meals to convey a sense of occasion. Tables should, therefore, always look orderly and food should always look attractive and appetizing. From the toddler stage onwards, a child should be given a reasonable choice of items. If he does not like green vegetables, for example, do not make an issue of it, simply offer an alternative such as carrot or an apple. Bear in mind that a child can be confused by too much choice; three or four items are probably the maximum that he can cope with at any one time. Remember, too, that large portions of anything are more likely to kill than to encourage appetite.

Children do not enjoy richly flavoured or too hot or spicy foods. Their sense of taste is, in fact, more alive than most adults and has not been blunted to the extent that they can only taste by covering everything with rich sauces or tomato ketchup. If their ability to taste is respected and is not dulled by over-strong flavours, the chances are that they will continue to enjoy subtle natural flavours for the rest of their lives. The same principle applies to sweetness. If a child is not offered artificial sweeteners in the form of sugar added to everything, he will enjoy the natural sweetness that is present in many foods and his dental and general health will be eternally grateful for your foresight.

A child should not, of course, be forced to eat any particular item, however good you think it is for him. This will only make him retch or wretched. It will also make him all the more determined. Battles of will quickly become a habit and will make mealtimes a misery for himself and everybody else or a battleground which, for psychological reasons, he begins to enjoy.

Do not worry if your child does not vary his choice of food as often as you would like him to. Many children who are known to exist on wholemeal bread, cheese, honey, yoghurt, apple, oranges and milk, day in day out, whilst refusing anything else, are perfectly healthy and do not suffer from any nutritional lack.

Another essential for avoiding fussy feeders is

always to allow the meal to go at a pace which is right for the individual child. Some children are, by their parents' standards, very slow eaters. If they are constantly rushed, mealtimes become a misery for them and problems set in. Mealtimes should always be relaxed happy occasions. This can be a difficult discipline for a parent who is prone to thinking ahead to the next activity on the agenda. In the long run, however, it is wiser to allow events to proceed at a pace which is right for the child, rather than to court time-consuming delays in the form of problems.

For the same reason, it is important not to rush a baby from this or that taste before he is ready to make the change. It is far wiser to allow him to take his time about being weaned from milk on to solids and to adjust slowly to one new flavour at a time. Fist-feeding and food-throwing is an inevitable part of a baby's development. A baby who is constantly checked from touching his own food will begin to protest and display behaviour problems. Give him a free hand and be prepared with plastic cover-ups for him and the surrounding area. Feeding himself may also take longer, but it is a vital step in his development and will have a strong influence on his general attitude and behaviour at mealtimes. If you are worried about him playing too much and eating too little, have two spoons—one for him to use and one for you to pop in the occasional crafty mouthful!

☐ **Loss of appetite** A sudden loss of appetite should always be taken seriously. This is usually a sign that the child is unwell or sickening for an infection. Thrush, for example, can make eating painful for a baby. Do not hesitate to seek your doctor's advice if you are worried.

A NORMAL APPETITE

Babies and young children react in one of two ways when they are pressurized to eat more than is natural for them. Some resist and begin to display behaviour problems at the table; others oblige and become overweight. It is now a medically accepted fact that babies and children can be encouraged to eat more food than is good for them and that the excess causes fat cells—adipose cells—to increase and multiply. Once this happens, the cells continue to demand food and it is then exceedingly difficult to transform a fat child into a thin child.

However much a parent wants to please a child by preparing appetizing food and being rewarded by a healthy appetite, it is essential to remember that there is a natural measure in everything. No child will thank its parents for a weight problem which will remain to trouble him for the rest of his life. Appetites which may seem small by a parent's standard should be respected as being right and natural for that particular child. If there is a true need for adjustment, this will become evident in the child's general health and behaviour.

It is only too easy for mealtimes to become a battle of wills between mother and child. The wisest approach when a child first begins to show faddiness is to appear unconcerned. If a child refuses one meal altogether, do not panic. Just clear the meal away, resist the temptation to offer in-between snacks and wait until the next mealtime. If there is a repeat performance, do not worry—the child's interest in how you will react may be stronger than his appetite. Keep calm, he will eat when he is hungry.

The Importance of Posture

Many ailments are created by faulty posture and unnecessary movements. It is not unusual, for example, for infants to complain about aches and pains in various parts of their bodies. If you ask a child to sit or stand, you can often see why. Correcting posture can often cure an ailment. A child, for example, who habitually adopts a twisted sitting position will soon begin to stand and walk in the same manner and cause a lateral curvature of his spine. The habitual contraction of finger joints when writing is the cause of some arthritic conditions. Tilted heads and stiff tense neck muscles can cause eye-strain and headaches. Poor posture can also contribute to stammering, digestive disorders and asthma.

Some children have naturally good posture, but this is rare. Most need the same kind of guidance for correct use of the body as that given to subjects like reading and writing. It helps to remember that children are great imitators. They will follow a parent's example—good and bad.

What becomes very clear when one considers posture is how closely it is related to state of mind. Whenever a person slumps physically, there is also an inner slump. The expression 'That made you sit up!' is very accurate. An alert mind equals an alert posture. An ideal approach is for parents to look beyond the physical slump to the state of mind that is creating it. Instead of saying: 'Do sit up', gain your child's interest and set him off on an activity. If he stops slouching, you will know that you have succeeded!

WALKING STRAIGHT AND TALL

If parents wish a child to walk with a natural grace then, from his very first steps, they need to drop all sense of rush and allow a natural measured pace. A child who is habitually hurried by a parent will either develop jumbo-sized steps that are out of proportion with the rest of his body, or absurdly fast mincing steps. To add insult to injury, he will be told: 'Do walk properly'! Rushing can also create a stooping gait. This reflects the habit of a person mentally straining to reach the destination at a speed faster than the body can convey him.

Many parents experience frustration when a child who has been making such good progress with walking suddenly refuses to walk and screams for a pushchair or to be carried whenever there is a necessity to go out. The reason is often

so simple: a child will only want to walk if he is allowed to enjoy walking and this, of course, entails walking at a pace which is right and proper for his physical stage of development. If walking always entails huffing and puffing and rushing, and turning a blind eye and ear to all that makes a walk delightful—a child will clearly not enjoy walking and will scream for a carry or his push-chair.

The most important physical principle to understand about posture is that if the head and spine are in true alignment, then all other parts come into position. One common misuse, apart from the usual ones of slumping and compressing the spine, is moving the head from the neck. It makes an incredible difference when a child is helped to realize that the head 'swivels' from a point somewhere between the ears. This correction alone will ease much tension in the neck.

Another common error is for children to 'carry' their shoulders too high. This creates tension, pain and restricted breathing. If the spine is fully 'eased up' throughout its length, this tension will disperse. A child often needs a reminder to straighten up, but to let his shoulders hang lightly.

Countless foot ailments are caused and aggravated by an off-balance stance and misuse of energy. Most adult foot troubles could be eradicated in childhood by parents giving attention to posture and the correct use of energy, such as cultivating a light tread. Well-fitting shoes are also essential.

'DO SIT UP STRAIGHT'

Look before speaking! Is the chair the right height for the child? If a child's feet are dangling several inches above floor level, he will compensate for this by slumping backwards, or by sagging at waist level. If the chair is too high, offer a footstool. Chairs that encourage a child to

use his spine are obviously preferable to chairs that encourage him to flop back for support. If a chair is too soft and spongy, it will not support the child's back, and will create a sag at waist level and cause aches and pains in the neck and back.

TABLE POSTURE

Children's posture often suffers at mealtimes because they are allowed to get into the habit of bringing their heads down to their plate, rather than raising the cutlery to their mouth. The initial cause of this insecurity is that the child is anxious lest the food should spill or fall from the spoon or fork during its passage from plate to mouth. If parents ensure that the chair is the right height and show the child how to avoid spills by picking up the right amount of food, this insecurity soon passes. The same principle applies to drinking. A child who is shown how to hold a cup and saucer at chest level, and how to raise the cup to his lips, is saved the awkward and ungraceful habit of lowering his head to the cup.

LIFTING WITH CARE

'Careful how you lift that'. The instruction is not enough. A child needs to be shown. Place an object on the floor. Ask your child to stand with his feet slightly apart. Now ask him to bend his knees and let his arms dangle loosely. Lower his trunk slightly forward at the same time until his finger-tips touch his knees. Repeat this, then ask him to pick up the object. Alternatively, stand him with one foot slightly forward and show him how to adopt the 'curtsy' position for picking up. As industrial doctors will tell you, if people were taught to lift and carry properly, then children, mankind and industry would be the richer for it. Countless days are lost every year because of strains, sprains and hernias. If parents spend a little time studying the body as a working instrument, their child will benefit for life.

Some children have naturally good posture, but this is rare. Most need the same kind of guidance for correct use of the body as that given to subjects like reading and writing.

It helps to remember that children are great imitators. They will follow a parent's example —good or bad. It also helps to check that tables and chairs are the right height for the child. If, for example a child's feet are left dangling several inches above floor level, he will compensate for this by slumping backwards or by sagging at the waist. Countless ailments, such as aches and pains in the neck, back, hip and thigh joints, are caused by faulty posture and could,

therefore, be easily eradicated.

The best time to encourage a child to move naturally and gracefully is in early childhood before bad habits have become established.

A Lifetime's Care

KNOWING, CARING AND LOVING

Looking back on the first three years of parenthood, most mothers and fathers agree that what makes it such an exceptionally memorable and satisfying period is that moments are as big as years. It is a time when every breath, sight, sound, taste, touch and smell count; a time when all the senses and other faculties throb with life and learning. Certainly, everyone agrees that early parenthood, like early childhood, is a process of constant growth; that never again (until the arrival of the next child) does one experience and achieve so much in so few years. Nor is any achievement so permanent or so valuable.

In one sense, of course, parents re-live their own childhoods along with their child; or, at least, caring for a child affords the opportunity to do so. No-one who has ever watched a father helping his son to launch an armada of twigs upon a puddle can doubt that the opportunity exists. Equally, no-one who has seen a mother help to bandage the arm of an injured doll before her daughter tucks it up in bed, can have any doubts.

Somewhere, recorded within each mother and father, is a very clear memory of childhood experience. This memory enables parents to help children to grow healthily and happily, at ease with themselves and others. Perhaps the most useful piece of knowledge arising from childhood memory to influence parenthood, is that the future—whether this be in terms of minutes, hours or years—is always purchased by the present. There is no better confirmation than childhood, that every moment well spent is a useful preparation for life. Lessons properly learned need never be learned twice—and this applies equally to parents and children.

Whether or not parenthood (and, for that matter, childhood) is to contain more happiness than unhappiness, more fulfilment than frustration, is decided very early on in a parent's and a child's life. One thing that parents and children would agree is that life begins well and that with the right kind of care—physical, mental, emotional and spiritual—it can remain so.

Knowing, caring and loving is the key to the whole human experience. Having prepared the soil and planted all the necessary seeds during the first three years of their child's life, parents simply need to ensure that both they and the home-environment continue to offer the right kind of nourishment for their child's physical, mental, emotional and spiritual growth throughout childhood to maturity.

Glossary

Abortion When a pregnancy ends before the completion of the twenty-eighth week, that is, before the foetus is legally capable of a separate existence, the mother is said to have had an abortion.

Abortions are, broadly speaking, of two types; spontaneous abortion, which is the same as a miscarriage, and therapeutic abortion, which is the same as a termination. Spontaneous abortions can be either threatened, inevitable, incomplete or septic, depending on the course of events. If an embryo dies within the uterus in early pregnancy, but is not expelled for several weeks afterwards, this is called a missed abortion.

Accidental haemorrage Bleeding from the uterus during pregnancy. It may be revealed or concealed.

Amino acids Chemical compounds that are necessary to proper growth.

Amniotic fluid This is the fluid which fills the amniotic sac and surrounds the foetus inside the uterus. It serves to protect the baby by acting as a cushion against outside pressures. The fluid is in constant circulation. It is secreted by the foetal surface of the placenta and membrances, and is swallowed by the foetus. The foetus also passes urine back into the amniotic fluid.

Amniocentesis This procedure involves taking a sample of the amniotic fluid by passing a needle through the front wall of the abdomen and into the uterus. Analysis of the amniotic fluid is helpful in diagnosing a number of conditions, especially mongolism.

Analgesic Drug used to relieve pain.

Antenatal This literally means 'before the birth' and is usually applied to such things as 'Antenatal Clinics, Classes and Preparation for Birth'.

Antibodies Special protein or globulins formed in the body to counteract the effects of bacterial antigens or toxins.

Binovular twins Non-identical twins derived from two ova; sometimes called fraternal twins.

Blood pressure The pressure created by the heart within the major blood vessels in order to circulate blood around the body.

Braxton Hicks' contractions Painless uterine contractions which occur every twenty minutes throughout pregnancy.

Breech This refers to the baby's bottom; a breech presentation is when the baby's bottom comes first during the birth instead of the head.

Caesarean section By Caesarean law, when a woman died in childbirth the uterus had to be cut open and the baby extracted in case it had survived. The modern Caesarean operation is a method of delivering the baby through a surgical abdominal incision which enables the baby to be removed without having to pass down through the cervix and vagina. The classical Caesarean section was an incision in the upper part of the uterus. The modern operation is the 'lower segment Caesarean section' in which the incision is made low down.

Catheter A hollow tube used to drain urine from the bladder.

Cephalic presentation A baby presenting head first during the birth, more usually called vertex presentation.

Cervical canal The canal in the cervix from the uterus to the vagina.

Cervix This is the lowest part of the uterus. It has a narrow canal running through it which dilates during labour to allow the passage of the baby into the vagina.

Chorionic gonadotrophin The hormone formed by the chorionic villi, that is initially responsible for the continuance of the pregnancy. Its presence in urine is used to diagnose pregnancy.

Chorionic villi The sponge-like structures on the outer surface of the developing ovum from which the placenta is formed.

Chromosome Filament-like structures which occur in pairs in the nucleus of every cell in the body. Each chromosome consists of hundreds of molecules of nucleo-protein called genes. There are twenty-three pairs of chromosomes in each human cell.

Circumcision Operation for the removal of the foreskin or prepuce of the penis.

Colostrum This is the secretion which the breasts produce during pregnancy and before normal breast milk is produced. Colostrum is particularly important for a baby. It is rich in antibodies which protect the baby for the first few months of life against all infectious diseases which the mother herself had had.

Congenital abnormality An abnormality present in the baby at birth.

Corpus luteum This is formed in the ovary after ovulation.

D & C Stands for dilatation and curettage. This refers to the small operation and the way in which the cervix is stretched with metal dilators to enable a curettage to be passed into the cavity of the uterus to remove any abnormal material there. The D & C is often used to diagnose problems within the uterus and after an incomplete abortion, when the residual products of conception are evacuated.

Decidua The thickened lining of the uterus which receives and protects the developing embryo during pregnancy.

Dilatation This refers to the extent to which the cervix is open during labour. It is commonly measured in centimetres or in fingers' breadths. In order to allow the baby to pass through, the cervix has to be fully dilated which represents a diameter of approximately ten centimetres or five fingers' breadths.

Ectopic pregnancy A pregnancy in which the fertilized ovum begins to develop in the Fallopian tubes instead of implanting in the uterus.

E.D.D. This is an abbreviation for 'expected date of delivery', which is calculated from the first day of the L.M.P., 'last menstrual period'. The calculation with a normal twenty-eight day cycle is to add seven days to the first day of the last menstrual period and then subtract three months. The resulting date is the E.D.D. nine months later. For example: L.M.P.: 1/6/78—E.D.D.: 8/3/79. E.D.D. is sometimes known as E.D.C.— Expected date of Confinement.

Embryo The embryo is the fertilized egg from the moment of fertilization until the completion of the first twelve weeks of intra-uterine (within the womb) life.

Endometrium The mucous membrane lining the uterus.

Engaged Head Towards the end of pregnancy, the foetus's head enters into the cavity of the pelvis. It is then said to be 'engaged'. In women having their first baby, engagement of the head commonly occurs between thirty-six and thirty-eight weeks. In women having second and subsequent babies, engagement usually occurs later and may not, in fact, happen until early labour.

Epidural anaesthetic An anaesthetic given into the epidural space surrounding the spinal cord.

Episiotomy An episiotomy is a surgical incision, made in the perineum, to enable the baby's head to pass through the vagina. The reason for an episiotomy is to facilitate the delivery of the baby and to prevent undue stretching or tearing of the perineum and lower vagina.

External cervical os The opening at the vaginal end of the cervix.

Fallopian tubes The tubes that connect the ovaries to the uterus.

Fertilization The union of the ovum and the sperm.

Fontanelle The upper part or vault of the baby's skull is made up of four separate bones which are joined together at their edges by a strong membrane. Where the four bones meet at the front of the top of the baby's head, there is a kite-shaped depression which is called the anterior fontanelle. At the back of the top of the baby's head three bones meet and so the depression—posterior fontanelle—is smaller and triangular in shape.

Foetus This word comes from the Latin meaning a young one. It applies to the baby inside the uterus from twelve weeks until it is actually delivered.

Full term This means the completion of the normal period of pregnancy which extends, on average, for 269 days from the day of conception. If the day of conception is not known, as is usually the case, the calculation is done from the first day of the last menstrual period. In this case, full term represents approximately forty weeks.

Genes The hereditary factors present in chromosomes which decide physical and mental make-up.

Gonadotrophins A group of hormones, produced by the anterior lobe of the pituitary gland, that are particularly responsible for the growth, development and function of the ovaries.

Gonads A sexual gland. The testicle or ovary.

Graafian follicles A Graafian follicle is the follicle which is formed in the ovary by the maturing egg. Each month one follicle from the ovary, enlarges, and the egg cell develops. About the middle of the cycle, the egg escapes from the follicle into the adjoining Fallopian tube. The follicle then becomes converted into a corpus luteum. Both Graafian follicle and corpus luteum are important in the production of the hormones which regulate the menstrual cycle.

Gynaecologist A doctor who specializes in diseases particular to women.

Haemoglobin The colouring matter of the red blood corpuscles. It also has a strong affinity for oxygen and helps to carry this round the body.

Haemorrhage This simply means bleeding—an escape of blood from its vessels.

Haemorrhoids These are 'piles'—small dilated varicose veins around the entrance of the anus (back passage).

Hypertension This is a rise of blood pressure above the normal level. The normal level varies from patient to patient, but if the top blood pressure (systolic) is above 140, and the lower blood pressure (diastolic) over 90, the woman has hypertension. Hypertension is a feature of toxaemia in pregnancy.

Induction Induction means the starting of labour artificially before labour starts naturally. It is employed by obstetricians when it is felt that the mother and baby will benefit from delivery before nature decides to bring this about.

Internal cervical os The opening of the upper end of the cervical canal.

Intravenous Within a vein.

Involution The contraction of the uterus after labour.

Labour The process of delivery of the baby.

Lanugo These are fine hairs which cover the baby during his life in the uterus. They disappear in late pregnancy and are not present at birth.

Liquor amnii The fluid in which the foetus floats in the uterus.

L.M.P. This is an abbreviation for 'last menstrual period'. It is commonly seen in obstetric notes and refers to the first day of the last menstrual period from which the E.D.D. (see E.D.D.) is calculated.

Lochia A blood-stained discharge from the vagina after delivery.

Meconium Greenish substance present in the baby's rectum before and after birth.

Membranes, Rupturing of The membranes rupture spontaneously during the course of labour, generally about half way through the first stage. Artificial rupture of the membranes, releasing some of the amniotic fluid, is a common method of induction of labour.

Micturition This simply means passing urine. Frequency of micturition is a common symptom of pregnancy.

Miscarriage This means the spontaneous termination of pregnancy prior to the completion of twenty-eight weeks. It is synonymous with spontaneous abortion.

Moulding The compression of the infant's head as it is forced through the maternal passages during labour.

Mucus A sticky substance created by special glands. It usually has a protective function.

Multigravida A woman during her second or subsequent pregnancy.

Obstetrician A doctor who specializes in pregnancy.

Oedema Swelling of the tissues of the body caused by fluid.

Oestrogen Female hormone formed by the developing ovum.

Operculum The plug of mucus that fills the cervical canal throughout pregnancy.

Ovulation This is the release of the ovum from the Graafian follicle in the ovary. It occurs about the fourteenth day of the cycle in a normal twenty-eight day cycle. After ovulation, the woman's body temperature rises slightly.

Ovum The reproductive cell of the female.

Oxytocic drug A drug which stimulates the uterus to contract.

Paediatrician A specialist in diseaseses and the care of babies and children.

Perineum The area of skin and underlying tissue which runs from the back of the entrance to the vagina and the front of the entrance to the anus. It is the area which is most under strain when the baby is delivered. In order to protect it from being torn or unduly stretched, an episiotomy is often performed.

Placenta This is the organ (also called the afterbirth) by which nutrients and oxygen are transferred to the baby from the maternal circulation. It is about the size of a small dinner plate and weighs approximately one-fifth of the baby's weight at the time of delivery. In most cases, it will weigh between 500–700 grams (1–1½ lb).

Placenta praevia A placenta which is attached to the lower part of the uterine wall.

Post-partum haemorrhage A haemorrhage that occurs after childbirth.

Pre-eclampsia A condition specific to pregnancy. It is characterized by a raised blood pressure, severe swelling of the fingers or ankles and protein in the urine.

Premature Mothers-to-be who go into labour prior to the completion of the thirty seventh week are said to have gone into premature labour. A premature baby is one that is born before this time or weighing less than 2.5 kg (5 lb 8 oz).

Presentation That portion of the foetus which is felt at the os (opening) during the onset of labour. The commonest presenting part is the vertex (head). When the baby is coming bottom first, this is said to be a breech presentation.

Primigravida A woman who is pregnant for the first time.

Progesterone Female hormones, secreted by the corpus luteum, which play an important part in the regulation of the menstrual cycle and during pregnancy.

Post-natal Means 'after the birth'. It is applied to such things as post-natal depression, and post-natal visit. The post-natal visit to the doctor some six to eight weeks after delivery is to ensure that the pelvic organs have returned to normal and to give an opportunity to discuss any problems, particularly those relating to family planning.

Postpartum Means after the birth of the baby. It is applied to such complications as postpartum haemorrhage.

Polyhydramnios This is an excess of the normal amount of amniotic fluid. The normal volume of fluid at full term is about 1 litre (2 pints). In cases of polyhydramnios, this figure may rise to 2 or 3 litres or even more.

Puerperium The first six weeks after the birth of the baby.

Quickening The first perceptible foetal movements felt by the mother.

Rhesus factor Rh factor. The red blood cells of most humans contain the Rhesus factor. Those that do not are said to be Rhesus negative. This is of importance as a probable cause of anaemia and jaundice in the newly-born when the infant is Rhesus positive and the mother Rhesus negative. Treatment is by blood transfusion.

Seminal count Examination of the quantity of sperm in the semen.

Seminal vesicles Small organs at the base of the prostate gland that store sperm prior to ejaculation.

Sperm The male reproductive cell.

Stillbirth The birth of a dead baby after twenty-eight weeks of pregnancy.

Subcutaneous fat The layer of fat that lies immediately beneath the skin.

Testes The male reproductive organs where sperm are formed.

Thrush A fungus infection of the vagina, sometimes affecting the lining of the mouth in newborn infants.

Trophoblast The outer layer of cells—chorionic villi—which are formed during the early stages of the development of an embryo. The cells of the trophoblast have the ability to penetrate into the special lining of the uterus of early pregnancy and are responsible for establishing the placenta in its final site in the uterus.

Toxaemia This is a condition which can occur in late pregnancy. It is characterized by raised blood pressure, protein in the urine and oedema (swelling of the face, legs and hands).

Twenty-four hour collection Refers to the common practice of collecting all the urine that is passed by a woman over twenty-four hours in order to measure the amount of oestrogen excreted in the urine. This, in turn, is a measure of the oestrogen produced by the placenta and foetus which gives a good indication of how the placenta is functioning.

Ultrasonic scan This is an examination, using an ultrasonic machine, to give information about all stages of pregnancy. In particular it is used to give an accurate estimation of the correct E.D.D.

Umbilicus This is the point at which the umbilical cord enters the baby. After the birth of the baby, the umbilical cord is tied or clamped and the stump then shrivels to form the adult umbilicus.

Uniovular twins Identical twins that are developed from one ovum.

Urethra The canal through which urine is discharged from the bladder.

Uterus This is the 'womb', the organ which is situated at the top of the vagina and in which the foetus grows.

Vas deferens The tube that links the testes to the seminal vesicles.

Vernix A white soap-like substance which covers the foetal skin when it is in the uterus. It prevents the skin from becoming unduly softened by the amniotic fluid.

Vertex presentation When the baby presents head first at delivery, this is called vertex presentation.

Viability The ability of the baby to exist after birth.

Vulva The external female genital organs.

Index

Figures in italics refer to illustrations.

Acknowledgments

We would like to thank the following people for their assistance with preparing the photography for this book, particularly the parents of the many children featured.

Vilma Barraclough and Charlie; Stewart and Jan Bishop and Alice; Mr and Mrs Bocon, Clair, Louise and Nicholas; Cathleen, Charlotte and Benjamin Bolton; Claire Bowen; Mrs Bozorgi and daughter; Felicity Brooks; Lynda Carnell and Simon; Mrs Chopin John and Adrian; Elisabeth Clark; Mary Clode and Suzanne; Mrs Conway and Catheryn; Mr and Mrs Crome and Joshua; George and Hugo Davies; Karen Denlon; Samantha Dodds; Clive and Coralie Dorman; Michael and Lena Frederick and John Michael; Jemima and Lucinda Garthwaite; Vanya Gibbons; Sara Jane Green; Kim Godfrey; Lavina Grimshaw and Chloe; Paul Gugenheim; Vicki Hallam and Nancy; Alexander, Edward and William Hamilton; Kirsty Hinton; Nicola Hobbs; Terence and Christine Hopcroft, Anthony and Daniel; Doreen Jacobs and Lucinda; Emily Knapp Fisher; Wai-Ling-Lamb; Phil and Olivia Lapworth, Ben and Chloe; Sara Legge; Dahlia Louis and Paul; Max Lousada; June Marsh and Helen; Jenny Mitchell and Kaitie; Charlotte Moore and Daisy; George Murray-Taylor; Andrew Nolan; Harry O'Sullivan; Val Perlmutter and Daniel; Dianah Ralph, Mark and Simon; Lis Ransom and Sara; Caro Redfern; Christian and Debbie Routh; Mrs Spencer and Darren; Mr and Mrs Stark and Heidi Jayne; Anna Stevenson and Laura; Jo Suchitsky and Rebecca; Gill Turney and Tullulah; Robert Ward; Vicki and Alex; Nick and Dinah Woods, Emily and Matthew; Fran Yorke, Griselda, Hester and Sophie.

King's College Hospital, London

Miss C. R. Clarke SRN SCM RSCN,
Sister Neo Natal Intensive Care Unit
Mrs B. C. Gilks SRN SCM,
Sister Antenatal Clinic
Miss D. Henschel SRN SCM MTD,
Senior Midwifery Tutor
Miss M. J. Lilley SRN SCM MTD,
Senior Nursing Officer
Miss D. Saggers SRN SCM MTD,
Midwifery Tutor
Miss M. A. Williams SRN RSCN,
Nursing Officer Neo Natal Intensive Care Unit
Antenatal Classes, King's College Hospital and Loughborough Health Centre
Sister Johnstone

Grove Way Day Nursery

Equipment available from over 200 Babyboots Departments at most major branches of Boots

Exclusive, practical and pretty clothes for children and mothers by Tigermoth, 166 Portobello Road, London NW11 and 425 Richmond Road, Twickenham and also by mail order.

Oliver Hatch and Whitecross Studio Ltd.

Artwork by Sally Launder, Lydia Malim and David Worth